Encyclopedia of Women
in the Middle Ages

Encyclopedia of Women in the Middle Ages

by JENNIFER LAWLER

McFarland & Company, Inc., Publishers

Jefferson, North Carolina, and London

Library of Congress Cataloguing-in-Publication Data

Lawler, Jennifer, 1965–
    Encyclopedia of women in the Middle Ages / by Jennifer Lawler.
      p.   cm.
    Includes bibliographical references and index.
    ISBN 0-7864-1119-8 (illustrated case binding : 50# alkaline paper) ∞
    1. Women — History — Middle Ages, 500–1500 — Encyclopedias.
HQ1143.L38   2001
305.4'09'02 — dc21   2001126809

British Library cataloguing data are available

Manufactured in the United States of America

Cover art ©2001 PhotoDisc

McFarland & Company, Inc., Publishers
  Box 611, Jefferson, North Carolina 28640
    www.mcfarlandpub.com

This book is dedicated to Jessica,
who makes everything worthwhile.

Acknowledgments

Many thanks to Dr. Michael Cherniss for putting up with my feeble attempts at noun declension for all those years; to Dr. Richard Hardin, who introduced me to Spenser, not a medieval poet but nonetheless a very good one; to Dr. Beverly Boyd, who pointed out that no one asked Emelye; and to Dr. Douglas Atkins, who once told me I was indeed a writer. All of you made this project possible.

Table of Contents

Preface

When I first began studying the Anglo-Saxon language (Old English), we learned vocabulary words according to their frequency of usage in Anglo-Saxon poetry. The first week, we learned *man*, *war*, *blood*, *warrior*, and *mead*. The second week, we learned *sword*, *slain*, *grief*, and, with morbid logic, *revenge*.

Something like twelve weeks later, we learned *woman*. Apparently, early medieval poets didn't have much to say about women.

You could look at the entire history of the Middle Ages — including the work of modern historians — and come away with the impression that there were three women in medieval Europe: Eleanor of Aquitaine, Joan of Arc, and the ghost of the Virgin Mary.

In the mid–1980s, more and more academics and other writers began investigating and reporting about women's lives in the Middle Ages. But there still was not a general guide, an encyclopedia, focusing on medieval women. Because of this lack, I have produced this *Encyclopedia of Women in the Middle Ages*.

In this book, I have included a brief introduction that describes the world in which medieval women lived, an A to Z reference to medieval women and the various aspects of their lives, a glossary that defines general terms that a reader may need to know, and a bibliography that includes suggestions for obtaining additional information in a variety of subject areas.

The *Encyclopedia of Women in the Middle Ages* is intended for use by general readers interested in the Middle Ages, by history students learning about the Middle Ages, and by others interested in understanding more about the history of women's lives. May this book inspire you to seek further information about women in the Middle Ages.

— Jennifer Lawler
Summer, 2001
Lawrence, Kansas

Note about Language, Transliteration, and Names

In the Middle Ages, the historical period from about AD 500 to about 1500, few people had last names. Sometimes, but not always, nobles had and used a family name. Most people were known by their first names. They were further identified by their job, their place of birth, or a personal trait. Sometimes a person's relationship to another person was used, such as "Will's son" (eventually, "Wilson"). Even many villages went unnamed.

Given names were part of a family tradition and were an inheritance, so many families had several members with the same name or slight variations of it. When consulting primary sources, this multitude of similar-sounding people can make it difficult to know to which person the reference attaches. This is especially true in the early Middle Ages. It can be difficult and even impossible to trace ancestry.

Further, it was not uncommon for women to change their given names upon marrying. This happened most often when a noble woman married a foreigner and went to live in a foreign land. For instance, Edith, upon her marriage, became Queen Matilda of Scotland.

In the later Middle Ages, around the twelfth century, when individual identity was becoming more and more important, people took their last names from their lord or from their occupation. The use of last names was by no means widespread until after the end of the Middle Ages. Last names then became inherited, except in Scandinavia and Eastern Europe, where surnames — patronymics — were not fixed.

The fact that women were often referred to as "the bishop's sister" or "the merchant's daughter" rather than by their given names increases the difficulty of learning about women in the Middle Ages. Even in modern histories of the period, writers, infuriatingly, continue to refer to women this way, without giving a name. Further, primary documents about women are difficult to find, since they had few legal rights and do not appear in chronicles focusing on wars and kings. Therefore, as thorough as one may attempt to be, many interesting women have, perforce, been overlooked.

3

To add to the confusion about names, there is a tendency for medieval historians to translate foreign names into the vernacular. Thus, in France, the legendary saint is known as Jeanne d'Arc, while in England, she is called Joan of Arc. Eirene, a spelling commonly used in the Byzantine Empire, becomes Irene when Europeans write about her. Zoë becomes the rather less obvious Sophia. Also, vernacular names have been Latinized. The Anglo-Saxon Chrotichildis becomes Clotilda when scribes writing in Latin refer to her.

Further, because of language evolution, names have come to be spelled differently. Bardas can also be read, perfectly logically, as Vardas. Thus, historians have used both spellings. In addition, spelling was not standardized in the Middle Ages. A person might even spell her own name differently when writing it on different documents. Therefore, there are references to Suabia and Swabia, Adrian and Hadrian, and other such examples abound. In this work, all women are listed by their most commonly used first names.

Different languages use different alphabets. Transliteration creates problems, as names spelled one way using the Cyrillic alphabet or the Arabic alphabet may reasonably be spelled three or four different ways using the Latin alphabet. Thus, Mohammad, Muhammad, Mahmud, Mahmet, and Muhammed have all at one time or another been used to identify the prophet of Islam.

In this book, the spelling most frequently encountered in sources has been used. Extensive cross-references have been included in order to reduce any possible confusion, but it is always wise to check alternate spellings before assuming that a specific woman is not listed.

For most of the women in this book, information on family lineage can be found in the appendix of genealogical charts.

Introduction

There are special problems in writing about women in history and particularly women in the Middle Ages. The sources we have are more interested in the male-oriented spheres and in the lives of the nobility than in women and non-nobles. Even many modern historians focus on warfare and royal reigns. Although we do know a great deal about how certain noblewomen lived, we know a great deal less about non-noble women — the vast majority of women who lived in the Middle Ages. But some general conclusions can be reached.

Women of the Middle Ages were considered inferior to men in all ways. They could not hold public office, they could not become priests, and they could not hold official positions in the church. They required advocates to appear in court on their behalf. They were considered minors throughout their lives, with their husbands or fathers holding authority over them. A woman's father and, later, her husband, was obligated to protect her, much like the relation between a lord and his vassal.

The church frowned on women, even though they often converted to Christianity before their male family members and then persuaded their husbands and fathers to convert as well. They were considered sexual, depraved, unscrupulous, shameless, manipulative, even evil. Church fathers viewed women as instruments of the devil and faulted them because they could cause men to fail in their devotion to God. Many theologians spent considerable time and energy detailing the failings of women. Thomas Aquinas was one such theologian. He argued that women were inferior to men and should be subject to them. He even went so far as to say that the father had a more active role in conception and childbirth than the mother and so should be more loved by the child.

Theologians blamed women for original sin. Eve — and hence every woman — was the reason humanity had been barred from the Garden of Eden. Canon law specified that women were inferior to men and that wives were subject to their husbands and subservient to them. Wife beating was encouraged as a way to control women; physical abuse was common among all classes and was acceptable as long as it did not lead to death.

Some church leaders disagreed with

the official view. Hugh of Saint Victor, for instance, pictured women as partners of men, although this was not a commonly held opinion. More typical were the instructions the Goodman of Paris compiled in a book for his wife-to-be in the fourteenth century: he counseled her to copy the behavior of a loyal dog who follows his master even if his master beats him.

In employment as well, women were considered inferior to men and were paid only half as much. However, they worked at many of the same trades as men did. They sometimes apprenticed in guilds and worked in shops owned by their husbands and fathers. They worked as domestics and as tavern and innkeepers. They had monopolies in some trades, such as ale-making, spinning, and other food and textile trades. Some craft guilds and occupations, however, specifically excluded women.

Women practiced as professors, physicians, and surgeons. Noblewomen served as regents for their young sons, managed households, and ruled in the absence of their husbands, who were often gone fighting wars, undertaking crusades, being held for ransom, or attending the king.

Although women worked, in general their purpose was to have children. If a woman failed to produce children — especially sons — she could be repudiated by her husband or forced to become a nun. The care of children, the sick, the injured, and the elderly was the province of women. A husband could have mistresses, but a woman who committed adultery could be repudiated, physically punished, and in some cases killed. A man's illegitimate children were generally raised and educated in his household.

In many (though not all) regions, women could not inherit land, make a legal will, or testify in court. They required a male advocate to represent their interests. Women could possess or administer a seigneury (fief) or rule an abbey, but throughout much of the world they were legally minors. "Unknown women" — those without a husband or father — were legislated against and expelled from villages and cities.

Women were often physically secluded from men. In France, they lived in the *chambre des dames*; in Greece and the Byzantine Empire, they lived in the gynaeceum. The romantic notion of a woman standing at a window or balcony waiting for a suitor to walk by is actually a realistic depiction of life for middle- and upper-class women. (If inappropriate relationships appeared to be forming, young ladies were kept away from the windows!) Until they were about twelve, they had some freedom to move about their home and village. After that time, they were closely supervised, even locked up. Often they were not even allowed to attend church.

Because marriages were arranged, strong, serious measures were taken to prevent unapproved elopements and sexual relationships that would reduce the woman's value on the marriage market. Women achieved their greatest independence as young servants or as widows. They derived all of their social status from men. Once widowed, they were expected to remarry soon, although traditionally they were allowed thirty days of mourning. Pregnant women were allowed special protection.

Unlike women in most other cultures, Roman women were legally independent of their male relatives. They could divorce their husbands and had inheritance rights. Some of this status was later conferred to the Germanic women who lived among them.

In the early Middle Ages, polygyny was common. Wives were bought, sold, and shared. Husbands could easily repudiate their wives. Only in the eleventh century did England finally pass a law banning the selling of women into marriage (although this practice continued for many years afterward).

Educated Germanic women were raised much the way men were: they fought in battles and hunted with men. Men provided a dowry to women upon marriage. Under law codes, however, Germanic women were always minors, although they could appear before law courts in their own right. The testimony of two or three women equaled that of one man. The Germanic notion that women needed protection melded with Christian doctrine and was assimilated by other groups throughout the Middle Ages.

Anglo-Saxon wives were purchased from their families. Nonetheless, they had considerable power over their property and could dispose of it as they wished. They possessed many legal rights and supervised the household. Divorce was through mutual consent. If an unmarried woman participated in sex, she was fined. If she was married, her lover was fined and bought her husband a new wife. Rape was treated like theft, also punished with fines.

The Burgundians gave women custody of their children and protected female inheritance. By the eighth century, Burgundian women were legally independent of their male relatives.

Frankish women were excluded from public office and from the official church. They were not allowed to actively participate in worship. Tribal law banned certain kinds of contact between men and women. A man who touched the finger of a free woman was fined fifteen shillings. For rape, he was fined forty shillings, double if the woman was married. The fine was payable to the woman's father or husband.

Around the year 1000, women in medieval Europe gained more rights. They commonly supervised households and attended guests. In some cases, they had legal liberty and could buy, sell, and hold land.

Gains and losses in women's legal rights and in their treatment at the hands of men were common throughout the Middle Ages. In many cases, women were more powerful and autonomous in the early Middle Ages than they were in the Renaissance. Whatever the time, there were always women of strong, fearless natures who managed to live their lives on their own terms.

THE ENCYCLOPEDIA

A

Abbess

The leader of a convent, a religious community of women. Only larger monasteries and convents, called abbeys, were ruled by an abbess (or the male equivalent, an abbot). Smaller communities had a prioress or prior as head.

Many well-known women of the Middle Ages, including Hildegarde of Bingen, were abbesses. They educated girls and women and served as protectors and patrons of culture and literature. While women in general had few political rights, abbesses were able to exercise political rights as the superiors of a monastic family. Sometimes they took over the functions of a priest, including celebrating mass, hearing confessions, and blessing novices, although the Catholic church forbade this practice. *See* Convents and Nuns; Hildegarde of Bingen.

Abduction

Abduction, or forcible kidnapping, was a recognized form of marriage in the Middle Ages and was common until the

twelfth century. Occasionally women aided their abductors. Depending on a woman's social position and value to her family, she could be kept imprisoned in her own home (to avoid liaisons of which the family did not approve and which might lower her value on the marriage market). For such women, being abducted was a form of liberation, and they were sometimes willing to go along with it.

Other women were not pleased to be kidnapped and forced into marriage, although they had little choice in the matter. The historical records show cases of married women being abducted for the purpose of marriage. Such was the situation of the queen of Breifne, a petty kingdom in Ireland, who was kidnapped by Dermot MacMurrough. The bloody conflict that followed led to Dermot's deposition and exile. *See* Marriage and Family.

Abuse

Physical abuse of women and children was common in the Middle Ages. It was encouraged by theologians as a way to keep women under control. The law did nothing to stop family members from inflicting pain and injury on each other, although causing the death of another person was always a crime, except in cases of punishment for a serious crime, such as adultery. Both men and women abused children and servants (or other dependents) in order to force them to obey. *See* Marriage and Family.

Acha of Deira (7th century)

The daughter of Ælle, the king of Deira, an early Anglo-Saxon kingdom. Instead of her brother Edwin succeeding to the throne of Deira, a rival, Æthelfrith, invaded and seized the throne. When this happened, Acha's mother fled with Edwin to Wales, where they lived in exile. Usurpers often murdered the rightful heir and his family in order to eliminate a possible focal point for rebellion.

Stranded in Deira and left unprotected, Acha was forced to marry Æthelfrith, who felt the marriage would help legitimize his otherwise specious claim to the throne. Little is known about her life. Æthelfrith himself was killed in 616 when he attempted to murder Edwin.

SUGGESTED READING: Geoffrey Ashe, *Kings and Queens of Early Britain* (Chicago: Academy Chicago, 1990); John Hines and Walter Pohl, *Anglo-Saxons from the Migration Period to the Eighth Century* (London: Boydell and Brewer, 1998).

Adela of Blois (d. 1137)

The daughter of William the Conqueror, she married Stephen, the count of Blois, with whom she had several children, including Theobald V and Stephen of Blois, who later became king of England by the expedient method of usurping the throne.

Adela of Champagne (d. 1206)

Also called Alix. Queen of France, the third wife of Louis VII. The marriage helped normalize relations between the king and the independent nobles of Champagne. Her son Philip II Augustus was Louis's first heir. He later became king of France.

Adelaide of Sicily (12th century)

Queen Mother. A wealthy widow and the mother of King Roger II of Sicily. After the death of her first husband, Roger of Sicily, she married King Baldwin I, the Latin king of Jerusalem, in 1113. According to their marriage agreement, if their marriage were childless, the crown of Jerusalem would pass to Roger, her son. Since both the bride and groom were older, children seemed unlikely.

Once Baldwin had spent Adelaide's enormous dowry, he had the marriage annulled and forced her to return to Sicily. She and Roger were much insulted, and relations between the two governments remained strained for many years. Baldwin's treatment of Adelaide was not an uncommon occurrence in the Middle Ages. *See* Marriage and Family.

Adelaide of Italy, Saint (931–999)

Queen of Burgundy, Empress consort of Emperor Otto I, and regent to her grandson Otto III. She was the daughter of Rudolf II, king of Burgundy, and Bertha of Suabia.

In 947, Adelaide married Clothar (Lothar), the Italian king of Burgundy. He died in 950, and Berengar II of Ivrea seized the throne, imprisoning Adelaide. Later, Berengar's son and co-ruler, Adalbert, attempted to force Adelaide to marry him, thus enhancing his claim to the throne of Burgundy. Adelaide escaped and appealed to the German king and emperor,

Otto I, for help. Otto invaded and married her himself. Otto's son, Liudolf, afraid that this union would affect his inheritance, rebelled against Otto. Otto soon suppressed the rebellion. A few years later, in 956, Liudolf died of malaria.

When, in 962, Otto was coronated as Holy Roman emperor, Adelaide became empress. Throughout his reign, Adelaide remained an important, trusted advisor.

Later, she became interested in Clunaic monasticism and worked to strengthen the bond between church and state. When Otto died, she tried to influence their son Otto II the way she had influenced him. Her perceived interference caused the two to become estranged, and she left Germany for the Burgundian court where she had grown up. Before his death, Otto II reconciled with Adelaide and named her as regent to his son Otto III. With her Greek daughter-in-law, Theophano, she served as co-regent. Theophano died in 991. Adelaide governed until Otto III became an adult, in 994. She retired afterward, founding churches and monasteries before her death. She was widely revered and became an unofficial saint. *See* Theophano (956–991).

SUGGESTED READING: Constance Brittain Bouchard, *Sword, Miter and Cloister: Nobility and the Church in Burgundy, 980–1198* (Ithaca, NY: Cornell University Press, 1987); Mary Erler, *Women and Power in the Middle Ages* (Athens: University of Georgia Press, 1988).

Adelheid *see* Adelaide of Italy, Saint

Adeliza of Louvain (12th century)

Queen of England. After the death of his first wife, Matilda of Scotland, Henry I, the king of England, still had no male heirs. The purpose of his marriage to Adeliza was to produce such an heir. None of his sons survived, so he named his daughter Matilda as his heir. Her claim was contested by male relatives, eventually leading to a civil war. *See* Matilda of England.

SUGGESTED READING: John Hudson, *The Formation of English Common Law: Law and Society in England from the Norman Conquest to the Magna Carta* (New York: Longman, 1996).

Adultery

Adultery and other sexual "sins" were legislated against throughout the Middle Ages, with women more stringently punished than men. *See* Crime, Punishment, and Violence; Law and Women; Marriage and Family; Sexuality.

Ælfgifu (10th century)

Queen of Wessex and later queen of England. She married Eadwig (also known as Edwy), the king of Wessex. His advisor, Saint Dunstan, considered the marriage illegal and repeatedly referred to Queen Ælfgifu as Eadwig's mistress. For this he was banished. Two years later, in 957, Eadwig died, and his brother Edgar succeeded to the throne. Ælfgifu withdrew from court life for some years.

In 975, Edgar died, and his son Edward the Martyr assumed the throne. Since Edward was only fourteen, Saint Dunstan took control of the kingdom. Edward was soon murdered; his half-brother Æthelred II the Unready and his stepmother, Ælfthryth, were implicated in his death. Æthelred became king of England in 979; at that time he married Ælfgifu. Although she was probably in her late thirties or early forties by that time, she had a child with him, Edmund II Ironside, who would become king of

England. Ælfgifu died shortly thereafter. *See* Ælfthryth.

SUGGESTED READING: Steven Bassett, *Origins of Anglo-Saxon Kingdoms* (New York: St. Martin's, 1989); Peter Hunter Blair, *An Introduction to Anglo-Saxon England* (New York: Cambridge University Press, 1992).

Ælfled *see* Æthelflæd

Ælfthryth (10th century)

Queen of England. She married Edgar, the king of England, and became stepmother to Edward the Martyr, who succeeded to the throne in 975, when he was fourteen. She had ambitions for her own son, Æthelred. When Edward was murdered in 979, it was assumed that she had a hand in the plot to kill him in order for her son to wear the crown. Æthelred indeed succeeded to the throne; he married Ælgifu and had a son, Edmund II Ironside, who would also become king of England. *See* Ælfgifu.

SUGGESTED READING: Anne Dugan, ed., *Queens and Queenship in Medieval Europe* (London: Boydell and Brewer, 1997).

Æthelburh (7th century)

Queen of Northumbria. The sister of Eadbald, king of Kent, she married Edwin, king of Northumbria, in 625. She was a Christian and succeeded in converting him within a few years of their marriage. She brought several Roman missionaries with her to Northumbria, where they began converting Edwin's subjects. This process of conversion angered Penda, the Mercian king, a pagan who despised the new religion. Penda allied with Cadwallon, another petty king, and they invaded Northumbria. At the battle of Hatfield Chase, Æthelburh's husband, Edwin, was killed and his army defeated. The Roman mission in Northumbria collapsed, and the kingdom itself was split into two parts. Æthelburh's fate is unclear, but with her help Christianity had established a foothold in England and would soon become the dominant religion.

SUGGESTED READING: David N. Dumville, *Wessex and England from Alfred to Edgar: Six Essays on Political, Cultural and Ecclesiastical Revival* (London: Boydell and Brewer, 1992); Richard Fletcher, *The Barbarian Conversion: From Paganism to Christianity* (New York: Henry Holt, 1998).

Æthelflæd (d. 918)

Also called Lady of the Mercians. Anglo-Saxon ruler of Mercia, a semiautonomous province; she also exerted authority in Northumbria and Wales. Æthelflæd was the eldest daughter of King Alfred the Great. In 886 or thereabouts, she married Æthelred, the ealdorman ("elder man," or ruler) of the Mercians. She effectively served as co-ruler before the death of her husband, strengthening Mercia against the Viking incursions. After Æthelred's death in 911, she assumed complete control of the kingdom.

She assisted her brother Edward the Elder, king of Wessex (ruled 899–924), to defeat the Vikings in eastern England. Æthelflæd built a fortress around Mercia while her brother Edward fortified the southeast Midlands. In 917, they attacked the Viking settlements in eastern England. She and her army captured Derby and Leicester, but she died before the end of the campaign. Edward took over her kingdom and finished driving out the Vikings. Mercia thus became part of Wessex. In the process Edward became ruler of much of Scotland, Wales, and Northumbria.

SUGGESTED READING: Richard P. Abels, *Alfred the Great: War, Kingship and*

Culture in Anglo-Saxon England (Reading, MA: Longman, 1998); Geoffrey Ashe, *Kings and Queens of Early Britain* (Chicago: Academy Chicago, 1990); George Phillip Baker, *The Fighting Kings of Wessex* (New York: Combined Publishing, 1996).

Æthelthryth (d. 679)

Also known by the Latin version of her name, Etheldreda, and the French version of her name, Audrée. Twice-married virgin and monastic founder. She was the daughter of King Anna of the East Angles. Converted to Christianity, she was married, against her wishes, to Tonbert, the prince of South Grywe. He acceded to her wishes that she remain a virgin. After he died, she lived on the island of Ely, part of her dower lands, and pursued a life of quiet contemplation. Her reputation for goodness and virginity commanded the attention of Ecgfrith, king of Northumbria. She found his attention distracting and offensive, but she was forced to marry him anyway. According to her biographers, she convinced him to live chastely with her, pointing out that the Virgin Mary and Joseph made an excellent model for leading a married life without the stain of sin. After some years of this arrangement, Ecgfrith grew angry with her. She refused to relinquish her vows of virginity and joined a convent ruled by Ecgfrith's aunt. He followed her there and had her expelled. With divine intervention, she was able to flee to Ely, where she established a monastery and became a nun. Finally, Ecgfrith married someone else.

After her death, her extreme asceticism was praised, and a cult grew up around her. When her body was moved sixteen years after her death, it was found to be uncorrupted, a sign of chastity. She was believed to be powerful even after death; she protected her lands and her monastery from destruction for many centuries. She became the example of virginity in Bede's *Ecclesiastical History.* More medieval vernacular lives or biographies were composed in England about her life than about any other native female saint. Several of her biographers were women. *See* Marriage and Family; Religion and Women.

SUGGESTED READING: Venerable Bede, *Ecclesiastical History of the English People* (New York: Oxford University Press, 1992); Gerald Bonner, *Church and Faith in the Patristic Tradition: Augustine, Pelagianism and Early Christian Northumbria* (New York: Variorum, 1996); David Hugh Farmer and J. F. Webb, *The Age of Bede* (New York: Penguin, 1983); Karen Winstead, *Chaste Passions: Medieval English Virgin Martyr Legends* (Ithaca, NY: Cornell University Press, 2000).

Agatha *see* **Matilda of Scotland**

Agnes (1024–1077)

Holy Roman empress. The daughter of Agnes of Aquitaine, who ruled Aquitaine as regent even after her son should have succeeded, and William V the Pious, the duke of Aquitaine, who died before Agnes married Henry III, the Holy Roman emperor, in 1043. In 1056, Henry died, and Agnes became regent for their young son, Henry IV. When he reached the age of majority, she refused to cede power to him, just as her mother had done with her brother. She was finally deposed in 1062, with the connivance of the German bishops. Afterward, she lived in Rome until her death; her son became a great enemy of the pope. *See* Agnes of Aquitaine.

SUGGESTED READING: H. Fuhrmann, *Germany in the High Middle Ages, c. 1050–1200* (Cambridge: Cambridge University Press, 1987); Theodor Ernst Mommsen, ed., *Imperial Lives and Letters of the Eleventh Century* (New York: Columbia University Press, 2000).

Agnes of Aquitaine (11th century)

Duchess of Aquitaine. She married William V, the duke of Aquitaine, called the Pious, and had a daughter and son with him.

William died while their son was still a minor, and Agnes married Geoffrey Martel in order to protect her son's interests in Aquitaine. Martel invaded Aquitaine and established her as regent. Later, she refused to give up power even after her son came of age. He united with Martel to depose her, which they accomplished in 1058.

Her daughter Agnes would become empress of the Holy Roman Empire and would also refuse to give up power when her son came of age. *See* Agnes.

SUGGESTED READING: Jane Martindale, *Status, Authority and Regional Power: Aquitaine and France, Ninth to Twelfth Centuries* (New York: Variorum, 1996).

Agnes of France (b. 1171)

The sister of Philip Augustus, king of France. In 1180, at age nine, she married Alexius II Comnenus, the ten-year-old son of Mary of Antioch and the Byzantine emperor, Manuel Comnenus. Alexius's mother, Mary, ruled as his regent until a coup in 1182 deposed Mary and Alexius; both were murdered. In 1183, Agnes, a twelve-year-old widow, was forced to marry the sixty-four–year-old usurper, Andronicus Comnenus. Despite her young age, he consummated the marriage. He made her change her name to the Greek Anna.

Andronicus was deposed by Isaac Angelus in 1185. He was murdered by an angry mob, and Agnes was again made a widow; this time she was only fourteen.

SUGGESTED READING: H. W. Haussig, *A History of Byzantine Civilization* (New York: Praeger, 1971); Alexander P. Kazdan and Ann Epstein, *Change in Byzantine Culture in the Eleventh and Twelfth Centuries* (Berkeley: University of California Press, 1990).

Agnes of Poitiers (12th century)

Queen of Aragón. The sister of Duke William IX of Aquitaine, she married Ramiro II, king of Aragón, known as Ramiro the Monk, in 1136. The marriage, for purely political convenience, enabled Ramiro to secure his claim to the throne. Because he was a member of a religious order, ordinarily he would not have succeeded to the throne after the death of his brother Alfonso I. Ramiro did not want to rule in his own right. Rather, he wanted to control succession.

Agnes gave birth to their daughter, Petronila, late in 1136, and in the following year an alliance with Barcelona was created when Petronila was betrothed to Ramon Berenger IV, the count of Barcelona. Ramiro gave him rulership of Aragón and withdrew to a monastery. Agnes returned to France. *See* Petronila.

SUGGESTED READING: Thomas N. Bisson, *The Medieval Crown of Aragon: A Short History* (London: Clarendon, 1991); Bernard Reilly, *The Kingdom of Léon-Castilla Under King Alfonso I, 1065–1109* (New York: Cambridge University Press, 1991).

Agrestizia *see* **Dindrane**

Ahkas

Spirit wives or spirit women associated with religious worship practiced by medieval Scandinavian women. *See* Religion and Women.

Alice of Jerusalem (12th century)

Princess of Antioch. The daughter of Baldwin, the Latin king of Jerusalem, she married Bohemund II, prince of Antioch, who was killed in 1130 at the age of twenty-two. They had a two-year-old daughter at the time.

Alice served as regent of Antioch after the death of her husband and barred her father from entering Antioch. Baldwin saw an opportunity to rule Antioch, so he resorted to force, took the throne, and exiled her to Laodicea. In 1135, four years after her father's death, Alice was finally allowed to return. Through trickery, her young daughter, Constance, then seven years old, was abducted and forced to marry Raymond of Poitiers, a son of Duke William IX, in order for Raymond to claim the lands. Alice returned to her place of exile and died almost immediately. *See* Constance of Antioch.

SUGGESTED READING: Thomas S. Asbridge, *The Creation of the Principality of Antioch: 1098–1130* (London: Boydell and Brewer, 2000); Steven Tibble, *Monarchy and Lordships in the Latin Kingdom of Jerusalem, 1099–1291* (London: Clarendon, 1990).

Alice Perrers (1348?–1400)

Called Dame Alice. Mistress to Edward III, king of England. She came to court as a ward of Queen Philippa and became Edward's mistress after Philippa's death. Like most royal favorites, she was despised at court. She was not of noble birth, which was also a cause of resentment.

Alice exercised enormous influence over the king and was a good friend to Chaucer and to John of Gaunt. Eventually, she married Sir William Windsor, who had served the king's sons in the military, and continued as the king's mistress.

Intelligent and clever, Alice was notorious for her manipulation of the king.

An act of Parliament finally banished her from court in 1376, but she was brought back by the duke of Lancaster to keep the king occupied during his declining years as the nobles sought to gain power at the expense of the English Crown. Alice's life is an example of the few routes women had to gain power and influence. *See* Philippa of Hainaut.

SUGGESTED READING: May McKisack, *The Fourteenth Century: 1307–1399* (New York: Oxford University Press, 1991); John Taylor, *Politics and Crisis in Fourteenth-Century England* (New York: Sutton, 1990).

Alix *see* Adela of Champagne

Amalasuntha (d. 535)

Ostrogothic queen of Italy. Her father was Theuderic, and her son Athalaric was heir to the throne. Because of his youth, she effectively administered the government, ruling over an Italian kingdom from the city of Ravenna. During her regency, there was unrest between the Goths and the subject Romans.

Like her father, she admired Roman culture and attempted to rule as he had. She was well educated and fluent in Greek and Latin. She tried to influence her son to become well educated and cultured as well, but he was removed from her control by a group of Gothic nobles who disapproved of her plan for educating him. Instead, Athalaric became a dissipated alcoholic and died at the age of seventeen.

After her son's death, the Ostrogoths opposed Amalasuntha's desire to remain in power, primarily because she was a woman. The Ostrogothic king was also the military leader; since a woman was not prepared to lead troops into battle, she could not rule.

The title passed to one of Theuderic's nephews, Theodehad, who Amalasuntha believed would rule jointly with her. To this end, she asked the emperor and the senate to approve this arrangement, which they did. Unknown to her, however, Theodehad had secretly negotiated separately with the Byzantine emperor, Justinian, promising him territory in Italy if he recognized Theodehad as sole ruler. Amalasuntha was imprisoned and later murdered by Theodehad, although he continued to insist to Justinian that he was treating her well.

SUGGESTED READING: Thomas Burns, *A History of the Ostrogoths* (Bloomington: Indiana University Press, 1991); Peter Heather, *The Goths* (Oxford: Blackwell, 1998); Thomas Hodgkin, *Theodoric the Goth* (New York: AMS Press, 1992).

Amazons

Race of warrior women in Greek mythology. In medieval legends, they were female Goths who traveled to Africa to establish their own country. They allegedly cut off their right breasts in order to practice archery. Their society excluded men; occasionally they would have intercourse with captive men or men from neighboring countries in order to reproduce. Male children were sent away or killed.

In the Middle Ages, stories about Amazons could be found in travelers' tales, Arthurian romances and even in Chaucer's *The Knight's Tale*.

SUGGESTED READING: Josine Blok, *The Early Amazons: Modern and Ancient Perspectives on a Persistent Myth* (Boston: Brill, 1994).

Anchoress

Female religious hermit. Anchoresses secluded themselves from contact with the outside world, often living in remote areas. Sometimes anchoresses were walled up in a chamber with only a window to the outside world through which food could pass. *See Ancren Riwle*; Convents and Nuns; Religion and Women.

SUGGESTED READING: Anne Savage, *Anchoritic Spirituality: "Ancrene Wisse" and Associated Works* (Mahwah, NJ: Paulist Press, 1991).

Ancren Riwle

Also *Ancrene Wisse* (Anchoresses' Rule or Anchorites' Rule). A twelfth-century religious work by an unknown author that describes how young women could seclude themselves for religious reasons. It was also used in some medieval convents as a rule of the order. Although didactic, the work is also energetic, realistic, and informative. *See* Anchoress; Religion and Women.

SUGGESTED READING: *"Ancrene Riwle": Introduction and Part I* (Binghamton, NY: Medieval and Renaissance Texts and Studies, 1984); Georgianna Linda, *The Solitary Self: Individuality in the "Ancrene Wisse"* (Cambridge, MA: Harvard University Press, 1982).

Ancrene Rule see *Ancren Riwle*

Ancrene Wisse see *Ancren Riwle*

Anna of Byzantium (10th century)

Byzantine princess of Kiev. Sister of Emperor Basil. She became betrothed to Vladimir, prince of Kiev, over the objection of the Byzantine people; no Byzantine royal person had ever married a foreigner (and a heathen at that.)

Nonetheless, in 989, she and Vladimir were married. Just before the wedding, Vladimir converted to Christianity. Their Kievan subjects soon followed. This was typical of conversion stories in the

Middle Ages: a woman would convert and convince her husband (or father) to follow suit. Once he did so, he would require his family, followers, and subjects to convert as well.

After their marriage, Vladimir gave up his other wives and mistresses and became Saint Vladimir. *See* Conversion.

SUGGESTED READING: Simon Franklin, *The Emergence of Rus: 750–1200* (Reading, MA: Addison Wesley Longman, 1996); Vladimir Volkoff, *Vladimir: The Russian Viking* (New York: Overlook Press, 1988).

Anna Comnena (1083–1153)

Byzantine princess and historian. The daughter of Alexius I Comnenus, the famous Byzantine emperor and Irene Ducas. When she was fourteen, she married Nicephorus Bryennius, a court official who eventually achieved the rank of caesar. With him, she had four children.

Anna believed she would be her father's successor, although she had a younger brother, John Comnenus, who was capable of inheriting the throne. When her father was dying, she and her husband conspired to kill her brother. In this, her mother, Irene, supported her. Anna's plot was discovered, her property was confiscated, and she was barred from court. Exiled, she sought refuge at the monastery of Kecharitomene, which her mother had founded. There, she became a nun, and when she was fifty-five, she wrote the *Alexiad*, a prose epic history of her father's reign and the First Crusade, one of the most famous and important histories of the Byzantine Empire. *See* Irene Ducas.

SUGGESTED READING: Anna Comnena, *The Alexiad of Anna Comnena* (New York: Viking, 1985); Thalia Gouma-Peterson, *Anna Komnene and Her Times* (New York: Garland, 2000).

Anna Dalassena (11th century)

Empress mother and regent for her son Alexius I Comnenus, Byzantine emperor. Her husband, the Byzantine heir, refused the throne after his brother abdicated. Anna was furious at his decision. The imperial crown then passed out of the Comnenus family. Michael VIII Ducas, who succeeded, was deposed by Nicephorus III and eventually abdicated in favor of Anna's son Alexius. Anna was elated at this turn of events.

Alexius married Irene, a member of the Ducas family to resolve tensions, but Anna encouraged him to insult the Ducas family by excluding his own wife from his coronation ceremony, which he did.

Alexius wanted his mother to rule in his place, and Anna served well in this capacity. Alexius conferred authority to her to rule when he left the empire to fight Robert Guiscard, the leader of a Norman invasion.

The Byzantine Empire came under attack from a number of enemies during this period, including Scythians, Muslims, and Europeans. Eventually Anna and Alexius were able to repel the invaders and strengthen the empire. Anna's granddaughter Anna Comnena schemed to rule the Byzantine Empire but was unable to do so. Forced into exile, she wrote the *Alexiad* about her father's reign. *See* Anna Comnena.

SUGGESTED READING: Lynda Garland, *Byzantine Empresses: Women and Power in Byzantium, AD 527–1204* (New York: Routledge, 1999); Barbara Hill, *Imperial Women: Byzantium, 1025–1204: Power, Patronage and Ideology* (Reading, MA: Addison-Wesley, 1999).

Anna Notaras Paleologina (d. 1507)

Eldest child of a wealthy Byzantine family. Her father, Grand Duke Loukas

Notaras, was a high official in Constantinople and served as ambassador to Venice and Genoa.

When Constantinople fell to the Turks in 1453, her father and most of her siblings were imprisoned by the sultan and later murdered. Anna and two of her sisters had been sent to Rome a few years earlier when trouble seemed imminent. Her youngest brother, Isaac, was able to escape the Turks and join his sisters.

During her years of exile, she remained Orthodox. In the 1470s, she tried to found a Greek colony in Siena, wanting to create a community of Byzantine refugees in order to maintain their language, culture, and religion. Although Italian officials approved of the plan, it was never carried out. After this failure, Anna moved to Venice.

She refused to marry and also refused to become a Catholic nun (many wealthy unmarried women did become nuns). No Orthodox convent existed in Venice. The Venetian authorities banned the public practice of the Orthodox faith on the grounds that it was error or heresy and to prevent angering the pope. Anna, after repeatedly complaining about the lack of Orthodox churches in Italy, finally built her own chapel in her own home where Orthodox mass could be celebrated. Throughout her life, she supported Greek scholarship and had a library of her own. *See* Religion and Women.

SUGGESTED READING: Robert de Clari, *The Conquest of Constantinople* (Toronto: University of Toronto Press, 1997); John Julius Norwich, *Byzantium: The Decline and Fall* (New York: Knopf, 1996).

Anna of Savoy (c. 1306–c. 1365)

Also known as Anna Paleologina. Known in the West as Joanna or Giovanna. Regent and empress. She was the daughter of Amadeo V, count of Savoy, and Marie of Brabant. She became a Byzantine through her marriage in 1326 to Andronicus III, who was at odds with Andronicus II. Andronicus III's wife had died, and the future of the Byzantine Empire depended on his marrying again and producing an heir.

Anna seemed a good choice. After her marriage, her husband pronounced her empress, and she converted to the Orthodox religion. During her husband's life, she played little role in the empire except to bear children. Her daughter Irene (Eirene) Paleologina was betrothed to John Asen, the fifteen-year-old son of the tsar of Bulgaria, when she was only five. Anna's son John was born in 1332 and eventually became Emperor John V Paleologus. Her second son, Michael Paleologus, became despot. She had two more daughters; little is known of them.

In 1330, Andronicus fell ill, and Anna ruled the empire on his behalf. In 1341, he died. Her oldest son, John, was only nine years old at the time. John Cantacuzene began acting as regent, but the patriarch, John Kalekas, opposed him and planned to serve as co-regent with Anna, which started a civil war. In the same year, John Cantacuzene's troops proclaimed him emperor. The conflict lasted almost six years. During this time, many problems plagued the Byzantine Empire. The economy suffered, Byzantine coinage was debased to pay for the war, and disastrous treaties with Italian cities were made. In 1343, with the troops of Umur (Turks) at the gates of the capital, Anna summoned help from Venice and Genoa, pawning the crown jewels to pay for the aid. No help came although the jewels disappeared. Many of Anna's supporters deserted her rather than allow the devastation to continue.

Anna grew more and more ruthless

as she attempted to consolidate her power. She eventually dismissed the patriarch when she thought she was losing his support. In 1347, she finally agreed to peace between her son John and John Cantacuzene. They reigned together as co-emperors. John married Cantacuzene's daughter Helena in order to stabilize the situation. Cantacuzene's son Matthew Cantacuzene thought he should be the heir and threatened to overthrow John. Anna convinced him and his allies to withdraw. She then reigned over Thessalonica as empress for fourteen years. In 1354, John Cantacuzene abdicated, and John V Paleologus ruled in his own right.

In Thessalonica, Anna issued decrees and minted coins. Later, she withdrew from public life and became a nun, taking the name Anastasia. She died around 1365. *See* Irene Asenina Cantacuzene.

SUGGESTED READING: Edmund Fryde, *The Early Paleologan Renaissance: 1261–1360* (Boston: Brill, 2000); Donald M. Nicol, *The Byzantine Lady: Ten Portraits, 1250–1500* (New York: Cambridge University Press, 1994); Donald M. Nicol, *The Last Centuries of Byzantium: 1261–1453* (New York: Cambridge University Press, 1992).

Anna Paleologina *see* **Anna of Savoy**

Anne de Beaujeau (c. 1460–1522)

French regent. Sister to Charles VIII, king of France. When their father, Louis XI, died, Charles was still a minor; Louis named Anne regent shortly before his death. Although she encountered some opposition, she ruled from 1483 to 1491, a lengthy period for any regent. Charles's cousin Louis, a rival claimant to the throne, attempted to depose Charles and Anne and was imprisoned for his efforts.

In 1491, Charles began to rule in his own right; Anne arranged his marriage to Anne of Brittany in order to acquire her territory. *See* Anne of Brittany.

SUGGESTED READING: Frederic V. Grufield, *The French Kings* (New York: Da Capo, 1988).

Anne of Bohemia (d. 1394)

Beloved wife to Richard II, the notorious king of England (1377–1399). Of royal blood, her brother was Wenceslas, king of Bohemia. By all accounts, Richard was much in love with her and after her death ordered their manor house at Sheen to be destroyed because she had died there.

Anne of Brittany (1477–1514)

Queen of France. Anne became duchess of Brittany in 1488 upon the death of her father. To maintain the duchy's independence from France, she married Maximilian of Austria, who became the Holy Roman Emperor Maximilian I. A few years later, the French set siege to Brittany. Since Maximilian seemed uninterested or incapable of looking after her interests, Anne annulled her marriage to him in 1491. She then married the French king, Charles VIII. Charles's sister Anne arranged the match in order to acquire the duchy and was willing to defend the territory.

In 1498, Charles died, and Anne married his cousin and successor, Louis XII. The duchy of Brittany was eventually subsumed and became part of French territory. *See* Anne de Beaujeau.

SUGGESTED READING: Michael C. E. Jones, *The Creation of Brittany: A Late Medieval State* (London: Hambledon, 1988).

Anne of Woodstock (d. 1438)

Countess of Stafford. Sole heir of Thomas of Woodstock, she inherited estates in Hereford, Essex, and Northampton.

She was married three times, first to Thomas of Stafford, the earl of Stafford; then to his brother and heir, Edmund, with whom she had three children; and finally, in 1419, to William Bourchier, a nobleman with whom she had five children. When William died in 1426, she became the wealthiest woman in England. Her estates, which she managed personally, were always profitable and well run.

Antonina (6th century)

Byzantine political figure. The daughter of circus performers, she married Emperor Justinian's brilliant military leader, Belisarius. Before their marriage, she had several children with different fathers. She remained unrepentant and unchanged after their wedding and continued to have numerous affairs. She accompanied her husband on most of his military campaigns and was with him when he reconquered the Vandal kingdom in North Africa. She was a practical and intelligent leader.

In 548, Belisarius sent her to seek more aid from Emperor Justinian, but Empress Theodora had just died, and Justinian, overcome with grief, was unable to respond. Belisarius and Antonina were forced to conclude the reconquest without additional aid.

SUGGESTED READING: Averil Cameron, *Changing Cultures in Early Byzantium* (New York: Variorum, 1996).

Arabian Nights

Also known as *One Thousand and One Nights*. A compilation of stories from Persia, Arabia, India, and Egypt, collected over hundreds of years. Originally, they were probably told as oral stories, folklore, and fables. The stories include tales well known to Westerners, such as "Ali Baba and the Forty Thieves," "Aladdin and the Lamp," and "Sinbad the Sailor."

The stories were grouped together and given a cohesive narrative in the Middle Ages. In the narrative, a sultan discovers that his wife has been unfaithful and has her murdered. So enraged is he by her infidelity that he decides to marry a new woman every night and have her killed in the morning so that he can be assured of her fidelity.

Scheherezade, an Arabian princess, agrees to marry the sultan. In order to prevent his killing her, she arranges to tell a story to her sister, who has accompanied her to the sultan's palace. That night, Scheherezade stops her story telling before finishing the tale. The following morning, the sultan allows her to live so that he can hear the rest of the story. She continues and begins a new story each night for one thousand and one nights. At the end of this time, the sultan decides to let her live.

The earliest extant version of *Arabian Nights* is an incomplete manuscript from the ninth century. It was added to over the following years, reaching a final form in the late fifteenth century. The stories are valuable sources of information about medieval Arabic civilization. *See* Scheherezade.

SUGGESTED READING: Ferial J. Ghazoul, *Nocturnal Poetics: The Arabian Nights in Comparative Context* (Cairo: American University in Cairo Press, 1996); Husain Haddawy, ed., *The Arabian Nights* (New York: Norton, 1995); Robert Irwin, *The Arabian Nights: A Companion* (New York: Viking Penguin, 1996).

Argante

In Arthurian legend, the queen of Avalon, with whom Arthur sought refuge after his last battle, according to the medieval historian Layamon.

Ariadne (5th century)

The daughter of Byzantine Emperor Leo, she married Zeno, an Isaurian chieftain. Her son Leo was named successor to her father. Ariadne felt her husband should have been so honored and forced her son to name Zeno co-emperor. Her son died shortly thereafter, and Zeno assumed sole rulership of the Byzantine Empire.

Ariadne's mother, Verina, and her uncle Basiliscus were implacable enemies to Zeno. Verina wished her lover, Patricius, to be emperor; Basiliscus wished to be emperor himself. The two contrived to depose Zeno, but Basiliscus had Patricius murdered. Two years later, in 477, Zeno returned and reclaimed the throne. Zeno's general, Illus, imprisoned Verina for her treasonous crimes. Notwithstanding the fact that her mother was the mortal enemy of her husband, Ariadne took offense at this act and attempted to have Illus assassinated. A few years later, Zeno broke with Illus and freed Verina, who helped establish a rival court under the usurper Leontius.

After Zeno died in 491, Flavius Anastasius became emperor, largely through Ariadne's manipulations. She married him soon after his elevation, although he was in his sixties at the time. *See* Verina.

SUGGESTED READING: Michael Grant, *From Rome to Byzantium: The Fifth Century AD* (New York: Routledge, 1998); Stephen Williams, *The Rome That Did Not Fall: The Survival of the East in the Fifth Century* (New York: Routledge, 2000).

Art of Courtly Love

De arte honeste amandi. Also called *Treatise on Love.* A work by Andreas Capellanus (Andrew the Chaplain) examining the ideal of courtly love, probably written about 1185. Andreas was chaplain to Marie, the countess of Champagne, who commissioned him to write the treatise.

In the work, Andreas tell his audience to be generous and Christian. He points out that clergy members make the best lovers and boasts of his own skills in this area, mentioning in particular his ability to seduce nuns, although he maintains that he has always declined to complete the seduction for fear of punishment in the next life.

Andreas also describes what courtly love is and how it should be conducted and ends, as is typical of such works in this period, with a retraction that lists all of the sins and vices of women, who, he decides, are not really worthy of such emotion.

The treatise was extremely popular as is evident by the number of manuscripts which exist. The work was also translated into a number of vernacular languages. *See* Courtly Love.

SUGGESTED READING: Peter L. Allen, *The Art of Love: Amatory Fiction from Ovid to the "Romance of the Rose"* (Philadelphia: University of Pennsylvania Press, 1992); Andreas Capellanus, *The Art of Courtly Love* (New York: Columbia University Press, 1990).

Asa (9th century)

Viking queen. Mother of Halfdan the Black, the famous Viking leader. According to legend, Gudrod the Hunting King abducted and forcibly married her, which was not uncommon at the time. When their child, Halfdan, was still an infant, one of Asa's sympathizers killed Gudrod. For safety, Asa raised Halfdan in the kingdom of Agdir, her homeland, where he became king. Later he defeated many Scandinavian kings and died in an accidental drowning.

SUGGESTED READING: D. Wilson,

ed., *The Northern World: The History and Heritage of Northern Europe* AD *400–1100* (New York: Abrams, 1980).

Astrid (10th century)

Mother of the Viking ruler Olaf I Tryggvason, the first Norwegian king to convert to Christianity. After her husband, Tryggvi Olafsson, was killed, Astrid, pregnant with Olaf, fled and gave birth to her son on an island, around 968. Astrid evaded her many enemies and made her way to the court of Kiev, where her brother Sigurd was a high-ranking court official. Astrid, her son, and many of their allies found sanctuary there. Olaf became a Viking adventurer in the Baltic and married a Polish princess. Around 994, he allied with Sveyn Forkbeard, the Danish king, in order to regain his lost inheritance.

SUGGESTED READING: D. Wilson, *The Vikings and Their Origins* (London: Thames and Hudson, 1980).

Athenais (d. 460)

Also called Eudocia. Byzantine empress. Her given name refers to the city of Athens, where presumably she was born. She married the Byzantine emperor, Theodosius II, in 421. A pagan, she converted to Christianity before her marriage. At that time, she changed her name to Eudocia. The following year, she had a daughter, who she also named Eudocia; her husband rewarded her with the rank of augusta. This annoyed Theodosius's sister Pulcheria, who wielded the true power in the empire.

Athenais transformed education, making Constantine's university (the University of Constantinople) a large and distinguished intellectual center.

Her daughter Eudocia married Valentinian, who would become emperor, in 437. Athenais then embarked on a pilgrimage to Jerusalem. Soon after her return, she was banished by her husband, probably owing to his sister Pulcheria's machinations. She died in 460 in Jerusalem, where she had lived in exile. *See* Eudocia (b. 422); Pulcheria.

SUGGESTED READING: Michael Grant, *From Rome to Byzantium: The Fifth Century* AD (New York: Routledge, 1998); Mark David Usher, *Homeric Stitchings: The Homeric Centos of the Empress Eudocia* (London: Rowman and Littlefield, 1998).

Avalon

In Arthurian legend, the island where the ladies of Avalon take Arthur after his last battle to recover from his wounds. Geoffrey of Monmouth calls it the Island of Apples; Malory calls it Avilion. It was also formerly known as a Celtic paradise.

B

Baldechildis (7th century)

Also known as Balthild of Chelles or Queen Batilda. Frankish queen and founding mother of Western monasticism. An English noble, she was captured during a siege and forced to marry Clovis II, king of the Franks. When he fell ill, she ruled the kingdom in his name. On his death in 657, she served as regent for her son and co-ruled with the mayor of the palace, Elboin.

She founded a community for women in Chelles in northern France. She entered that monastery when her son technically gained his majority, in 664 or 665. She was noted for her humility.

SUGGESTED READING: Jacques le Goff, *Medieval Civilization, 400–1500* (Oxford: Blackwell, 1990); E. James, *The Origins of France* (New York: St. Martin's, 1982).

Balthild of Chelles *see* Baldechildis

Beatrice Portinari (1266–1290)

Florentine noblewoman believed to be the Beatrice referred to in Dante's *Divine Comedy*, who he loved passionately and could not forget even after her death from the plague. They met in 1274 when Beatrice was only twelve.

Beatrix de Montpellier
(12th century)

A French noblewoman most noted for disinheriting her son in favor of her daughter and her granddaughter in 1171.

Beatriz of Castile (13th century)

Queen of Portugal. The illegitimate daughter of Alfonso X, king of Castile, she married Afonso III, king of Portugal, in 1253, even though he was still married to his first wife, Matilda of Boulogne. Matilda charged him with bigamy, and the pope placed his lands under interdict, but the king and Beatriz refused to separate. After Matilda died in 1263, their marriage was recognized ,and their children were made legitimate. Beatriz's son, Dinis, became king of Portugal. *See* Matilda of Boulogne.

SUGGESTED READING: Heath Dillard, *Daughters of the Reconquest: Women in Castilian Town Society, 1100–1300* (New York: Cambridge University Press, 1985).

Beatriz of Portugal (14th century)

Heiress to Portuguese throne. She was betrothed to John (Juan) I, the king of Castile, but in order to preserve the independence of Portugal, her father, Fernando, insisted that she inherit the crown, that John should be the ruler, but that Queen Mother Leonor should act as regent until a male child of Beatriz and John reached the age of majority and could rule in his own right. This way, Fernando hoped to circumvent any problem with female succession without granting the territory to John outright. John himself could only assume the throne in the case of Beatriz dying childless. The two were betrothed according to these conditions in 1383.

Despite the conditions of the betrothal, John immediately tried to take control of Portugal. In resistance, the citizens of Lisbon elected João of Aris, the illegitimate son of King Peter (Pedro), as defender of the realm. John invaded in 1384 and laid siege to Lisbon. Six months later, he was forced to withdraw. The Portuguese decided that Beatriz was illegitimate and therefore could not claim the throne, so João of Aris was crowned king in 1385 and became João I. This prevented John from making any further claim to the throne. Nonetheless, John invaded again, but this time his army was routed at Aljubarrota.

Beatriz thus lost her inheritance. It is possible she could have kept the throne or at least participated in a succession decision if John had not interfered. *See* Leonor of Aragón.

SUGGESTED READING: James Maxwell Anderson, *The History of Portugal* (Westport, CT: Greenwood, 2000).

Beauty

Highly valued in the Middle Ages, when the idea of "love at first sight" first became common. The beauty of a woman was believed to be the primary reason for a man to fall in love. Andreas Capellanus, the author of *The Art of Courtly Love*, accordingly believed a blind man to be incapable of love.

Most people in the Middle Ages believed that a person's outward appearance reflected the nature of his or her soul; therefore, a beautiful woman had a charitable, Christian nature. The most highly prized features were blonde hair with grey eyes. Cosmetics were used to enhance one's natural appearance. *See Art of Courtly Love*; Cosmetics; Courtly Love.

Béguinage

A communal house for Béguines. *See* Béguines.

Béguines

Women's religious movement. The word is used to describe many different types of religious movements under the control of women, but the Béguines were actually a specific religious group. In northern Europe in the thirteenth century, the group appealed to single and widowed women who wished to live a religious life without becoming nuns; convents rarely had room for women without ample endowment. Members of this lay religious order followed conventional monastic rules. They lived alone, in groups, or with their families and taught, performed manual labor, preached, and wrote. Their philosophy was to "live neither in the world nor out of it." Many lived together in béguinages; some cities had as many as a hundred of these houses.

Members took no vows. A person could join the order simply by taking an oath in front of a clergyman, but the order was never sanctioned nor made official by the church; in fact, their insistence on preaching and writing pious and mystical works brought them into continual conflict with church authorities. One of the most famous Béguine writers was Mechthild of Magdeburg. The Béguines were condemned for heresy in 1312, and the movement subsequently disappeared.

In Bavaria, similar communities were called Gottesfreunde, "friends of God," and members attempted to live in direct imitation of Christ. Because these communities remained in close association with the church, they did not come into conflict with authorities as the Béguines did. *See* Convents and Nuns; Mechthild of Magdeburg; Religion and Women.

SUGGESTED READING: Marie Conn, *Noble Daughters: Unheralded Women in Western Christianity, Thirteenth to Eighteenth Centuries* (Westport, CT: Greenwood, 2000); Ernest W. McDonnell, *The Beguines and Beghards in Medieval Culture with Special Emphasis on the Belgian Scene* (New Brunswick, NJ: 1954, 1969).

Belota the Jewess (14th century)

Early fourteenth-century physician. She was prohibited from practicing medicine because she was a woman and was repeatedly arrested for continuing to treat patients. *See* Medicine and Health.

Berengaria of Castile *see* Berenguela

Berengaria of Navarre (1165?–1230)

Queen of England. The daughter of the king of Navarre, Sancho VI, she married Richard I (the Lionhearted) in 1191 even though Richard had previously been betrothed to Alice, the daughter of the French king, Louis VII. At the time of their marriage, Richard had already embarked on the Third Crusade, so Berengaria traveled to Italy to meet him. They were married in Cyprus. She stayed at

Acre while Richard continued crusading. On his return from the Middle East, he was taken prisoner by the Germans. Berengaria then moved to France to attempt to ransom him. Although Richard was ransomed in 1194, the couple were never reunited. Richard died in 1199, and Berengaria spent the rest of her life in France. *See* Crusades.

SUGGESTED READING: Ann Trindade, *Berengaria: In Search of Richard the Lionhearted's Queen* (Dublin: Four Courts Press, 1999).

Berenguela (1180–1246)

Also Berengaria of Castile. Spanish queen. Daughter of Queen Leonor of Castile (Eleanor Plantagenet) and Alfonso VIII, king of Castile. To settle a dispute between her father and Alfonso IX, king of León, she married Alfonso IX and as dowry brought with her some disputed lands. The marriage took place in 1197; this was the second marriage for both. Friendlier relations between the two kingdoms then followed. But Berenguela and Alfonso were too closely related for their marriage to be approved by the pope, so in 1198, he excommunicated them and placed León under interdict. In 1204, after the birth of their five children, they dissolved their marriage and were reconciled with the pope. Hostilities between her former husband and her father followed but by 1209, they had settled their differences.

In 1214, after the death of her father, Berenguela's brother Henry (Enrique) I succeeded to the throne of Castile. He was eleven years old. She served as his regent and earned praise as a wise and prudent ruler. He died three years later while playing; Berenguela then recalled her son Ferdinand III, called the Saint, from León, where he was living with his father. Although she was heiress to the kingdom of Castile herself, she renounced her claim in favor of her son at the request of the people.

Alfonso IX went to war against them, apparently feeling he had a claim to the Castilian throne. Berenguela and Ferdinand easily defeated him, and when Alfonso died in 1230, Ferdinand permanently united the two kingdoms.

SUGGESTED READING: Simon Barton, *The Aristocracy of Twelfth-Century Leon and Castile* (New York: Cambridge University Press, 1997).

Berhta *see* **Bertha**

Bertha (6th century)

Also Berhta. Queen of Kent. The daughter of Charibert, king of Paris, she married Æthelberht, king of Kent. She was a Christian, and Æthelberht agreed to allow her to continue practicing her faith. There was probably a group of similar believers in Kent at this time. Æthelberht tolerated the missionaries of Gregory the Great and later, under his wife's influence, converted to Christianity himself and was baptized by Saint Augustine of Canterbury. *See* Conversion.

SUGGESTED READING: Richard Gameson, *St. Augustine and the Conversion of England* (New York: Sutton, 2000).

Bertha of Sulzbach (12th century)

Byzantine empress. She married Byzantine Emperor Manuel Comnenus and took the Greek name Irene. She was a diplomatic asset, although unloved by her subjects. She concluded an alliance between the Western emperor, Conrad, and her husband in 1148. She was noted for her virtue and chastity.

Bertrada of Montfort (d. after 1114)

Notorious noblewoman. She married

Fulk the Surly of Anjou, becoming his fifth wife; his first had died, and he had repudiated three others. The union was not a happy one, and she took the king of France, Philip I, as her lover. During one of his visits to Tours, in 1093, she let herself be abducted by him and later bore him two sons. As a result, she and King Philip were excommunicated. They stubbornly remained unrepentant lovers even after the pope laid France under interdict. Fulk threatened to kill the king but eventually calmed down. After Philip died in 1108, Bertrada returned to Fulk, then decided she wanted to become a nun. The next year, she became prioress of Notre Dame convent in Haute-Bruyère and abandoned her former scandalous life. *See* Convents and Nuns.

Bieris de Romais (13th century?)

One of the most famous female troubadours of the thirteenth century, she is known to have lived in the Languedoc region of France. She is best known for writing a *chanson* (love poem) to another woman, an occurrence that has for centuries caused scholars to speculate wildly in order to avoid the simple conclusion that one woman could be in love with another. Little else is known about her except that she was born in Rome.

Birgitta of Sweden, Saint *see* Bridget of Sweden, Saint

Blanche of Bourbon (14th century)

French queen of Castile and León. Member of the famous French Bourbon family whose members ruled several European countries. She was the sister of Joanna, the queen of France (1337–1378). She married Peter (Pedro) I the Cruel, king of Castile and León. Immediately after their marriage, Peter imprisoned her

so that she would not interfere with him and his mistress; later he simply abandoned her. Blanche died soon thereafter, and the French accused Peter of murdering her; he was quite capable of it. This act prompted the French to support Henry (Enrique) II, one of Peter's illegitimate brothers, in his claim to the Castilian throne. The English therefore supported Peter, and the two countries fought each other by proxy in what became known as the War of Spanish Succession.

SUGGESTED READING: Clara Estow, *Pedro the Cruel of Castile: 1350–1369* (Boston: Brill, 1995).

Blanche of Castile (1188–1252)

Also Blanche of France. Queen of France. The daughter of Alfonso VIII of Castile and Leonor of Castile (Eleanor Plantagenet); her grandmother was Eleanor of Aquitaine, and Blanche was nearly as influential as that woman. She was the mother of and regent for Saint Louis.

Blanche married Louis VIII, the future king of France, in 1200, when she was twelve. Louis was thirteen; neither had any choice but the marriage turned out to be quite happy. Blanche and Louis had twelve children; seven did not survive to adulthood.

The marriage pacified hostilities between England and France. Blanche took an active role in the government, appealing to Louis's father, Philip Augustus, the king of France, to aid her when she raised troops to send to her husband, who was supporting the rebellion against King John in England in 1216.

The two were crowned king and queen in 1223 after the death of Philip. Only three years later, Louis died of dysentery and Blanche ruled as regent for her son, earning a reputation as a pious and responsible ruler. She was also known for her sympathy for the plight of serfs and freed many of them. Her own household included many Castilians but she was intelligent enough not to give important posts to friends and relatives, since this would cause resentment among the French nobles. She provided dowries for poor girls, such as the relatives of servants, and she was generous to strangers.

During her rule, the nobles revolted. She raised an army and suppressed the rebellion. One of the rebellious barons, Count Thibaut of Champagne, afterward fell in love with her and wrote many poems dedicated to her. He came to be known as "le Chansonnier," or the Songwriter.

When Blanche summoned the count of Brittany to court to answer charges, he did not appear. Immediately, in the dead of winter 1228, she and her son Louis marched on the count's castle; in January 1229, they laid siege. Blanche had the village razed, and the count soon surrendered. Shortly thereafter, her cousin Henry III, the king of England, invaded. Blanche, with the support of Thibaut, drove his troops off and negotiated a peace treaty with Henry.

Next, the barons struck at Thibaut, invading his territories in Champagne. Blanche led an army against the rebels, forcing them to leave Champagne and eventually forcing each of the barons to agree to peace.

When disputes with the archbishop of Rouen led to an interdiction on royal chapels and the excommunication of government officials, Blanche seized the prelate's lands and won a hasty settlement. She seized the lands of French barons who supported Pope Innocent IV's Crusade against Conrad, the Holy Roman Emperor (who refused to support Innocent's Crusade to the Holy Land). When the

chapter of Notre Dame illegally taxed peasants and then imprisoned those who complained, Blanche led a band of soldiers against them, rescuing the serfs.

In 1229, she put down a student riot in Paris; in the process, several students were killed. She refused the university's demands for reparations. Many students and masters left the university in protest, but within two years, most had returned.

In 1236, her son Louis IX achieved his majority and began ruling in his own right. Blanche remained an important, trusted advisor. When he embarked on the Seventh Crusade in 1248, she again served as regent. In 1250, he was captured by Turks and eventually ransomed. He died of the plague in North Africa, after the death of his mother.

In the last few days of her life, she became a Cistercian nun. Her heart was enshrined in a tomb at the abbey of Lys in 1253; the remainder of her body was interred at the abbey of Maubuisson. Both were abbeys she had supported throughout her life.

SUGGESTED READING: Georges Duby, *France in the Middle Ages, 987–1460: From Hugh Capet to Joan of Arc* (Oxford: Blackwell, 1991); Theodore Evergates, ed., *Aristocratic Women in Medieval France* (Philadelphia: University of Pennsylvania Press, 1999).

Blanche of France *see* **Blanche of Castile**

Blanche of Lancaster (d. 1369)
Duchess of Lancaster. The daughter of Henry of Lancaster, she married John of Gaunt, the third son of King Edward III, in 1359, when she was eighteen. They had five children together. After Henry's death, she inherited the Lancaster estates, and John became duke of Lancaster. This

established the House of Lancaster, which fought the rival House of York for control of England during the Wars of the Roses.

When Blanche died of the plague ten years after their wedding, John's intimate friend, Geoffrey Chaucer, wrote *The Book of the Duchess* to commemorate her. *See* Kathryn Swinford; Wars and Warfare.

Blanche of Navarre (d. 1441)

Queen of Navarre and Aragón. She married John (Juan) II, king of Aragón, in 1420. She was the heiress of Navarre, and after the death of her father in 1425, John succeeded to the throne. Their son Charles of Navarre rebelled against John on several occasions; even after Charles's death, his supporters continued their rebellion.

John spent most of his time focused on Aragón, and Blanche ruled Navarre alone until her death.

Blanche of Navarre (15th century)

Spanish noblewoman. Daughter of John (Juan) II of Aragón and Blanche of Navarre. She married Henry (Enrique) IV, the heir to Castile, in 1440. After he succeeded to the throne in 1454, he repudiated Blanche to marry Juana of Portugal in order to form a political alliance. Later, her marriage was officially set aside on the grounds of Henry's impotence. *See* Juana of Portugal.

Book of the City of Ladies

A work written by Christine de Pizan in 1404. Based loosely on the allegorical structure of Saint Augustine's *City of God*, *The Book of the City of Ladies* attempts to show virtuous women leading good lives. It was written in response to the misogynistic attack on women by Jean de Meun in his continuation of Guillaume de Lorris's famous work, *Romance of the Rose*.

The Book of the City of Ladies was Christine's defense of women. It consists primarily of example, or stories of examples. Using a logical and rational approach, Christine undermined arguments supporting the inferior status of women. She also encouraged women to use their own intelligence and understanding of what women were like instead of being influenced by the writings of ignorant men. *See* Christine de Pizan.

SUGGESTED READING: Christine de Pizan, *The Book of the City of Ladies* (New York: Persea Press, 1998).

Book of the Three Virtues see Treasure of the City of Ladies

Booke of Margery Kempe

First extant autobiography in the English vernacular. Margery Kempe, a famous 14th-century mystic, narrated the story of her life to scribes, who recorded her memories of her life and adventures as a spiritual teacher. *See* Margery Kempe.

SUGGESTED READING: Margery Kempe, *The Book of Margery Kempe* (Harmondsworth, England: Penguin, 1985).

Bouga

With her sister Touga, part of a legendary family that included five brothers. They drove the Avar rulers from Croatia and subjected the others. They were from "White Croatia," possibly an area north of the Carpathians. They were probably ethnically Iranian. The story is probably based on a migration that took place about the seventh century.

SUGGESTED READING: John V. A. Fine, *The Early Medieval Balkans: A Critical Survey from the Sixth to the Late Twelfth Century* (Detroit: University of Michigan Press, 1991).

Brethren of the Free Spirit

A religious movement of the fourteenth century whose major gospels were written by women. Followers considered themselves to be saved without the intervention of priests or the sacraments of the church. They sought personal salvation through a direct connection with God and believed God to be in themselves. Like other anticlerics, they interrupted church services and otherwise disrupted the work of the church. For these reasons, they earned the enmity of church authorities.

Followers took vows of poverty and believed themselves to be perfect, without sin, even if they engaged in intercourse or other traditionally restricted or prohibited acts. They lived in communal residences which allowed free love and adultery. Followers were encouraged to practice nudity and to be free from shame.

They called themselves "holy beggars" who could take what they wanted. Some followers believed they had the right to kill anyone who interfered with them.

Members were usually literate and well spoken, from the middle and upper classes. Both genders were admitted, but the major gospels were written by two women, Schweister Katrei and Marguerite Porete.

In 1372, the Inquisition condemned the movement. One female leader, Jeanne Dabenton, was burned at the stake. The sect was finally suppressed a few years later. *See* Marguerite Porete; Schweister Katrei.

SUGGESTED READING: Marguerite Porete, *The Mirror of Simple Souls* (Mahwah, NJ: Paulist Press, 1993); Raoul Vaneigem, *The Movement of the Free Spirit* (New York: Zone Books, 1994).

Bride *see* Brigid of Ireland, Saint

Bride Ale

Festivity in which friends and family of a bride-to-be gathered to sell ale, with the proceeds going to the new bride. "Help ales," as these were called, were also held for other members of the community when they were in need of financial help. *See* Marriage and Family.

Bride Payment

Male dowry. Gift of money or property given by a husband to his wife (or her family) at the time of marriage. Common in the early Middle Ages, sometimes bride payment was indistinguishable from purchasing a bride from her family. Later, the bride payment was intended for the bride to use for her support should she became a widow. *See* Dowry; Marriage and Family.

Bride Show

Traditional means by which Byzantine rulers chose their wives. Well-born women from all over the empire presented themselves at a designated time and place. Recruiters went throughout the countryside to find suitable candidates. *See* Marriage and Family.

Bridget *see* Brigid of Ireland, Saint

Bridget of Sweden, Saint
(c. 1303–1373)

Also Saint Birgitta of Sweden. Holy figure and patron saint of Sweden. The founder of an order of nuns, the Brigittines, Bridget was also a mystic. She married Ulf Gudmarsson and had eight children, including Saint Catherine of Sweden. When she was about forty, she traveled to Santiago de Compostela on pilgrimage, which had a profound spiritual effect on her. Her husband died later that year, and

Bridget joined a Cistercian monastery where she revealed her mystic visions. Thereafter, she received a divine message to start a new order, which she called the Order of the Holy Savior, but which is known as the Brigittine Order. The order was confirmed by the pope in 1370. Renowned for her kindness and generosity, especially to the poor, she denounced the corruption of the church and was a zealous reformer. She worked to restore the papacy to Rome and predicted Pope Urban V's unexpected early death. *See* Religion and Women.

SUGGESTED READING: Bridget of Sweden, *Saint Bride and Her Book: Birgitta of Sweden's Revelations, with Interpretive Essay and Introduction* (London: Boydell and Brewer, 2000); Bridget Morris, *St. Birgitta of Sweden* (London: Boydell and Brewer, 1999).

Brigid of Ireland, Saint

(453?–524?)

Also called Bridget, Bride, and Brigid of Kildare. Irish nun and founder of four monasteries, including a double monastery (one that admitted men and women) at Kildare. She became one of the three patron saints of Ireland (along with Saint Patrick and Saint Columba). She was instrumental in the conversion of Ireland.

According to legend, her father tried to arrange her marriage to a wealthy man, but she refused. She also gave away much of her father's money, arousing his anger. As a compromise, he allowed her to become a nun.

Brigid was a healer; some stories about her works have druidic overtones. As abbess of the monastery at Kildare, she may have assumed the functions of a priest, hearing confessions, celebrating mass, and ordaining clergy. According to near-contemporary accounts, she was made a

bishop. A cult formed around her after her death. *See* Religion and Women.

SUGGESTED READING: Mary Low, *Celtic Christianity and Nature: Early Irish and Hebridean Traditions* (Edinburgh: Edinburgh University Press, 1997); Joseph Falaky Nagy, *Conversing with Angels and Ancients: Literary Myths of Medieval Ireland* (Ithaca, NY: Cornell University Press, 1997); Richard Sharpe, *Medieval Irish Saints' Lives: An Introduction to Vitae Sanctorum Hiberniae* (Oxford: Clarendon, 1991).

Brigid of Kildare *see* Brigid of Ireland, Saint

Brigittine Order *see* Brigittines

Brigittines

Also known as the Brigittine Order. A religious order founded by Saint Bridget of Sweden, it was officially known as the Order of the Holy Savior. Saint Bridget established the order after receiving a divine message directing her to do so. The order was confirmed by the pope in 1370 and became popular in northern Europe. In the beginning, Brigittine monasteries admitted both men and women with an abbess over all, but in the sixteenth century the houses were split. *See* Bridget of Sweden, Saint; Convents and Nuns.

Brunhild (550?–613)

Also Brunhilda and Brunhilde. Visigothic queen of the Frankish kingdom of Austrasia. She was the daughter of Athanagild, king of the Visigoths in Spain. She married Sigebert I, king of Austrasia, in 567. Brunhild's sister, Galswintha, married Chilperic, Sigebert's brother and the king of Neustria, a neighboring Frankish kingdom. Chilperic's former mistress, Fredegunde, had his new wife murdered and married Chilperic herself. This strained tense relations even further, as Brunhild attempted to revenge her sister's death. The two women carried on a vicious hostility for many years.

In 575, Fredegunde had Brunhild's husband, Sigebert, murdered. Brunhild then ruled Austrasia as regent for her son, Childebert II. She negotiated his adoption by his uncle Guntram, and he later succeeded to the territories ruled by Guntram, including Burgundy and Orléans. When Childebert died while trying to capture all of the Frankish lands, Brunhild ruled as regent for her grandson. She is known for expelling the monk Saint Columbanus from Austrasia at the request of the Gallic bishops who were angered by his proselytizing. Her reign was legendary for her conniving acts and bloody deeds.

A group of Frankish nobles led by Arnulf, the bishop of Metz, and Pippin the Elder plotted to overthrow her. In 612, their plot succeeded, and she was overthrown by the Neustrian king, Clothar (Lothar) II, son of Fredegunde. Pippin the Elder then became mayor of the palace. Brunhild was tortured, then dragged behind a wild horse until she died. *See* Fredegunde.

SUGGESTED READING: Peter Heather, *The Goths* (Oxford: Blackwell, 1998); Herwig Wolfram, *History of the Goths* (Berkeley: University of California Press, 1990).

Brunhild

Legendary queen of Iceland. A character in the medieval Austrian epic *Nibelungenlied*, which was produced by an unknown writer around 1203. The work incorporates Norse and German mythology as well as legendary and historical material. In the story, the hero Sigurd (Siegfried), a German warrior, helps King Gunther win Brunhild by defeating her in battle. He has the advantage; he is wearing a magic cape. Brunhild, believing King Gunther has defeated her, consents to marry him. The theme of the warrior-king defeating a warrior-princess through trickery in order to marry her is a common one in folklore.

Later, Brunhild discovers the trick by which she was convinced to marry Gunther. In her anger, she has Sigurd killed; Sigurd's wife, Kriemhild, vows vengeance, eventually murders Gunther and his allies, and then is murdered in turn.

SUGGESTED READING: Francis G. Gentry et al., eds., *German Epic Poetry: The Nibelungenlied, the Older Lay of Hildebrand and Other Works* (New York: Continuum, 1995); Katherine Morris, *Sorceress or Witch? The Image of Gender in Medieval Iceland and Northern Europe* (New York: University Press of America, 1991).

C

Caesaria (6th century)

Abbess of first known convent for women. In 512, the convent was established by her brother, Bishop Caesarius of Arles, who then appointed her its abbess. *See Rule of Nuns.*

Cataline de Lancaster *see* **Catherine of Lancaster**

Caterina *see* **Thamar**

Caterina Benincasa *see* **Catherine of Siena, Saint**

Catherine of Lancaster (d. 1418)

English queen mother of Castile. She shared the regency of her son John (Juan) II with his uncle Fernando de Antequera, king of Aragón; they divided the administration of Castile in half to resolve tension between them in 1407. After Fernando died in 1416, Catherine ruled as sole regent until her death in 1418, after which time the pope declared John to be of age.

Catherine was known for enforcing restrictive legislation aimed at Muslims in Castile, including the requirements that Muslims wear an identifying symbol on their garments and live away from Christians. They were also banned from holding public office and from practicing a trade or profession. Many Muslims lived in rural areas, working as sharecroppers; many others were slaves. Catherine restricted Jews in a similar way. In 1412, she specified that Jews and Moors (Muslims) must live in enclosed ghettos. Jews were required to wear yellow garments and could not be physicians, pharmacists, nor money lenders nor, even more specifically, could they take a meal with Christian friends. Further, she required that Christians in high church or government positions show they had no Jewish ancestry, mostly as a result of a popular belief that Christian blood was made impure by marriage to Jews. *See* Religion and Women.

SUGGESTED READING: Ana Echevarria, *The Fortress of Faith: The Attitude towards Muslims in Fifteenth-Century Spain* (Boston: Brill, 1999); Angus MacKay, *Love, Religion and Politics in Fifteenth-Century Spain* (Boston: Brill, 1998); Mark D. Meyerson and Edward D. English, eds., *Christians, Muslims and Jews in Medieval and Early Modern Spain: Interaction and Cultural Change* (Notre Dame, IN: University of Notre Dame Press, 2000).

Catherine of Sebastopol

One of the best-known slave traders in the Middle Ages. *See* Slavery and Women.

Catherine of Siena, Saint
(1347–1380)

Patron saint of Italy. A noncloistered Dominican nun, born Caterina Benincasa. She was the youngest of twenty-three children in a family of middle-class wealth. She practiced self-deprivation from a young age, living austerely and in a state of penance almost continually. She saw her first visions at the age of seven.

Catherine fell into trances, saw visions, and bore the stigmata of the five wounds of Christ (visible, however, only to her). She thought God spoke directly to her. She wrote the work *Dialogues;* her conversations with God were taken down by her many followers. Evidently a charismatic person, people who came to see her trances and then became devoted to her, calling her "Mama."

She repeatedly described the ecstasy of her union with Christ, which she considered similar to a marriage bond. In one of her visions, Jesus wed her in a ceremony presided over by the Virgin Mary.

As she became more famous, she settled quarrels and converted nonbelievers. She became increasingly interested in public life, influencing kings and popes. She chastised the cardinals for electing the anti-pope. In 1376, she began campaigning for Pope Gregory XI to return to Rome as a symbol of reform in the church. The city of Florence asked her to intercede and negotiate with the pope.

Catherine died of self-inflicted deprivation in 1380 and was canonized in 1461.

SUGGESTED READING: Karen Armstrong, *Visions of God: Four Medieval Mystics and Their Writings* (New York: Bantam,

1994); Caterina da Siena, *Catherine of Siena: The Dialogues* (Mahwah, NJ: Paulist Press, 1988); Elizabeth Alvida Petroff, *Body and Soul: Essays on Medieval Women and Mysticism* (New York: Oxford University Press, 1994).

Catherine of Valois (1401–1437)

Queen of England from 1420 to 1422. The daughter of Charles VI, king of France, she married Henry V, king of England, as part of an unsuccessful attempt to end the Hundred Years' War.

Henry demanded an immense dowry plus the duchies of Aquitaine and Normandy as part of the marriage bargain. Charles VI refused these terms. In 1415, Henry invaded France. Five years later, he married Catherine, after forcing the French to agree to his terms. The following year, Catherine had a son, who would become Henry VI, the inept king who sparked the Wars of the Roses.

Catherine's husband died in 1422. Catherine then married Owen Tudor, a Welsh squire. They had five children, one of whom would become Henry VII, the first Tudor king of England, who ended the Wars of the Roses. *See* Wars and Warfare.

SUGGESTED READING: R. L. Storey, *The End of the House of Lancaster* (New York: Sutton, 1999); Alison Weir, *The Wars of the Roses* (New York: Ballantine, 1996).

Chambre des Dames

"Women's room." In France, the part of the house where women lived in seclusion from men. Similar to a harem or gynaceum. *See* Harem; Women's Quarters.

Chastity Belt

Device, similar to a girdle but with locks, used to protect virginity. The device was invented in the Middle Ages, stemming from the Muslim custom of attaching a padlock to a woman's labia to preserve virginity. The chastity belt eventually made its way from the Middle East to Europe. In medieval times, it was more a literary conceit than a device that was actually used. Chastity belts did not actually come into common use (relatively speaking) until the Renaissance. *See* Marriage and Family; Sexuality.

Childbirth

According to canon law, childbirth was the sole purpose of marriage for women. Women who attempted to use birth control were considered fornicators and even murderers. This did not stop them from attempting to control their fertility.

Childbirth was a mortal hazard. Many women died during childbirth or suffered grave injuries. Contraception and abortion were adopted with limited success; the female role in conception was not well understood.

For nobles, childbirth was an occasion of much importance. The bedchamber would be elegantly appointed, and special rituals would be conducted. The noblewoman would be surrounded by attendants to help her give birth. *See* Marriage and Family.

Childcare

Parents had little understanding of child safety in the Middle Ages. Children were left alone while their parents worked in the fields or conducted their business. Often, fires broke out or accidents occurred that could have been prevented with adult supervision. As many children died in household accidents as died of diseases.

In wealthier families, a nurse was

hired to look after young children. She often kept the children in her own home. *See* Marriage and Family.

Children *see* Marriage and Family

Chivalry

Code of behavior and order of knighthood that developed in Europe in the Middle Ages. As a moral system for war and love, it influenced all areas of noble life. The principles of chivalric behavior were to some degree unattainable ideals, but the concept served as a way to bring the religious and moral aspects of medieval society into harmony with the warrior and martial aspects of medieval society.

The ideal of chivalry was for the knight to serve the ends of justice. He was to be a servant of the church and a liberator of the oppressed. Courage, strength, and ability were imperative. The admired virtues included loyalty, truthfulness, honor, and courtesy. Chivalry also influenced the development of courtly or romantic love, particularly as expressed in medieval literature. The chivalrous lover was polite and generous.

Many of these ideals derived from the history of the warrior. For instance, in the early Middle Ages, the only form of law and government derived from the loyalty a lord and his vassal pledged to each other. From this came the insistence on the importance of loyalty and fulfillment of oaths and vows. The feats and tests of physical strength in which a chivalrous knight might participate during a tournament derived from the fact that it required real strength to wear armor and real skill to battle opponents on horseback.

Of course, chivalric behavior was not always positive. It encouraged violence and the defense of one's honor against small or imagined slights. Some scholars argue that the romantic ideals of chivalry actually encouraged misogynistic attitudes, particularly since few real women could live up to the ideals imposed by the philosophers of chivalry and courtly love. Certainly, the ideals did not apply to women of the lower classes, who could be used or abused however a higher-ranking man desired.

Chivalry reached its peak in the thirteenth century and then entered a decline in the fourteenth and fifteenth centuries. Much of the substance of chivalry had been lost, as can be seen in the number of defeats inflicted on knights during battles in this period. The ideals of chivalry and knighthood later became the foundation for the ideal gentleman: the courtly gentleman or courtier. *See* Courtly Love.

SUGGESTED READING: C. Stephen Jaeger, *Origins of Courtliness: Civilizing Trends and the Formation of Courtly Ideals, 939–1210* (Philadelphia: University of Pennsylvania Press, 1990); Richard W. Kaeuper, *Chivalry and Violence in Medieval Europe* (New York: Oxford University Press, 1999).

Chlothildis *see* Clotilda

Christine de Pisan *see* Christine de Pizan

Christine de Pizan (1361–1431)

First professional female writer and a woman of extraordinary talent. A well-respected writer during her lifetime, her work was admired and widely imitated. She became the official biographer of the French king, Charles V; her father, Thomas of Pisano, called Thomas the Astrologer, was a professor of astrology at the University of Bologna until he was retained by King Charles as court astrologer. It was through this relationship that Charles became aware of Christine's talents.

After the death of her husband, Christine became the sole support of her family, and she made a living as a copyist, later writing "for the market."

Her military treatise, *The Book of Deeds of Arms and of Chivalry*, was so wildly popular that even eighty years later, the English king, Henry VII, asked the venerable printer William Caxton to translate the work into English and to distribute it to his soldiers. A copy of this treatise was even owned by Napoleon Bonaparte's aide-de-camp.

During her lifetime, Christine enjoyed influential patronage. Much of her work survives in lavishly illustrated and bound manuscripts that circulated widely at court. Her works were translated into many other languages while she was alive. She was also respected as a literary critic.

Many of her manuscripts deal with "women's issues," and she argues that male writers present a negative and hostile picture of women. She encourages women to use their own experience to guide them instead of listening to the defamations of men, and she offers stories of good, honorable women as role models (although, of course, the term is not one she would have understood).

For nearly a century after her death, Christine's works continued to be read, as the example of her military treatise shows. Both her prose and her poetry were copied and circulated throughout the courts of various lands. New editions continued to be produced. Her popularity peaked in two different places at two different times. Around the mid–fifteenth century, her writings became popular at the Court of Burgundy. The first two dukes collected all of her works, manuscripts of which resided in the court library for many years. A number of the manuscripts circulated not only among members of the court but also among middle-class officials and their families.

In the second half of the fifteenth century, Christine's popularity increased in the Houses of Bourbon, Brittany, and Orleans. Again, copies of her manuscripts were ordered and kept in the libraries of these houses. Anne of Brittany, in particular, enjoyed Christine's work and was instrumental in getting some of the manuscripts printed.

The printer records — that is, the number of printed manuscripts that survive — show that during the latter part of the fifteenth century, Christine's most famous work was "Othea's Letter to Hector," followed by *The Book of Three Virtues*.

During the century following her death, readers considered Christine's writings practical and wise. Her works on philosophy, politics, and religion are comprehensive and encyclopedic as medieval works tend to be. She touched on social and political issues that seemed contemporary even one hundred years later; her reasoned, calm approach and sensible solutions were admired. Her advice was valued even several generations after her death. As tastes changed, however, her writings fell out of favor.

Her works include one commissioned by Philip II, the history of his brother Charles V., *Livre des fais et bonnes meurs due sage Roy Charles V* (Deeds and Good Manners of the Wise King Charles V). Among her other works are: *Avision Christine, Epsitre au dieu d'Amours* (Epistle to the God of Love), *Epitre d'Othéa, Livre de cité des dames* (The Book of the City of Ladies, long considered her major work), *Livre des corps de policie* (On the Body of Policy), *Livre des trois vertus* (The Book of

Three Virtues), *Livre du chemin de long es-tude* (Book of the Long Road of Study), and *Mutacion de Fortune.*

SUGGESTED READING: Christine de Pizan, *The Book of the City of Ladies* (New York: Persea, 1998), *The Book of Deeds of Arms and of Chivalry* (University Park: Pennsylvania State University Press, 1999), *The Treasure of the City of Ladies; or The Book of the Three Virtues* (New York: Penguin, 1985); Marilynn Desmond, *Christine de Pizan and the Categories of Difference* (Minneapolis: University of Minnesota Press, 1998); Maureen Quilligan, *The Allegory of Female Authority: Christine de Pizan's Cite des Dames* (Ithaca, NY: Cornell University Press, 1991); Charity C. Willard, *Christine de Pizan: Her Life and Works* (New York: Persea, 1990); Margarete Zimmerman and Dina de Rentiis, eds., *The City of Scholars: New Approaches to Christine de Pizan* (New York: Walter de Gruyter, 1994).

Christine of Markyate (d. between 1155–1166)

Anglo-Saxon noblewoman and local saint whose biography gives glimpses of a vanishing culture. (In 1066, the French Normans conquered England, becoming the dominant culture.)

Christine wished to become a nun although her family had arranged a marriage for her. She was forced to become betrothed but she refused to live with her husband. She later accused her family of trying to corrupt her and influence her away from the religious life. Vowing to remain a virgin, she fled her family to become a nun; her family incited her husband to rape her. She suffered many terrifying experiences, including at the hands of a local bishop, before she was allowed to live independently. Her story mirrors that of many virgin martyrs who maimed

themselves or allowed themselves to be killed to escape the violations of sexual intercourse. *See* Convents and Nuns; Martyrs, Martyrdom and Martyrology; Religion and Women.

SUGGESTED READING: Cindy L. Carlson, *Constructions of Widowhood and Virginity in the Middle Ages* (New York: St. Martin's, 1999); Kathleen Coyne Kelly, *Performing Virginity and Testing Chastity in the Middle Ages* (New York: Routledge, 2000); Karen A. Winstead, *Chaste Passions: Medieval English Virgin Martyr Legends* (Ithaca, NY: Cornell University Press, 2000).

Chrodechilde *see* **Clotilda**

Chrotichildis *see* **Clotilda**

Clare of Assisi, Saint (1194–1253)

Italian nun inspired by Saint Francis of Assisi. When she was about seventeen years old, she heard Saint Francis preach. Inspired, she entered the Franciscan Order. Under the tutelage of Saint Francis, Clare established the first order of Franciscan nuns, called the Order of the Poor Ladies. They are also known as the Poor Clares. Several hundred monasteries of the order still exist. Clare was canonized in 1255. *See* Poor Clares; *Rule of Saint Clare.*

SUGGESTED READING: Regis J. Armstrong, *Clare of Assisi: Early Documents* (Mahwah, NJ: Paulist Press, 1988).

Clothing

In the Middle Ages, clothing designated status. Because people had no way of knowing who strangers were, they felt it was important to be able to identify others on sight. That way, everyone knew the status of everyone else. At least, that was the ideal. To ensure that people were exactly what they seemed to be, the authorities spent considerable time and effort passing laws that detailed what people could wear, what they could eat, and even how much money they could spend. These were called sumptuary laws.

In Europe, the laws specifically stated what people of different social classes, conditions, and professions could wear. Lepers, for example, were required to wear grey coats and red hats. Clergy members wore cassocks. Physicians wore purple robes and red gloves. Peasants wore blouses or tunics and little else. Prostitutes wore red clothing. Public penitents (such as criminals sentenced to penance) were required to wear white robes. Reformed heretics were forced to wear embroidered crosses on their clothing. Jews were identified by patches on their clothes, usually yellow circles.

One of the reasons sumptuary laws were necessary was that nobles were offended by aspiring classes imitating them. So they tried to prevent others from looking like nobles if they were not nobles. People in the middle class, for instance, could not wear certain kinds of fur. Peasants could only wear brown or black. Sumptuary laws even limited the number of new outfits that individuals could purchase annually. The laws detailed exact specifications for clothing, furs, jewelry, and other ornamentation, such as lace. Even cloth color depended on rank and income. People who violated the laws were subject to fines and the confiscation of the objects they could not legally possess. Documents, however, show that people were willing to risk the fine and confiscation in order to wear clothing outside their designated rank.

The sumptuary laws worked in another way as well. By legislating that only aristocrats could wear silks, furs, fine wools, and expensive jewelry, they also implied that aristocrats should wear these things or risk degrading themselves.

People of certain ranks received clothing privileges. Knights could wear signet rings and fur. Doctors and their spouses were allowed to purchase more clothes annually than other members of the middle class.

The sumptuary laws tried to fix identity by governing how people in various classes could dress, eat, and consume. But in the end, the laws were unenforceable.

Typical dress was quite consistent throughout the Middle Ages. Gentlemen wore close-fitting garments that could be worn under armor, such as a doublet and hose. In cold weather, they wore fur-lined jackets or cloaks. The codpiece was an especially ornate accessory that only gentlemen wore, designed to enhance and draw attention to the male anatomy. Women of noble rank wore elaborate dresses that consisted of a long undergarment and an overgarment with wide sleeves, usually a kirtle and mantle or gown and surcoat, plus as many rings, amulets, and necklaces as possible. Most gowns were brightly colored. For special occasions, women wore jeweled or fur-trimmed gowns of velvet and brocade. They usually wore their hair loose until they were married. Married women wore scarves or veils. Women of the middle class or of the lower nobility wore linen and wool housedresses over petticoats.

For special occasions, women wore wimples as nuns traditionally have done. Headgear also indicated rank. The king and queen wore crowns. Bishops wore miters, and the pope wore a tiara. Nobles, squires, and magistrates wore pointed hats called hennin. The taller and more pointed these were, the more elegant they were considered to be. For special occasions, the hats were made of gold and silver tissue. Wealthy women wore jeweled circlets or bandeaus instead of more elaborate headdresses. Doctors wore hoods. Wealthy landowners wore coifs, while farmers wore round brimmed hats, and rural people wore caps. Jews wore yellow pointed hats.

For shoes, commoners wore heavy boots or wooden clogs with leather laces, while nobles wore heelless slippers. These slippers fit tightly and came to a point with long curling toes.

Clothing was usually secured with laces, clasps, and brooches. Europeans did not know about buttons until the thirteenth century. Pockets were also unknown, so all members of society carried purses that contained their belongings. Undergarments were not often worn; if an undergarment was worn at all, it consisted of a linen shift.

Clothing was handed down from generation to generation. Although fashions did change over time, a fine gown was a permanent investment, passed down from mother to daughter.

Clothing varied in different parts of the world. In the Byzantine Empire, an oriental influence was apparent in decorations such as embroidery, fringes, and extensive needlework. Cloaks and tunics were commonly worn, as were caftans and long-sleeved robes. Imperial documents described appropriate court garments. Courtiers were expected to adhere to these regulations.

Clothing was more traditional and more practical in some parts of the world. This meant draped tunics, which could be elaborately decorated. In the Middle East, this garment was modified into a sewn robe often worn with an overrobe. Variations of the sari were worn in India and Asia. Persians and some eastern tribes wore trousers (easier for mounting horses).

In Southeast Asia, trousers and vests or waistcoats were worn. Trousers were also common in China, although rarely worn in Japan. China, Japan, and Korea all had variations of the kimono which could be layered in cold weather. These could be ornamented and decorated to a great degree.

SUGGESTED READING: Hans-Werner Goetz, *Life in the Middle Ages* (Notre Dame, IN: University of Notre Dame Press, 1997); Alan Hunt, *Governance of the Consuming Passions: A History of Sumptuary Law* (New York: St. Martin's, 1996); Karel C. Innemee, *Ecclesiastical Dress in the Medieval Near East* (Boston: Brill, 1997); C. M. Woolgar, *Household Accounts from Medieval England* (New York: Oxford University Press, 1993).

Clotilda (6th century)

Frankish noblewoman. Daughter of Saint Clotilda and Clovis I, king of the Franks. Her brother Childebert became the king of Paris.

Clotilda married Amalaric, king of the Visigoths, in order to ease tensions between the Franks and Visigoths. The opposite condition occurred when Amalaric, an Arian Christian, refused to allow Clotilda to practice orthodox Christianity. This gave her brother Childebert an excuse to wage war on the Visigoths. Amalaric subsequently died in battle, possibly murdered by his own soldiers. *See* Clotilda, Saint.

Clotilda, Saint (c. 470–545)

Burgundian princess. The daughter of the Burgundian noble Chilperic, she was also the niece of the king of the Burgundians, Gundobad. She married Clovis I (also known as Chlodwig), king of the Salian Franks, in 493. According to legend, she converted her husband to Christianity in

496, after he won a battle against the Ala-mann, a Germanic tribe, when she prayed to God for his success. Clovis was baptized that year. He forcibly converted his subjects to Christianity, thus establishing Christianity in the West, directly influencing the course of Western civilization. After Clovis's death in 511, the kingdom was divided among their four sons. Their daughter, also called Clotilda, was the cause of a war between the Franks and the Visigoths.

After the death of her husband, Clotilda withdrew to a monastery and was canonized shortly after her death. *See* Clotilda; Conversion.

SUGGESTED READING: John W. Currier, *Clovis, King of Franks* (Milwaukee: Marquette University Press, 1997); J. N. Hillgarth, *Christianity and Paganism, 350–750: The Conversion of Western Europe* (Philadelphia: University of Pennsylvania Press, 1986).

Colette, Saint (15th century)

Religious figure and political and spiritual advisor. She served as advisor to the Burgundian court as well as to the French court of Philip the Good and his mother, Margaret of Bavaria. She negotiated political and diplomatic matters among the noble families of Burgundy, Savoy, and France. Many powerful people, including Margaret, Charles the Bold, and Maximilian of Hapsburg, sought her canonization.

When Colette was four, her mother, during her daily prayers, felt the sufferings of Christ; the memory of her mother's pain created a lasting influence. For her entire life, Colette herself felt pain during the hour of the crucifixion and whenever she read or heard about the sufferings of Christ.

Colette was hypersensitive to many things. She could not stand the sight of fire and could not tolerate heat, nor insects; the thought of sexual intercourse repelled her. She preferred to remain a virgin and wanted her followers to be virgins, too. She despised married saints and faulted her own mother for marrying her father, particularly as it was a second marriage. Later she was denounced as a hypocrite and a manipulator, but her influence was nonetheless important. *See* Religion and Women.

SUGGESTED READING: Dyan Elliott, *Fallen Bodies: Pollution, Sexuality and Demonology in the Middle Ages* (Philadelphia: University of Pennsylvania Press, 1999); Aviad M. Kleinbert, *Prophets in Their Own Country: Living Saints and the Making of Sainthood in the Later Middle Ages* (Chicago: University of Chicago Press, 1992).

Constança *see* Constanza

Constance

Also Custance. A literary figure popular in the Middle Ages, Constance typifies the medieval ideal of womanly virtues. She, along with Griselda, another archetypal literary figure, portrays the patience and meek submissiveness desired (but infrequently obtained) of medieval women.

In Chaucer's retelling of the Constance story, *The Man of Law's Tale*, Custance (Constance), the beautiful emperor's daughter, is desired by a "sowdan [sultan]." He becomes Christian in order to marry her. The sultan's mother, a "welle of vices," is angered that her son has renounced his old religion and vows vengeance. She puts Custance in a boat and for "yeres and dayes fleet this creature / Thurghout the See of Grece" (lines 463–64). God protects Custance from danger and even though she is without food and water, she does not starve. She is blamed for the death of her friend Hermengyldes, but many are converted to Christianity by miracles and her example. She is banished this way not just once, but twice. Each time, as her name suggests, she patiently ("constantly") endures her hardships. At the end, reunited with the sultan, "they lyven alle, and never asunder wende" (line 1157). This involuntary exile serves to test Custance and determine whether she is able to serve in community. Her exile allows her true virtue to become apparent. *See* Griselda.

SUGGESTED READING: Geoffrey Chaucer, *The Riverside Chaucer* (New York: Houghton Mifflin, 1987); Kathleen Coyne Kelly, *Performing Virginity and Testing Chastity in the Middle Ages* (New York: Routledge, 2000).

Constance of Antioch (b. 1128)

Heiress to Antioch. Daughter of Bohemund II of Antioch and Alice of Jerusalem. After her father died, Constance and her mother were exiled to Laodicea. In 1135, they were allowed to return to Antioch. Almost immediately, through trickery, Constance was abducted and forced to marry Raymond of Poitiers, who wanted to claim her territories. She was seven years old. The two had four children; one of their daughters, Mary of Antioch, became empress.

Raymond died in battle against the Muslims in 1049, and Constance needed a new husband to secure her right to Antioch. In 1153, she married Reynald of Châtillon, a Crusader. He proved unfaithful and unreliable. *See* Alice of Jerusalem; Mary of Antioch.

Constance of Castile *see* Constanza of Castile

Constance of Sicily (c. 1154–1198)

Queen of Sicily and Holy Roman empress. The daughter of Roger II, king of Sicily, she became his heiress. She married Henry VI, son of Frederick Barbarossa, the Holy Roman emperor, in 1184. Five years later, she succeeded to the Castilian throne but was opposed by Tancred of Lecce, her nephew. The Sicilians supported his claim. Henry invaded on Constance's behalf, but was unable to consolidate his power. He withdrew and returned to Germany to put down a revolt by German nobles.

In 1191, after the death of his father, Henry was crowned Holy Roman emperor and Constance was named empress consort. When she was forty years old, she bore her first and only child, Frederick. Frederick was called Stupor Mundi, the Astonishment of the World.

In 1194, Tancred died, and Constance claimed the Sicilian throne with no further dispute. She and Henry were crowned queen and king of Sicily. Three years later, Henry died, and Constance tried to ensure her son's succession, but she died the following year. Pope Innocent III became Frederick's guardian; Frederick became the Holy Roman emperor. He inherited the Sicilian throne from his mother and kept a court there.

SUGGESTED READING: Donald Matthew, *The Norman Kingdom of Sicily* (New York: Cambridge University Press, 1992); Hiroshi Takayama, *The Administration of the Norman Kingdom of Sicily* (Boston: Brill, 1993).

Constance of Sicily (13th century)

Queen of Aragón and Sicily. The daughter of Manfred of Sicily, she married Peter (Pedro) III (the Great), king of Aragón. By 1268, after the deaths of her brother and father, she was referred to as heiress in official documents. After her marriage in 1262, she and Peter became embroiled in a succession dispute over control of Sicily. After the revolt of the Sicilian Vespers in 1282, in which the Sicilians revolted against Angevin (Norman/French) rule and murdered a party of French soldiers, Peter used his marriage to Constance to seize the throne by supporting the Sicilians against the French military and Italian clergy.

SUGGESTED READING: Steven Runciman, *The Sicilian Vespers: A History of the Mediterranean World in the Later Thirteenth Century* (New York: Cambridge University Press, 1992).

Constanza of Aragón (14th century)

Aragonese heiress. Daughter of Peter (Pedro) IV of Aragón, who named her his heir in 1347 with the consent of the Aragonese nobles. In an unusual step, he consulted with civil and canon lawyers to ensure the legality of her succession.

Constanza of Castile (d. 1394)

Castilian heiress. The daughter of Peter (Pedro) the Cruel, king of Castile, who was murdered in 1369. She became heir to the throne and married John of Gaunt in 1372 to cement an alliance between England and Castile. According to Spanish law, this made John of Gaunt the king of Castile, if he could regain the throne from the usurper Henry (Enrique) of Trastamara, who was supported by the French as part of the so-called War of the Spanish Succession.

Constanza and John were recognized by the English parliament as king and queen of Castile, although they were never able to take power. After Constanza's death, John of Gaunt withdrew his claim.

SUGGESTED READING: Clara Estow, *Pedro the Cruel of Castile, 1350–1369* (Boston: Brill, 1995); Angus MacKay, *Society, Economy and Religion in Late Medieval Castile* (Brookfield, CT: Ashgate, 1987).

Convents and Nuns

Convents are communities organized for women (nuns) to devote themselves to spiritual life. Throughout the Middle Ages, religious people withdrew from the temptations of the world, living alone or in monasteries, where they tried to attain salvation through prayer, penance, and in some cases, good works.

Although monasticism had existed before Christianity, it flourished during the Christian era. The first full-scale religious community for both men and women was founded in Egypt in the fourth century. Hermits, who withdrew to live alone, were especially common in the early Middle Ages and in the East. Friars, who went out into the world to preach, became more and more visible as the Middle Ages continued. Hospitals, also religious communities, had lay brothers and sisters who assisted with the care of the sick. Hermits and friars, along with monks and nuns, became the most enduring symbols of Christianity during the Middle Ages.

Nuns usually entered a certain religious order or monastery (the term was used to refer to religious communities of men or women) as teenagers and later took vows that bound them to the order. Sometimes babies or young children were given to monasteries to be raised; these children were called oblates. Often, oblates were disabled or simply lacked physical beauty, which made it difficult for them to survive in the outside world. Too many children in a family resulted in a tremendous burden, so "extra" children were sent to a monastery. It was often cheaper to purchase an entry to a monastery than to provide a dowry for a daughter.

Usually, however, a person would decide as a teenager to enter a monastery, a comparative oasis of calm and order in a violent world. Such communities lived by a "rule," specific guidelines for behavior. The age of majority for girls professing monastic vows was fourteen. They took a triple vow: obedience, poverty, and chastity. They cut their hair in order to become less attached to earthly beauty. Women who had their hair shorn could not continue to live in the outside world without embarrassment — everyone would know they had violated their vows. Women forced to enter monasteries would have their hair cut immediately as a symbol to them — and to the outside world — that they now belonged in a monastery. There was no way to hide short hair nor escape the meaning of it.

There were fewer monasteries for women than for men, and female monasteries had fewer members than male monasteries. For example, in the thirteenth century, there were one hundred English female convents as opposed to six hundred male monasteries. Eighty to one hundred nuns was not uncommon for a house; there was a definite trend toward social exclusiveness. Convents were poorer than male monasteries because nuns had a limited role in Christianity. Male monasteries had larger endowments and received more money from the church.

Most nuns were the unmarried daughters of a noble family or one of many daughters in a family. Widows often entered convents after their husbands died. Byzantine convents especially brimmed with cast-off mistresses, inconvenient wives, and former empresses. Some married couples entered monastic life together, although they had to set aside their marriage vows and agree to be celibate. This rule was almost certainly broken on occasion. Some women left unhappy marriages to become nuns; this required their husbands' consent. Sometimes unwanted wives were forced to join a monastery, although this did not mean their husbands were free to remarry.

Convents also provided a place for female intellectuals to live. The most scholarly women were usually nuns; this scholastic tradition was especially strong in Germany. Many German abbesses made their convents into centers of culture, learning, and piety. Abbesses were extremely powerful, particularly in Saxony in the tenth and eleventh centuries. The abbesses of Quedlinburg and Gandersheim were powerful enough to strike their own coins. Abbesses like these ruled convents that owned large tracts of land and had their own knights and their own law courts. Important abbesses highly influenced the surrounding community, and people would name their children after them.

Most nuns saw themselves as religious people first and as women second. Very religious women would follow ascetic practices, such as fasting, which may have induced hallucinations (therefore, "visions"). Women in monasteries were thought of as brides of Christ — the consecration ceremony stressed this — whereas male monastics were identified as emulating Christ himself.

It was not uncommon for women to enter a convent, then leave to marry, bear children, and return, depending on political expediency. Sometimes they were known to have affairs and bear illegitimate children.

Kings and queens established royal monasteries. These secular rulers influenced monastic policy; by the same token, abbesses became integral to the secular government. Because they were educated, nuns wrote letters, acted as advisors, and served as diplomats. Nobles also established private monasteries, often for their unmarried daughters, who would become abbesses. The founder would often enter the monastery as well, after turning over worldly affairs to her children.

Political prisoners and inconvenient claimants to the throne were sometimes confined to monasteries. Clerics who were criminals were forced to live in monasteries as prison sentences. Women also became nuns to answer a call or vocation, to escape criminal penalties through lifelong penance, or if no other livelihood were available.

The purposes of life in a convent were prayer, work, and study. People gave donations in order to have prayers said for them or for their loved ones. Burial in hallowed ground in a convent was much sought-after and could be purchased for the right price.

Abbesses and nuns founded almshouses to care for the poor and hospitals to care for the sick. Some medical training was given to nuns who were expected to take care of the other members of the community. Convents often accepted orphans, and nuns taught the girls in the outside community. Nuns also served as stewards of property and executors of wills and assisted with other legal affairs. They issued mortgages, lent money, and engaged in trade.

Abbesses — indeed, all members of a convent — had to enlist the support of the surrounding community, as they were defenseless in times of war. Their property was at risk, although physical harm to nuns occurred less often than to lay women. Nuns often played political roles, but if they found themselves on the losing side,

their convent could be dissolved. They used their spiritual clout as a political tool.

A limited number of nuns could be admitted to an order, depending on the wealth of the monastery. If a nun brought her own wealth, she could be admitted. Often one nun had to die in order for another to be admitted. Although requiring an entry fee was condemned by the church as simony, and male monasteries stopped accepting such fees in the thirteenth century, women's monasteries received little financial support from the church and continued to require them. Although nuns were supposed to be personally poor, the monastery had to be financially solvent in order to support its members. Early monasteries were self-sufficient, raising their own food and making their own clothes, but over time this became more difficult. Money was needed to pay for cloth and to purchase the services of laborers and other employees. Donations and entry fees were therefore important. Novices were accepted for their money, not for their suitability for religious life. Private property was "loaned" to nuns to ensure their survival. Papal exemptions were sometimes sought in order to hold inherited property. Nuns were more likely to have personal property than monks; their orders had fewer financial resources, and their families were likely to try to support them by giving them private incomes or control of what would have been their marriage dowries.

Gifts often came with strings. Donors could have the final say over who was elected abbess, for instance, or pressure the convent to accept certain novices.

A monastery was organized on hierarchical grounds. The abbess was the master of the monastery. She was usually much superior to the nuns over whom she presided. Abbesses were almost always members of the nobility. They often had their own separate houses and participated in the secular world. They were supposed to be elected by the nuns in a monastery, but were usually appointed by a secular ruler or the pope. In smaller convents, the prioress was the leader. A sub-prioress assisted her. A treasurer kept track of the convent's funds. Obedientiaries, the officials who managed various aspects of community living, included the chantress, who organized church services; the sacrist, who was responsible for vestments, altar cloths, candles, and sacred utensils; the fratress, who was responsible for chairs, tables, linens, and dishes; the almoness, who was responsible for almsgiving; the chambress, who was responsible for making, cleaning, and repairing clothing and bed linens; the cellaress, who was responsible for food and for gardening/farming; the kitcheness, who was responsible for food preparation and was subordinate to the cellaress; the infirmaress, who was responsible for nursing the sick; and the novice mistress, who educated and oversaw novices. In small convents, one person could have multiple duties; in larger convents, the officials had assistants. Convents also hired a chaplain who lived outside the convent grounds; he was responsible for saying mass and hearing confessions.

It was the bishop's responsibility to oversee monasteries and make sure they were run correctly. Documents show that some monastics were unwilling to follow the bishop's instructions. There are records of nuns having children, sometimes more than one, taking in novices they could not afford, and otherwise bending, if not breaking, the rules of the order. Exemptions from Episcopal oversight, which some powerful abbesses eagerly sought, made the house directly responsible to the pope. These nuns often challenged the authority of male superiors although in general nuns accepted their place in a patriarchal society.

The church encouraged cloistering and enclosure because authorities believed women were extremely susceptible to temptation. Although strict cloister was the ideal, in reality nuns needed to maintain ties with their families and friends and to oversee worldly business. Thus, there were two kinds of cloister, active and passive. In active cloistering, nuns were not allowed to leave the convent. In passive cloistering, outsiders were not allowed in. Nuns were forbidden to attend weddings and baptisms because such events encouraged dancing, drinking, and other merriment. Nuns were not allowed to go on pilgrimages, since they could easily be led astray during such a trip; nonetheless, as Chaucer's *Canterbury Tales* tells us, this rule was not strictly obeyed. The cloistering of nuns was considered more important than the cloistering of monks, although many monastic rules imposed cloistering on men, too.

Most nuns remained firmly attached to their families and visited them even if officially in cloister. Nuns needed to leave the cloister for their own interests as well as to see to the convent's interests. Relying on male proxies often resulted in disaster. More than one convent that relied on proxies quickly found itself bankrupt. Nuns were criticized for leaving the cloister to attend to these needs, although the nuns and abbesses rarely saw anything wrong with it.

Often many relatives lived in the same convent. Convents were not just spiritual places, but institutions created and existing for the well-being of family members.

Often monasteries consisting of one gender had some members of the other who lived in affiliation with them because they were related — brother and sister, mother and son. Sometimes lay people who were relatives lived closely with professed monastics.

Unlike the traditional plan of a monastery composed of individual cells in which each monk slept, nuns were supposed to sleep in cubicles separated by low walls to prevent them from yielding to sexual temptation. In the Benedictine Order, nuns were supposed to stay silent except during service or during chapter meetings. All orders had chapter meetings, in which misbehavior was discussed and punishment and penance meted out.

Often, however, nuns had private chambers and had their food specially prepared for them. They ate their meals in their chambers and even entertained guests there.

In the ninth century, the Second Council of Aix-la-Chapelle (836) denounced some convents, saying they resembled brothels and asserting that nuns frequently broke their vows of chastity. In many cases, only a small number of monastics were incontinent, possibly those whose reasons for joining the convent were not religious. It is also likely that nuns were occasionally coerced by male clergy and male laborers as well.

Poverty and unchastity were linked; the poorer houses suffering financial hardship had less control over their members. Small and isolated houses were more prone to this problem as well. Low morale and a difficult life made unchastity more common. All convents had male staff — a chaplain, priest, lay brothers, laborers, overseers — so it was not difficult for a nun to find a sex partner.

When monks were sexually active, they tended to have fleeting relationships and were thus less likely to be discovered, although by the fourteenth century, the male clergy had a notorious reputation for lewd behavior. Nuns who were involved in sexual relations were likely to enter long-term relationships and also ran the risk of becoming pregnant; for these reasons, they were more likely to be discovered in their error.

Anyone who left a monastery denied a binding vow, and therefore it was a reprehensible act to leave a monastery in order to marry. Having an affair, on the other hand, was considered a temporary human failing and could be forgiven with penance and a vow to do better in the future.

Besides becoming nuns in convents, women could follow a religious life in other ways. Canonesses lived in convents and were celibate and obedient to the order's rule, but they did not take a vow of poverty and were not cloistered. Béguines were free to leave the sisterhood when they wished.

When orders of friars became more common, many women embraced this type of religious vocation, but the church was slow in accepting female friars. (Female Franciscans and Dominicans lived like other nuns, unlike male Franciscans and Dominicans, who lived as friars.) Women sometimes chose to become anchoresses in cells built adjacent to churches, monasteries, and even castles. A mass for the dead would be celebrated and earth scattered over her to show her soul's "death" to the world. There were twice as many female anchoresses and recluses as there were male.

Women sometimes took vows of virginity (performed in front of the parish priest and witnesses) and remained with their families; although such vows were binding, they usually did not offer a woman protection if her family wanted her to marry someone. *See* Anchoress; Béguines; Religion and Women.

SUGGESTED READING: Anne Boyd, *Life in a Medieval Monastery: Durham Priory in the Fifteenth Century* (New York: Cambridge University Press, 1987); W. Braunfels, *Monasteries of Western Europe* (London: Thames and Hudson, 1972); Jean le Clerq, *Love of Learning and the Desire for God: A Study of Monastic Culture* (New York: Fordham University Press, 1982); Roberta Gilchrist, *Gender and Material Culture: The Archaeology of Religious Women* (New York: Routledge, 1997); Penelope Johnson and Catherine R. Stimpson, *Equal in Monastic Profession: Religious Women in Medieval France* (Chicago: University of Chicago Press, 1991); F. Donald Logan, *Runaway Religious in Medieval England, c. 1240–1540* (New York: Cambridge University Press, 1996); Marilyn Oliva, *The Convent and the Community in Late Medieval England: Female Monasteries in the Diocese of Norwich, 1350–1540* (London: Boydell and Brewer, 1998); Miriam Schmitt, ed., *Medieval Woman Monastics: Wisdom's Wellsprings* (Collegeville, MN: Liturgical Press, 1996).

Conversion

In the Middle Ages, Christian women were often credited with converting powerful men, who would then impose Christianity on their subjects. A great deal of evangelization was done by women, although little of this was authorized or sponsored by the church. Women converted to Christianity more quickly than men did. They would then attempt to convert the men in their lives, including brothers, fathers, sons, and husbands. Christianity appealed to women because it promised them autonomy — they could save their own souls. It also offered an alternative to marriage, in that they could become nuns and enter a religious community.

Christianity was well established in Europe by the eighth century, but in Eastern Europe, for example Hungary and Poland, Christianity was slow in coming, and even by the fourteenth century some Balkan rulers were still pagan.

Conversion had a darker side in the Middle Ages. When pagans, Muslims, or Jews refused to convert, they often were forced to leave their homes; sometimes they were murdered or their children kidnapped if they refused to convert. Muslims also forcibly converted subject peoples, particularly in the seventh and eighth centuries. *See* Religion and Women.

SUGGESTED READING: J. N. Hillgarth, *Christianity and Paganism, 350–750: The Conversion of Western Europe* (Philadelphia: University of Pennsylvania Press, 1986); Henry Mayr-Harting, *The Coming of Christianity of Anglo-Saxon England* (University Park, Pennsylvania State University Press, 1991); James Muldoon, ed., *Varieties of Religious Conversion in the Middle Ages* (Gainesville: University Press of Florida, 1997); Norman Roth, *Conversion, Inquisition and the Expulsion of the Jews from Spain* (Madison: University of Wisconsin Press, 1995).

Cooking *see* Food and Cooking

Cosmetics

Because beauty was so highly prized in the Middle Ages, women went to no end of trouble to adorn their faces. To this end, they frequently used cosmetics, although the church condemned such artificial enhancements. Because a pale white face was prized, women used lead as a whitening agent. Byzantine ladies used enamel on their faces. In order to redden their cheeks, they used roots of vines mixed with rosewater. To conceal wrinkles, they used the juice of swordplant. Freckles were bleached by using dragonwort and bones of cuttlefish mixed with water or eggs and vinegar. For pimples, they applied leeches. Women bleached their hair using extracts made from ashes in order to achieve the much-admired blonde hair. Perfumes were also popular, often made from spices.

Cosmetics could be purchased from merchants. The ingredients used—such as arsenic—were often dangerous, even deadly. *See* Beauty.

Countess of Dia (b. c. 1140)

Famed female troubadour. Although four of her *chansons* are extant, no record of her life has been found. She was probably related to the powerful Burgundian aristocracy and married a lord of Dia.

Courtly Love

A code of behavior for noble lovers to follow; it was love for its own sake, romantic love, even true love, as opposed to the purely convenient, businesslike marital relationships in which most couples found themselves participating. It flourished as an ideal between the eleventh and thirteenth centuries, when the concept of chivalry also flourished. The idea was originally taken from the Roman poet Ovid, who set forth many of the rules in his poem *Ars Amatoria* (Art of Love). Courtly love was celebrated in the *chansons* of the French troubadours, who were the first poets to write about women as exalted figures.

Courtly love was a component of chivalry and, like chivalry, required adherence to certain rules. Usually another man's wife was the focus of courtly love. A lover proved his devotion by performing anonymous heroic deeds and feats of strength. Courtly love was believed to make a man better, since he would try to

be a more generous, honorable person. He would present a clean and neat appearance and be more interesting. Other typical elements of courtly love included lovesickness, jealousy, insomnia, and loss of appetite.

Secrecy was essential to courtly love, since it was by its definition adulterous. Love was irrelevant to marriage—it got in the way of political arrangements—and so it was reserved for relationships outside marriage. The faithlessness of lovers was considered more shameful than adultery.

The prevailing misogynistic attitude of the Middle Ages was at odds with this ideal. On the one hand, women were considered faithless, shrewish, unintelligent, and unkind, and on the other hand, they were considered beautiful, constant, considerate, and worthy of any sacrifice. Some historians consider courtly love a secular counterpart to the Cult of the Virgin Mary; it has been called the Cult of Women and the Cult of the Lady.

Historians disagree over the actual practice of courtly love. Since in reality adultery was a sinful and criminal act, some historians believe that courtly love was little more than a literary convention, not for everyday purposes. Others contend that it was an ideal that many people tried to follow. In actual practice, courtly conduct simply meant that upper-class women should not be physically abused, coerced, or raped; lower-class women did not have even this flimsy protection. In essence, the ideal of courtly love recognized the upper-class woman's independent existence, even though it objectified her at the same time.

Courtly love was the topic of a considerable amount of writing, from the romances of Chrétien de Troyes to the *Roman de la Rose* of Guillaume de Lorris and Jean de Meun, which tells the story of a love affair through the literary device of a dream-vision. The ideal of courtly love was also celebrated in Arthurian romance.

Some historians argue that courtly love ideals actually encouraged misogynistic attitudes toward women in two ways: first, by creating a standard any real woman would be incapable of attaining, and second, by making her an object and not a person, capable in her own right. *See* Chivalry; Cult of the Virgin Mary; *Roman de la Rose.*

SUGGESTED READING: Peter L. Allen, *The Art of Love: Amatory Fiction from Ovid to the "Romance of the Rose"* (Philadelphia: University of Pennsylvania Press, 1992); Andreas Capellanus, *The Art of Courtly Love* (New York: Columbia University Press, 1990); R. Howard Block, *Medieval Misogyny and the Invention of Western Romantic Love* (Chicago: University of Chicago Press, 1991).

Crime, Punishment, and Violence

In the Middle Ages, crime and violence were inescapable; murder was the leading cause of death. Twice as many homicides occurred as accidental deaths. Vicious assaults were routine. Art and literature frequently depicted blood, violence, and cruelty.

Some historians have suggested that a combination of factors created such a violent culture, including the idealization of violence in the form of chivalry, an exceptionally martial culture borrowed from imperial Rome, and the fact that few people lived beyond a young age — adolescents and teenagers made life-and-death decisions every day. Enormous power was concentrated in the hands of children, ultimately leading to a breakdown in authority, to unchecked impulsiveness, and

to an emphasis on short-term satisfaction rather than long-term gains. Thus, an insult was answered with an act of violence, which in turn required a violent response, engendering a devastating spiral of destruction.

In Europe, each lord dispensed justice for these people under his control or on his lands. He kept fines for himself. The lord or his steward determined guilt or innocence and assessed penalties. Women were rarely in this position; when they were, it was almost always as regent for a husband or son. Little in the way of evidence was used. People who served as witnesses to the proceedings had to remember the details and dates since written records were rare. Therefore, they would often be beaten to impress the day and its details on their memories. Violence was an officially recognized means of ascertaining the truth; torture was acceptable. To extract confessions, accused people could be brutally beaten.

Women usually could not appear in court and required a male advocate to protect their interests. They usually could not testify in court cases, although in Anglo-Saxon society, women could appear before the law assembly. The testimony of two or three women was considered equivalent to that of one man.

A woman's husband or father was considered responsible for her conduct and would answer accusations against her. In some cases, a woman who worked in a trade different from her husband's would be legally responsible, separately from her husband. The prevailing belief was that a father or husband should not be responsible for a woman's business debts.

For minor crimes, such as disturbing the peace, the criminal would be subject to a period in the stocks or the pillory in the town square, where neighbors could ridicule the criminal and pelt him or her with rotten vegetables. In other cases, public penance would be demanded, with the criminal/penitent forced to wear sackcloth and ashes, to walk barefoot for miles, or even to live in a monastery for the rest of his or her life.

Punishment for crimes was usually quite severe. In the later Middle Ages, the death penalty was often used, especially for crimes against property. People were hanged for stealing eggs, for instance. Thieves had their arms and legs amputated. Those conspiring to commit crimes would have their ears cut off and their eyes put out. Accused and condemned criminals could be racked, burned, flayed, flogged, or drawn-and-quartered. In cases of adultery, the woman involved usually suffered more severe punishment than the man. This ranged from a fine to death. In some cases, a woman convicted of adultery was turned over to her husband or father, who could dispose of her as he wished. Cases of violence against women were usually treated like property crimes. Fines would be imposed, depending on the severity of the abuse. Touching a woman inappropriately received a smaller fine than raping a woman; injuring a married woman was a more serious crime than injuring an unmarried woman.

Physical punishments were usually performed in the town square so that an audience could watch. The belief was that seeing a criminal hanged would deter others from committing crimes. However, these gruesome entertainments did little to prevent crime but drew large crowds, including very small children.

The medieval dungeons that loom large in modern imagination really played little role in punishment. Although each lord had a dungeon and could keep suspected criminals, prisoners of war, and political prisoners jailed for months or even years without a trial, most often punishment was quicker, more direct, and more brutal.

Of course, condemning a person and actually carrying out the sentence were two different things, especially in the Middle Ages, when the machinery of law was not sophisticated. A convicted criminal could escape and become an outlaw. A criminal could seek sanctuary in a church, where secular law could not reach; from there the criminal could easily take to outlawry. The criminal might also bribe authorities to escape punishment or embark on a pilgrimage instead of submitting to a sentence. Sometimes a guilty person could enter a monastery to expiate his or her crimes. Occasionally, clerics were condemned to living their lives in a monastery.

Every object had a legal status and was responsible for its actions. Thus, animals were brought to trial for causing property damage. Saint Louis put the Talmud, a Jewish religious book, on trial for blasphemy. The Talmud was convicted. *See* Law and Women.

Suggested reading: Barbara Hanawalt, *Medieval Crime and Social Control* (Minneapolis: University of Minnesota Press, 1999); Guy Halsall, ed., *Violence and Society in the Early Medieval West* (London: Boydell and Brewer, 1997); Timothy S. Haskett, *Crime and Punishment in the Middle Ages* (Victoria, BC: University of Victoria Medieval Studies, 1998); Richard W. Kaeuper, *War, Justice and Public Order: England and France in the Later Middle Ages* (Oxford: Clarendon, 1988); Mitchell B. Merback, *The Thief, the Cross and the Wheel: Pain and the Spectacle of Punishment in Medieval and Renaissance Europe* (Chicago: University of Chicago Press, 1999).

Crusades

Military campaigns by European Christians conducted to regain Jerusalem and the Holy Land from Muslim hands; they took place from 1095 to 1270. In the thirteenth century, Crusades were also undertaken against pagans, heretics, and political opponents. The Crusades began after the Seljuk Turks expanded their territory in the mid–eleventh century. They conquered Syria and Palestine — the Holy Land. Western Christians felt shocked and threatened by this. At the same time, Turkish forces captured parts of the Byzantine Empire, which meant that many Eastern Christians became subject to their rule. The Crusades began as a response to these events. They gave unlanded noblemen and knights the opportunity to take territory. The Crusades also opened up commerce and trading opportunities, especially for the Italian cities.

Women frequently embarked on Crusades, either in connection with their husbands or independently. Often, they went out of religious conviction or to take advantage of the indulgences offered by the pope, but sometimes they went to be free from the restrictions of their families and communities. Women who went crusading sometimes found themselves sold into slavery or forced into prostitution. The church, recognizing these problems, considered forbidding women from embarking on Crusades but was unsuccessful in this endeavor.

Eleanor of Aquitaine accompanied her husband, Louis VII, on the Second Crusade (1145–1148). She earned notoriety for allegedly engaging in a number of affairs along the way; they were divorced shortly after their return from crusading, and Eleanor married the English king. The Albigensian Crusade (1208–1229), which was intended to suppress the Cathari heresy, widespread in the Languedoc area of southern France (specifically in Albi; hence, "Albigensian"), was especially hard on women, many of whom were killed during the fighting. Other women, widowed or unmarried, were forced to attempt to live on the devastated land without the assistance of their male relatives. This was the first Crusade that encouraged Christians to fight against other Christians.

The Children's Crusade (1212) included women and children of mostly lower social classes. Early in the thirteenth century, two twelve-year-old boys, Stephen of France and Nicholas of Germany, preached a Crusade for children. They told their followers that angels would guide them and part the seas for them. Thousands of children, along with clergy members, thieves, prostitutes, and other marginalized people, flocked to join the Crusade. Some of the German Crusaders reached Palestine, where they disappeared, probably sold as slaves. The rest died or returned home. The French Crusaders were offered transport by two notorious French criminals, Hugh the Iron and William of Posquères. Instead of bringing the Crusaders to the Holy Land, the two brought the children to North Africa, where they were sold as slaves to the Arabs.

SUGGESTED READING: Penny J. Cole, *The Preaching of the Crusades to the Holy Land, 1095–1270* (Cambridge, MA: Medieval Academy of America, 1991); Francesco Gabrieli, *Arab Historians of the Crusades* (Berkeley: University of California Press, 1984); Norman Housely, *The Avignon Papacy and the Crusades* (New York: Oxford University Press, 1986), *The Later Crusades* (New York: Oxford University Press, 1992); Steven Runciman, *The First Crusade* (New York: Cambridge University Press, 1992); Kenneth Setton, *History of the Crusades* (Madison, WI: University of Wisconsin Press, 1969); Geffroi de Villehardouin, *Memoirs of the Crusades* (Westport, CT: Greenwood, 1983).

Cult of the Lady *see* Courtly Love

Cult of the Virgin Mary

Also known as the Cult of the Virgin. Medieval obsession with worshipping the Virgin Mary; many of the ideals were similar to those embraced by courtly love. The Virgin was envisioned as a medieval royal lady and was called the Queen of Heaven. Although she had been a minor figure in the Bible, she became a figure of great importance in the Middle Ages, rivaling her son.

According to church officials, Mary's sanctity benefited all women. Saint Augustine, the early Christian theologian, was the first to teach that sex was evil;

therefore, Mary's virginal status was to be admired and emulated. In addition, he taught that salvation could be attained only with the intervention of Saint Mary. Later, in the twelfth century, Bernard of Clairvaux first stated that Mary herself had been born without sin. This doctrine became known as the Immaculate Conception.

The Virgin Mary was seen as a vindication of women, who, through Eve, were responsible for the Fall. But a dichotomy existed. Women were treated as either saints or sinners, not as ordinary individuals. *See* Courtly Love.

SUGGESTED READING: Gonzalo de Berceo, *Miracles of Our Lady* (Lexington: University Press of Kentucky, 1997).

Cult of Women *see* Courtly Love

Custance *see* Constance

D

Dame Alice *see* Alice Perrers

Danielis (8th century)

Wealthy Byzantine widow, patron of Basil the Macedonian, who became emperor. She held vast tracts of land and built shops and entire villages. She was well known for her textile production facilities. She held hundreds of slaves to work her holdings. Contemporary accounts claim she gave gifts to Basil that were richer than kings could give to one another.

Dervorguilla (13th century)

Scottish noblewoman affiliated with

the king's family. She married John Baliol the Elder, and their son John Baliol the Younger became king of Scotland in 1292. After the death of Margaret, Maid of Norway, he became embroiled in a succession dispute and was chosen by the king of England, Edward I, to succeed to the Scottish throne.

Desideria *see* Hildegarde of Suabia

Dhuoda (800–after 844)

Frankish noblewoman who wrote a treatise on education. She married a court official, Bernard of Septimania, in 824.

During this period, Charlemagne's empire disintegrated. Dhuoda bore a son, William, in 826, and was imprisoned in Uzés by her husband. Although not a common occurrence, such mistreatment of medieval women has extensive documentation.

While in prison, she wrote a manual for her son (c. 841–843); this is the oldest extant treatise on education. Further, a lay female author was quite unusual at this date. The manual urges her son to love wisely, exercise self-control, and act with integrity.

Dhuoda was forced to remain in Uzés while her children were in Aquitaine with their father; bad health and other dangers kept her from her family. The manual records her longing to see her children again. Little is known about her life except what is told in the manual. She was clearly well versed in biblical and church teachings and knew Greek and Hebrew sources.

Her husband, Bernard, was accused of treason and executed in 844; five years later Dhuoda's son William was also executed for treason. Nothing is known of her after this date.

SUGGESTED READING: Dhuoda, *Handbook for William: A Carolingian Woman's Counsel for Her Son* (Washington, DC: Catholic University of America Press, 1999); Marie Anne Mayeski, *Dhuoda: Ninth-Century Mother and Theologian* (Scranton, PA: University of Scranton Press, 1995).

Dindrane

Also called Agrestizia. In Arthurian romance, sister to Perceval. With a group of knights, including Perceval, she set out on the Grail quest. The group came upon a castle with a leprous châtelaine. The residents of the castle demanded the blood of any passing woman in order to cure her. Dindrane volunteered her blood and died donating it; this enabled Perceval's success in the Grail quest.

Dísir

Old Norse word for household spirits, always female, who received sacrifices in the home. Such female household spirits were prevalent in medieval Scandinavian religious lore. *See* Religion and Women.

Dowry

Gift of money, land, or other property, which a woman brought to a marriage. Dowries appeared in the later Middle Ages; earlier, bride payment was the norm.

In addition to attracting prospective bridegrooms, the dowry was supposed to support the wife should she become a widow, and it became part of the inheritance passed on to her children. Dower lands were sometimes specified in a marital agreement. This was property to which the wife would retire on the death of her husband, allowing her son to succeed to the principal estates. The laws of dowry allowed widows to use their husband's estates during their lifetimes, although they could not arrange the disposition of it. *See* Bride Payment; Marriage and Family.

SUGGESTED READING: Marion Kaplan, *Marriage Bargain: Women and Dowries in European History* (Binghamton, NY: Haworth, 1984).

Drífa

Legendary queen of "Finnland." In the *Ynglingasaga,* an Icelandic epic, she hires a seiðr (divination) practitioner to disturb the mind of her unfaithful husband, King Vanlandi of Sweden. The magic works; the king wishes to return to

Finnland but his retainers prevent him. Enraged by his lack of response, Drífa tells the seiðr practitioner to send an incubus, who kills the king.

SUGGESTED READING: Robert Kel-logg and Jane Smiley, trans., *The Sagas of the Icelanders* (New York: Viking, 2000).

Droit de Cuissage
"First night." *See* Jus Primae Noctis.

E

Edith (11th century)

Anglo-Saxon noblewoman. The daughter of Godwin, earl of Wessex, she married Edward the Confessor, king of England. Tension between her husband and her father caused her father's exile. He later invaded England. Edward was forced to restore Godwin's land and title.

Edith's life illustrates a typical problem in medieval marriage. Although marital alliances were supposed to ease tensions and reduce hostilities, this did not always happen. Often, a woman was forced to watch her husband war against her father or brothers. It was not uncommon for a woman in this position, who had no choice in her marriage, to support her birth family in opposition to her husband. *See* Marriage and Family.

SUGGESTED READING: J. Campbell, ed., *The Anglo-Saxons* (Oxford: Phaidon Books, 1982); Pauline Stafford, *Queen Emma and Queen Edith: Queenship and Women's Power in Eleventh-Century England* (Oxford: Blackwell, 1997).

Edith, Queen *see* **Matilda of Scotland**

Education

Formal education was denied to most women in the Middle Ages. Occasionally noblewomen and wealthier peasants learned to read at convent schools. Women were not allowed to attend universities. In great households, a tutor was often employed; occasionally the girls could take lessons with the boys. In towns, girls could sometimes attend elementary schools, although this was not considered necessary. The wisdom of educating women was often debated. Moral education — chastity, humility, and modesty — was instead emphasized.

Girls were taught certain skills, such as embroidery, weaving, music, cooking, and sewing. Daughters of nobles were sent to another castle for this training. They learned how to handle finances, select servants, make and care for clothes, choose and tend wines and food, and plant and tend gardens. They also learned first aid since they served as both doctor and pharmacist in their households.

The degree of education and literacy varied widely among social classes in the Middle Ages. Many peasants received no education at all, while the wealthier peasants, artisans, and tradespeople went to church schools or popular schools where they learned reading, writing, and simple math, usually in the vernacular.

At around the age of seven, many non-nobles became apprenticed to a craft or a trade; whether they received further schooling was largely up to the master with whom they apprenticed.

In church schools, the trivium was taught — grammar, rhetoric, and logic. Promising students, in addition, were taught the quadrivium — astronomy, arithmetic, geometry, and music. Those who were destined for the clergy went to traditional schools and universities, where the curriculum was taught in Latin, the universal language of nobles and clergy members. Women who professed monastic vows were sometimes taught Latin, too. Abbesses were usually literate and often taught nuns how to read Latin and the vernacular.

As paper became cheaper and copying became the province of tradespeople, not monks, more and more books were distributed. This, coupled with the power of printing presses, spread the printed word. Increasing numbers of people wanted to learn how to read and write. In the early Middle Ages, it was not essential for a peasant to be able to read; in the closing years of the medieval period, it had become considerably more important. This led to a rise in the number of popular schools, which were often held in the home of an educated villager and led by itinerant teachers.

By the fifteenth century, most higher-ranking clergy and professionals could read and so could many nobles. Of yeomen, craftsmen, and merchants, about half could read. Less than twenty percent of laborers and peasants were literate. In the later Middle Ages, it was common for people — nobles, clergy, and commoners — to be literate in the vernacular language, but not Latin. This led to an increased interest in vernacular versions of the Bible and associated commentaries, but the church opposed writing in the vernacular, primarily because it feared that people

would misinterpret the Bible or feel they no longer needed the intercession of the church or the priests. For many years, possession of a Bible in a vernacular language was considered heresy.

Books

In the early Middle Ages, books were written by monks and clergy members for other monks and clergy members and for secular leaders. Most of these works were versions of the Bible and Bible commentaries, plus sermons, religious stories, and saints' lives. Classical Greek and Roman texts were also fairly common. They were written down and copied by monastic scribes.

Many books were illustrated ("illuminated") with brilliant colors and bound with wood or leather covers with metal clasps. These covers could be painted or enameled and decorated with jewels. Only a small number of people could read and afford books until late in the Middle Ages.

By the fourteenth century, professional copyists and illuminators, many of them women, worked as scribes. Greater literacy and a wealthier middle class meant a greater demand for books. Books of encyclopedic proportions were favored, but all books of knowledge were in demand, covering subjects such as science, alchemy, hunting, war, and strategy. Romances and satires were also popular, as were cookery books, advice and etiquette books, phrase books, and how-to books that taught accounting, hiring and training servants, and treating illnesses. Gardening books, bestiaries, and herbals were all popular. Wealthy women were often patrons of writers and poets, and they purchased many books for their private libraries.

In Asia, scrolls were favored over books with bound leaves during the medieval period. The Chinese invented woodblock printing in the sixth century, so books could be more easily reproduced than in Europe. The first printed Chinese books were religious. In the eleventh century, the Chinese invented movable type. Thus, more people had access to books. These inventions came slowly to Europe but revolutionized education when they did.

SUGGESTED READING: Michael van Cleave Alexander, *The Growth of English Education 1348–1648* (University Park: Pennsylvania State University Press, 1990); J. W. Drijvers and A. A. MacDonald, eds., *Centers of Learning: Learning and Location in Pre-Modern Europe and the Near East* (Boston: Brill, 1997); Heinrich Fichtenau, *Heretics and Scholars in the High Middle Ages* (University Park: Pennsylvania State University Press, 1998); C. Stephen Jaeger, *The Envy of Angels: Cathedral Schools and Social Ideals in Medieval Europe* (Philadelphia: University of Pennsylvania Press, 1994).

Eir

Medieval Scandinavian goddess of healing, in particular, childbirth. *See* Religion and Women.

Eirene *see* **Irene**

Elaine the White *see* **Lady of Shalott**

Eleanor *see* **Leonor Plantagenet**

Eleanor de Montfort (1215–1275)

Noblewoman who served as inspiration for the thirteenth-century story *Jehan et Blonde*, a courtly romance by Philippe de Remi Beaumanoir. The youngest daughter of King John of England and Isabella of Angoulême, she was the sister of King Henry III.

In 1224, when she was just nine years old, she married William Marshal II, a man in his thirties, who was one of Henry's chief vassals. At sixteen, still childless, Eleanor became a widow. Because there were no children of the marriage, William's estate reverted to his family. Nonetheless, she claimed one-third of his estates as her dower land and battled the Marshal family all her life over this, although she eventually settled for an annual tribute of 900 pounds.

After her husband's death, she took a vow of chastity, though she did not became a nun. However, a life of religious contemplation did not suit her.

In 1236, when she was twenty-one, she attended the wedding of her brother Henry in Canterbury and met a French knight, Simon de Montfort, earl of Leicester. He had pursued other potential partners but these had fallen through. He soon became interested in Eleanor. In 1238, they married in secret. Rumor presumed she was pregnant. The wedding took place in the king's private chapel, because of the embarrassment of her violating her vow of chastity. English nobles had every right to object to the marriage — she should have married a native noble or at least someone of royal blood. The king had apparently arranged the hasty wedding in secret, so that no one could object. The nobles were nonetheless affronted by what they termed "the underhanded marriage." By bribery, cajolery, and flattery, Simon convinced the barons to accept the marriage.

Still, some clergy said the marriage could not be acknowledged because of Eleanor's previous vow of chastity, which was considered binding. Because of this, Simon sought a papal dispensation, which, for the right price, was granted. When Eleanor did not have a child until eleven months after her marriage, no one understood the reason for the secret and hasty marriage.

Soon, the two had earned the king's enmity; without permission, Simon had named Henry as a guarantor for money he had borrowed. They were thus evicted from the castle Henry had given them and escaped in the middle of the night to avoid imprisonment in the Tower. They fled to France, where they settled at the Montfort family castle. In 1244, Henry had forgiven them, and they returned to England.

Eleanor blocked a treaty in 1257 because of the dispute over her dower lands; she continued to refuse to give up her family's claim to certain French lands. After her mother's death, she sued her stepsiblings for a share of Isabella's estates. Only after she had received ten manors did she agree to the treaty in 1259.

In 1264, the nobles, under the leadership of Simon de Montfort, went to war against King Henry; the battle of Lewes was a decisive victory for the barons. The king, his son, and his brother were all taken prisoner. Eleanor, who supported her husband's ambitions, ruled the castle in his absence and sent gifts to her imprisoned relatives. Forces loyal to the king battled back and attacked. In August of that year, Eleanor traveled to the stronghold of Dover castle. Her husband and son Henry were killed in battle. Her remaining sons continued to fight against the king's forces. She kept royalist prisoners at Dover under her power and kept the treasury of the barons under her lock and key.

The following year, Prince Edward attacked her garrison, and Eleanor was forced to surrender. She was banished and her land confiscated. She was fifty years old at the time. Afterward, she sought to repair relations with her brother the king, but he did not respond to her overtures.

Finally, she joined the convent at Montargis. Later, her two sons killed Richard of Cornwall's son in revenge for betraying the barons' cause; one son died in hiding within a few months; the other ended his days in a Sicilian prison. *See* Wars and Warfare.

SUGGESTED READING: Alan Harding, *England in the Thirteenth Century* (New York: Cambridge University Press, 1993); Douglas Kelly, *The Art of Medieval French Romance* (Madison: University of Wisconsin Press, 1992); Roberta L. Krueger, *The Cambridge Companion to Medieval Romance* (New York: Cambridge University Press, 2000).

Eleanor of Aquitaine (1122?–1204)

Queen of France and England and the mother of Richard the Lionhearted. One of the most famous medieval women. The heiress to the duchy of Aquitaine, a separate kingdom, she married Louis VII, the French king, in 1137. She was about fifteen years old at the time.

The introduction of the ideals of courtly love are often attributed to her. In her so-called Court of Love, men and women disputed questions of appropriate romantic and chivalric behavior. Her daughter Marie of Champagne commissioned Andreas Capellanus to record the results of their discussions in *The Art of Courtly Love*.

When Eleanor's husband embarked on the Second Crusade, she went with him. She was accused of committing adultery, causing a scandal. In 1152, because of the scandal and because she had not produced a male heir, her marriage to Louis was annulled. The pope approved the annulment on the basis of a blood relationship between the two that had not existed before the marriage. In the Middle Ages, such relationships were conveniently "discovered" when a husband wished to repudiate his wife and be free to remarry.

The duchy of Aquitaine, an important territory, reverted to Eleanor's holding. In the same year, she married Henry of Anjou, who became Henry II, king of England, in 1154. Upon her marriage to Henry, he assumed control over the duchy of Aquitaine.

In 1170, Eleanor convinced Henry to grant their son Richard her French holdings, which he did. Three years later, Richard the Lionhearted and his brother John, called Lackland, fomented a rebellion against Henry with Eleanor's support. She was imprisoned for her part in the rebellion and was not released until after Henry died in 1189. At that time, she gained control of the kingdom, which she ruled as regent for Richard, who had embarked on the Third Crusade. In Richard's absence, John Lackland attempted to usurp the throne with the aid of the French king. When Richard returned in 1194, Eleanor affected a reconciliation between the two brothers. She then withdrew from public life, retiring to a monastery.

After Richard's death, she played an important role in protecting John, now King John, from the machinations of her grandson Arthur of Brittany. She arranged the marriage of her granddaughter Blanche to Louis, the son of the king of France, and again withdrew to her monastery at Fontevrault, where she died in 1204.

After her death, stories circulated that she was mistress to everyone from Saladin, the famous sultan, to Gilbert of La Porrée, an elderly scholar, and to this day she is notorious for her behavior. *See* Marie of Champagne.

SUGGESTED READING: D. D. R Owen, *Eleanor of Aquitaine: Queen and Legend* (Oxford: Blackwell, 1996); Alison Weir, *Eleanor of Aquitaine: A Life* (New York: Ballantine, 2000).

Eleanor of Castile (1244?–1290)

Queen of England. The daughter of the king of Castile and León, she married Prince Edward in 1252. Twenty years later, he became king of England after the death of his father, Henry III. At that time, Eleanor and Edward were in the Middle East on the Seventh Crusade. They were not officially crowned king and queen until they finally returned to England in 1274.

SUGGESTED READING: John Carmi Parsons, *Eleanor of Castile: Queen and Society in Thirteenth-Century England* (New York: St. Martin's, 1995).

Eleanor of Provence (1223?–1291)

Queen of England. She married the English king, Henry III, in 1236. She caused considerable resentment by awarding offices and favors to her many relatives. This resentment turned into the Barons' War, in which Henry was captured by the forces of the nobles. Eleanor raised an army in France and invaded. Her son Edward won the decisive battle of Evesham. When Henry died in 1272 and her son Edward I succeeded to the throne, she withdrew to a monsatery where she later died. *See* Wars and Warfare.

SUGGESTED READING: Margaret Howell, *Eleanor of Provence: Queenship in Thirteenth-Century England* (Oxford: Blackwell, 1998).

Elene *see* **Helena entries**

Elizabeth of Bavaria (1371–1435)

Called Isabeau by the French. Of the Wittelsbach dynasty in Germany, she was the granddaughter of Bernabò Visconti. In 1385, she married the French king, Charles VI, known as Charles the Mad. She was the mother of Charles VII, called the Dauphin, who made Joan of Arc famous; she had nine other children as well.

During her husband's episodes of insanity, he could not endure Elizabeth's presence. She supplied him with a substitute, Odette de Champdivers, whom the public took to calling "the little queen." During these episodes, Elizabeth served as regent, allying with Louis, the duke of Orléans and the king's younger brother.

Elizabeth pursued extravagance, adultery, and political intrigue. She amassed a personal fortune and established a Court of Love to discuss questions of courtly love and noble behavior.

She became mistress to Louis during one of Charles's fits of madness. When Louis was murdered in 1408, she became mistress to his murderer, John the Fearless (Jean de Nevers), the son of the duke of Burgundy. The two effectively ruled France.

When her son Charles became an adult, he rebelled against her and imprisoned her. Her lover, John, came to her rescue in 1417.

As a result of Charles's madness, the English were able to conquer a considerable amount of French territory. In 1420, she agreed to the Treaty of Troyes, which effectively disinherited her son Charles. Shortly thereafter, John switched sides, abandoned Elizabeth, and allied with Charles. Elizabeth's power came to an end, and she retired from public life.

The notorious marquis de Sade became her biographer. *See* Joan of Arc; Odette de Champdivers.

SUGGESTED READING: R. C. Famiglietti, *Royal Intrigue: Crisis at the Court of Charles VI, 1392–1420* (New York: AMS Press, 1987).

Elizabeth of Hungary, Saint
(1207–1231)

Princess of Thuringia. Daughter of Andrew II, king of Hungary. In 1221, she married Louis IV, prince of Thuringia; they had three children. During her marriage, she practiced asceticism and was generous in giving alms to charity. When Louis died, she was exiled from Hungary by her brother-in-law, who claimed her generosity was bankrupting the estate. With the aid of the bishop of Bamberg, her uncle, she was later restored as regent for her son. However, she gave up the regency and became a Franciscan nun. She devoted the rest of her life to the practice of asceticism and to charitable works.

Elizabeth of Schönau (12th century)

Intellectual nun and mystic. She knew and corresponded with the famous abbess Hildegarde of Bingen. She experienced revelations, mostly dealing with humility, tolerance, and abandoning worldly temptations. She carefully recorded these revelations. *See* Hildegarde of Bingen.

Elizabeth of York (15th century)

Queen of England. In 1486, she married Henry Tudor, who became King Henry VII, the first ruler from the House of Tudor. Their marriage unified the Houses of York and Lancaster and ended the civil war known as the Wars of the Roses. *See* Margaret Beaufort; War and Warfare.

Elizabeth Woodville (1437–1492)

Queen of England. Elizabeth, a commoner, secretly married Edward IV, the king of England, in 1464. She manipulated Edward into awarding her family and favorites important positions and financial rewards. He elevated a number of commoners to the nobility. This caused considerable resentment among the established gentry, in particular, Richard Neville.

After the death of Edward in 1483,

their son Edward V succeeded to the throne, but he was imprisoned by his uncle Richard III, who seized the throne, claiming that he was ruling as regent. Richard declared Elizabeth's marriage to the king void because of a prior betrothal, making the children of the marriage illegitimate and therefore not eligible to succeed to the throne. He confined her two young sons to the Tower of London, where they were murdered; history accuses Richard of their deaths, although there is no evidence of this. He forced the unpopular Woodvilles out of their positions of power, and Parliament recognized him as king of England.

The story is told in Shakespeare's play *King Richard III*.

SUGGESTED READING: Bertram Fields, *Royal Blood: Richard III and the Mystery of the Princes* (New York: Regan, 1998); William Shakespeare, *King Richard III* (New York: Cambridge University Press, 2000).

Elsa, Princess

Character in medieval German romances. Lohengrin, the son of Perceval, was a knight of the Holy Grail. He married Princess Elsa after rescuing her, but was then doomed to abandon her.

Emma of Normandy (11th century)

Queen of England. Daughter of Richard I, duke of Normandy. She married Æthelred the Unready, king of England. Both of her sons, Edward the Confessor and Alfred, became kings of England.

In 1013, invading Danes forced Emma and her children to flee to the Continent. Æthelred soon joined them. The following year, the Danish king of England, Svein Forkbeard, died, and Æthelred returned and resumed ruling England.

After Æthelred died in 1016, Edmund II Ironside, Æthelred's son, was named king. Cnut II, called the Great, the son of Svein Forkbeard, defeated Edmund at the battle of Ashingdon. Edmund died a few weeks later, and Cnut became king of England. Emma then married Cnut, who was king of England, Denmark, and Norway. Cnut reconciled with the English people and made peace with the Norman rulers on the Continent.

SUGGESTED READING: Alexander R. Rumble, ed., *The Reign of Cnut: King of England, Denmark, Norway* (Madison, WI: Fairleigh Dickinson University Press, 1994); Pauline Stafford, *Queen Emma and Queen Edith: Queenship and Women's Power in Eleventh-Century England* (Oxford: Blackwell, 1997).

Ermengard (d. 1147 or 1149)

Countess of Narbonne. Known as Duchess Ermengard. The daughter of Fulk of Anjou, she was considered slightly unstable. She married William of Aquitaine, who was also known as William the Troubadour for the poetry he wrote. She ruled Aquitaine in her own right for fifty years, leading troops as a member of the French royalist party that opposed the English.

In 1112, she and her second husband separated, he to become a monk and she to become a nun at Fontevrault. A reconciliation was attempted in 1119, but she returned to the monastery, this time at Larrey. In 1132, she embarked on a pilgrimage to Jerusalem to visit her brother Fulk V, who was then king of Jerusalem. On her return to France, she founded a Cistercian nunnery near Nantes.

Esclarmonde (d. 1240?)

Noblewoman who was an important member of the Cathari sect, a heretical group that believed an ongoing war between good and evil was being fought on earth. The group abhorred anything worldly.

A widow and the mother of six, Esclarmonde devoted her later years to the Cathari cause, debating with Catholic priests and preachers about the Cathari beliefs.

After her death, her castle became a stronghold of the Cathari and was the focus of a Crusade in 1243, which put the castle under siege. In 1244, the Cathari asked for terms, and the Crusaders said those who gave up their beliefs would be saved; those who did not would be burned. Over two hundred Cathari, many of them women, were subsequently imprisoned and burned at the stake, effectively destroying the sect. *See* Religion and Women.

SUGGESTED READING: Michael Costen, *The Cathars and the Albigensian Crusade* (Manchester, England: Manchester University Press, 1997); Jonathan Sumption, *The Albigensian Crusade* (New York: Faber and Faber, 2000).

Esther, Queen

Character from an Old Testament story. Esther was a Hebrew girl who became a Persian queen and used her feminine wiles to influence the king and save the Jews in Persia from a murderous plot. She became the medieval model of the queen who influences political decisions. The ideal queen was seen as an intercessor and as more merciful than the king.

The story, popular in the Middle Ages, made worldly riches acceptable as long as they were used properly. Esther was also the model of wifely obedience, a woman who earned the trust of her husband through her virtues and then risked her life for her people. *See* Queens and Queenship.

Etheldreda *see* Æthelthryth

Eudocia *see* Athenais

Eudocia (b. 422)

Byzantine empress. Daughter of Athenais (also known as Eudocia) and Theodosius II, she married Emperor Valentinian III in 437. He was the son of Placidia and Constantius; his mother ruled in his place because he was weak and ineffectual.

After Valentinian was killed in 455, leaving no son to inherit, an elderly senator, Petronius Maximus, was the choice of the army to succeed him. Petronius Maximus attempted to marry Eudocia to secure his claim. According to legend, she was repelled by the idea and enlisted the aid of Gaiseric, king of the Vandals. Gaiseric invaded, and the Byzantine army mutinied against Petronius. Unfortunately, Gaiseric forced Eudocia and her two daughters to accompany him on his return to Carthage. *See* Athenais; Placidia.

SUGGESTED READING: Michael Grant, *From Rome to Byzantium: The Fifth Century AD* (New York: Routledge, 1998).

Eudocia (11th century)

Byzantine empress. She married Constantine X Ducas, Byzantine emperor. Before his death in 1064, he made her swear she would not remarry. She agreed. However, to ensure the legitimacy of the next emperor — and to ensure that she would remain in power — she needed to marry. To get the necessary dispensation, she lied to the senate and said she intended to marry the patriarch's brother. Once the senate released her from her oath, she announced her intention to marry Romanus Diogenes, who became emperor in 1068.

Romanus went on to lose the battle of Manzikert against the Seljuk Turks, the greatest military disaster in Byzantine history. In 1071, on his return to Constantinople after he was ransomed for a high price, he was deposed, and Eudocia was exiled and forced to become a nun.

Eudokia *see* Eudocia

Eudoxia (d. 403)

Roman empress. A beautiful woman of unknown origin, she married Arcadius, the co-ruler of Rome, in 395 with the help of a eunuch named Eutropius, who selected her as part of his attempt to manipulate Arcadius.

It soon became clear that Eudoxia detested her husband. Eutropius was soon named consul. The army troops resented the elevation of a corrupt eunuch, and Eudoxia encouraged Arcadius to surrender Eutropius to the troops, which he did.

Eudoxia was noted for her love of luxury and her depraved sensuality and was said to wear a fringe on her forehead, the mark of a courtesan. She caused considerable talk when she ordered a silver statue of herself to be erected just outside Saint Sophia.

Her reign was noted for her hostilities with Saint John Chrysostom, the bishop of Constantinople, who denounced her at every turn. Soon, she refused to allow her husband to communicate with Saint John at all. John was banished and died in exile.

Eudoxia died in 403, after suffering a miscarriage. Her son Theodosius succeeded to the throne when he was seven.

SUGGESTED READING: Tony Honore, *Law in the Crisis of Empire, 379–455 AD: The Theodosian Dynasty and Its Quaestors* (New York: Oxford University Press, 1998); J. H. W. G. Liebschuetz, *Barbarians and Bishops: Army, Church, and the State in the Age of Arcadius and Chrysostom* (New York: Oxford University Press, 1991).

Eulogia *see* Irene Choumnaina Paleologina

Eve

In biblical stories, the first woman who God made. In the Middle Ages, she was held up as a negative model of what women were like. Because she was tempted by the devil and seduced by him, all women were thought to be instruments of the devil.

As justification for the subordinate position of women in the church hierarchy, church fathers pointed out that Eve was made from Adam's rib, was the first to be seduced by Satan, and was the cause of expulsion from the Garden of Eden. *See* Religion and Women.

F

Family *see* Marriage and Family

Fatima (606?–632?)

The daughter of Muhammad the Prophet and his first wife, Khadija. She was his only child to produce children: two sons, Hasan and Husayn. She married

Ali of Arabia (Ali ibn Abi Talib), Muhammad's cousin and a caliph.

The Fatimids, a medieval caliphate of Shi'ite Muslims in North Africa, claimed to be descended from her. They overthrew the Aghlabid dynasty in the tenth century and eventually ruled over a large territory; they were overthrown by Saladin, sultan of Egypt, in the twelfth century. The Idrisids, another North African Muslim dynasty, was founded by Idrisis ibn Abd Allah, a descendant of Fātima and Ali. This dynasty flourished between the eighth and tenth centuries. After becoming embroiled in a rivalry between the Fātimids and another Muslim dynasty, the Umayyads, the Idrisids lost power.

Muslims consider her one of the Four Perfect Women. *See* Religion and Women.

SUGGESTED READING: M. Bonner and Heinz Halm, *The Empire of the Mahdi*: *The Rise of the Fatimids* (Boston: Brill, 1997).

Fausta (4th century)

Roman empress. Daughter of the Byzantine emperor, Maximian. She became the second wife of Constantine the Great, who converted Rome to Christianity, in 307. The alliance helped cement her father's claim to rulership. When her mother-in-law, Helena, was given the rank of augusta, which she herself bore, Fausta became resentful. Helena disliked her because Fausta's adopted sister, Theodora, had "stolen" Helena's husband, Constantius the Pale. The two women were enemies throughout their lives.

In 310, Constantine killed Fausta's father and seized the Eastern throne. Despite this contretemps, the two had three sons, all of whom became caesars.

In 326, during a ceremonial trip to Rome, Fausta's husband had her put to death in the bathhouse, although the exact method is not known. The reason is open to debate: some sources claim she was having an affair with Constantine's son Crispus, who was also murdered at the same time, while others say that she made the accusation that Crispus had attempted to seduce her, and when her lie was discovered, she was put to death.

Feudalism and Women

A form of social structure and hierarchy in medieval Europe, feudalism was a system of social, political, and military relationships based on reciprocal obligations. In its most basic terms, it was simply the exchange of service and loyalty for protection and justice. In practice, the ruler awarded his favored subjects with grants of land. Feudalism was based on land since it was the only true capital in the Middle Ages, which, by and large, did not have a money-based economy until the fourteenth century. The French law stated specifically, "No lord without land, no land without lord."

Middle- and upper-class women lived largely outside the feudal system. The reciprocal obligations that bound a knight to his king had no equivalent for women. Thus, their role in the feudal world was as the property of men. They were defined primarily in relation to their fathers, brothers, husbands, and sons.

Feudal estates came with military obligations, thus they passed to men. Only if no male heirs existed could women inherit. A woman's father was her guardian until marriage; if he died, the father's lord served as her guardian until she was married. Such wardships could be lucrative. The lord kept any money generated by a ward's estate, and she had to marry whoever he said or lose her inheritance. These conditions were fairly universal throughout Europe. The lord "sold" the ward's marriage to a prospective bridegroom interested in taking control of an heiress's estate. Wardship was considered an investment and, like goods, could be bought and sold.

In the feudal structure, a peasant

owed a certain amount of service to the lord in exchange for protection and a small plot of land to work. The lord owed service to his king — military service during wartime and administrative service during peace — in exchange for the fief or the grant of land. The obligations were supposed to be reciprocal, with the king protecting the lord and the lord protecting the peasant, but it did not always work this way. The reciprocal obligations, called vassalage, were not that different from an employer-employee relationship. Some were good, some were bad, some were prosperous and some were not. In the Byzantine Empire and the Arab world, forms of sharecropping were common. In this case, the person working the land did not own it. Instead, the farmer (a peasant) gave most of the harvest to the landowner, keeping a small percentage for himself. Female peasants and serfs were expected to work the land alongside their fathers and husbands. Little allowance was made for pregnancy, childbirth, or childrearing.

Feudalism succeeded in tying land-holding nobles to the king; the alternative would have been states fractured into dozens of tiny, independent duchies contending with one another. The church was also part of the feudal system. Bishops and abbots acted as lords, even fulfilling military obligations as required.

By the fourteenth century, the institution was obsolete and weak. Wealth was no longer concentrated in land. The nobility had sold their land to raise funds, discontinued the practice of manorialism or communal farming, as it was no longer cost efficient, and sold serfs their freedom.

The merchant class arose outside the feudal world of the Middle Ages. Lords granted liberties to towns because the towns brought them considerable revenues. Towns, and the merchants in them, moved the medieval world from a land-based economy to a currency-based economy. Women were involved in all aspects of trade, often in conjunction with their husbands. If her husband were absent on a trading trip, she would run the business. As a widow, she would take over all trading and merchant functions. Women were also involved in the production of goods, particularly textiles and foods. *See* Guilds; Marriage and Family; Occupations.

SUGGESTED READING: Marc Block, *Feudal Society: The Growth of the Ties of Dependence* (Chicago: University of Chicago Press, 1988); Michael Hicks, *Bastard Feudalism* (London: Longman, 1995); Joel Kate, *Economy and Nature in the Fourteenth Century: Money, Market Exchange and the Emergence of Scientific Thought* (New York: Cambridge University Press, 1998); Jean-Pierre Poly, *The Feudal Transformation, 900–1200* (New York: Holmes and Meier, 1991); Peter Spufford, *Money and Its Use in Medieval Europe* (New York: Cambridge University Press, 1989).

First Night *see* Jus Primae Noctis

Fontevrault

Also Fontevraud and Fontevraut. A famous French double monastery in which the monks were subordinate to the nuns and came under the authority of the abbess. It was founded as a refuge for women forced into political marriages, as well as for widows and abandoned wives. The monastery was renowned for accepting women in trouble, such as those fleeing their husbands, At Fontervrault, Eleanor of Aquitaine professed her vows and died. *See* Convents and Nuns; Eleanor of Aquitaine.

Food and Cooking

People in the Middle Ages had an

abiding preoccupation with food, not surprising given the precarious line between
feast and famine that usually existed. This
preoccupation was reinforced by church
strictures regarding when and how food
should be eaten and by secular sumptuary laws that dictated what foods the various social classes were allowed to eat.

Women, then as now, had a difficult
relation to food, which has always represented more than merely a source of energy. Studies have shown that nuns and
other religious women often inflicted severe self-deprivation by fasting for days,
weeks, and even months in order to "pu-
rify" themselves. Such fasting may have
caused hallucinations, the "visions" so
prized by medieval holy women. It also
killed several well-known mystics. In more
mundane fashion, female children had
less to eat than male children, and women
were the first to starve in times of famine.

Preparing and serving food in the
vast households of the nobles fell to servants, usually women, who devoted most
of their time to it. The largest expenditure
in most households was for food. The
wealthy consumed large quantities of
wine and spices, meat and fish. Game was
highly prized as it symbolized the aristocratic way of life. Serfs and the lower
ranks of yeomanry subsisted on potage, a
kind of stew. They also ate bread and
drank ale.

Households did their own baking and
sometimes their own brewing, purchasing other foodstuffs from vendors. In
towns, food was usually purchased by all
classes, except the nobles, who maintained
kitchens and cooks. Street vendors and
shops sold already prepared food. In these
areas, women often brewed and sold ale to
supplement the family income. Alewives,
as they were called, outnumbered most
other merchants. Ale was graded accord-

ing to quality and sold at strictly controlled prices.

Something like bake sales were held
to help others. "Help ales," as these activities were called, consisted of groups of
friends and family members purchasing
and then selling ale with the net proceeds
going to the person in need. Usually these
were hosted by guilds for guild members.
"Bride ales" were essentially the same
thing, with the proceeds going directly to
the new bride.

For aristocrats, who spent up to eighty
percent of their total expenditures on food
alone, the cook was indispensable. She
(sometimes, he) was relied upon to turn
the ordinary into the extraordinary. The
more unusual and exotic, the better. Foods
were prepared in the shapes of animals,
were heavily garnished, or were decorated
with coloring. A meat dish might be divided into quarters, with one quarter colored yellow, one red, one green, and one
blue. Gold and silver foil were also used
to decorate food, as were elaborate spun-
sugar confections.

The cook was charged with keeping
the lord's meals as far away as possible
from peasant life and peasant food. Cooks,
therefore, thought of themselves as crafts-
people, spending hours preparing food
each day. Good cooks, never easy to find,
held a great deal of power, for they could
make life miserable for the household. *See*
Households; Marriage and Family; Sumptuary Laws.

SUGGESTED READING: Grenville Astill
and John Langdon, eds., *Medieval Farming and Technology: The Impact of Agricultural Change in Northwest Europe* (Boston: Brill, 1997); Caroline Walker Bynum,
*Holy Feast and Holy Fast: The Religious
Significance of Food to Medieval Women*
(Berkeley: University of California Press,
1988); Bridget Ann Henisch, *Fast and*

Feast: Food in Medieval Society (University Park: Pennsylvania State University Press, 1986); Odile Redon et al., trans., *The Medieval Kitchen: Recipes from France and Italy* (Chicago: University of Chicago Press, 2000); Del Sweeney, *Agriculture in the Middle Ages: Technology, Practice and Representation* (Philadelphia: University of Pennsylvania Press, 1995).

Francesca de Rimini (d. 1285?)

Italian noblewoman whose life became the basis for legendary romances. The daughter of Guido da Polenta, the ruler of Ravenna, she married for political reasons. According to legend, her husband, Giovanni Malatesta de Rimini, was unattractive and unkind. She began an affair with Giovanni's younger brother, Paolo. When Giovanni discovered the affair, he murdered his wife and his brother. The tragic story inspired a famous episode in Dante's *Divine Comedy*. It was also the basis for numerous other works of literature, especially in the nineteenth century.

Frauenturnier *see* Ladies' Tournament

Fredegunde (d. 597)

Frankish queen. Fredegunde, the mistress to Chilperic I of Neustria, instigated the murder of his wife, Galswintha, and married him herself. Galswintha was the sister of Brunhild, who was married to Sigebert I, the king of Austrasia and half brother of Chilperic. The murder of Galswintha led to bitter hostility between the two kingdoms and, more viciously, between the two women.

Fredegunde eventually connived at the murder of Sigebert and succeeded in killing him in 575. Her son Clothar (Lothar) II succeeded to the Neustrian throne in 584, with Fredegunde acting as his regent.

After Fredegunde's death, most of the territory was lost to Clothar's two cousins, but both were dead by 613. This, coupled with Brunhild's murder in the same year, ended the conflict between Austrasia and Neustria. *See* Brunhild.

SUGGESTED READING: Rosamond McKitterick, *The Frankish Kings and Culture in the Early Middle Ages* (New York: Cambridge University Press, 1995).

Freyja

Medieval Viking goddess. Ruler of a realm of the afterlife to which slain warriors went (Sessrúmnir). She was associated with the seiðr ritual (divination). *See* Religion and Women.

Frigg

Medieval Scandinavian goddess; in the poetic *Eddai*, she was a healer. *See* Religion and Women.

Friðgerðr

Viking woman depicted in *Kristnisaga* as worshipping at a pagan temple while her husband, Þorvaldr Koðránsson, was preaching Christianity at the Althing. The story depicts the tension between Christianity and paganism that persisted in Scandinavia and Iceland for centuries after the rest of Europe had converted. *See* Conversion; Religion and Women.

G

Games and Entertainment

Throughout the Middle Ages, people sought to entertain themselves with games and other entertainment whenever they had spare time, conducting a social life centered around friends and family. They played board games, such as backgammon, as well as card and dice games. People frequently gambled on the outcome of these games, which led to some thundering denunciations by the church.

Medieval people played games with balls, performed ring dances, and wrestled. They also competed with each other in shot put, archery, and slingshot. They participated in practical sports such as fencing and horsemanship. They played a form of croquet without hoops and enjoyed blindman's bluff. By the fourteenth century, a form of field hockey called soules had developed.

Women went to alehouses tended by women who brewed ale. They enjoyed soaking in public baths. The garden was a favorite place of retreat for women; later, gardens gained a reputation as places to carry on illicit affairs.

Medieval people also played tennis and chess. However, both were outlawed in the fourteenth century because tennis tournaments incited riots and chess even provoked murder.

Most cities had playing fields. Citizens would form teams and play a kind of baseball with a bat and leather ball, a bowling game, or golf. They also played a game similar to American football, using a pig's bladder. They also watched bull baiting, bear baiting, and cockfighting, betting on the outcome of all of these events.

They participated in dances, sang songs, produced plays and pageants, listened to storytellers, and staged tournaments. Hunting was the most popular sport for nobles, with hawking a close second. Most nobles designated certain lands on their property for hunting. Poachers were tortured and killed to prevent them from interfering with the nobles' sport. Nobles hunted with hounds and with trained falcons. A man devoted to hawking would carry his favorite hawk on his wrist, bringing it to meals, to church, or anywhere possible.

SUGGESTED READING: John Marshall Carter, *Medieval Games* (Westport, CT: Greenwood, 1992).

Garden

Highly prized by medieval women, an orchard or garden was considered a place of refuge. Many women hosted social gatherings there, away from the household. Gardens were popularly believed to be a place where women went to meet their lovers. *See* Games and Entertainment.

Garsenda de Forcalquier

(c. 1175–after 1257)

Female troubadour. She was born into one of the leading families of Provence and married Alfonse II, a great lord of Provence and the brother of Peter (Pedro) II, king of Aragón. She was forced into the marriage because her family had rebelled against Alfonse; she was the family's offer of submission. Later, her grandfather revoked part of her dowry, provoking a war. In 1209, her husband died. She ruled Provence after his death as regent for her infant son, who had been kidnapped by the Aragonese. She did not regain custody of him until 1213, when her late husband's brother Peter was killed. After her son married and assumed rulership of Provence, Garsenda retired from active political life, joining the abbey of La Celle in 1222 or 1225. She was reportedly still alive in 1257; she would have been in her eighties. Through all of her trials and tribulations, she wrote lyric poetry famous in the region.

SUGGESTED READING: Meg Bogin, *The Women Troubadours* (New York: Norton, 1980); Kathryn Reyerson and John Drendel, eds., *Urban and Rural Communities in Medieval France: Provence and Languedoc, 1000–1500* (Boston: Brill, 1998).

Gefjun

Medieval Viking goddess of the afterlife; unmarried women entered her service after death. *See* Religion and Women.

Geneviève, Saint (c. 422–500)

Patron saint of Paris. At a very young age, she devoted her life to religious practice. According to legend, she prophesied the invasion of the Huns and saved Paris by praying. She is credited with converting Clovis I, the Frankish king. *See* Conversion.

Germanic Invaders

Groups of tribes who conquered most of Western and Central Europe around the fifth century AD, largely responsible for the fall of the Roman Empire. By about 200 BC, Germanic groups had controlled northern Germany and southern Scandinavia, and for the next several centuries they came into repeated contact with the Roman Empire.

Early in their history, Germanic tribes were organized around extended family groups. Over time, these family groups developed into clans with military leaders or chieftains. As the tribes grew more powerful, a leader along with an advisory council would rule even in times of peace. Women, elders, and children followed the Germanic warriors and settled with them in newly conquered territories.

During the third century, Roman legions used Germanic mercenary soldiers. The Germanic migrations increased during this period, straining the Roman Empire as Goths, Alamanni, and Franks put pressure on frontier and border areas. Under Diocletian and Constantine the Great, this pressure ceased but when the Huns arrived from central Asia in the fourth century, the migrations again increased. In 376, the Visigoths crossed the lower Danube, bringing women, children, and elders with them. They were not intending to raid the territory; they planned to settle there. They found Italy unable to support them, so they traveled to Spain, where they established a Visigothic kingdom that lasted into the eighth century. They were followed by the Vandals, who went through Gaul and Spain, plundering and sacking cities and monasteries en route. The Vandals sacked Rome in 455, having arrived by ship as the Vikings later would. The Vandals established a North African kingdom at Carthage but it did not endure long.

The Huns invaded Gaul in 451. They traveled to Italy and reached the walled city of Rome, but Pope Leo the Great withstood them. Attila, the famed leader of the Huns, died suddenly, and the Huns left Italy.

The German Franks went south, establishing Frankish kingdoms in the areas that are now Germany and France. The Burgundians established the kingdom of

Burgundy. When the Roman army withdrew from Britain early in the fifth century, the Picts attacked the land as did Scottish tribes and the Saxons (later known as the Anglo-Saxons). The Britons fought the Saxons for many years but succumbed by the end of the sixth century. Many Britons fled to Wales, Cornwall, and Brittany, which lay across the channel.

Other Germanic tribes settled in Northern Europe, forming kingdoms in Scandinavia and becoming the dreaded Vikings. Some of these Scandinavian tribes scattered across the world, ending up as far away as Kievan Russia, Iceland, and North America. Around the seventh century, the majority of the Germanic invasions and migrations had concluded, with the exception of the Viking invasions, which would continue throughout Europe, off and on, for the next several hundred years. *See* Indigenous People.

SUGGESTED READING: Andrew Bell, *The Role of Migration in the History of the Eurasian Steppe*: *Sedentary Civilization versus "Barbarian" and Nomad* (New York: St. Martin's, 2000); John B. Bury, *Invasion of Europe by the Barbarians* (New York: Norton, 2000).

Gerðr

In Viking mythology, a female giant who lived in the mountains and was courted by the god Freyr. The story is described in the medieval Eddaic poem *För Scirnis*. Gerðr was associated with winter, mountains, and the god's ultimate triumph over frigidity. *See* Religion and Women.

Gertrude of Helfta *see* Gertrude the Great, Saint

Gertrude the Great, Saint
(d. c. 1302)

Also Gertrude of Helfta. German mystic and religious woman. She was given to the convent at Helfta as an oblate when she was five years old. Well educated there, she became a scribe. When she was about twenty-five, she devoted her life to quiet contemplation. She received many visions, including visions of the Sacred Heart. She wrote many influential religious and mystical works, the most important being *The Herald of Divine Love*. Her writings earned her the title "the Great." *See* Religion and Women.

SUGGESTED READING: Mary Jeremy Finnegan, *The Women of Helfta: Scholars and Mystics* (Athens: University of Georgia Press, 1991).

Gisela (10th century)

Frankish queen. She married the German king and emperor, Conrad II. Together they founded the Frankish Salian dynasty. Although Conrad's reign was troubled with continuing conflict with the nobles, he was able to expand his territories to include Burgundy. Gisela was active in the government, drawing up documents and participating in the ruling decisions. This may have been because Gisela was well-educated while Conrad was illiterate. She was able to encourage her own traditions at court as opposed to his, and she made certain their son Henry III received an excellent education.

After Conrad was killed trying to suppress a rebellion in the north, she withdrew from political life.

SUGGESTED READING: Theodore John Rivers, *Laws of the Salian and Ripurian Franks* (New York: AMS Press, 1987).

God the Mother

The mystic Julian of Norwich stated the controversial belief that God is both father and mother and that this dual nature was revealed to her in a vision. *See* Julian of Norwich; Religion and Women.

SUGGESTED READING: Julian of Norwich, *Revelations of Divine Love and the Motherhood of God* (London: Brewer, 1998).

Godiva, Lady (1040?–1080?)

Anglo-Saxon noblewoman. She married Leofric, earl of Mercia. They founded monasteries throughout England. She is most famous for an incident in which she persuaded her husband to lower the heavy taxes he had imposed on Coventry by riding naked through the town with only her long hair to protect her modesty. Although she requested that the citizens not watch her, one man, Tom the Tailor, did so, earning him the name of "Peeping Tom."

SUGGESTED READING: Peter R. Coss, *The Early Records of Medieval Coventry* (Oxford: Oxford University Press, 1986).

Grendel's Mother

One of the more famous monsters in medieval legend, she appears in the Anglo-Saxon epic poem *Beowulf.* In the story, Beowulf, a prince of the Geats, travels to Heorot, the hall of the king of the Danes. The Danes are suffering from the depredations of the monster Grendel, who has visited the hall by night for twelve years, murdering anyone there. Beowulf destroys Grendel. In revenge, Grendel's mother attacks the hall. Beowulf follows her to her home beneath the sea and kills her. He is rewarded by his king; later he is killed while destroying a dragon. The poem ends with the funeral of Beowulf and the uncertainty of the now-leaderless tribe.

SUGGESTED READING: Seamus Heaney, trans., *Beowulf* (New York: Farrar Straus and Giroux, 2000).

Griselda

Like Constance (Custance), Griselda is a literary figure who typifies the medieval ideal of feminine virtue. Chaucer tells the story in *The Clerk's Tale.* Here, Griselda, who is virtuous and "womanly," swears to obey her husband, Walter. A peasant woman, she is raised in status by her marriage, and her husband, the "markys," wants to test her. This he does by pretending to murder her children and then by driving her away. Eventually, satisfied as to his wife's virtue, he reunites his family, and they live happily ever after. The moral is "for sith a woman was so pacient / Unto a mortal man, wel moore us oghte / Receyven al in glee that God us sent / For greet silke is he preeve that he wroghte" (lines 1149–52). Of course, Griselda's faith is never in question, nor is her faith a motive for Walter's actions. Nonetheless, it is her ability to suffer with Christian patience that is celebrated. *See* Constance.

SUGGESTED READING: Geoffrey Chaucer, *The Riverside Chaucer* (New York: Houghton Mifflin, 1987); Glenda McLeod, *Virtue and Venom: Catalogs of Women from Antiquity to the Renaissance* (Detroit: University of Michigan Press, 1991).

Gudrun

Character in the Icelandic prose saga *Laxdæla Saga.* The saga is best known for its tragic love story of Gudrun and Kjartan Olafsson and their two warring families.

Guilds

Associations of people in similar professions, trades, or crafts, developed to protect themselves. Medieval guilds were the forerunners of modern labor unions. They began as religious associations whose members pledged mutual aid and protection. At first, just one guild existed per town, but more developed over time. Some of these associations became merchant guilds, with bands of merchants traveling together to prevent outlaws from attacking them. In addition to physical protection, they promised to stand by each other in law courts. From these beginnings, trade associations, then craft guilds, evolved.

Medieval craft guilds had the power to set wages and to accept or decline apprentices. If there were too many bricklayers in a city, for instance, their value would be reduced, so the bricklayers' guild kept tight control over membership. It was the same for all of the guilds. People who were not members of a guild were not allowed to practice that guild's trade or profession in a city with a guild. Merchants who were not members of guilds had to abide by restrictions on what they could sell and for how much, and they were subject to special taxes. In male-dominated guilds (which included most of them), women were usually not accepted; if they were, they were treated as second-class members. Wives and daughters of guild members were treated like household members although they did much of the work.

Craft guilds accepted three types of members: masters, apprentices, and journeymen. Masters owned the materials, the tools, and the buildings in which the trade or craft took place or was produced. Apprentices were young people learning the trade. Once they had achieved a certain level of skill, they became journeymen. Apprentices and journeymen usually lived with the master or on the master's property. Journeymen were paid a fixed wage for their work. Because it was in the interest of the masters to keep their numbers small, they instituted many rules and restrictions so that by the fourteenth century, it was almost impossible to become a master in any trade. At this point, jour-

neymen organized their own associations in order to improve their working conditions. These were called journeymen or yeomen guilds. They sometimes banded together to go on strike. Most guilds regulated the length of apprenticeship and the number of apprentices a master or mistress could take on at one time. If the work turned out by a guild member was of poor quality, the guild would order it destroyed.

In order to control competition, guilds established rules about fair practices. Guild members were not allowed to compete on price; this was strictly regulated so that all guild members could make a living. Work was usually prohibited after dark, since one could not see well by candlelight and the quality of work produced at this time would probably be inferior. Members could not purchase supplies from Jews. Infractions were punished with fines or a period of time at the pillory.

Masters were not allowed to advertise, in case one master served more customers than another. If a new tool or technology were discovered that made production cheaper or more efficient, a master could not use it unless all masters used it. The goal of such restrictions was to make it completely fair for all members of the guild to earn a livelihood. Guilds also ensured a very high quality of goods and services, since the entire craft or trade would be embarrassed by one person's poor handiwork.

In some guilds, such as the Fullers Guild, a wife could continue to do the work after her husband died; otherwise, women were not allowed to do the work. If a widow married a man who was not a member of the guild to which her late husband had belonged, she could no longer do the work. A few guilds, such as the

Bathhouse Guild, did not distinguish between male and female members; both could run bathhouses.

Craft guilds existed for everything from baking to ale-making to shoemaking to manuscript copying. There were guilds for bellringers, minstrels, candlemakers, grocers, road menders, and weavers.

Guild members often contributed generously to charity and provided entertainment and religious instruction for the towns where they were located. They demanded dues according to income, but they also paid for the funerals of members and would support the widows and families of deceased guild members. *See* Feudalism and Women; Occupations.

SUGGESTED READING: Clifford Davidson, *Technology, Guilds and Early English Drama* (Kalamazoo: Western Michigan University Press, 1997); Steven A. Epstein, *Wage Labor and Guilds in Medieval Europe* (Chapel Hill: University of North Carolina Press, 1995).

Guinevere

In Arthurian romance, the wife of King Arthur. After taking the throne, Arthur married Guinevere. As dowry, her father gave Arthur the Round Table, which eliminated quarrels over precedence.

In Geoffrey of Monmouth's version, Guinevere was kidnapped by Arthur's nephew Mordred (in some versions, Mordred is Arthur's son), while Arthur battled the Romans. Arthur put down Mordred's rebellion and saved the queen.

In later versions of the Arthurian legends, she had an adulterous affair with Lancelot, Arthur's favorite, or first knight. In various stories, Lancelot sought to win her affection and embarked on many adventures for her. In Malory's version, after

their adulterous affair was revealed by various conniving knights, Lancelot fled from the king's wrath, and Guinevere was sentenced to burn to death. Lancelot rescued her from this fate and battled Arthur. While Arthur was thus occupied, his son Mordred rebelled. Arthur returned to battle Mordred, who he killed, but was mortally wounded in the effort. Guinevere became a nun.

In other versions, Guinevere died during Arthur's reign. In one story, she became a prisoner of the Picts and died in captivity. In yet another tradition, she had a child with Mordred. In another, she was killed by Lancelot for going willingly with Mordred. One story tells how Guinevere and Mordred were brother and sister, although in this story, Mordred was not Arthur's son.

Guinevere was frequently abducted in stories, and Lancelot often came to her rescue. Sometimes she was replaced by the False Guinevere and had to be reinstated. Sometimes she was shown as shrewish, lying, and compulsively faithless. Other times, she was depicted as having great dignity and beauty. In almost all of the stories, she served as the catalyst that caused the final battle between Arthur and Mordred, which invariably resulted in Mordred's death, Arthur's mortal injury, and the end of the dream of Camelot. *See* Chivalry; Courtly Love.

SUGGESTED READING: Sir Thomas Malory, *Malory: The Morte Darthur* (Evanston, IL: Northwestern University Press, 1968); Lon Walters, *Lancelot and Guinevere: A Casebook* (New York: Garland, 1996).

Guinevere, False

In Arthurian romance, Guinevere's identical half sister. Like many twins and half siblings in medieval literature, she was evil. She claimed to be the real Guinevere and replaced her. Eventually she admitted her deception, and the real Guinevere was returned to her rightful place.

Gülbehar (15th century)

Mother of Bayezid II, the famous Ottoman ruler. A slave girl of either Albanian or Greek heritage, she was a Christian and became the mistress of Mehmed II the Conqueror around 1450. *See* Slavery and Women.

Gunnhild

Legendary queen of Iceland, she was the character in the Icelandic sagas who possessed the magical ability of divination. She used her ability to control the poet Egil's mind. Under her control, he left Iceland and went to Scotland, where his enemy, Gunnhild's husband (King Erik Bloodaxe), resided.

Gynaeceum

Women's quarters. Greek women were confined to the gynaceum; Islamic women lived in harems, which were essentially the same thing. Turkish women lived in the seraglio. In France, this was called the *chambre des dames*. In Europe, in the early Middle Ages, women laborers lived as a group in women's quarters instead of with their families. *See* Women's Quarters.

H

Hagiography

Literary works that purport to relate the biographical details of the life of a saint. Especially popular in the Middle Ages, these saints' lives presented highly idealized and fictionalized accounts that showed how a good Christian should live. Women preferred to read about the lives of female saints as models of strong, devout women with courage and conviction. *See* Martyrs, Martyrdom, and Martyrology; Religion and Women.

SUGGESTED READING: Gail Ashton, *The Generation of Identity in Late Medieval Hagiography: Speaking the Saint* (New York: Routledge, 2000); Lynda L. Coon, *Sacred Fictions: Holy Women and Hagiography in Late Antiquity* (Philadelphia: University of Pennsylvania Press, 1997).

Harem

Women's quarters. In the Arabic world, as in much of Europe, women were secluded from men and from public life. They were sometimes literally imprisoned in the women's quarters. Although the word *harem* has taken on a titillating sexual connotation, it was simply the place where all the women in a household lived, including daughters, wives, mistresses, and other female relatives. Very young boys also lived in the harem. On occasion, the harem was protected and guarded by a eunuch, a male warrior who had been castrated so he would be less likely to yield to sexual temptation. *See* Women's Quarters.

Hedwig *see* Jadwiga of Poland

Hel

In medieval Scandinavian mythology, the daughter of the god Loki. She rules the land of the dead. *See* Religion and Women.

Helena (3rd–4th century)

Byzantine political and religious figure. An innkeeper's daughter from Bithynia, she was probably a prostitute for her father. After converting to Christianity, she married Constantius the Pale, a general in the Byzantine army, who later abandoned her to marry Theodora, the adopted daughter of Emperor Maximian. Helena became a bitter enemy of Empress Fausta, Emperor Maximian's natural daughter, who eventually married Helena's son Constantine the Great, the first emperor of Rome to adopt Christianity. Constantine transferred the capital of the empire to Constantinople, thus creating the Byzantine Empire.

Helena was elevated to the rank of augusta by her son and became one of the most revered women in the Byzantine Empire.

Helena remained an Arian Christian, despite her son's attempts to eradicate this heresy. Essentially, Arianism was the belief that Christ was human, not divine, and so was therefore subordinate to God the father, not coequal with him.

In 327, when Helena was more than seventy years old, she made a pilgrimage to Jerusalem, where she found the "true cross." According to legend, she placed it on a dying woman. When the woman was returned to health, Helena knew it was the true cross. Helena probably died while still in Jerusalem. She is the first known Christian pilgrim. After her death, she was canonized. Her story was repeatedly retold throughout the Middle Ages, including the Anglo-Saxon poet Cynewulf's version, *Elene*.

SUGGESTED READING: Cynewulf, *Cynewulf's Elene* (London: University of Exeter Press, 1996); Julia Bolton Holloway, *Essays on Pilgrimage and Literature* (New York: AMS Press, 1990).

Helena (11th century)

Norman noblewoman. Daughter of Robert Guiscard, the Norman duke of Apulia, Calabria, and Sicily. In 1074, she was betrothed to Michael VII's son Constantine, an infant. She was forced to remain in the gynaceum until her fiancé became old enough to marry. In 1078, Michael was overthrown, and she was confined to a convent.

Because of her treatment, her father prepared to invade the Byzantine Empire, and in 1081 his fleet sailed. The war that followed lasted several years.

Helena Cantacuzena Comnena (d. c. 1463)

Empress of Trebizond, an empire along the coast of the southern shore of the Black Sea in present-day Turkey. A member of the famous Byzantine Cantacuzene family, Helena married Grand Duke David in 1440. He became emperor when his brother died in 1458.

David refused to pay tribute to the sultan, Mehmet, in 1460. Mehmet invaded Trebizond, and the following year, David was forced to surrender the empire. Helena, David, and their children were captured and sent to Constantinople. Later they were exiled to Adrianople, where they were expected to live out their lives quietly. Soon, David was accused of conspiring against the sultan, and he, Helena, and their children were again imprisoned. This time, the sultan had all male members of the family killed.

According to legend, after the execution, Mehmet ordered the bodies of the men to be thrown outside the castle walls and left unburied. He confiscated all of David's property and demanded a ransom for Helena. Her family and friends tried to raise the money, but she was no longer interested in living. Instead, she defied the sultan by burying her husband and children with her own hands. Within days, she died.

SUGGESTED READING: Vryonis Speros, Jr., *The Decline of Medieval Hellenism in Asia Minor and the Process of Islamization from the Eleventh through the Fifteenth Century* (Berkeley: University of California Press, 1986).

Helena Doukaina (1241–1271)

Queen of the Two Sicilies. The Greek daughter of Michael II, the despot of Epiros, who was at war with several enemies and sought an alliance with Manfred of Sicily. Michael offered his daughter Helena in marriage. Her dowry included considerable lands in Epiros, which Manfred coveted. Having no male heir, Manfred was eager to remarry. The son of the notorious Frederick II, Manfred was despised by the pope and other Western heads of state. A cultured and educated man, he nonetheless had a scandalous reputation—as did his court. Even so, Helena was betrothed to him in 1258, and the following year they were married. As a result, she became queen of the Two Sicilies, as well as the duchess of Apulia and the princess of Taranto.

Michael lost his war against the armies of Nicaea, but Manfred continued to support him. Still, the Latin Empire of Constantinople collapsed, and Byzantine rule was restored to Constantinople. Later, in 1262, Pope Urban IV incited Charles of Anjou to take Sicily, which he did in 1266, killing Manfred in battle.

After the death of her husband, Helena was arrested by soldiers of Charles of Anjou. None of her family came to her support, although two friends tried to arrange a ship to transport her and her four children away. She escaped with the children to Trani, where the ship was supposed to be waiting to bring them to Greece, but weather delayed the journey, and she and her children were discovered and imprisoned at the castle. Her children were taken from her. She died in 1271, barely thirty.

Her daughter, Beatrice, became a prisoner at Naples and was not released for thirteen years. Helena's sons were imprisoned in a tower in Bari and kept in shackles and chains since they were potentially dangerous to Charles of Anjou. In 1300, they were moved to Naples, and two of them died soon after. The third son survived eighteen more years in prison.

SUGGESTED READING: Jean Dunbabin, *Charles I of Anjou: Power, Kingship and Statemaking in Thirteenth-Century Europe* (Reading, MA: Addison-Wesley, 1998); Donald Matthew, *The Norman Kingdom of Sicily* (New York: Cambridge University Press, 1992).

Helena Lecapenus (10th century)

Byzantine empress. Daughter of Romanus Lecapenus, who seized power in the Byzantine Empire in 919. She married the true successor, Constantine VII Porphyrogenitus, a minor, to cement her father's claim. Thus Empress Zoë Carbonopsina was forced out of power, and Symeon, the Bulgarian ruler who wanted his own daughter to marry Constantine, was thwarted.

Helena was forced to constantly defend Constantine against her own family's intrigues. Constantine became emperor after Helena's father was deposed by her brothers in 944; they sought the throne for themselves, but the Byzantine people decided otherwise. The following year, Helena arranged to have her brothers arrested and exiled. They were forced to enter a monastery just as they had forced their father to do. *See* Zoë Carbonopsina.

Héloïse (c. 1102–1164)

French noblewoman. Niece to Fulbert, a canon of the Cathedral of Notre Dame, and mistress to Peter Abelard, a noted scholar and one of the founders of the University of Paris, with whom she bore a son. She was a member of a high noble French family fighting for eminence in the court of King Louis VI.

From childhood, she was interested in her studies and, according to her biographers, surpassed most men with her learning and intelligence. In 1120, Peter became a tutor to Héloïse, and soon thereafter they began their affair, although Peter was more than twenty years older than she. Héloïse became pregnant. Sources differ regarding what happened then. Some say the two eloped and secretly married; others say Peter abducted her and agreed to marry her, but Héloïse, a proponent of free love, refused marriage because it enslaved both members and made what should be a freely given gift into a duty. Whatever the case, the two were eventually married, probably after their son, Astrolabe, was born. Astrolabe was raised by Peter's sister.

Upon learning about the affair, Héloïse's uncle hired several men to attack Peter. They castrated him. Later, Héloïse retired to a convent and Peter to a monastery, although their relationship continued through a series of poignant letters. Historians speculate that Peter put her in the nunnery since he was worried about his reputation; he seemed to expect her to continue her education as if nothing had transpired. Even though a nun, Héloïse remained passionately in love with Peter all of her life. She reproached him with her opinion that since he was castrated, he did not care about her because he could not have sex with her. They continued their separate lives.

In 1129, she was the prioress of a convent in Argenteuil when it was dissolved. She led several of the nuns to Champagne and became abbess of a new community near Peter, at Le Paraclet. The "Forty-two questions" that she put to Abelard became famous questions of theology.

After her death, she was buried next to Peter. Her story inspired Rousseau, Diderot, Voltaire, and Rilke; the Romantic poets were said to meditate on her grave. *See* Convents and Nuns; Religion and Women.

SUGGESTED READING: Pierre Abailard, *The Letters of Abelard and Heloise* (Reading, MA: Addison Wesley Longman, 1998); Bonnie Wheeler, ed., *Listening to Heloise: The Voice of a Twelfth-Century Woman* (New York: St. Martin's, 2000).

Heresy

The opposition to orthodox doctrine. In the Middle Ages, dozens of sects sprang up that offered differing interpretations of the nature of Christ, the atonement of sins, and all aspects of Christianity. Many heresies were suppressed by the church, often by the use of force. The Albigensian Crusades — undertaken against a region in France whose population adhered to the Cathari heresy — were the first battles between Christians sanctioned by the pope.

The egalitarian systems often present in heretical sects appealed to women. Indeed, women comprised the largest number of heretics, and the church decried how easily women were led into error. However, it was their subordinate and unwelcome position in the church hierarchy that forced them to find more meaningful ways to express their religious beliefs. *See* Crusades; Religion and Women.

SUGGESTED READING: Malcolm Lambert, *Medieval Heresy: Popular Movements from the Gregorian Reform to the Reformation* (Oxford: Blackwell, 1992); Shannon McSheffrey, *Gender and Heresy: Women and Men in Lollard Communities, 1420–1530* (Philadelphia: University of Pennsylvania Press, 1995); R. I. Moore, *The Birth of Popular Heresy* (Toronto: University of Toronto Press, 1995); Edward Peters, *Heresy and Authority in Medieval Europe: Documents in Translation* (Philadelphia: University of Pennsylvania Press, 1980).

Herleva (11th century)

Mother of William the Conqueror, the first Norman king of England. She was not married to his father, Duke Robert I of Normandy. After Robert's death in 1035, she married Herluin de Conteville and had two sons: Odo, the bishop of Bayeaux, and Robert, the count of Montain.

Hermengard *see* **Ermengard**

Herrad of Landsberg (12th century)

Well-known intellectual, mystic, and abbess of a convent in Hohenberg. She wrote and illustrated *Hortus delicarum* (Garden of Delights), an encyclopedic work, around 1175–1185. The compendium, several hundred pages long, includes everything she felt was necessary for the instruction of her nuns and describes everything from horseshoeing to clothing. Unfortunately the manuscript was destroyed in the nineteenth century. *See* Convents and Nuns.

Hilda of Whitby, Saint (614–680)

English abbess. The niece of Edwin, king of Northumbria. In 627, she was baptized with him; he became the first Christian king of Northumbria. He was soon assassinated, but she survived the political machinations and became a nun when she was thirty-three years old. A few years later, she became abbess of a convent. Ten years later, she founded the double monastery called Streaneshalch (Whitby and became abbess over it. Whitby was a dependent of the monastery at Lindisfarne. Cædmon, the first Anglo-Saxon Christian poet, was a lay member of Whitby. A humble groom, he had a vision in which he was told to sing about the creation. He was able to do so and thus revealed his talent to Hilda, who encouraged him to enter the religious life, where he was allowed to nurture his talent as a musician and a poet.

Hilda was highly influential in the church and hosted at Whitby the ecclesiastical assembly known as the Synod of Whitby in 664. The assembly established the precedence of Roman Christian practices over Celtic practices. *See* Convents and Nuns; Religion and Women.

Hildegarde of Bingen (1098–1187)

German abbess and musician. When she was eight years old, she was given to a convent near Bingen, Germany. A contemporary biographer said she was her parents' "tithe." As their tenth child, she was the one they contributed to the church. She was fourteen years old when she made her profession.

Hildegarde became abbess of this Benedictine convent and established several others throughout Germany.

When she was in her forties, she began writing a book, *Scivias*, which described her mystical visions and became popular in Europe. Her most famous work, it was a compendium of poems and visions, in which Christ speaks through her. The work was accepted as canonical by the church although it claims full equality for women. The work established her position as the leading feminist theorist of the Middle Ages.

Hildegarde was also outspoken in approving of sexual love in the context of marriage and even equated nuns with the church fathers. In her writings and teachings, she emphasized that women had a special visionary role in Christianity.

In response, she was lectured by church authorities about staying cloistered. She challenged church authority on occasion, such as when she buried an excommunicated man in consecrated ground. Her convent was placed under interdict. Although she was eighty years old at the time, she traveled to Mainz in order to appeal to a clerical tribunal. The case was resolved only when the archbishop involved died.

Later, she compiled all of her poetry and musical works in another popular manuscript. Her musical works are sophisticated and unconventional. She wrote a morality play that is also a musical composition.

Hildegarde was a healer, physician, and pharmacologist. She wrote treatises on nature and medicine. She developed an early theory of evolution and knew that the earth is round. She propounded theories of the role of women. She was interested in scientific interpretations of the world and was even interested in tackling the question of sexuality, its purpose, and its meaning. Her theory of conception was remarkably accurate.

In her visionary writing, she expressed her conviction that humans have the capacity to be more perfect. She believed the soul has both male and female aspects, and that men and women, while possessing different characteristics from one another, should attempt to develop the characteristics of the opposite gender.

Because of her formidable intellect and her mystical writings, she was considered a prophet and advised secular rulers and religious leaders. Although she suffered many illnesses, they did not prevent her from becoming involved in political and diplomatic dealings. Her fame spread throughout Germany and to Flanders, France, England, Italy, and even Greece. She was never canonized although she is often called Saint Hildegarde. Miracles were attributed to her both before and after her death. *See* Religion and Women.

SUGGESTED READING: Hildegarde of Bingen, *Book of Divine Works, with Letters and Songs* (Sante Fe: University of New Mexico Press, 1987), *Explanation of the Rule of Benedict* (Toronto: University of Toronto Press, 1990), *Illuminations* (Sante Fe: University of New Mexico Press, 1985).

Hildegarde of Suabia (8th century)

Also Desideria. Lombard queen of the Franks. Her father was the famous Lombard king, Desiderius. In order to create an alliance between the Franks and the Lombards, she married Charlemagne in 771. Charlemagne wanted an alliance with the Lombards in order to reduce his brother Carloman's power and lands. In that same year, Carloman died. When Desiderius encroached on papal lands and threatened to invade Rome in 774, Charlemagne repudiated Hildegarde (as often happened in the Middle Ages when it was expedient) and fought a war against the Lombards. Desiderius was forced to surrender, and Charlemagne became the king of the Lombards. Hildegarde returned home to her defeated family. *See* Marriage and Family.

SUGGESTED READING: Richard Hodges et al., *Mohammed, Charlemagne and the Origins of Europe* (Ithaca, NY: Cornell University Press, 1983).

Homosexuality *see* **Sexuality**

Honoria (5th century)

Daughter of Placidia, the effective ruler of the Western Empire (in place of her son Valentinian III). She was known for offering herself in marriage to Attila the Hun. *See* Placidia.

Hospitals

Institutions for the care of the sick, wounded, and dying, which were semireligious communities in the Middle Ages. In general, they were supervised by monks and nuns, with lay brothers and sisters performing the work. In the thirteenth century, Paris even had hospitals with maternity wards. *See* Convents and Nuns; Medicine and Health.

SUGGESTED READING: Nicholas Orme and Margaret Webster, *The English Hospital, 1070–1570* (New Haven, CT: Yale University Press, 1995).

Households

The typical medieval peasant household was similar to the nuclear family known today but, just as today, it had infinite variations. Typically, a husband and wife plus their young children lived and worked together. Sometimes members of an extended family lived together under one roof. Merchants and artisans housed apprentices and journeymen in their homes.

The medieval aristocratic household was mostly male. It consisted of the lord, his wife, and their young children, possibly the lord's mother, a few female companions, and one or two female servants. Sometimes after the death of the lord, his widow (sometimes his mother or daughter) would rule in his place. The rest of the members of the household included male officers and mostly male servants.

Dukes and earls had between fifty and two hundred members in their households. Bishops and abbots usually had between forty and eighty. A royal household had three or four hundred. Barons and petty nobility had as few as twenty members in their households. Knights might have half that number.

The noble household consisted of the inner household, which was the stable, unchanging, main household, and the riding household, which consisted of the lord and a small group of retainers who traveled on the lord's business. The inner household usually consisted of the wife or widow, plus the youngest members of the family, a few companions, and some servants. Relatives, important advisors, and officials also joined the household on a changing basis. Gentlemen, yeomen (called valetti, from which the word *valet* comes), grooms (called garciones or garçons, "waiters"), pages, and guests also lived in the household at different times and in varying numbers.

The more servants a noble had, the more glory and social standing he or she acquired. Servants and affiliated members of the household wore livery and badges to identify with whom they were associated.

A royal household consisted of a chancellor who served as chief of staff; a constable who supervised the outside staff; a marshal who kept the discipline at court; a grand butler who supervised the inside staff; a personal bodyguard consisting of several well-trusted retainers; a master of falconry and the hunt; a master of stables; a master of forests; grand stewards of the kitchen, bakery, cellar, fruit, and furnishings; a physician; an astronomer; a chamberlain who saw to the private needs of the king; barbers; priests; painters and other artists; musicians; minstrels and storytellers; secretaries; copyists or scribes; jesters and other entertainers; pages, usually the sons of favored nobles; squires; a chatelaine or estate manager; a treasurer and other ministers; knights with attendants; and servants, such as cupbearers, carters, and launderers. This often meant a permanent household or court of hundreds. In the early Middle Ages, this retinue traveled from place to place in order to reduce the burden such a number of people placed on limited resources.

The biggest expenditure for every household was food. As much as half the budget (in some cases, more) was spent on food, regardless of social class. Another ten percent was spent on clothing and textiles, which would be passed down from one person to another and even from generation to generation. Clothing was so valuable that lords gave clothing or cloth to retainers as a reward for service. Wages also equaled about ten percent of the budget; much pay was given in kind. Little was spent on fuel, since firewood and peat were easily collected.

The poor lived in huts and hovels or in one- or two-room houses. The middle class lived in larger buildings with stone walls and gardens. Outbuildings included stables, pigpens, and chicken coops. A bakehouse was connected to the kitchen. The house itself consisted of a central hall, a great parlor with smaller rooms off of it, privy, cellar, larder house, buttery, cloth house (closet), and often a chapel. Above stairs was the bedchamber. All of the rooms were small and sparsely furnished and were designed for working in.

Nobles lived in castles that were larger versions of the middle-class home and more lavishly decorated. Toward the end of the medieval time period, they lived in manor houses in towns. *See* Food and Cooking; Marriage and Family.

SUGGESTED READING: David Her-lihy, *Medieval Households* (Cambridge, MA: Harvard University Press, 1985); Marjorie Rowling, *Life in Medieval Times* (New York: Perigee, 1973).

Hrotswitha of Gandersheim
(late 10th century)

Benedictine nun in the western part of Germany. She wrote short dramas modeled on Roman drama. Her work is notorious for its depiction of violence and sexuality as well as science and theology. Her notable play is *The Martyrdom of the Holy Virgins*, which has sadomasochistic overtones. *See* Convents and Nuns; Religion and Women.

SUGGESTED READING: Hrotswitha of Gandersheim, *The Plays of Hrotswitha of Gandersheim* (Oak Park, IL: Bolchazy Carducci, 1986).

Hugh of Saint Victor (1096–1141)

French theologian, one of the few medieval Catholic theologians to argue for the equality of women. At a very young age, he joined the Augustinian Order at the monastery of Hamersleven. When he was about twenty, he entered the monastery of Saint Victor in Paris and stayed there for the rest of his life. He established a school of mysticism that made Saint Victor a famous center.

Hugh developed a theory of the contemplative life which depicted the stages one most go through to achieve union with God. He wrote on various scientific subjects. He was one of the few medieval men who pictured women as partners of men. Using the biblical story of the creation of Eve to support his belief, he pointed out that Eve had been made from Adam's rib in order to be at his side, not from his head in order to be his lord, nor from his foot in order to be his slave. He contrasted the sinfulness of Eve with the purity of

Mary as a way to show that not all women were evil and corrupt. He always portrayed the church as a woman. *See* Cult of the Virgin Mary; Religion and Women.

SUGGESTED READING: Jerome Taylor, *The Didascalicon of Hugh of St. Victor: A Medieval Guide to the Arts* (New York: Columbia University Press, 1991).

I

Igraine

The mother of King Arthur in Arthurian romance. She was married to Gorlois, who fought with Uther, the king of England. Uther, who coveted Igraine, made her pregnant by appearing to her as her husband, helped by Merlin's magic. Gorlois was killed in battle with Uther. Later, Uther married Igraine, but the child Arthur was given to Merlin, who had him raised by a foster father.

Imma *see* Emma of Normandy

Indigenous People

During barbarian incursions, indigenous people throughout Europe could not repel the invaders and suffered in various ways. They were killed or forced to flee to walled cities, mountains, and islands. Often, women were forced into marriage or concubinage with the conquering invaders. Some groups, such as the Thracians, disappeared from the historical record. Others remained where they had lived or resettled nearby and were assimilated. Forcible relocation was a common practice of the Byzantine Empire. In Greece, the indigenous people became Hellenized.

Inés de Castro (1320?–1355)

Castilian noblewoman whose tragic fate became the subject of many Spanish songs and poems. Sometime around 1340, Inés went to live with her cousin Constantia, who had married Peter (Pedro) I, called the Severe, the son of King Alfonso IV of Portugal. After Constantia died in 1345, Peter began an affair with Inés. According to some sources, he secretly married her. The two had four children before King Alfonso had Inés murdered, apparently afraid that her children would interfere with the legitimate succession of his first grandson, Constantia's child. Peter conducted a brief civil war against Alfonso but later appeared to reconcile with him and the murderers. Once he succeeded to the throne, however, he had them executed. Peter also had Inés's body exhumed and reburied in a tomb befitting a queen.

Infanta Isabella *see* Isabella the Catholic

Infanta Juana *see* Juana, Infanta

Infanticide

Method of controlling family size, common early in the Middle Ages. Female infants were more often murdered than male infants. The typical method was by exposure to the elements. The primary reason for infanticide was economic. Many households could not support more than a few members. Because female children had less value than male children, they were more likely to be viewed as disposable. Daughters married, which required a dowry. Daughters did not contribute substantial economic benefits to the birth family — they were more valuable to the husband's family. Throughout the Middle Ages, the Catholic church condemned the practice as murder. *See* Marriage and Family.

Ingeborg (12th century)

Danish queen of France. A noblewoman, she married Philip Augustus, king of France, thirteen years after he succeeded to the throne. She was almost immediately repudiated. Philip claimed she had secret vices and tried to annul the marriage. This caused turmoil in the kingdom for some years. Philip was even accused of being possessed by the devil. The pope placed France under interdict when Philip married again. Ingeborg retreated to a monastery for women.

Ingeborg Eriksdottir (13th century)

Sister of Erik, the king of Sweden, she married Birger of Bjalboa, a Swedish nobleman. Subsequently, he was named jarl, chief of earls, in 1248. From then on he controlled the country. Under Ingeborg's influence, he wrote laws that improved the condition of women in his realm.

Inheritance

Depending on where she lived, a woman might be able to inherit property or the right to rule, but the way a woman usually controlled property or assumed power was as a regent for her minor son (sometimes for a minor brother or an absent husband). In most cases, if there were no male heir, the property was divided among daughters, whose husbands would then administer the land. In the case of a title, it was rarely passed to the eldest daughter and thence to her husband. More often, a title passed to a distantly related male.

Among the Burgundians, the mother's personal possessions went to her daughters; sons had no share. An unmarried woman's belongings went to her sisters; if she had no sisters, then to her brothers. In the fourteenth and fifteenth centuries, legal developments made the position of women stronger, especially in England and France. They had more claim to their husband's estates and could hold property in their own right. Throughout the Middle Ages, the right of female succession was problematic and was frequently challenged by men. This was true in the Byzantine Empire as well as in the West. The roots of this bias probably stem from the military nature of feudalism. A woman was not considered capable of fulfilling the military obligations she owed her lord and so could not possess the lands according to the feudal contract. *See* Feudalism and Women.

SUGGESTED READING: Andrew Lewis, *Royal Succession in Capetian France: Studies on Familial Order and the State* (Cambridge, MA: Harvard University Press, 1982); Eileen Spring, *Law, Land and Family: Aristocratic Inheritance in England, 1300–1800* (Chapel Hill: University of North Carolina Press, 1997).

Inquisition

System established in the Middle Ages for the purpose of investigating and suppressing heresy, which had been common from the fourth century, but did not earn its vicious reputation until the late Middle Ages.

The vigorous persecution of heresy began when Christianity became the official religion of the Roman Empire. Any deviation from orthodox Christianity was an opposition to the state. A heretic was therefore an enemy of the state.

For many years, the penalty for heresy was excommunication. That changed in the twelfth century, when heretics became a more serious threat. Heresy became more organized. Now entire villages and cities held ideas in opposition to the church.

Since women tended to gravitate toward heretical sects, which were more egalitarian than the Catholic church and offered more autonomy, they often found themselves the targets of inquisitors.

A person who came forward and confessed heresy suffered lesser penalties than one who did not confess and had to be tried. Any person could be accused of heresy, although the targets were mostly Jews (and in Spain, Muslims) and old women who were a burden to their families. Any contact with a known heretic made one immediately suspect.

At first, the accused was not even allowed to know the name of the accuser, although after some years this practice was suspended. Accusers could be liars, convicted criminals or heretics themselves. Guilt was assumed if two people accused the same person. The accused were not always told the charges or the specific offenses for which they were being tried, and they were forced to defend themselves by guessing. In 1252, Pope Innocent IV instituted the practice of torturing suspected heretics in order to prompt confessions. Accused heretics could summon character witnesses to swear they were orthodox; these character witnesses could be tortured as well. Some thirteenth-century Crusades, especially against the Cathari, were military actions undertaken against towns and territories that had many heretics. These Crusades were the first church-sanctioned wars between Christians.

Inquisitors were charged with bringing heretics back to orthodoxy through persuasion, argument, and threat. If a heretic recanted and then returned to heresy, he or she could be punished with loss of property and a period of imprisonment. If a heretic recanted and remained orthodox, the penalty was lighter. Accused heretics who did not confess or did not recant faced the ultimate penalty: death by burning. Estimates range widely, but some historians believe as many as ten million people were put to death during the Inquisition, which raged until the seventeenth century. *See* Crusades; Heresy; Religion and Women.

SUGGESTED READING: James Buchanan Given, *Inquisition and Medieval Society: Power, Discipline, and Resistance in Languedoc* (Ithaca, NY: Cornell University Press, 1997); Bernard Hamilton, *The Medieval Inquisition* (New York: Holmes and Meier, 1982); B. Netanyahu, *Toward the Inquisition: Essays on Jewish and Converso History in Late Medieval Spain* (Ithaca, NY: Cornell University Press, 1998); Albert Clement Shannon, *The Medieval Inquisition* (Wilmington, DE: Michael Glazier, 1991).

Irene *see* Bertha of Sulzbach

Irene, Emperor (752–803)

Byzantine ruler. A native of Athens, she married Emperor Leo IV. She was an Iconodule (image venerator) although for some years Iconoclasm had been the policy of the Byzantine Empire. After the death of her husband in 780, she served as regent for her son Constantine VI, who was only ten. She demanded to be called "emperor" and used the masculine form of the title. During the following decade, she put down numerous rebellions and restored monks who had been exiled during the Iconoclastic Controversy. In 787, she convened the Seventh Ecumenical Council, which condemned Iconoclasm.

In 790, she declared herself superior to her son. Because of this, her enemies conspired to seize power. She learned of the plot, had those responsible executed, and imprisoned her son. She was overthrown in a military rebellion later that year. Constantine took power in his own right and exiled Irene. Constantine restored Irene in 792, and she immediately began plotting against him. In 795, Constantine suddenly and unexpectedly divorced his wife, Mary of Amnia, and married his mistress, causing a scandal. The Byzantine clergy disapproved of second marriages in general, even of widows and widowers. This act enraged them.

Irene seized the opportunity to instigate a palace coup in 797. Constantine had undermined his own regime, not only with the unpopular divorce and remarriage, but also by threatening to restore Iconoclasm, which made him unpopular among the people.

Irene captured her son and had his eyes put out. He did not survive this brutality and left no heir to the throne. Irene became sole ruler, the first woman to rule over the Byzantine Empire in her own right.

In 802, Charlemagne asked her to marry him after the pope had coronated him as emperor of the Roman Empire (Western Europe). The Byzantines denounced the pope's act, as there could only be one emperor and they had her: Irene (even if they did detest her). Irene initially refused to recognize Charlemagne as the emperor of the Roman Empire, but appeared to consider his offer of marriage seriously as a means of solidifying her power.

Before anything could be done, however, Charlemagne died.

Popular sentiment had turned against Irene because of her treatment of her son. In addition, no woman had ever ruled the Byzantine Empire in her own right, so this generated considerable opposition. She was deposed in 802 in a coup and exiled to Lesbos, where she died the following year.

SUGGESTED READING: Lynda Garland, *Byzantine Empresses: Women and Power in Byzantium AD 527–1204* (New York: Routledge, 1999); R. Jenkins, *Byzantium: The Imperial Centuries, 610–1071* (New York: Random House, 1966); Jaroslav Pelikan, *Imago Dei: The Byzantine Apologia for Icons* (Princeton, NJ: Princeton University Press, 1990).

Irene Asenina Cantacuzene
(d. after 1363)

Also Eirene. Byzantine empress. One of the great-grandchildren of Emperor Michael VIII and the daughter of Andronicus Paleologus Asen, the son of the Bulgarian tsar. She was probably raised in Constantinople. She married John Cantacuzene, the future emperor, in 1318. They had six children.

At first, she lived in Gallipoli, where John held estates. In 1320, Emperor Andronicus III was disinherited by his grandfather Andronicus II. Many nobles protested this action, and Irene's husband, John, led a rebellion against Andronicus II. While he was at war, Irene was responsible for affairs in Gallipoli.

In 1328, Andronicus II abdicated in favor of Andronicus III. John became his commander in chief. When Andronicus died in 1341, he had a young son, John V Paleologus. His widow, Anna of Savoy, expected to be regent, but John Cantacuzene attempted to seize power himself. A group of rebels named him emperor. He was unable to secure his claim and was forced to flee to Serbia.

Abandoned by John, Irene and her brother Manuel Asen defended the city of Didymoteichon, seeking help from the Bulgars and Turks. In 1343, John was finally able to return to Didymoteichon and continued to press his claim to the throne. Shortly thereafter, he won the civil war against John V Paleologus's supporters and was crowned emperor. Irene became empress at the same time.

In 1346, their daughter Theodora married Orhan, the emir of Bithynia in Asia Minor, a "barbarian" who was a Muslim. This created an ally, but many Byzantines felt it was a distasteful match. In 1347, Anna of Savoy, the widow of Andronicus III, surrendered Constantinople to John, and he reigned there as senior emperor. He allowed John V Paleologus to reign as junior emperor. To cement the alliance, Irene's daughter Helena married John V Paleologus.

However, Irene's son Matthew thought he, not John Paleologus, should be heir to the throne. He was temporarily appeased when he was presented with lands in Thrace. In the same year, Irene's youngest son, Andronicus, died of the plague.

In 1348, John Cantacuzene went to war with the Bulgarians, leaving Irene to administer imperial affairs and to defend Constantinople. The Genoese took the opportunity to attack, but Irene refused to negotiate and defended the city against their repeated attacks. Around 1350, her son Matthew went to war against John V Paleologus, against her wishes. By 1353, John Cantacuzene had succumbed to the pressure and named his son emperor. In the following year, the Turks, who were supposed to be Byzantine allies, occupied

Gallipoli. During the ensuing war, John Paleologus returned to Constantinople and was acclaimed emperor; John Cantacuzene abdicated and later entered a monastery. Irene entered a convent, taking the name Eugenia. Their son Matthew was finally forced to renounce the imperial title. *See* Anna of Savoy.

SUGGESTED READING: Edmund Fryde, *The Early Paleologan Renaissance: 1261–1360* (Boston: Brill, 2000); Donald M. Nicol, *The Last Centuries of Byzantium: 1261–1453* (New York: Cambridge University Press, 1993), *The Reluctant Emperor: A Biography of John Cantacuzene, Byzantine Emperor and Monk, c. 1295–1383* (New York: Cambridge University Press, 1996).

Irene Choumnaina Paleologina
(1291–1355)

Also Eirene and Eulogia. Byzantine princess and abbess. The second daughter of Nicephorus Choumnous, a scholar and prime minister to Emperor Andronicus II Paleologus, Irene grew up in a wealthy household, a scholar and a devoted Christian.

In 1303, when she was twelve years old, she married John Paleologus, the emperor's son, who had already been given the title of despot. The emperor's wife, Irene, violently disapproved of the match.

Four years later, when John died, Irene was just sixteen. She could not marry again without losing rank, a thought inconceivable to her father. After some time, she decided to become a nun. She founded a convent at her expense and determined to live on her own terms. She was about twenty-one at the time. She took the name Eulogia and served as abbess at a double monastery. Her spiritual advisor, Theoleptus, served as abbot. The convent soon became fashionable and more than one hundred nuns joined it. By 1327, her parents and Theoleptus were dead. Five years later, when she was about forty years old, Emperor Andronicus II died, and she fell victim to depression and despair. Fortunately, she found a new advisor.

Her spiritual advisors thought she was too concerned with her social standing and her family and accused her of being proud, arrogant, and stubborn. This was illustrated when she opposed the usurper John Cantacuzene, who had made himself emperor of Constantinople. She mobilized her considerable resources against him, and he abdicated in 1354. She died the following year. *See* Anna of Savoy; Convents and Nuns.

SUGGESTED READING: Angela Hero, ed., *A Woman's Quest for Spiritual Guidance: The Correspondence of Princess Eulogia Chomnaina Palaiologina* (Holy Cross Orthodox Press, 1986).

Irene Ducas (11th century)

Member of a powerful Byzantine ruling family, she married Alexius I Comnenus, who became emperor after deposing Nicephorus III, the Ducas emperor, in 1081. They married almost immediately after Alexius took power. Their daughter Anna Comnena became a well-known historian of the First Crusade.

Alexius, as the adopted son of Empress Mary of Alania, succeeded to the throne once the usurper Nicephorus Botaneiates abdicated. Irene was forced to live in a different building while Alexius lived at the palace with Empress Mary. Mary and Alexius were suspected of carrying on an affair. Irene was even excluded from the imperial coronation ceremony. After protests from the patriarch, however, she was crowned a few days later.

Eventually, Irene and her husband settled into a happily married life and had nine children. *See* Anna Comnena.

SUGGESTED READING: Lynda Garland, *Byzantine Empresses: Women and Power in Byzantium AD 527–1204* (New York: Routledge, 1999).

Irene Paleologina (c. 1273–1317)

Also called Eirene and Yolanda of Montferrat. Italian empress of the Byzantine Empire. She was a Lombard, an ethnic group very powerful in Italy; her father, William, was the marquis of Montferrat and the king of Thessalonica. Alfonso X of Castile was her grandfather. She married the Byzantine emperor, Andronicus II Paleologus, in 1284, when she was about eleven. She was given the Greek name of Eirene or Irene at the time of her marriage. She then started an ambitious program of intrigue against her husband.

Her dowry was the kingdom of Thessalonica in northeastern Greece. Over time, her husband gave her additional lands in Macedonia. Although her husband had become emperor in 1282, she was not elevated to the status of empress until the birth of her first son in 1286. She had several more children, three of whom died in infancy.

Andronicus II had two sons from a previous marriage, and he intended his firstborn, Michael, to succeed him. In 1294, he crowned Michael as co-emperor. He gave his second son the title of despot. Irene felt her sons were left out, so her first son was also named Despot. She wanted the empire divided into principalities for her sons to inherit, but this idea horrified the emperor and his subjects.

Irene disliked her husband, finding him demanding and unfaithful. Their relationship grew strained especially after their daughter Simonis became the bride of Stephen Milutin, the ruler of Serbia, when she was only five years old. This scandalous marriage took place in 1299. Milutin consummated the marriage, and the injuries that Simonis sustained made her unable to bear children. Next, Irene's husband married her son John to Irene Choumnaina (Paleologina), not an illustrious match for him and certainly not what Irene had in mind for her son.

In 1303, she went to Thessalonica to live, holding court as empress in her own right. Two years later, her brother, who had inherited the title of marquis, died, and Irene wanted to give the title to her son John. But the emperor was persuaded by the anti–Latin patriarch of Constantinople to do otherwise. Two years later, John was dead. She asked that her second son inherit Montferrat, which he did in 1306; he died in 1338.

In Thessalonica, which she regarded as her own property, she continued to control matters of state and foreign policy without her husband's assistance. He placed a spy in her court and learned of the vicious rumors and accusations she circulated against him. Surprisingly, Stephen Milutin, who had brutalized her daughter, soon became her closest ally. As she continued to denounce her husband, the patriarch reprimanded her for setting a bad example of marriage. She died in Thessalonica in 1317.

Her daughter Simonis, who traveled to Thessalonica for her mother's funeral, did not want to go back to Serbia. Her husband sent a delegation to bring her back, and her father insisted that she return. She tried to escape, dressed as a nun, but her half brother Constantine betrayed her. She was forcibly returned to Serbia. Her husband died three years later. In 1321 she returned to Constantinople and became a nun. She died twenty years later. *See* Simonis Paleologus.

SUGGESTED READING: Donald M. Nicol, *The Byzantine Lady: Ten Portraits, 1250–1500* (New York: Cambridge University Press, 1994).

Isabeau of Bavaria *see* **Elizabeth of Bavaria**

Isabel *see* **Isabella the Catholic**

Isabel of Portugal (15th century)
Queen of Castile and Portuguese noblewoman. She married John (Juan) II, king of Castile, at the arrangement of Alvaro de Luna, the constable of Castile and essentially the ruler during John's reign. The marriage was arranged without consulting the bridegroom, which of course caused problems, but he was eventually persuaded to participate. Isabel soon became one of Alvaro's most troublesome opponents, bent on his destruction. History does not explain why.

She managed to convince her husband to banish Alvaro from court. When Alvaro delayed, she had him arrested and charged with usurping the throne. He was beheaded in 1453.

After Alvaro's death, King John was obsessed with the murder he had authorized and was unable to govern. Isabel happily did so in his place until his death in 1454, when the throne passed to Henry (Enrique) IV.

SUGGESTED READING: Angus MacKay, *Love, Religion and Politics in Fifteenth-Century Spain* (Boston: Brill, 1998); L. J. Simon, *Iberia and the Mediterranean World of the Middle Ages* (Boston: Brill, 1995).

Isabella of Angoulême (d. 1246)
The daughter of a French nobleman, she married John Lackland, king of England, in 1200, becoming his second wife.

She had been betrothed to Hugh of Lusignan, but married John instead. As a result of this insult, Philip II Augustus, king of France, seized her territories in Normandy.

Isabella was widowed in 1216. Her son Henry III then succeeded to the throne. Isabella married Hugh of la Marche. In 1242, they planned a rebellion against the French king, Louis IX, by blockading La Rochelle. Louis's mother, Blanche of Castile, discovered the conspiracy. Henry III invaded, joining Isabella, Hugh, and their followers, but because Blanche was prepared, Louis defeated the English.

Later, Isabella hired servants to poison Louis, but the plot was again discovered. The servants were executed, and she was forced to pledge her loyalty to the king. Her plots earned her the nickname "Jezebel."

SUGGESTED READING: Christopher Allman, *Society at War: The Experience of England and France During the Hundred Years' War* (London: Boydell and Brewer, 1999); Robert C. Stacey, *Politics, Policy and Finance under Henry III, 1216–1245* (New York: Oxford University Press, 1987).

Isabella of England (1332–1379)

The second child and eldest daughter of Edward III and Queen Philippa, who tried and failed five times to arrange a marriage for her.

With her brother Edward and younger sister, Joanna, Isabella had her own household as a child, with governesses, cooks, clergy, and servants. She indulged in ostentatious luxury from childhood until her death.

The first marriage negotiations King Edward undertook on her behalf were with Peter (Pedro), king of Castile, when she was three years old, but this fell through. Then she was considered as a potential wife of the son of the duke of Brabant, but this was delayed because they were too closely related and needed a papal dispensation. A third match was proposed with the count of Flanders, Louis de Male, but he refused to marry her and fled to France in order to avoid it. Next, her father attempted to betroth her to Charles IV of Bohemia, but this also fell through. When she was nineteen, she became betrothed to Bérard d'Albret, a lord of Gascony, but she jilted him.

Possibly as a reaction to this lack of success in arranging an appropriate match, her father endowed her with lands, revenues, and gifts. Even though he was quite generous, she was extremely extravagant and chronically ran short of money.

Isabella was eventually married in 1365 at age thirty-three, to Enguerrand de Coucy, a French lord who was being held as a guarantee for King John II's ransom. Coucy was given the earldom of Bedford to tie him more closely to England.

SUGGESTED READING: Barbara Tuchman, *A Distant Mirror: The Calamitous 14th Century* (New York: Ballantine, 1987).

Isabella of France (1296–1358)

Queen of England. The daughter of Philip IV, king of France, when she was twelve years old she married Edward II, king of England, whose most notable achievement was the complete breakdown of law and order during his reign. Isabella's uncle, the duke of Lancaster, was an implacable opponent of Edward's, but although he controlled much English territory and called himself "steward of England," he was unable to keep the support of other nobles. Isabella supported her uncle's opposition to Edward. Edward marched against him in 1322, and the duke was captured and executed for treason.

Isabella had four children with Edward despite the fact that he was homosexual. Her son Edward would become king of England.

Mistreated, humiliated, and neglected throughout her marriage, she grew to despise her husband. She hated the royal favorites, the Dispensers, who tried to annul her marriage to Edward and had sequestered her estates.

In 1325, Edward sent her to France to arrange an agreement between Edward and Isabella's brother Charles IV, then king of France. Isabella stayed in France, plotting against Edward. In France, Isabella met Roger Mortimer, a Welsh nobleman and rebel who opposed Edward and who had fought against him in 1320 and again in 1321. Mortimer had escaped from the Tower of London and was living in exile in France. Isabella also met other powerful English exiles. They began to assemble an army. Her brother King Charles IV also aided her in her quest. In 1326, Edward II sent his son Edward III, the heir to the crown of England, to join Isabella. Once he was safely in her possession, Isabella and Mortimer, with the support of William II of Holland, invaded England. Edward II and the Dispensers fled, but Isabella's army hunted them down. The Dispensers were murdered immediately, and Edward was imprisoned. In 1327, Parliament deposed him; he was murdered later that year. Isabella's son Edward III was acclaimed king of England by Parliament, but the country was effectively ruled by Mortimer. Mortimer brokered a hated peace settlement with Scotland, the Treaty of Northampton, which caused a revolt in 1329.

The following year, in 1330, Edward III overthrew Mortimer and killed him. He placed Isabella under house arrest, where she died, insane, many years later.

SUGGESTED READING: Sandra Raban, *England under Edward I and Edward II* (Oxford: Blackwell, 2000); Nigel Saul, *Fourteenth-Century England* (London: Boydell and Brewer, 2000); Scott L. Waugh, *England in the Reign of Edward III* (New York: Cambridge University Press, 1991).

Isabella of France (1349–1372)
French noblewoman. Daughter of King John II of France. She was betrothed to Gian Galeazzo, the son of the Visconti family, when she was eleven, for a payment of 600,000 gold coins. This scandalous arrangement helped pay King John's ransom to the English, but the marriage to the family of an Italian tyrant was startling and was widely regarded as a measure of how far France had fallen from its glory days. Most people felt that Isabella had been sold to the Italians. Isabella died at the age of twenty-three in childbirth. *See* Marriage and Family.

Isabella of France (b. 1389)
Queen of England. In 1396, she married Richard II, king of England, who supposedly fell in love with her after seeing her portrait. She was only seven years old at the time, and the marriage was conducted by proxy. The marriage caused grave doubts concerning succession. This story is told in Shakespeare's play *Richard II.*

Isabella the Catholic (d. 1504)
Also called Infanta Isabella. Spanish queen and the sister of Henry IV of Castile. In 1468, rebellious Castilian nobles tried to proclaim her queen in opposition to her brother, but she refused to be used as a puppet. Instead, she signed a treaty with Henry, who recognized her as heir to the throne. She agreed to marry someone of Henry's choosing but married Ferdinand

of Aragón, her cousin and heir to the throne of Aragón. This marriage took place in 1469 with a forged papal dispensation and without her brother's agreement. He denounced the marriage and declared it nullified.

In 1470, Henry took the further step of declaring his daughter Infanta Juana as his true daughter and his heir (her legitimacy had been called into question because of his well-known impotence). He did this specifically to thwart Isabella's designs. A civil war ensued. Isabella's father-in-law, John (Juan) II, aided her claim.

Henry died in 1474. Immediately Isabella was proclaimed queen, although Juana's supporters opposed her. Some opponents claimed that females could not inherit the throne, but the archbishop of Toledo and Seville confirmed the right of female succession.

Juana was betrothed to Afonso V of Portugal, called the African, who invaded Castile on her behalf in 1475. Isabella's forces defeated him in 1476, and in 1478 Isabella was acknowledged queen. Afonso and Juana renounced all claim to Castile in exchange for Portugal's right to exclusive conquest of Africa.

Ferdinand, Isabella's husband, succeeded to the throne of Aragón in 1479. He and Isabella became formidable rulers, best known for launching the Spanish Inquisition and sponsoring Christopher Columbus. During her reign, the unification of Aragón and Castile became a reality; the unification of all Spain followed. Religious intolerance increased. More than 150,000 Jews were expelled, and others were forced to convert in 1492. A significant increase in slavery, especially of Africans, also took place. In 1502, Isabella expelled the Muslims as well, although most remaining Muslims chose to convert.

Intelligent and determined, she re-formed the government, created a standing army, and promulgated a book of law. She favored protectionism in trade. Eventually, she secured the right of appointment, effectively placing the church under state control in an effort to reform the church. She was responsible for the conquest of Granada.

The Spanish Inquisition was established in 1483, and it had the worst features of the Inquisition: secrecy, torture, property confiscation, and execution.

She was the only woman in Iberian history to ascend to the throne in her own right. She and her husband were referred to as the "two Catholic kings" by Pope Alexander in 1494. She is often considered a Renaissance figure rather than a medieval one. *See* Inheritance; Inquisition; Juana, Infanta.

SUGGESTED READING: Warren Carroll, *Isabel of Spain: The Catholic Queen* (Front Royal, VA: Christendom Press, 1991); Henry Kamen, *The Spanish Inquisition: A Historical Revision* (New Haven, CT: Yale University Press, 1999); Nancy Rubin, *Isabella of Castile: The First Renaissance Queen* (New York: St. Martin's, 1992).

Iseult

In Arthurian romance, the daughter of the king of Ireland. She married King Mark of Cornwall but, after accidentally drinking a love potion, fell in love with Tristan, King Mark's nephew. The two began an affair. She died of a broken heart after Tristan's death. In some versions of the story, Mark killed Tristan on learning of the affair; in another version, Lancelot did so. In at least one version, King Mark was responsible for destroying Camelot and the Round Table.

Iseult was also the name of Tristan's wife, who he married after leaving Iseult of Ireland. This Iseult was called Iseult of the White Hands. But because he still loved the first Iseult, his marriage suffered. When he was wounded and in danger of dying, he sent a message asking Iseult of Ireland to come and heal him. Iseult of the White Hands deceived him into believing that Iseult of Ireland was not coming, and he died without seeing her. *See* Courtly Love.

SUGGESTED READING: Joseph Bedier and Hilaire Beloc, trans., *The Romance of Tristan and Iseult* (New York: Vintage, 1994).

Ithamar *see* **Thamar**

Ivette of Huy (1159–c. 1224)

Also Juette. Famous visionary. The daughter of a tax collector, she was thirteen years old when arrangements were made for her marriage. Shortly thereafter, she told her confessor that she disliked marriage, intercourse, and childbirth and wanted her husband to die. After five years of marriage and three sons, he did die. Although Ivette preferred to remain a widow, family members wished her to remarry since she had an attractive dowry. Opposed to another marriage, she refused to become a slave, as she put it. Around this time, she began to see visions, including devils. Because of her opposition to marriage, she was forced to defend herself in the bishop's court, where she said she had vowed to serve Christ through holy chastity and so could not remarry. The bishop, believing she might be a holy visionary, agreed to let her remain unmarried. She was eighteen.

A relative of her late husband tried to seduce her, and she rebuffed him. Some time later when she was staying overnight at the home of a friend, he appeared there as well. Afraid that he would rape her, she appealed to the Virgin Mary for protection and was safe.

As a devout Christian, she gave away much of her property, but her father, horrified, took over management of her affairs. She wished to withdraw from the world but could not find a means to do so. Few convents existed. Those that did accepted only noblewomen with large dowries. Finally, she sought refuge at a leper house and began ministering to the patients there. After ten years, she became a recluse, walled up in a little house built next to the leper house, where she lived for the next thirty-seven years. A maidservant was walled up with her (no one asked how she felt about this turn of events). The leper house became a community for women, where they enjoyed relative freedom of action.

Ivette slept near the window, received supplicants, and passed on messages. A large company of women sought her protection. Her followers saw her as a holy visionary. After her enclosure, her visions became more and more frequent. She came to be seen as a medium between the spiritual world and the temporal world. Many people asked her to make pronouncements on thorny theological issues. Her main power was that she could discern the secret faults of others, such as jealousy and lust. These skills served her well.

After a time, her power threatened the canons and the clergy — male power. They denounced her and were clearly pleased when she died. Authorities refused the requests of her followers to be walled up like her. *See* Hagiography; Religion and Women.

SUGGESTED READING: Kathleen Coyne Kelly, *Performing Virginity and Testing Chastity in the Middle Ages* (New York: Routledge, 2000); Rosalynn Voaden,

God's Words, Women's Voices: The Discernment of Spirits in the Writing of Late Medieval Women Visionaries (London: Boydell and Brewer, 1999).

J

Jacoba Felicia (14th century)

Also Jacqueline Felicia. Parisian woman who practiced medicine and a form of faith healing. She was charged as a criminal for practicing medicine without a license in 1322. The University of Paris controlled licensure, and by the fourteenth century women were simply not allowed to practice medicine, although prior to this time, they had been able to do so. Jacoba nonetheless continued to help others who needed her medical services. *See* Medicine and Health.

Jacqueline Felicia *see* Jacoba Felicia

Jadwiga of Anjou *see* Jadwiga of Poland

Jadwiga of Poland (1374–1399)

Also Hedwig; Jadwiga of Anjou. Queen of Poland and Lithuania. She married Vladislav (Wadysaw) Jagiełło of Lithuania in 1386; he had became grand duke of Lithuania in 1377 after the death of his father. She was the heiress to Poland, and the two become queen and king of Poland. Thus, their marriage united the kingdoms of Poland and Lithuania. She convinced Vladislav to convert to Christianity because his new subjects were Christian. In the year after their marriage, he introduced Christianity to Lithuania and suppressed paganism. Because of this, Jadwiga was credited with converting the Baltic countries.

The Jagiełło dynasty they founded provided many rulers to Poland, Lithuania, Hungary, and Bohemia before dying out in 1572. *See* Conversion.

SUGGESTED READING: Oskar Halecki and Tadeusz Gomada, *Jadwiga of Anjou and the Rise of East Central Europe* (East European Monographs, 1991); Jean W. Sedlar, *East Central Europe in the Middle Ages, 1000–1500* (Seattle: University of Washington Press, 1994).

Jakvinta (11th–12th century)

Italian noblewoman. She married Constantine Bodin, ruler of Duklja, also called Zeta (now Montenegro); at the time, this was all that remained of the earlier Bulgarian Empire. A former captive of the Byzantines, Constantine was released in 1078, and upon the death of his father in 1081 or 1082, he came to power, consolidating his claim by 1085. The marriage, which took place in 1081, probably strengthened the alliance between him and the Normans in Bari, Italy.

Jakvinta was a powerful force and significant influence. Fearing for her sons' inheritance, she urged Constantine to jail his cousin Branislav and his family. This was done around 1093–1095. Branislav died while in prison, but he had sons who were free and sought asylum in Dubrovnik, where Constantine laid siege. At Jakvinta's urging, Constantine beheaded Branislav's brother and one of his sons at the town walls.

After Constantine's death, sometime between 1101 and 1108, Jakvinta became the target of much hostility. In order to advance her son Juraj's claim to the throne of Duklja, she poisoned the elected Dukljan king, Vladimir, and tried to blame it on Constantine's brother Droboslav, who was also vying for the throne. After Vladimir's death, Jakvinta felt threatened by Droboslav and had him attacked while he was in jail. At her command, he was castrated, blinded, and immured in a monastery. Her son became ruler around 1118.

Branislav's relatives sought revenge and appealed to the Byzantine Empire for aid. The Byzantines sent an army. Jakvinta was arrested and died in Constantinople.

SUGGESTED READING: John V. A. Fine, *The Early Medieval Balkans: A Critical Survey from the Sixth to the Late Twelfth Century* (Detroit: University of Michigan Press, 1991).

Jeanne *see* Joanna of Bourbon

Jeanne I *see* Joan I

Jeanne II *see* Joan II

Jeanne Dabenton

One of the leaders of the Brethren of the Free Spirit movement. Followers of this movement sought personal salvation through a direct connection with God. They considered themselves to be saved without the intervention of priests or the sacraments of the church. They practiced free love and called themselves "holy beggars." The church condemned the movement in 1372, and Jeanne was burned at the stake for refusing to recant. *See* Brethren of the Free Spirit; Heresy; Religion and Women.

SUGGESTED READING: Raoul Veneigem, *The Movement of the Free Spirit* (New York: Zone Books, 1994).

Jeanne d'Arc *see* Joan of Arc

Jelena (12th century)

Serbian queen of Hungary. Daughter of Uroš, grand župan (ruler) of Raška (present-day Serbia). She married Belá II (the Blind), king of Hungary, in 1130; he had been blinded by his uncle King Koloman, who wanted his own son Stephen to succeed him. Her dowry included part of northern Serbia. The Serbs hoped to gain help against the Byzantines by this alliance.

Belá required Jelena's assistance to rule. Thus she held an important position in Hungarian diplomacy. In 1141, Belá died and their son Geza II succeeded. Jelena and her brothers — ethnic Serbs — ruled in Geza's place. Jelena's brother Beloš became the official regent. Their aid to Serbia infuriated the Byzantine Empire, which sought to control Serbia. The Byzantine emperor went to war against Hungary, but Geza, who reached the age of majority during the conflict, signed a treaty and ended the war.

SUGGESTED READING: John V. A. Fine, *The Early Medieval Balkans: A Critical Survey from the Sixth to the Late Twelfth Century* (Detroit: University of Michigan Press, 1991).

Jimena (11th–12th century)

Also Ximena. Spanish ruler of Valencia. Famous for her marriage to Count Rodrigo Díaz de Vivar, known as El Cid, a Castilian exile who fought on behalf of King Alfonso VI against the Muslims. He died in 1099, and a famous epic recounting his exploits was written. According to the poet of *El Cid*, he never took a mistress, loved his wife, and was never defeated in battle. He symbolized the virtues appreciated by Castilian society.

For three years after her husband's

death, Jimena ruled Valencia, but the Al-moravids (a Muslim dynasty) set siege to the city, and she was eventually forced to withdraw.

Joan I (c. 1273–1305)

Also called Jeanne. Queen of Navarre from 1274 and queen of France from 1285. The daughter of Henry I of Navarre, she inherited the throne of Navarre after his death in 1274. The nobles of Castile and Aragón threatened her reign, and she sought refuge with King Philip III of France, who aided her.

She married his son Philip IV of France in 1284, thus uniting both kingdoms. Navarre became a territory of France for many years. The immediate result was a civil war in Navarre. Joan's three sons became French kings — Louis X, Philip V, and Charles IV. Her daughter Isabella became queen of England. *See* Isabella of France.

Joan II (1309–1349)

Also called Jeanne. Queen of Navarre from 1328. The daughter of Louis X, king of France, who had inherited Navarre from his mother and France from his father, and the granddaughter of Joan I.

Joan's father died in 1316, when Joan was seven. Her claim to the French throne was set aside by her uncle Philip V, who claimed that women could not inherit the French throne under Salic law. He usurped the throne of Navarre as well.

After Philip VI came to the French throne in 1328, he granted Navarre to Joan. She and her husband, Philip of Evreaux, were well regarded by their new subjects. Her son Carlos (Charles II) succeeded to the throne of Navarre. The line continued until the middle of the fifteenth century. *See* Joan I.

SUGGESTED READING: Theodore John

Rivers, *Laws of the Salian and Ripurian Franks* (New York: AMS Press, 1987).

Joan, Pope

Legendary female pope. According to different versions of the story, she was pope in the ninth, tenth, or eleventh century. According to one legend, she fell in love with a monk, with whom she eloped, disguising herself as a man to escape detection. When her lover died, she entered the priesthood and was eventually elected pope, as John VIII. She later died in childbirth.

The first published version of the story appeared in the thirteenth century, told by the writer Stephen of Bourbon. For several centuries, the story was believed, even by the church, to be true.

Joan of Arc (1412–1431)

Also Jeanne d'Arc. Known as the Maid of Orléans and La Pucelle. Patron saint of France and military leader during the Hundred Years' War.

As a peasant girl, Joan began to hear voices and have visions from the time she was thirteen. When she was just sixteen, Joan heard voices from God ordering her to expel the English from France and have the disenfranchised dauphin made king. Charles VII, called Charles the Dauphin, was the eldest surviving son of King Charles VI of France, but he did not succeed to the throne upon his father's death. Instead, Henry VI of England, an infant at the time, inherited the throne, as had been agreed upon in the Treaty of Troyes, which had been negotiated in the hopes of ending the Hundred Years' War. Notwithstanding the treaty, the English continued their military campaigns against the French, winning several major battles.

A prophecy, of which Joan knew, predicted that a virgin from the Lorraine marches would save France during its time of greatest need. She felt certain that her mission was to have Charles crowned the true king of France.

She appeared first in 1428 and convinced a board of theologians that her claims of experiencing religious visions were true. She led the army that delivered Orléans from a protracted siege in May 1429. Doing so, she united the country and played a pivotal role in turning the tide of the Hundred Years' War in favor of the French. Shortly after the siege was broken, she and her followers won the decisive battle of Patay. In the following years, the French pushed the English out of France. The last battle of the Hundred Years' War occurred in 1453 at Castillon.

Although Joan succeeded in preserving the throne of France for Charles, he had no wish to continue the fight against the English, so she conducted a battle at Compiègne without his sanction. She was captured by Philip the Good, the duke of Burgundy, at Compiègne in 1430. He and his pro–English allies turned her over to an ecclesiastical court in Rouen to be tried on charges of heresy and sorcery. She was interrogated and tortured for more than a year and was found guilty of wearing men's clothing (she said she wore men's clothes to avoid the danger of rape). She was also convicted of believing she was responsible to God, not the Roman Catholic church. She was sentenced to death but after she confessed her errors, she was instead condemned to life in prison. Once in prison, she relapsed. This time, Pierre Cauchon, the bishop of Beavais, found her guilty of heresy and ordered her to be executed.

Joan was burned at the stake in May 1431. None of the French royalty or nobles tried to save her, possibly because they were ashamed that it took a village girl to lead them to victory. Twenty-two years after her execution, the French army recaptured all of French territory. In 1456, Pope Calixtus II retried her case and found her innocent. In 1920, she was canonized.

SUGGESTED READING: Harold Bloom, ed., *Joan of Arc* (New York: Chelsea House, Publishers, 1992); Willard Trask, *Joan of Arc: In Her Own Words* (New York: Turtle Point Press, 1996); Bonnie Wheeler and Charles T. Wood, eds., *Fresh Verdicts on Joan of Arc* (New York: Garland, 1996).

Joan of England (13th century)

The daughter of King John of England, she married Llewelyn the Great, the prince of Wales and a legendary hero, in 1205. The marriage did not prevent her father from invading when he suspected the prince of planning to seize English holdings in Wales. In response, Llewelyn sided with the English nobles against John, forcing him to sign the historic Magna Carta.

Joan of Kent (14th century)

Called the Fair Maid of Kent. Princess of England and the subject of scandal. She was betrothed to the earl of Salisbury but married his steward instead. Around the same time, she fell in love with Prince Edward, called the Black Prince, the son of King Edward III of England. When her husband, the steward, died in 1361, she went to the Black Prince, who married her even before receiving the necessary papal dispensation. Notorious and scandalous in her behavior, she had probably been King Edward's mistress before she became Prince Edward's wife. She was distrusted by Queen Philippa, who thought her too extravagant. She had four children; one of whom became Richard II.

SUGGESTED READING: Richard Barber, *Edward, Prince of Wales and Aquitaine: A Biography of the Black Prince* (Rochester, NY: University of Rochester Press, 1999).

Joanna I (1326–1382)

Queen of Naples. The granddaughter of the well-regarded King Robert, she became queen after his death. She married Andrew of Hungary, who was murdered at Joanna's instigation in 1345.

When James (Jaume) III, king of Majorca, was captured by Peter (Pedro) IV of Aragón in 1344, he was forced to sell his rights to Montpellier to France in order to raise his ransom. Joanna, sympathetic to his cause, supplied him with a fleet of ships with which he attempted to regain Majorca, but he died in battle.

In 1347, Joanna married Louis of Taranto. The Hungarians invaded, and she fled the country. She sold Avignon to the pope while she was in exile, returning to Naples in 1352. Louis died ten years later.

After tensions had died down, she married James IV of Majorca, the son of James III, who she had earlier aided. James died in battle in 1375, and Joanna, a widow for the third time, then married Otto of Brunswick. Still childless, she named Charles of Durazzo (also known as Charles III of Naples) her heir, then repudiated him in favor of Louis of Anjou.

Pope Urban VI excommunicated her for giving refuge to the anti-pope, Clement VII, when he fled Rome. He declared her deposed in favor of Charles of Durazzo. Charles invaded and captured her. He was then crowned king. When Louis of Anjou came to Joanna's aid, Charles strangled her.

SUGGESTED READING: Norman Housely, *The Italian Crusades* (New York: Oxford University Press, 1982).

Joanna II (1371–1435)

Queen of Naples from 1414. She succeeded her brother King Lancelot to the throne. She married Jacques de Bourbon in 1415. He murdered one of her lovers, resulting in a furor. Louis III of Anjou claimed the throne (it had been promised to his ancestor by Joanna I). To prevent this, Joanna named Alfonso V of Aragón as her heir. In 1420, Alfonso came to her assistance in the fight against Louis III. Later she repudiated Alfonso and named Louis as her heir, thus sparking a war of succession after her death in 1435. Alfonso eventually defeated the Angevins and was recognized as king of Naples by the pope in 1443. *See* Joanna I.

Joanna of Bavaria (14th century)

Also Joanna of Bohemia. Queen of Bohemia. She married Wenceslas IV, the king of Germany and Bohemia and Holy Roman emperor. He was regarded as a cruel and incapable king. According to legend, one of his dogs, as vicious as he was, killed Joanna.

The patron saint of Bohemia, John of Nepomuk, was allegedly the confessor to Queen Joanna. When Wenceslas demanded to know the queen's confessions, John refused, citing the secrecy of the confessional. Wenceslas then had John murdered. Modern historians believe that the two had religious differences that led to the murder.

SUGGESTED READING: H. Cole, *History of Women in Germany from the Medieval Time to Present* (Berlin: German Historical Institute, 1990).

Joanna of Bohemia *see* Joanna of Bavaria

Jorð

Medieval Viking deity, comparable to Mother Earth. *See* Religion and Women.

Juana, Infanta (1462–1530)

The heiress to the kingdom of Castile. In 1464, when she was two years old, the nobles claimed that she was illegitimate and that the master of Santiago, Beltrán de la Cuera, was her father. They nicknamed her "la Beltraneja" and demanded that the king, Henry IV, name his brother Alfonso as successor.

The king was known to be impotent. His first marriage, to Blanche of Navarre, had been set aside for that reason. Infanta Juana's mother, Juana of Portugal, was married to him for six years before the child was born. Thus her legitimacy was and will always be in doubt.

In 1470, Henry declared Juana his true daughter and heir in order to thwart his sister Isabella's ambitions. A civil war ensued. When Henry died in 1474, Isabella's supporters proclaimed her queen.

Juana was betrothed to Afonso V of Portugal, called the African, who prepared to invade Castile on her behalf. Isabella's forces defeated him in 1476, and in 1478 Isabella was acknowledged queen.

Afonso and Juana then renounced all claim to Castile in exchange for Portugal's right to exclusive conquest of Africa. Isabella's husband, Ferdinand, became king of Aragón in 1479, and he and Isabella became formidable rulers, uniting Spain and driving the Muslims from Granada.

Juana then rejected marriage to Afonso — and anyone else — and went to a convent where she called herself Queen Juana. She died in 1530. *See* Isabella the Catholic; Juana of Portugal.

SUGGESTED READING: Warren Carroll, *Isabel of Spain: The Catholic Queen* (Front Royal, VA: Christendom Press, 1991); Nancy Rubin, *Isabella of Castile: The First Renaissance Queen* (New York: St. Martin's, 1992).

Juana Enriquez (15th century)

Queen of Navarre and Aragón. She married John (Juan) II, king of Navarre and Aragón, becoming his second wife. He did not designate his son Charles (Carlos) of Viana as his heir. Tension between father and son nearly caused a civil war.

Juana championed her own son's cause; later he would become Ferdinand the Catholic, the most famous king of Spain. In 1460, John had his son Charles arrested for treason. In this he was opposed by Henry IV, the king of Castile, who prepared to invade. John reluctantly released his son in 1461. Finally, John agreed to the Capitulation of Vilafranca del Panadés, in 1461, naming Charles his heir and Juana's son the next heir.

When Charles died the following year, both John and Juana were suspected of poisoning him. Eventually Ferdinand and his wife, Isabella, inherited and unified most of the Iberian peninsula. *See* Isabella the Catholic.

SUGGESTED READING: Thomas N. Bisson, *The Medieval Crown of Aragon: A Short History* (London: Clarendon, 1991).

Juana of Portugal (b. 1438?)

Queen of Castile. She married Henry (Enrique) IV, king of Castile, after he repudiated his first wife, Blanche of Navarre; that marriage was later set aside because the king was impotent. Juana's marriage to Henry sealed a political alliance between Castile and Portugal.

In 1462, after six years of marriage, Juana had a daughter, called Infanta Juana. The Castilian nobles declared the child illegitimate because of the king's notorious impotence and demanded that Henry name his brother Alfonso as his successor. Henry did nothing to refute the charges against Juana and her daughter until 1470, when he named Infanta Juana his true daughter and successor in order to thwart his sister Isabella's ambitions. A civil war ensued. Isabella was ultimately successful. *See* Isabella the Catholic; Juana, Infanta.

Juette *see* **Ivette of Huy**

Juksáhkká

Female household spirit in Scandinavia common in medieval folklore. She protected unborn male children and lived near the entrance of the house. *See* Religion and Women.

Julian of Norwich
(1343–1416 or 1419)

English mystic. Born in Norwich, she suffered a serious illness when she was thirty. During her recuperation, she experienced many visions and had direct experience of God's goodness. She recorded her revelations in several texts, including *Shewings* and *Revelations of Divine Love*. One of her famous statements was that God was both father and mother and that God had revealed this nature to her. Many manuscripts of her texts survive, which indicates their enormous popularity.

After her recovery, she lived as an anchoress in a cell attached to the Church of Saint Julian in Norwich. A servant was walled up with her. The rite of enclosure was conducted like a burial service for the soul. One had to die to the world in order to live a more Christlike life.

Julian gained a reputation for holiness and wisdom and was visited by that other famous English mystic, Margery Kempe. *See* Margery Kempe; Mystics and Mysticism.

SUGGESTED READING: Frederick Christian Bauerschmidt, *Julian of Norwich and the Mystical Body Politic of Christ* (Notre Dame, IN: University of Notre Dame Press, 1999); Jennifer Heimmel, *God Is Our Mother: Julian of Norwich and the Medieval Image of Christian Feminine Divinity* (New York: Prometheus, 1983); Julian of Norwich, *Revelations of Divine Love* (London: Brewer, 1987).

Juliana Berners (15th century)

Noblewoman who wrote a hunting treatise in which she clearly stated that Providence had ordered class distinctions. She was able to construct a genealogy showing that Christ was a gentleman on his mother's side.

Jus Primae Noctis

"First night." The legendary right of the lord to spend the first night with a peasant bride. The "right" may be more fable than truth, but female serfs were considered chattel and could be raped at will.

Justinian Code

Law code compiled in the early sixth century at the command of Emperor Justinian. This code attempted to impose a uniform legal system on all territories in the Roman Empire. The code reformed laws regarding land ownership, which was the primary source of wealth and power. Under the influence of Theodora, his wife, Justinian reduced the husband's right to his wife's dowry to that of a *ususfructus*—he could use the dowry but could not own it nor pass it on to his heirs. The code allowed women more autonomy and control over their lives and had a lasting impact on the development of the Byzantine Empire.

K

Kalmar Union

The unification of the three crowns of Scandinavia (Denmark, Sweden, and Norway), which was arranged by Margaret of Denmark in 1397. Rulers of these countries were elected, however, so the union could not be maintained. Margaret's successors ruled over Sweden until 1523. *See* Margaret of Denmark.

Kathryn Swinford (1350–1403)

Also Swynford. Beloved mistress of John of Gaunt, she had several illegitimate children with him, including Henry Beaufort, the bishop of Lincoln and Winchester, who became a cardinal. Her children were granted legitimacy by Parliament after she and John were eventually able to marry (1396). He had two wives before her. Both were marriages of political convenience, although according to contemporaries he loved his first wife, Blanche of Lancaster, very much. *See* Blanche of Lancaster; Marriage and Family.

Kathryn Swynford *see* Kathryn Swinford

Khadija (7th century)

The first convert to Islam. She married Muhammad the Prophet, becoming the first of his several wives. After he founded Islam, she became his disciple. *See* Conversion; Religion and Women.

Anna Komnena *see* Anna Comnena

Kosara (10th century)

Daughter of Samuel, the Bulgarian leader of Macedonia. According to legend, Samuel's brother Aaron went to war against him. Samuel murdered Aaron and his family with the exception of one son, John Vladislav. Kosara fell in love with John while he was a prisoner of her family. Her father relented, released John, and allowed the two to marry, even restoring John's former territory to him.

It is likely that the two were in fact married, but probably it was in order to smooth relations between Samuel and his brother's relatives and supporters.

Later, Kosara's husband murdered Samuel's son and heir, Gabriel Radomir. In 1018, John was killed while fighting the Byzantine Empire. The story of Miroslava mirrors the story of Kosara. *See* Miroslava.

Kriemhild

Character in the medieval Austrian epic *Nibelungenlied*, which was probably written in 1203. The hero, Sigurd (Siegfried), is a German warrior who journeys to the court of King Gunther, where he falls in love with Kriemhild. By helping King Gunther win the reluctant Queen Brunhild, Sigurd is allowed to marry Kriemhild. An evil councilor, Hagen, turns Gunther against Sigurd, claiming that Sigurd is trying to usurp the throne. With Gunther's approval, Hagen kills Sigurd. Kriemhild swears vengeance but is unable to raise an army since Hagen has stolen all of Sigurd's gold. Some years later, Kriemhild marries Attila the Hun and invites Hagen and Gunther to Attila's court, where she has them murdered. She is killed by a German supporter of Gunther in revenge.

Krum's Army

Ninth-century strategy of the Bulgarian leader Krum. Outnumbered by the Byzantine army, which threatened his territory and his rule with harassing raids, Krum armed women as well as men and attacked a Byzantine army encampment. They succeeded in killing Nicephorus, the Byzantine emperor, and emerged victorious from the fighting. *See* Wars and Warfare.

L

Ladies of the Garter

Royal and noble women who supported the male members of the Order of the Garter. They wore similar robes and garters and celebrated magnificent ceremonies with them. The Order of the Garter, a military order founded by Edward III, king of England, in order to develop a coterie of loyal military men, was officially established in 1349 with twenty-six knights who were not allowed to leave England without the king's permission. A garter was worn at the knee to remind the members to behave with loyalty, honor, and bravery.

Ladies' Tournament

Das Frauenturnier. German mären composed in Eastern Franconia by an anonymous author around 1300. The events take place in a German city with an ideal society and chivalrous knights. These knights, numbering about forty, are brutally attacked. Instead of responding with force, they go to make peace with the enemy, leaving their weapons and the women behind.

The women form a community. They gather in the meadow to exchange stories, finding themselves pleased with their autonomy and the absence of men. As they talk, they debate how men's conception of honor relates to them. Some of the women say there is no difference between men's honor and women's honor: one should enhance one's reputation by carrying weapons and participating in battles and tournaments. A wise woman says that honor and public acclaim are not related. She suggests that women gain honor through piety and chastity.

The women agree to participate in a tournament in order to resolve the debate. They dress in men's armor, ride their warhorses, and joust with each other. They also assume male names. The daughter of a man too poor to engage in chivalry and too poor to provide her with a dowry emerges as the winner. She has taken the name of Duke Walbren, the ruler of Limburg.

The knights return and learn of the tournament. They compliment the women but make them promise not to do it again. The news of the tournament spreads, and Duke Walbren hears of it. He meets the woman who won the tournament and provides her with a dowry and a husband.

Lady of Shalott

Also known as Elaine the White. In Arthurian romance, she died of unrequited love for Lancelot. After his death, she was brought by boat up the Thames to Camelot with a note explaining the reason for her death. She is the subject of numerous poems, especially by the nineteenth-century Romantic poets.

Lady of the Lake

In Arthurian romance, the woman who gave Arthur the sword Excalibur. She also raised Lancelot and cured him of madness. Probably based on folkloric lake fairies or nymphs.

Lady of the Mercians *see* Æthelflæd

Laura (14th century)

French noblewoman. Famous as the beloved of Petrarch, the Italian poet, scholar, and humanist. In 1327, he traveled to Avignon and became a clergyman. While there, he saw Laura and immediately fell in love with her. She inspired his vernacular love lyrics. He wrote two collections of sonnets, *Canzoniere* and *I Trionfi*, for her.

Law and Women

In the Middle Ages, law was primarily a private concern. Blood feuds and monetary compensation (wergild) were common in Europe and the Arab world. The person who presided over a court, such as the king, was merely an arbiter. Two kinds of law developed, common law and statute law. Common law depended on custom and precedent and could vary from neighborhood to neighborhood. It could not be applied uniformly, but it was as important as statute law. Statute law — written law — derived from edicts and proclamations issued by those in authority, although such laws could not always be enforced. Statute law consisted of both civil law, which was secular, and canon law, which was religious. Clergy members could not be tried under civil laws and had to be turned over to church authorities for prosecution. Ecclesiastical courts could pass judgments of imprisonment and even death on someone who had violated canon law, but such a criminal was turned over to the civil authorities for execution of the sentence.

Each culture had legal experts who advised parties in law cases. In Frankish lands, these were the Rachinburgii, and in Anglo-Saxon England, they were the doomsmen. In Scandinavian countries, they were called the lawspeakers. These legal experts often wrote tracts and treatises about law so that the law could be appropriately applied in different cases.

The law applied to women although generally they could not sue nor testify and required a male advocate in court. Men and women were treated differently under the law, which considered women to be minors all of their lives.

According to tenth-century canon law, freewomen who had affairs with male servants suffered death. A freeman who had a sexual encounter with a female servant had to do penance for one year. The female servant had to do penance for forty days, unless she had been willing, in which case the penalty was more severe. Clearly the church recognized that women were frequently forced to engage in sexual intercourse but still held them responsible for it. A woman who was raped had to be punished for her part.

In Sicily, female adulterers and madams were punished by slitting their noses. Male adulterers and those involved in the prostitution trade as procurers and the like did not suffer the same penalty. In Burgundy, a woman who left her husband could be killed; a man who left his wife could pay her the amount of her marriage price and escape further punishment. If the divorce was for cause, such as adultery, no compensation was to be paid.

Women proved their innocence of adultery by undergoing an ordeal or by appointing a champion to undergo trial by combat. In Salic law, a woman who married a slave forfeited her property and was exiled. If her family killed her for her marriage, no fine was assessed to them.

Women who were victims of crimes were entitled to less compensation than men. This was true even before birth. In Sicily, if a pregnant woman was beaten and the fetus died, a fine was paid (to her husband). If the fetus was female, half of the compensation was necessary. As a group, fines for killing young children and women were much less than fines for killing men. Among women, fines were highest for killing pregnant women, lower for women who were of childbearing age, and lowest for women who could not have children because of age, disease, or injury.

Married women and unmarried women were treated differently as well. This was because a man's wife was considered his property. In the case of rape, the fine was paid to the woman's husband. A lower fine was paid for the rape of unmarried women (to her father or guardian). Rape of one's own wife was not recognized as a crime. If a prostitute was raped, her usual price was paid. Concubines and widows had less recourse. If there were no witnesses to the crime, it was presumed not to have happened. In most areas, if a man agreed to marry the woman he raped, no crime was considered to have been committed. If a maidservant was raped, the fine went to her employer.

Non-Christians were expected to abide by the laws of the places were they lived. Many areas had restrictive legislation aimed at Jews and Muslims. Disputes between Jews were usually settled according to Jewish law. Muslims adhered to Sharia law. Jews and Muslims could not sue Christians nor testify against them. Women who married outside their faith were subject to fines, property confiscation, and other punishments; their children could be taken from them. *See* Crime, Punishment, and Violence; Religion and Women.

Suggested reading: Manlio Bellomo, *The Common Legal Past of Europe, 1000–1800* (Washington, DC: Catholic University of America Press, 1995); James A. Brundage, *Medieval Canon Law* (Reading, MA: Addison Wesley Longman, 1995); Anthony Musson and W. M. Ormrod, *The Evolution of English Justice: Law, Politics and Society in the Fourteenth Century* (New York: St. Martin's, 1999); J. W. Tubbs, *The Common Law Mind: Medieval and Early Modern Conceptions* (Baltimore: Johns Hopkins University Press, 2000).

Legend of Good Women

Poem written by Geoffrey Chaucer in which he defends women and female virtue, probably composed between 1380 and 1387. It is a dream-vision composed in the decasyllabic couplets Chaucer later used for *The Canterbury Tales*. He tells the stories of Cleopatra, Medea, Ariadne, and Dido, among others, as examples ("exempla") of womanly virtues. Christine de Pizan used a similar approach in her *Book of the City of Ladies*.

Legend of Good Women was apparently written at the request of Queen Philippa. The poem has moments of beauty and vibrancy, but it does not have the reputation of Chaucer's other work. *See* Christine de Pizan; Philippa of Hainaut.

Suggested reading: Geoffrey Chaucer, *The Riverside Chaucer* (New York: Houghton Mifflin, 1987).

Leonor Plantagenet (d. 1214)

Queen of Castile. The daughter of

Henry II, king of England, and Eleanor of Aquitaine. She married Alfonso VIII, the king of Castile, in 1169. Her dowry was the duchy of Gascony, but it was never surrendered to her husband and thus became a focal point of controversy. During her lengthy reign, she arranged advantageous marriages for her children, including her daughters Berenguela and Blanche (the mother of Saint Louis) and her son Henry (Enrique) I. She also conducted diplomatic affairs and defended her territory against Muslim incursions. She and her husband died within a month of each other in 1214. *See* Berenguela; Blanche of Castile.

SUGGESTED READING: Simon Barton, *The Aristocracy of Twelfth-Century Leon and Castile* (New York: Cambridge University Press, 1997).

Leonor de Guzmán (d. 1350)

Mistress to Alfonso XI, king of Castile. She bore ten of his illegitimate children, including Henry (Enrique) of Trastámara, who later deposed the rightful heir to the throne, Peter (Pedro) the Cruel. As soon as Peter succeeded to the throne, his mother, Maria of Portugal, ordered Leonor's execution so that she could not conspire against him. This murder started a conflict that ended in Peter's murder. *See* Maria of Portugal.

Leonor López de Córdoba
(15th century)

Spanish noblewoman, the grandniece of King Alfonso and cousin to Peter (Pedro) the Cruel. She wrote one of the earliest known autobiographies by a woman.

At the age of seven she was married to Ruy Gutiérrez de Henestrosa, the son of the king's chamberlain. When she was eight years old, she was imprisoned along with the rest of her family for political reasons. Her father was beheaded by

Henry (Enrique) of Trastámara, who had usurped the throne. Later, after Henry's death and Peter's restoration, Leonor returned to court. She and her husband tried to regain their property but were again exiled in 1412.

In her autobiography, she tells of murdering a servant who had crossed her. She also describes how she took a Jewish orphan in a raid on the Jewish quarter, forced him to be baptized as a Christian, and then raised him herself. He contracted the plague, but survived, although the people assigned to watch over him died — thirteen in all, including her own son.

SUGGESTED READING: Angus MacKay, *Love, Religion and Politics in Fifteenth-Century Spain* (Boston: Brill, 1998).

Leonor of Aragón (d. 1445)

Queen mother. Sister of Alfonso V of Aragón and regent for her son Afonso V. Her son became king of Portugal while he was still a minor. Leonor married Duarte of Portugal to strengthen her son's claim to the throne and to strengthen her own position. Her regency became increasingly precarious after Duarte died in 1438.

Her brothers were power-hungry men, and the nobles were afraid that, when she became regent for Afonso V, her brothers would turn their attention to Portugal. A meeting of nobles in 1439 replaced Queen Leonor with Peter (Pedro), duke of Coimbra, the king's uncle. Leonor asked her brothers for help, but they did not fulfill their promises to aid her. Fearing for her life, she fled to Castile, where she died in 1445.

Leonor of Castile (d. 1358)

Queen of Aragón. She married Alfonso IV of Aragón and became queen; it was Alfonso's second marriage. He was unable to grant her wish that her son Ferran be given territory to rule. She began a bitter animosity with her stepson Peter (Pedro) IV, Alfonso's eldest son. When Alfonso died, Peter tried to arrest her but she escaped. She was murdered by him in 1358.

SUGGESTED READING: Clara Estow, *Pedro the Cruel of Castile: 1350–1369* (Boston: Brill, 1995).

Lesbianism, Lesbians *see* **Sexuality**

Lupicina Euphemia (d. 524)

Byzantine empress. A slave, she had been the mistress to the man who sold her to Justin, an illiterate peasant with remarkable military abilities. Justin, who became her husband, was appointed commander of the Excubitors and became, quite improbably, emperor when Anastasius, after fervent prayer, chose him as successor. Lupicina's nephew Justinian became emperor after Justin's death. She continued to exert considerable influence at court and managed to prevent the marriage of Theodora to Justinian during her life. *See* Theodora.

M

Mab, Queen

In the Middle Ages, the legendary queen of the fairies, wife of Oberon.

Madame d'Or

Famous blonde dwarf in the entourage of Philip of Burgundy. She wrestled with the acrobat Hans to the amusement of the court. Her life was consistent with the treatment of the handicapped, ill, and disabled: they were treated harshly, laughed at as oddities, or forced into monasteries or leper houses where the general public would not have to see them. *See* Medicine and Health.

Magdalene Cult

Veneration of Mary of Magdalene, the prostitute who became one of Christ's earliest followers. She was the patron saint of female sinners. The idea of venerating her was first initiated by Peter Abelard, who felt she was worthy of prayers because of her relationship with Christ and the possibility that she could intercede on behalf of sinners. According to the New Testament, she was a prostitute who developed a close relationship with Jesus and was the first to see him after the resurrection. A cult of worshipers grew up around her legend. *See* Cult of the Virgin Mary.

Maid Marian

Character in the later legends of Robin Hood. A yeoman's daughter, she became entangled with Robin Hood when he rescued her from a knight; they fell in love with each other. Many trials and tribulations kept them apart, although in some stories they eventually married.

Maintenance Agreements

Agreements by which widowed women surrendered their holdings to their children in exchange for upkeep until death. *See* Dowry; Marriage and Family.

Malleus Maleficarum

The Witches' Hammer. A handbook

that detailed how to identify and destroy witches, written by the Inquisitors James Sprenger and Heinrich Kramer in 1486. The document states that even those who are merely different, such as the mentally ill, should be burned at the stake. *See* Heresy; Inquisition; Religion and Women.

SUGGESTED READING: Henricus Institoris and Montague Summers, *The Malleus Maleficarum of Heinrich Kramer and James Sprenger* (New York: Dover, 1971).

Manorialism

Also called the seigneurial system. Manorialism is frequently confused with feudalism although the two are not the same. Feudalism existed throughout Europe and even as far afield as Japan. It primarily established the relation between the lord and his vassal. Manorialism, which existed primarily in France, was concerned with the relation between the vassal and the tenants of his land.

The manor itself consisted of a village and its surrounding lands and was a concept older than the idea of a medieval fief. It was even older than the Roman concepts of land ownership and rulership. The manor was essentially a farming unit, as self-sufficient as possible. The workers were bound to the land. They received a portion of the land to work themselves, similar to sharecroppers in the American South. The demesne was the part of the land that belonged to the lord. The workers were required to work on the demesne several days a week, and its care took precedence over their own plots of land. *See* Feudalism and Women.

Mara Branković of Serbia
(c. 1414–1487)

Also known as Maria. Her father, George Branković, was despot of Serbia. He ruled Serbia on the sufferance of the

Ottoman Turks. He pretended to be their willing vassal while plotting ways to destroy their power. Mara was his daughter with his first wife.

In order to show his amenability, he married Mara to Murad II, the Muslim ruler of the Ottoman Turks. Murad demanded most of Serbia as a dowry. In 1433, the two were betrothed, and a short-lived peace between the Serbs and Turks followed. Two years later, they were married. Mara was twenty-one. Murad already had another wife.

Although the marriage ceremony was Islamic, Mara remained a Christian. She tried to help her father further his political goals. She also tried to further the Christian cause. She ministered to the needs of Christians living within Murad's empire and served as an intermediary for her husband. Like other women in Islamic countries, she lived in a harem with his first wife.

In 1436, the year after their marriage, conflict between the Turks and Serbs increased, and the Ottomans invaded Serbia. Three years later, Smederevo, the last remaining Serbian stronghold, fell. Mara's brothers, who had helped stir up the conflict, were imprisoned and blinded. Later they were able to return to Serbia after Mara helped arrange a treaty (1444).

Soon thereafter, Murad retired, allowing his eldest son from his first marriage to rule. He had lived an intemperate life and died of his excesses in 1451. Mehmed II, his son, who was about thirteen at the time of his succession, had come to think of Mara as a second mother and even addressed her as "Mother." Mehmed's dependence on Mara had increased after his own mother died in 1449. Mara had no children of her own. Mehmed frequently consulted her during his reign.

When Mara returned to Serbia after

the death of her husband, it was decided that she should marry the widowed Byzantine emperor, Constantine. She refused, saying she had promised to live a celibate and chaste life if ever she were released from the infidel Murad. After her father and her stepmother died under mysterious circumstances in 1456 and 1457, rumors of poisoning abounded. Afraid she would be poisoned next, Mara fled the city and returned to the Turks, asking Mehmed, now ruler of Constantinople, to protect her. In 1459, the Turks invaded Serbia again, finally ending the despotate of Serbia. Mara lived with her stepson, who treated her with honor and respect, settling her on a large estate and granting her a monastery with all of its revenues. She maintained a court with other exiled Serbians at Ježevo, where she may have maintained a workshop of scribes and artisans. She continued to serve as an intermediary, this time between the Turks and the Venetians. Her influence extended even to the appointment of church officials. Her belief that she had a duty to provide support and aid to Christians living in Muslim lands never wavered.

SUGGESTED READING: John V. A. Fine, *The Late Medieval Balkans: A Critical Survey from the Late Twelfth Century to the Ottoman Conquest* (Detroit: University of Michigan Press, 1994); J. C. S. Runciman, *Byzantine Civilization* (New York: St. Martin's, 1966); Peter F. Sugar, *Southeastern Europe Under Ottoman Rule* (Seattle: University of Washington Press, 1983).

Margaret, Maid of Norway
(1283–1290)

Heiress to Scotland. Daughter of the Norwegian king, Eric II, and Margaret of Scotland; granddaughter of Alexander III, king of Scotland. In 1284, the Scottish nobles proclaimed her Alexander's heir,

even though she was female and an infant, presumably to prevent the throne from falling into Norwegian hands. After Alexander's death in 1286, she succeeded to the throne.

A regency formed, and Edward I, king of England, arranged a marriage between his son Edward and Margaret. In 1290, the Scots agreed to the marriage as long as Scotland remained independent. The Treaty of Birgham specified these conditions. Thus, at age seven, Margaret left Norway to assume the throne in Scotland, but she became ill and died during the voyage. A struggle between Robert the Bruce and John Baliol ensued, and Edward I stepped into the breach, naming John as the next king.

SUGGESTED READING: B. Webster, *Medieval Scotland* (New York: St. Martin's, 1997).

Margaret Beaufort (1443–1509)

Countess of Richmond and Derby. She was a member of the House of Lancaster. She married her second husband Edmund Tudor in 1455 and had a son, Henry Tudor. Henry Tudor became King Henry VII of England after winning the Wars of the Roses.

After he succeeded to the throne, Margaret arranged a marriage between him and Elizabeth of York, which united the two houses. Margaret married twice more but had no other children.

A patron of the arts and of learning, Margaret sponsored William Caxton, the English printer. She endowed professorships at Oxford and Cambridge, among the oldest in the history of the universities. In the early sixteenth century, she established Christ's College and Saint John's College at Cambridge. *See* Elizabeth of York; Wars and Warfare.

Margaret of Anjou (1430?–1482)

Queen of England. The daughter of

the duke of Anjou, she married Henry VI, king of England, in 1445. Henry, a weak ruler who suffered fits of insanity, soon allowed her to rule England in his place. The court seethed with backstabbing, hatred, suspicion, and secret murders. Margaret became increasingly unpopular and lost the support of the nobles, who turned instead to Richard Plantagenet, who had a legitimate claim to the throne. Richard was of the York line; Henry was of the Lancaster line. Various factions of nobles controlled the country, and soon a civil war broke out.

In 1455, Henry was captured by the York forces. This marked the beginning of the Wars of the Roses, the conflict between the Houses of York and Lancaster for control of the English throne. During Henry's imprisonment, Parliament agreed that Richard was the legitimate heir, and Henry was forced to agree that he should succeed after Henry's death. Margaret, however, did not agree. She wanted her son Edward to succeed.

In 1460, Richard was killed, and his son Edward became leader of the York opposition. Richard Neville, the earl of Warwick, supported the York claim to the throne and helped depose Henry, putting Richard's son Edward on the throne. In 1461, Edward named himself King Edward IV, and Henry was denounced as a usurper and a traitor.

Margaret struggled to ensure her son's succession, even asking the French for help. Henry had fled to Scotland, where he remained until 1464, when he invaded England. Relations between Richard Neville, known as the kingmaker, and Edward grew strained. Edward was forced to leave England. In France, he allied with Margaret and helped restore Henry to the throne.

For a short period in 1470–1471, Henry remained on the throne, but then he was deposed, captured, and imprisoned. He died in the Tower of London. Most historians believe he was murdered on Edward IV's orders.

In 1471, Margaret's son Edward was killed in battle (he may have been murdered; the actual facts of his death are unclear). Edward Plantegenet was crowned king. One of his first acts was to imprison Margaret in the Tower of London for five years. Louis XI ransomed her (some sources say he bought her). She agreed to cede her French territories to him. *See* Wars and Warfare.

SUGGESTED READING: Keith Dockray, *Henry VI and the Wars of the Roses: A Sourcebook* (New York: Sutton, 2000); Phillipe Erlanger, *Margaret of Anjou: Queen of England* (Miami: University of Miami Press, 1970); Philip Haigh, *The Military Campaigns of the Wars of the Roses* (New York: Sutton, 1999).

Margaret of Denmark, Norway and Sweden (1353–1412)

Scandinavian queen. The daughter of King Waldemar IV of Denmark, she married Håkon VI, the king of Norway, when she was still a child. Her son Olaf became king of Denmark when he was five years old (1375). Margaret engineered his succession to the throne, despite his youth. Five years later, Håkon died. Margaret took control of Norway and Denmark as regent for her son. When Olaf died in 1387, she became queen. In 1389, the Swedish nobility revolted against their elected king, Albert of Mecklenburg, and named Margaret as regent, deposing Albert.

After Olaf's death, she had no heir, so she named Eric of Pomerania as her heir in 1397. He was crowned that year, founding the Kalmar Union (the unification of the thrones of the three Scandinavian countries). Although nominally king, Eric held no real power until after Margaret's death in 1412. *See* Kalmar Union.

SUGGESTED READING: Brigit and Peter Sawyer, *Medieval Scandinavia: From Conversion to Reformation, circa 800–1500* (Minneapolis: University of Minnesota Press, 1993).

Margaret of Scotland, Saint
(c. 1045–1093)

Also Margaret Ætheling the Exile. Scottish queen. The daughter of English King Edward Ætheling and the granddaughter of Edmund II Ironside, she was raised in Hungary, the place of her father's exile. In 1057, she returned to England, but the arrival of the Normans in 1066 forced her to flee to Scotland. She married Malcolm III, king of Scotland. They had five children. Three sons became kings of Scotland, and one daughter, Matilda (originally named Edith), became queen of England through her marriage to King Henry I.

A pious and austere woman, she reformed the Scottish church, restored monasteries, and introduced English customs to the court. She foretold the date of her own death and was canonized by Innocent IV in 1250. *See* Matilda of Scotland.

SUGGESTED READING: A. D. M. Barrell, *Medieval Scotland* (New York: Cambridge University Press, 2000); Lavinia Byrne, *Margaret of Scotland* (London: Hodder and Stoughton, 1999).

Margareth *see* Margaret entries

Margery Kempe (c. 1373–c. 1440)

English mystic. Born in Norfolk, she married a local man, John Kempe, when she was about twenty. Together they had fourteen children. After her first child was born, she suffered a serious illness and underwent a conversion. She started to see visions. As a result, she sought to live a more austere, religious life.

In 1413, after twenty years of marriage, Margery decided she was meant for a spiritual life, and she and her husband took vows of chastity. The following year, she began a number of pilgrimages throughout Europe and to the Holy Land. She began her autobiography, *The Booke of Margery Kempe*, about 1420. It was dictated to two scribes and describes her visions and her ecstatic behavior. It is the first known autobiography written in English. The manuscript was not discovered until the twentieth century.

Margery came into conflict with church authorities for interrupting services and arguing with clergy members. Local authorities were skeptical of her claims, and she was imprisoned for heresy, although she was eventually found innocent. Later, she visited the famous mystic Julian of Norwich, who confirmed Kempe's grace. *See Booke of Margery Kempe*; Julian of Norwich; Religion and Women.

SUGGESTED READING: Louise Collis, *Memoirs of a Medieval Woman: The Life and Times of Margery Kempe* (New York: HarperCollins, 1983); Margery Kempe, *The Book of Margery Kempe* (Harmondsworth, England: Penguin, 1985); Lynn Staley, *Margery Kempe's Dissenting Fictions* (University Park: Pennsylvania State University Press, 1994).

Marguerite of Provence (b. 1221)

Queen of France. She married Louis IX (Saint Louis), king of France, in 1234, when he was twenty. She was thirteen years old. The wedding ceremony was a three-day celebration remembered for years afterward. Blanche of Castile, Louis's mother, became jealous of Marguerite and did all she could to prevent the two from spending time together. Marguerite and Louis nonetheless managed to produce four daughters and six sons.

Marguerite traveled with him to Damietta, Egypt, on crusade. She stayed there after he was captured; she was pregnant. She instructed a knight of her acquaintance to kill her if the city fell to the Muslims, rather than allow her to be taken prisoner. Before this extremity was reached, Louis was ransomed and joined her at Acre.

After Blanche died in 1252, Marguerite tried to serve as an advisor to Louis, but he did not trust her judgment as he had his mother's. Instead, she turned to her son Philip, who would become the king of France. She attempted to influence him throughout his reign. Her taste for such power was apparent throughout her life. *See* Blanche of Castile.

SUGGESTED READING: Maureen Slattery, *Myth, Man and Sovereign Saint: King Louis IX* (New York: Peter Lang, 1985).

Marguerite Porete (d. 1310)

A prominent member of the Brethren of the Free Spirit, she formulated one of the gospels of the sect. She felt her soul had been destroyed and then created anew by God. Such a soul, she believed, was no longer capable of sinning, and so any act would be an expression of divine will and therefore could not be wrong. Her book, *The Mirror of Simple Souls*, was highly influential. She was excommunicated and burned at the stake in 1310. *See* Brethren of the Free Spirit; Heresy; Religion and Women.

SUGGESTED READING: Marguerite Porete, *The Mirror of Simple Souls* (Mahwah, NJ: Paulist Press, 1993); Raoul Vaneigem et al., *The Movement of the Free Spirit* (New York: Zone Books, 1994).

Maria *see* Mara Branković of Serbia

Maria (11th century)

Byzantine noblewoman and Bulgarian tsarina. Granddaughter of Emperor Romanus Lecapenus and the daughter of Christopher. She married the Bulgarian tsar, Peter, when she was still very young. Peter, the son of the legendary Bulgarian ruler Symeon, succeeded him. The marriage, in 1027, solidified the treaty between Bulgaria and the Byzantine Empire.

Maria introduced many Byzantine customs to the Bulgarian court. She manipulated Peter easily and exerted influence on his dealings.

Maria de Luna (14th century)

Queen of Aragón. She married King Martin the Humane of Aragón. She was related to Pope Benedict XIII (Pedro de Luna) and for this reason helped perpetuate the papal schism by supporting the Avignon pope against the Roman pope. With her support and that of her husband, Benedict was able to withstand the pressure of the French, English, and Castilian diplomats seeking to end the schism.

Her son Martin the Younger married Maria of Sicily and eventually became king of Sicily. *See* Maria of Sicily; Religion and Women.

Maria de Molina (d. 1321)

Queen of Castile. She married Sancho IV, king of Castile. Because she was Sancho's cousin, the pope refused to recognize the marriage and declared that any children of the union would be illegitimate and denied inheritance. Nonetheless, the two remained married. Later, Maria suggested that Sancho accommodate France instead of Aragón in a dispute, and this removed French opposition to their marriage. Sometime later, the pope recognized their marriage.

Her son Fernando IV of Castile inherited the throne when he was very young.

Maria served as his regent. Nobles opposed Fernando, claiming he was illegitimate and not the rightful heir to the throne. After his succession, many invasions followed, some almost simultaneous, from Portugal, Aragón, and the Muslims. Portugal was appeased with additional territories. The pope was convinced to pronounce Maria's children legitimate and so Fernando's enemies were thwarted. In 1301, Fernando reached the age of majority and severed all ties with her.

He died in 1312, when he was twenty-eight years old. His son Alfonso XI was just a one-year-old infant. Alfonso's mother had already died, so Maria defended him and his claim to the throne. The nobles recognized her as Alfonso's regent. After she died in 1321, a civil war broke out. She had been the only person able to keep the warring factions under control.

SUGGESTED READING: Joseph F. O'Callaghan, *A History of Medieval Spain* (Ithaca, NY: Cornell University Press, 1983); Bernard Reilly, *The Medieval Spains* (New York: Cambridge University Press, 1993).

Maria de Padilla (d. 1362)

Mistress to Peter the Cruel. She was installed in the royal household, and her family obtained preferments. She died at age twenty-eight in 1362. Peter then claimed that they had been secretly married ten years before, and the nobles acknowledged the rights of their four children to succeed to the throne.

Maria de Ventadorn (b. c. 1165)

An important patron of the troubadours in Languedoc, France, she was herself a troubadour from Limousin. She married Viscount Ebles de Ventadorn as a teenager. Much troubadour activity flourished in the region. She was well known,

highly regarded as both a poet and a hostess. Her poems are sophisticated examples of troubadour verse.

Her husband became a monk in 1221, and there is no further record of her.

Maria of Castile (15th century)

Queen of Aragón and Sicily. She married Alfonso V, king of Aragón and Sicily, called the Magnanimous. She was sister to the king of Castile, John (Juan) II. When Queen Joanna II of Naples adopted Alfonso as her heir, he went to Naples to protect his interests, leaving Maria to rule Aragón in his absence. She raised a considerable amount of money to support his claim to the Neapolitan throne. During his lengthy absence, the nobles grew increasingly frustrated and demanded his return. *See* Joanna II.

Maria of Portugal (14th century)

Queen of Castile. She married Alfonso XI, king of Castile. She suffered his mistresses, in particular the notorious Leonor de Guzmán, who bore ten of his children. After Alfonso died, Maria ordered the execution of Leonor, which was carried out. She then withdrew from political life and returned to Portugal, although the murder ignited a civil war between Peter (Pedro) the Cruel, her son, and Henry (Enrique), Leonor's son. *See* Leonor de Guzmán.

Maria of Sicily (d. 1401)

Heiress to Sicily. Daughter of King Frederick of Sicily and Constanza of Aragón. In 1377, she became heiress to her father's kingdom, but Peter (Pedro) IV of Aragón claimed it, saying females were not allowed to inherit. The pope, the traditional overlord of Sicily, denied Peter's claim; although he was not officially recognized, Peter did rule there. Maria eventually married Martin the Younger, the son of Martin the Humane, king of Aragón, and Maria de Luna. Martin the Younger later became recognized as the king of Sicily. *See* Maria de Luna.

Marian Cult

Mariolatry or the veneration of the Virgin Mary. *See* Cult of the Virgin Mary.

Marie de France (12th century)

French poet. Little is known about her history or her personal life. In fact, the name Marie de France is not even her name. She was given this name by a French writer in the sixteenth century, and it has been used for convenience ever since.

Marie was probably an educated woman from a good family. She could read and write Latin as well as French. She also knew English and apparently lived and wrote in England. Her writings are mostly in vernacular French.

Twelve short story poems, called *lais* or *lays*, are attributed to her, as is a collection of over one hundred fables. Her lays were based on Breton stories about love, romance, and the problems that arise from them. They challenge the ideal of courtly love, for they depict happily married women and bold lovers instead of timid ones. Marie's lays were popular among the aristocrats of the time. The lays usually attributed to her are *Guidemar, Equitan, Le Fresne, Bisclavret, Lanval, Les Deus Amanz, Yonec, Laüstic, Milun, Chaitivel, Chevrefoil,* and *Eliduc.*

Her collection of fables was also well received by her contemporaries. This collection, simply called *Fables,* was even more popular in the Middle Ages than her lays. They are the earliest vernacular versions of these stories in existence. Marie drew from a wide variety of sources, including Aesop, other Greek and Latin writers, and folk traditions from Germany, France, and the Middle East. As she retold the stories, she injected her own sense of humor and astute social commentary. More than twenty medieval manuscripts of the *Fables* exist.

The stories follow the fable tradition. They are short, clearly fictional tales with common people or animals as the main characters. Each has a message or moral to it. This was in keeping with the medieval tendency to place value on instruction rather than entertainment, although the fables are also enjoyable to read.

SUGGESTED READING: Marie de France, *The Lais of Marie de France* (New York: Penguin, 1986).

Marie of Champagne

Countess of Champagne. She was the daughter of Eleanor of Aquitaine and Louis VII, king of France. She held "courts of love" and commissioned *The Art of Courtly Love* by Andreas Capellanus. *See* Art of Courtly Love; Courtly Love; Eleanor of Aquitaine.

Mariolatry

Veneration of the Virgin Mary. *See* Cult of the Virgin Mary.

Markatum (14th century)

Daughter of a Muslim qadi or judge. In 1300, she married Osman, the Turkish ruler of a small state. According to legend, the ceremony was performed by a holy whirling dervish in strict accordance with Islamic law.

Their subjects were called Osmanlis, later Ottomans, as distinct from Turks, who were simply these people who inhabited Turkestan in general. The two founded the Ottoman Empire, which would dominate southwest Asia, southeast Europe, and parts of Africa, eventually surpassing even the Byzantine Empire.

Marozia (d. 935?)

Senator of Rome. Mistress, mother, and grandmother of popes. The daughter of Theophylact, commander of the Roman militia, who was also a nobleman and senator. She eventually inherited his senatorial seat. Theophylact held considerable power in Rome and controlled the papacy. Marozia apparently derived her taste for intrigue and political manipulation from him. When she was fifteen, she allegedly had an affair with Pope Sergius III, bearing his son. Sergius was forced from Rome by a rival anti-pope. He allied with Theophylact.

In 904, Sergius deposed the anti-pope, Christopher, in order to regain the papacy, seeking the aid of Marozia's husband, Alberic I, duke of Spoleto.

Alberic II, Marozia and Alberic's son, played an important role in Italian politics. Alberic I was murdered, probably sometime early in 928.

In that year, Marozia deposed Pope John X with the aid of her second husband, Guido, duke of Marquis. According to legend, she had an affair with John, but when she was unable to influence him, she and her husband decided to eliminate him. Also according to legend, he had been her mother's lover. In his place, Marozia and Guido elevated Stephen VII (VIII). They murdered John the following year. When Stephen died in 931, Marozia installed her son (allegedly the son of Sergius III) as Pope John XI.

In 932, she married Hugh of Arles, king of Lombards, who murdered his own wife and blinded his brother in order to marry her. Her grandson was later elevated to the papacy as John XII.

Her son Alberic II masterminded a coup that drove Hugh from power in 932. Alberic became the ruler of Rome. He imprisoned Marozia and Pope John XI. Both died in prison a few years later.

SUGGESTED READING: Paul Heatherington, *Medieval Rome: A Portrait of the City and Its Life* (New York: St. Martin's, 1994); Martinus, *The Chronicles of Rome* (London: Boydell and Brewer, 1999).

Marriage and Family

In the Middle Ages, many people married and started families while in their teens. One reason was because life expectancy was short. Half of all Europeans died before they were thirty years old. The life expectancy for a woman was twenty-four years because of the dangers of childbirth. Fourteen- or fifteen-year-olds often married and began their families right away.

Canon law stipulated that women had to be twelve years old and men fourteen in order to consent to marriage. The average age of a man at his marriage was twenty to twenty-four, depending on social class; for women it was fourteen to sixteen. Because men outnumbered women about 115 to 100, women did not stay widowed or unmarried for long. Because childbirth killed so many women, men often had several wives throughout their lives. (In the Byzantine Empire, the clergy disapproved of second marriages, even after the death of one's spouse, so second marriages were rare; third and fourth marriages were almost nonexistent.) Most marriages lasted between eight and twelve years.

Even though there was a great emphasis on marriage for political and religious reasons, there were many different kinds of households. As many as fifteen percent of all households consisted of single people. About fifty-five percent of households were nuclear families — father, mother, and their children. The remaining households consisted of extended families and multiple nuclear families living together.

After marriage, a husband and wife were considered "one flesh." A married woman had no freedom or autonomy. Early in the Middle Ages, marriages were entered into by families. The consent of the proposed husband and wife was considered irrelevant. Later, families began to seek the consent of the groom and only later the consent of the bride. It was the twelfth century before it was generally accepted that women should be allowed to refuse a marriage. In the early period, a wife's relatives were as important as her husband's. Depending on the situation, such as when she was a wealthy heiress, the husband might take his wife's name.

Because childbirth was so deadly, on a woman's wedding day, her mother traditionally gave her a length of cloth to be made into the dress in which she would be buried.

In the early Middle Ages, several kinds of marriage took place other than the traditional type arranged by the families of the spouses. These marriages were frequently legislated against, but they were commonly practiced. Marriage by abduction took place without the woman's consent. Marriage by elopement took place with the woman's consent, but without the approval of the families. The oldest Frankish law extant provides for the death penalty for those who assist an elopement. An additional form of marriage was sanctioned concubinage. A man could have a legal, wedded wife and several recognized friend-wives, who went through a public ceremony similar to a wedding ceremony. Women could not have friend-husbands. It required wealth to have friend-wives. A man might have a wedded wife for dynastic, political reasons and a friend-wife who was a love match. The friend-wife had more rights than a concubine, since she had a recognized position, but the church disapproved of the practice since it did not appear to be much different from concubinage, and the church did not recognize more than one spouse at a time.

Among the nobles, marriage was a source of territory, wealth, rulership, political advantage, and alliance. Marriages were arranged simply as part of medieval diplomacy. It was thought that people related by marriage would be less likely to war with each other, which helped to keep society peaceful. However, since most of the history of the Middle Ages consists of interminable warfare, this ideal did not work well in reality.

Noble and royal people were not consulted about whom they would like to marry. Peasants seldom had much control over their marriage partners, either. Personal preference was immaterial. The individual was subordinate to the family's interests. Because marriages were arranged, marriage brokers became common in cities, especially among members of the middle class for whom the traditional means of arranging marriages had become almost impossible.

The idea of falling in love with one's marriage partner was alien, although some couples managed to grow to care about each other. Even the ideals of courtly love specifically stated that it was impossible to love one's marriage partner and that true love could only come outside marriage.

As legal minors all of their lives, women had little say in how their lives were arranged. If a woman's father died before she married, she became the ward of her father's lord. It did not matter how old she was. The lord then received any revenues her property generated and could dispose of her in marriage as he wished. He could also sell her wardship to someone else, even to a prospective bridegroom. In order to gain the right to choose her own husband, a woman would have to pay a certain sum to her feudal lord.

A widow also became a ward of her late husband's lord. The lord would sell her remarriage to a prospective bridegroom. If a woman paid him to remain single, he would retain wardship of her children and could dispose of them as he chose.

Canon law allowed for wife beating as long as the husband did not maim or kill his wife. The "marriage debt" was the obligation to be available for sexual intercourse with one's spouse. Enjoying sex was considered a minor sin as long as it was done for the purpose of procreation. These conjugal rights were enforceable by law, and a marriage could be set aside if one partner consistently refused to pay the marriage debt or was unable to do so because of impotence.

Betrothal

A betrothal, similar to an engagement, was as legally binding as marriage. When marriage partners were very young and could not technically agree to a marriage, they would be betrothed or promised to one another. According to canon law, betrothals could not be contracted before the age of seven, because consent was necessary, and younger children did not have the understanding to consent. At the time of betrothal, the marriage agreement was entered into official records. The dower from the groom and the dowry from the bride were stated.

Betrothal meant that sexual intercourse was acceptable. Therefore, the children of a betrothed couple were usually considered legitimate, although in the case of disputed succession, rivals would insist these children were not legitimate.

When children were betrothed, consummation of the marriage would not take place until after the wedding itself. Both betrothal and wedding could be entered into by proxy.

Weddings

Weddings and marriages were secular events in the early Middle Ages, but the priest became increasingly involved over time. Among Christians, the wedding took place at the church door, and a wedding mass was celebrated afterward. The ring symbolized the man's dower; he gave that and a gift of money to the bride as a pledge (in Anglo-Saxon, a wed). Vows were exchanged. A child was placed in the bride's arms and a coin was placed in her shoe to symbolize fertility and riches. After the wedding mass, friends and family members brought the newly married couple to their bedchamber, amid much laughing and joking. The purpose of this arrangement was to prove that the marriage had been consummated, and thus it could not later be annulled on those grounds.

Clerical Marriage

Early in the Middle Ages, clergy members could marry and have families. By the eleventh century, church authorities disapproved of clerical marriage and were beginning to demand chastity. In 1072, however, there were still priests' wives and concubines, at least in Rouen, where they lynched the archbishop for preaching against them. The First Lateran Council of 1123 banned clerical marriage. In 1139, celibacy became mandatory because church offices were becoming inheritable, which created a problem.

The papacy fought against clerical marriage for centuries. The result was that clergy members kept mistresses. By the end of the thirteenth century, clerical concubinage was uncommon, but sexual escapades among priests were frequent, at least judging from the complaints that were registered against them. Many reform movements in the Middle Ages centered around the sexual behavior of clergy members.

Dissolution of Marriage

Early in the Middle Ages, divorce was easily obtained, either through mutual agreement or by the husband repudiating the wife. In the ninth century, the church began restricting it. The Gregorian reforms of the eleventh century stated that marriage was a monogamous institution, indissoluble, and a church sacrament. Soon the church officially allowed only annulments, in which case the church decided that, for one reason or another, a marriage (freely contracted between two unrelated individuals) had never actually taken place.

Nonetheless, divorce was still widely practiced. Remarriage was not allowed while the former spouse was still alive. If, for political reasons, a divorce was not practical, a noble could arrange to have a marriage annulled, usually by paying a fee to the pope. If one's wife had a servile ancestor, this was sufficient cause to annul a marriage. Consanguinity was not allowed; the risks of intermarriage were well known in the Middle Ages. People who were related within seven degrees could not marry. Men would invent genealogies in order to annul a marriage for this reason. However, for a fee, the church would set aside this rule (or enforce it, depending on the needs of the particular noble). It was not uncommon for a husband to spend his wife's fortune, then discover they were too closely related, have the marriage annulled, and force his penniless former wife to return to her family or enter a convent, so that he could find a new wife to marry.

In some parts of the world, it was not uncommon for a husband to spend the dowry and then murder his wife, particularly if he felt the dowry had not been not rich enough. Dowry death, as this practice is called, still occasionally occurs in India.

Early in the Middle Ages, if the wife could not or did not produce a son, she could be repudiated and sent back to her parents' home. The bride payment was returned to the husband. Later, when dowries became more common, the husband kept the dowry.

Remarriage

Although the church recognized only one true marriage, to prevent fornication, another marriage after the death of one's spouse was acceptable. For practical purposes, widowed women could not remain unmarried for long, particularly if they controlled property. Since female ownership of property after marriage was forbidden except under certain circumstances, a wealthy widow was highly sought. In 1215, the English king, John, finally declared that widows would no longer be forced to marry against their will.

Sexuality and Marriage

Virginity and celibacy were preferred to marriage, according to the church, because these practices allowed one to keep total focus on God. Marital relations were allowed only for procreation. Otherwise intercourse was considered a sin against God. This led to many complicated questions for theologians, although it was less problematic for ordinary people. For instance, theologians had to determine if intercourse during pregnancy was unlawful, as well as whether intercourse after menopause was acceptable between spouses. After all, one was required to pay the marriage debt.

Adultery could result in the death penalty for women but not for men. The death penalty was more common if a woman had an affair with a man of a lower social class.

Children

Nobles and well-off members of the middle class married at younger ages than poor people and had more children. Since such women employed wet nurses, their fertility returned sooner, and they could become pregnant more quickly after childbirth.

Women were considered little more than "breeders" in popular opinion, and they had few rights regarding their own children. They did not have legal custody of their children even after their husbands died. The husband's family was responsible for raising the children. A woman was expected to remarry, and her obligation would be to her new family. A new husband would not want the burden of stepchildren. Unfortunately, the late father's family often would not or could not care for the children. Therefore, abandonment and infanticide were common. Many so-called orphans actually had one living parent, and as many as one-third of all foundlings and orphans were children of slave women and their masters. Orphans had no status in society.

After the plague of 1348, infanticide increased dramatically, and many children were abandoned by families no longer able to care for them. Many orphanages, usually sponsored by convents and monasteries, opened during this period.

Childhood

Childhood was a particularly deadly time. In Europe in the Middle Ages, the mortality rate for children ran as high as seventy percent. Depending on the area and conditions, about twenty percent of all children died before they were two years old; fifty percent died before they

were age seven. The average woman gave birth to about four children. For this reason, medieval people were less sentimental about children and understood that they would likely die before reaching adulthood. Parents did not nurture their children in ways that are considered typical today. By the time they were six or seven, they were expected to contribute significantly to the family. Some historians speculate that the barbarity and cruelty of the Middle Ages was a direct result of the way medieval children were raised. Other historians believed that medieval children were cherished and nurtured since they were so often lost.

Boys were raised more gently than girls. Girls were considered a burden and were disposable. Women were responsible for childcare, but noblewomen usually hired wet nurses to care for their babies. Often, the infant was raised in the wet nurse's own home and did not return to his or her family until weaned, which was often not until the age of two or three. Fostering was common in France, England, Scotland, and Scandinavia. This ensured alliances among families, since the children could be used as hostages.

Little attention was paid to most children. They were frequently left without caregivers while their parents worked or attended to their duties. They did have toys, however. Peasant children used mice to haul toy carts. They played with wooden soldiers and weapons and made clay shapes that were then baked. They played with balls, see-saws, and the like. They also had pets, such as lapdogs, squirrels, and birds. Noble children might have monkeys. Cats were not kept as pets because they were believed to be the familiars of witches.

At age seven, childhood ended. Children had to contribute in some way to the function and economics of the family. Peasant girls hired out as maids when they were as young as five or six, certainly by the age of seven. Children were held culpable for their actions from the time they were seven, although they did not reach the age of legal majority until later — twelve years for girls and fourteen for boys.

Between the ages of eight and fourteen, noble boys served as pages at the manor of a nearby lord. Noble girls were sent to be companions or ladies-in-waiting, where they learned the domestic arts and received a basic education. Fostering — sending a child to be raised in another household — was common among nobles. Fostered children were different from royal hostages, who were often raised as foster children but were kept captive in order to maintain their family's loyalty.

Lower-class children became apprentices or servants. As they grew older, they became journeymen and then, after many years of experience, masters of an occupation.

By the age of fourteen or fifteen, noble boys became squires and personal servants. This was not considered demeaning in any way. In exchange, they would receive an education, learn the arts of war, and be counseled in religious matters. Eventually they would earn knighthood.

Some noble girls were also highly educated. They learned Latin and were often better educated than men. Women who might become nuns and abbesses were given a basic education.

Neither the king nor the rule of law had any authority to interfere with the legitimate rights of the head of the household over the family. Only when more two or more households fought would public authority intervene, although even in this case, such help had to be requested.

Thus, abused women and children had little recourse, although women sometimes had relatives and other supporters who would try to protect them.

Upon the death of a noble, the eldest son usually inherited. Early in the Middle Ages and throughout the medieval period in some parts of the world, all sons inherited, dividing the land and wealth among themselves. This proved untenable, as land became divided and subdivided into parcels too small to support a lord, his family, and his retinue. Soon inheritance of land and title passed only to the eldest son.

Daughters generally inherited if there were no sons. Widows were supposed to yield all property to their sons, although their sons were supposed to take care of them. If the heir was a minor, the widow administered the estate and served as regent.

In the absence of the lord, the lady was mistress and defender of the castle and leader of the hunts. She retained her rights to her dower lands, the territory she brought to the marriage as a dowry. She could possess and rule over a seigneury or fief or rule over an abbey, but she was technically a minor all of her life, under her father's protection first and then her husband's. Men were encouraged to beat women for their own good. In turn, women slapped and beat their inferiors, companions, and children and, if their husbands went too far, them as well.

Rejecting Marriage

Women had little opportunity to choose their own husbands or to remain single if they preferred to do so. Nonetheless, a certain percentage of women refused to marry. Sometimes they entered convents and led religious lives. They occasionally broke their marriage bonds in order to become nuns, although this required spousal consent. Often, as a couple neared the end of their lives they would enter monastic life together. The church supported married women who wanted to escape marriage by becoming nuns.

Unmarried women sometimes underwent fasts to protest an impending marriage. They sometimes mutilated themselves so that they would not be attractive to potential marriage partners (beauty was extremely important in the Middle Ages).

Remaining a virgin proclaimed a woman's liberty and autonomy. Defying a father's marital arrangements for the sake of remaining chaste (or simply for the sake of remaining unmarried) was an act of rebellion the magnitude of which is difficult for modern people to understand.

Some writers discouraged women from marriage and encouraged them to enter convents by telling them what marriage was like. They contended that a woman's husband would "beat and maul" her and treat her like a "thrall and a slave." A married woman must endure her husband's attentions no matter how unwanted, "vile and odious."

Although some women could remain unmarried by taking vows of virginity (or, in the case of widows, vows of chastity) or by entering a convent (if wealthy enough), more usually she had little say in the matter. Wealthier women had less control over their lives than middle-class and peasant women, whose marriages were less important in economic and political terms. *See* Households; Law and Women; Religion and Women; Sexuality.

SUGGESTED READING: Christopher N. L. Brooke, *The Medieval Idea of Marriage* (New York: Oxford University Press, 1994); Georges Duby, *Love and Marriage in the Middle Ages* (Chicago: University of Chicago Press, 1996); Francis Gies and Joseph Gies, *Marriage and the Family in the Middle Ages* (New York: HarperCollins, 1989); Katrien Heene, *The Legacy of Paradise: Marriage, Motherhood and Woman in Carolingian Edifying Literature* (New York: Peter Lang, 1997); Constance M. Rousseau and Joel Thomas Rosenthal, eds., *Women, Marriage and Family in Medieval Christendom* (Kalamazoo: Western Michigan University Press, 1998).

Martina (7th century)

Byzantine empress. In 612, just after the death of his first wife, Fabia, she married her uncle Emperor Heraclius. In 638, he began losing his sanity. His subjects thought it was the wrath of God descending on him for his incestuous marriage. The two had nine children: four died in infancy, one was deformed, and another was deaf and mute. Martina was publicly scorned for this.

Martina wanted her son Heraclonas to be co-ruler with Heraclius's firstborn son, Constantine. This was arranged in 638. Heraclius made a will naming the three — Martina, Heraclonas, and Constantine — as joint rulers. Martina wanted to consolidate power, so she arranged the murder of Constantine in 641, after he had reigned only three months.

Her subjects despised her, and soon Constantine's son was crowned emperor. She and Heraclonas were arrested. Her tongue was cut out and her nose slit. Both were exiled to Rhodes.

SUGGESTED READING: Lynda Garland, *Byzantine Empresses: Women and Power in Byzantium, AD 527–1204* (New York: Routledge, 1999); J. F. Haldon, *Byzantium in the Seventh Century: The Transformation of a Culture* (New York: Cambridge University Press, 1991).

Martyrs, Martyrdom, and Martyrology

Martyrs — those who chose death rather than renounce religious principles — were celebrated in the Middle Ages. Stories about their lives and deaths were extremely common and were often written as edifying works, meant to educate an audience on appropriate behavior. The martyrdom of Christian virgins made particularly violent and titillating reading, as story tellers described in intimate detail the lengths to which a Christian woman went in order to preserve her virginity, including self-mutilation, exile, and, of course, death. For women, the moral of the story was clear: death was preferable to losing one's virginity, at least in the eyes of the church. Accounts of the deaths of martyrs and the official lists of martyrs are called martyrology. *See* Religion and Women.

SUGGESTED READING: Jessica Coope, *The Martyrs of Cordoba: Community and Family Conflict in an Age of Mass Conversion* (Lincoln: University of Nebraska Press, 1995); Patrick J. Geary, *Living with the Dead in the Middle Ages* (Ithaca, NY: Cornell University Press, 1994); Patricia Healy Wasyliw, *Martyrdom, Murder and Magic: Child Saints and Their Cults in Medieval Europe* (New York: Peter Lang, 1998).

Mary, Virgin

Mother of Christ. In the Middle Ages, she became the focus of many people's religious and spiritual lives. *See* Cult of the Virgin Mary.

Mary of Alania (11th century)

Byzantine empress. A renowned beauty of the Ducas line, she married Emperor Constantine VI. A poor ruler, Constantine was eventually deposed by his mother, Empress Irene. Nicephorus Botaneiates seized the throne in 1078, but he knew nothing of politics and abdicated in 1081 in favor of Alexius Comnenus.

Mary may have fallen in love with Alexius Comnenus because in 1080, she adopted him as her son. She did not leave the palace after his arrival there in 1081; his wife and family stayed in a different building while he stayed with her. Historians speculate that they were lovers. Soon, however, they parted. Her son Constantine became co-emperor. *See* Irene.

Mary of Antioch (d. 1183)

Byzantine empress. The daughter of Constance of Antioch and Raymond of Poitiers, who Constance had been tricked into marrying when she was seven years old. Mary married Manuel I, the Byzantine emperor, in 1161. She ruled as regent for her son Alexius II Comnene after Manuel died in 1180. Alexius married Agnes of France in the same year; he was ten. Mary was the first Latin to rule in Constantinople.

Her nephew Andronicus Comnenus, a military leader, invaded Constantinople in 1182, to support a rebellion against Mary that had already started. Almost every Latin person in the empire was murdered: children, the sick, the elderly, and even those in hospitals. Mary was strangled, and Andronicus became Emperor Andronicus I. *See* Agnes of France; Constance of Antioch.

SUGGESTED READING: John Kinnamos, *Deeds of John and Manuel Comnenus* (New York: Columbia University Press, 1976); Paul Magdalino, *The Empire of Manuel I Komnenos, 1143–1180* (New York: Cambridge University Press, 1993).

Mary of Burgundy (1457–1482)

Duchess of Burgundy. Daughter of the duke of Burgundy, Charles the Bold, she inherited his land, an important and powerful duchy in medieval Europe. Charles's goal was to restore the kingdom of Burgundy, and he went to war against France on several occasions. During the siege of Nancy in 1476, he was killed. After she inherited the lands, Mary was forced to cede territory to the French Crown. The rest became part of the Holy Roman Empire after her marriage to Maximilian of Austria, which she undertook to keep Burgundy from falling into French hands. The two founded the Hapsburg line of rulers.

Mary of Cleeves (15th century)

French noblewoman. She married Charles of Orléans, who succeeded to the duchy of Orléans after his father was murdered by Burgundians in 1407. During the battle of Agincourt, he was captured and imprisoned by the English. He was ransomed by his wife-to-be. Upon his release, he married her; they had a son who became King Louis XII.

Mathilda *see* **Matilda**

Matilda of Anjou (1105–1154)

English noblewoman. The daughter of Fulk V, she entered the Fontevrault monastery when she was eleven. Her father subsequently arranged her marriage to William Ætheling, the heir to Henry I, king of England. The marriage took place in 1118. She was thirteen years old at the time. William died in a channel crossing when she was fourteen years old. She longed to return to Fontevrault, and she was allowed to do so. She died there in 1154.

Her experience was typical of noblewomen in the Middle Ages — sent to a convent when convenient, entered into an arranged marriage when expedient, and returned to the convent when her usefulness ended. *See* Marriage and Family.

Matilda of Boulogne (d. 1263)

Countess of Boulogne and queen of Portugal. She married Afonso III, king of Portugal. After the death of Sancho II, his brother, in 1248, he claimed the throne. Afonso married another woman — Beatriz of Castile — in 1253, while Matilda was still alive. She complained to the pope, who imposed an interdict although this did not convince Afonso to leave Beatriz. Matilda died in 1263. *See* Beatriz of Castile.

Matilda of England (1102–1167)

Also called Maud. Queen of England and Holy Roman empress. The daughter of Henry I, king of England, and Matilda of Scotland, she married Henry V, the Holy Roman emperor, when she was seven and he was almost forty. After his death in 1128, she wished to remain a childless widow, but her father still had no heir. Therefore, she was forced to marry Geoffrey of Anjou (also known as Geoffrey Plantagenet), who was the son of Fulk of Anjou. Geoffrey was fifteen at the time; she was in her late twenties. Because Geoffrey was only a baron, and she had been empress of the Holy Roman Empire, she resented the lower status to which the alliance subjected her. Nonetheless, the marriage eased hostility between the House of Anjou and the Normans and established the Angevin line of kings in England. With her claim to the throne to add legitimacy, Geoffrey conquered Normandy. After the birth of their son Henry, she left her husband for several years.

When her father, the king of England, died in 1135, leaving the throne to her, her cousin Stephen of Blois, grandson of William the Conqueror, at first supported her claim. Allegedly, the two conducted an affair. Soon, however, Stephen usurped the throne. Four years later, Matilda and her half brother Robert, earl of Gloucester, opposed Stephen, landing with an army at Arundel. A civil war erupted. In 1141, Stephen was captured by Robert, and Matilda reigned as queen for several months, but Stephen was soon returned to the throne. In 1142, Matilda was forced from Oxford after a lengthy siege by Stephen.

A five-year period of anarchy and chaos ensued, with neither Matilda nor Stephen able to assert control over the country. The great lords tried to take advantage of this situation and constantly switched allegiances. Robert continued to fight on Matilda's behalf until his death in 1147. Unable to press her claim, she withdrew in 1148 in favor of her son Henry of Anjou, who would later rule as Henry II. Henry continued the war against Stephen until 1153, at which time Stephen named Henry his heir. *See* Matilda of Scotland.

SUGGESTED READING: Marjorie Chibnall, *The Empress Matilda: Queen Consort, Queen Mother and Lady of the English* (Oxford: Blackwell, 1993); Keith J. Stringer, *The Reign of Stephen: Kingship, Warfare and Government in Twelfth-Century England* (New York: Routledge, 1993).

Matilda of Flanders (d. 1083)

Queen of England. She married William the Conqueror in 1053 against the wishes of the pope, who believed they were too closely related. The alliance strengthened William's claim to the throne. He invaded England in 1066, initiating the Norman Conquest. He was acknowledged king of England in that year, and she was crowned queen of England in 1068. The famous Bayeux tapestry, a needlework panel commemorating the invasion of England and created by Norman artists around 1080, is attributed to her, but it was probably made for Odo, the bishop of Bayeux and half brother to William. Matilda bore seven children, two of whom would become kings of England: William and Henry.

SUGGESTED READING: Ann Williams, *The English and the Norman Conquest* (London: Boydell and Brewer, 1997).

Matilda of Scotland (d. 1118)

Queen of England. The daughter of the king of Scotland, Malcolm III, and Margaret, granddaughter of Edmund II Ironside, king of England. Her name was originally Edith, but she took the name Matilda when she married Henry I, king of England and son of William the Conqueror. Her marriage, which took place in 1100, united the Anglo-Saxon line with the Norman line in England. Matilda and Henry had several children, but no male heirs survived. When Matilda died, she was greatly mourned by her subjects because she had been greatly loved.

Henry eventually named their daughter Matilda as his heir, but after his death, his nephew Stephen of Blois seized the throne. A civil war followed; eventually her daughter Matilda of England's son Henry II succeeded to the throne. *See* Margaret of Scotland, Saint; Matilda of England.

Matilda of Tuscany (1046–1115)

Countess of Tuscany. She married her stepfather's son Geoffrey the Hunchback, duke of Lorraine, in 1069. She ruled

Tuscany with the help of her mother, Beatrice of Lorraine. Geoffrey and Matilda divorced in 1071.

A political supporter of Pope Gregory VII, she opposed Henry IV, the Holy Roman emperor, during the investiture controversy. It was at her castle in Canossa that Henry was forced to perform his public penance. When Henry was excommunicated in 1080, she financed the pope's actions.

In 1089, she married Welf (Guelph) V, duke of Bavaria, and became a leading figure in the Guelph cause. She supported Conrad's rebellion against his father, Henry IV. She continued to war against the emperor until he died in 1106, leading her own anti-imperialist troops in battle.

Matilda had left her land to the pope, but in 1111, she reconciled with Henry V, the son of Henry IV and the new Holy Roman emperor. Her titles, which Henry IV had revoked, were restored. After her death, Henry seized the Italian territories she had left to the pope, sparking another conflict between the pope and the Holy Roman emperor. As a tireless supporter of the papacy, her body was interred at St. Peter's in Rome.

SUGGESTED READING: U. R. Blumenthal, *The Investiture Controversy: Church and Monarchy from the Ninth to the Twelfth Century* (Philadelphia: University of Pennsylvania Press, 1991); Danial Bornstein and Roberto Rusconi, *Women and Religion in Late Medieval and Renaissance Italy* (Chicago: University of Chicago Press, 1996).

Máttaráhkká

Mother of the household spirits venerated by medieval Scandinavian women; they lived under the floor. Comparable to Mother Earth cults. *See* Religion and Women.

Maud *see* Matilda of England

Mechthild of Magdeburg
(c. 1207–1282)

German mystic. Famous nun at a convent in Helfta in Saxony. She was a copyist and writer. She is known for her lyric poetry in which she described the soul at the Court of God, using much of the terminology of courtly love with erotic overtones.

Born to a noble family, she left her home in her early twenties so that she could live as a Béguine. This monastic movement did not require its members to take formal vows or orders. Members led lives of quiet contemplation and poverty. The group aroused the suspicion of the church, although the official church was often unable to meet the spiritual and moral needs of women.

Subject to visions, Mechthild wrote a book about her experiences, *The Flowing Light of the Godhead*. Her writings reveal a kind of Franciscanism. She denounced clergy members for corruption and for straying from God's will. She was received with hostility and eventually sought refuge at Helfta monastery. A cult formed around her, especially after her death. *See* Courtly Love; Religion and Women.

SUGGESTED READING: Amy Hollywood, *The Soul as Virgin Wife: Mechthild of Magdeburg, Marguerite Porete and Meister Eckhard* (Notre Dame, IN: University of Notre Dame Press, 1995); Ulrike Wiethaus, *Ecstatic Transformation: Transpersonal Psychology in the Work of Mechthild of Magdeburg* (Syracuse, NY: Syracuse University Press, 1995).

Medicine and Health

In the early Middle Ages, medicine in the West was largely confined to tribal lore. Even in the East before the seventh century, little could be done to heal the sick. In the seventh century, however, the Arabs began learning about classical medicine and developed an Islamic system of treating disease and injury. The Middle Ages saw the first medical schools, the first hospitals, and the development of a theory of contagion.

Arab physicians first identified smallpox and measles in 910, and they understood at that time that blood played an important role in infectious diseases. They understood how parasites worked and the importance of diet and hygiene. They also required physicians to be trained and licensed.

In Europe, medicine never reached the heights attained by Islamic medicine. Monks and nuns often ministered to the ill and became active in caring for lepers and victims of other diseases. Although some medical research was conducted, it was complicated by theologians, such as Bernard of Clarivaux, who banned clergy from studying medicine and required them to use only prayer.

Women were rarely allowed to become licensed physicians, and they could not attend universities. Fewer than five percent of official or licensed physicians were women. Nonetheless, for practical purposes, women learned a great deal about medicine in order to treat their families and other dependents. Female healers were common in all societies throughout the Middle Ages. Many of them were midwives, but they did not limit themselves just to childbirth and its associated problems, and they were able to treat the medical problems of both men and women.

There were few surgeons. It was not a well-regarded profession, so barber-surgeons with limited training practiced it. There was little understanding of anat-omy. The church, because it disapproved of bloodshed, disapproved of the practice of surgery, and in the thirteenth and fourteenth centuries the church banned clerics from performing surgery. By the fifteenth century, many women, especially in Paris, had taken up the profession of surgery. They had difficulty obtaining licenses so they usually worked unlicensed.

Medical treatment for female problems and for childbirth was not well developed. Conception was poorly understood. Most physicians believed that women contributed semen, too; women, therefore, were thought to possess smaller testes than men and to ejaculate. Both partners then had to experience sexual pleasure for conception to result. For this reason, people did not believe rape could result in pregnancy.

Female sperm was thought to be gathered up and excreted during menstruation. At the time of conception, if the sperm gathered on the left side of the uterus, the fetus would be a girl; if it gathered on the right side, it would be a boy. If conception occurred at or near the center, the fetus could be either, but if it were a boy it would possess female characteristics, and if it were a girl, it would possess male characteristics.

Menses, commonly called flowers, started around the age of thirteen and lasted to the age of fifty or sixty. The function of menopause was understood, and premature menopause was diagnosed and treated. Many diseases of the reproductive organs were diagnosed, although they were not well understood. Types of premenstrual stress were diagnosed and treated. Physicians knew endometriosis was caused by blood remaining clotted in the body instead of being expelled. Lack of menstruation was thought to be related to stress, excessive grief, anger, excitement, or fear.

Women with painful menses were helped with belonica, pennyroyal, wormwood, mint, rue, laurel, ginger, and warm wine. Damp warmth was used to ease cramps. Fennel, dill, and nettle helped start late periods and may intentionally have been used as abortives. Heavy menses were treated by inserting a suppository into the vagina; this suppository consisted of burned laurel ashes. Eating cooked camphor and sage or nettle and wine was also supposed to help heavy menses.

Ulcers of the womb, which included uterine infections and tears from childbirth, were treated with mulberry and oil of roses. Baths in roses, myrtles, chickpeas, and lentils were also considered useful. For an infection, physicians or midwives prescribed snake's blood, myrrh, and mushroom.

To prevent conception, women wore the womb of a female goat that had not had a litter against their skin. They also used a stone called galgates, either worn or tasted, to prevent conception. The testicles of a weasel worn under the breasts were also believed to prevent conception. After childbirth, women routinely applied barley on the afterbirth to prevent conception. Cucumbers, pennyroyal, and dittany were used as abortives.

It was commonly believed that women with narrow vulvas and "tight wombs" should not marry since they were likely to die in childbirth. It was thought that slender hips were a sign of this. Overweight women were known to have trouble during pregnancy and childbirth.

Iris and sugar were given to prevent miscarriage. It was believed that if a woman wanted something that was unavailable, a miscarriage might result, so husbands were cautioned not to talk about things that were not readily accessible. For difficult labor, baths with chickpeas, barley, or flax-seed were given. Vinegar or sugar was mixed with powdered mint and absinthe and given as a drink. Sneezing was thought to be helpful to labor, so the midwife would hold pepper under the pregnant woman's nose. For a breech birth, the midwife would attempt to rotate the fetus into the proper position. To extract afterbirth, sneezing was induced. The medications used to force menstruation were also used to force the afterbirth.

The Vikings had special medications for expelling stillborns. The French and English used rue, mugwort, absinthe, and black pepper in wine to expel stillborns.

After birth, henbane, iris, licorice, and hemp were given for sore breasts from nursing. Wealthy women and noblewomen usually employed a wet nurse. The choice of wet nurse was important. For noblewomen, the wet nurse was usually also a noble; a non-noble could taint the child. According to written guides, the wet nurse was not supposed to be too fat, too slender, too near pregnancy, or too far from the preceding childbirth. She was not supposed to eat sharp or acidic foods, such as garlic, and she was supposed to exercise and avoid stress.

Life Expectancy

Medieval life expectancy ranged widely throughout the period and from one country to another. In general, men lived longer than women. At any given time, one-half of the population was under twenty-one, and one-third of the population was under fourteen.

A slight majority of Europeans died before they were thirty. Women had a life expectancy of twenty-four years because of the dangers of childbirth. Men lived, on average, until the age of thirty. Many infants and children died. The highest mortality rate was for those age seven and under. In some regions, as many as seventy percent of children died before reaching age five.

Once past childhood and the dangers of young adulthood (e.g., warfare, childbirth), medieval adults could expect to live into old age.

Plague

The worst disaster of the Middle Ages was not a war nor a storm. It was a sickness called the black plague. This disease was also known as the bubonic plague since it left sores called buboes, or the black death, because of the color of the sores it caused.

The plague devastated Asia during the fourteenth century. It destroyed Hopei Province in China in 1331 and had spread to Russia and the Crimea by 1346. It was brought to Europe from the Crimea by Genoese trading ships in 1347. The disease was carried by fleas, which bit infected rats and then bit humans. The bite of either an infected flea or an infected rat could infect a person. The plague arrived in three different forms. The first, the bubonic form, was characterized by black swellings in the armpit and groin, which could become the size of an orange. Blood and pus leaked from the buboes, which spread over the body. Black patches showed on the skin from internal bleeding. Severe pain and death occurred within five days. This form infected the bloodstream and was spread by physical contact. A variation, the pneumonic, caused continuous fever and the spitting of blood and led to death in as little as twenty-four hours. This type infected the lungs and was spread by respiratory excretions. A third type, septicemic, entered the bloodstream. A person who contracted it died before symptoms showed. It was spread through physical contact. The three types struck at once, which caused the high death rate and increased the rate of infection.

The plague gave rise to superstitions. People believed the Pest Maiden flew from the mouth of a dead person to infect the living. Such superstitions were believed since people were unable to explain the cause of the plague. The author William Langland's Piers Plowman said the plague was caused by sin; many people did in fact believe this. Jews were also blamed, accused of infecting the wells. Christians began murdering Jews for this "crime" in 1348.

Other people thought the air was somehow poisoned, perhaps as a result of a terrible earthquake that had happened or an adverse alignment of planets. The plague was variously ascribed to the wrath of God or the hand of Satan. At least every decade from the fourteenth century on saw a recurrence of outbreaks. *See* Marriage and Family; Midwifery.

SUGGESTED READING: Darrel W. Amundsen, *Medicine, Society and Faith in the Ancient and Medieval Worlds* (Baltimore: Johns Hopkins University Press, 1995); Paul Binski, *Medieval Death: Ritual and Representation* (Ithaca, NY: Cornell University Press, 1996); Robert S. Gottfried, *The Black Death: Natural and Human Disaster in Medieval Europe* (New York: Free Press, 1985); David Herlihy and Samuel Kline Cohn, *The Black Death and the Transformation of the West* (Cambridge, MA: Harvard University Press, 1997); Tony Hunt, *The Medieval Surgery* (London: Boydell and Brewer, 1992); Colin Platt, *King Death: The Black Death and Its Aftermath in Late Medieval England* (Toronto: University of Toronto Press, 1996); Manfred Ullmann, *Islamic Medicine* (New York: Columbia University Press, 1997).

Midwifery

The practice of assisting women in childbirth. In the Middle Ages, midwives — some well trained, most not — helped women during labor and delivery, performed abortions, and provided contraceptive medications and devices. Midwives were always women. Male physicians sometimes aided women, especially during important births, but this was rare. *See* Medicine and Health.

Miroslava (11th century)

Bulgarian noblewoman. Her story mirrors that of Kosara. According to legend, she too was a daughter of Samuel, the tenth-century Bulgarian ruler, and she too fell in love with one of his prisoners — Ashot, the son of the Byzantine governor. In this story, Samuel allowed the two to marry and made Ashot the governor of Durazzo.

Ashot then plotted to turn Durazzo over to the Byzantines; the conspiracy was successful in 1005. Ashot and Miroslava had already left the city, and they avoided being caught and tried for their part.

It is likely that the two were in fact married, probably in order to reduce tensions between the Byzantine Empire and Bulgaria. *See* Kosara.

Morgan le Fay

Also Morgause. In Arthurian romance, Arthur's half sister. She learned magic from Merlin, fell in love with Lancelot, and imprisoned him when he did not return her love.

In some stories, as a result of unwitting incest, she gave birth to Arthur's son Mordred. Arthur, unaware of his parentage, did not know Morgan was his half sister. In other stories, she hated Arthur because Arthur's father had killed her father, and she passed her hatred on to her son Mordred.

Motherhood *see* Marriage and Family

Murasaki Shikibu (978?–1031)

Japanese novelist. One of Japan's greatest writers, she wrote what is considered the world's first novel, *Tale of the Genji*. Little is known about her life, except that she lived at court during the Heian period in the service of Empress Akiko. Her real name is unknown. *See Tale of the Genji*.

SUGGESTED READING: Doris G. Bargen, *A Woman's Weapon: Spirit Possession in the "Tale of the Genji"* (Honolulu: University of Hawaii Press, 1997).

Mystics and Mysticism

Believers in religious intuition. Mystics have visions or moments of understanding of the ultimate nature of God. These experiences of communion result in ecstasy and adoration. In the Middle Ages, believers thought mystics could heal others simply based on faith.

The majority of medieval mystics were women, such as Julian of Norwich and Margery Kempe. Historians posit that this was because women were marginalized in orthodox Christianity and traditional Christian worship. Mysticism became an outlet and a way for religious women to circumvent the paternal and patristic teachings of the church and seek an independent connection with God.

Islam also produced mystics, although they were less likely to be women. Some Islamic sects cultivated the mystical elements of the religion. *See* Julian of Norwich; Margery Kempe; Religion and Women.

SUGGESTED READING: Karen Armstrong, *Visions of God: Four Medieval Mystics and Their Writings* (New York:

Bantam, 1994); Oliver Davies, *God Within: The Mystical Traditions of Northern Europe* (Mahwah, NJ: Paulist Press, 1988); Reynold Alleyne Nicholson, *The Mystics of Islam* (New York: Viking Penguin, 1990); Elizabeth Alvida Petroff, *Body and Soul: Essays on Medieval Women and Mysticism* (New York: Oxford University Press, 1994).

Nornor

Old Norse word for female spirits associated with fate, similar to the Greek Fates. There are three: Urðr, Verðandi, and Skuld, equivalent to Past, Present and Future. *See* Religion and Women.

Nunnery *see* Convents and Nuns

Nuns *see* Convents and Nuns

O

Occupations

In the Middle Ages, women could be employed in a variety of occupations. Peasant women worked as maids and houseservants. They could also be spinners (thus "spinsters"), weavers, dyers, bakers, and alebrewers. Occasionally, they were leather and wool merchants, shopkeepers, shoemakers, bookbinders, and goldsmiths. They had an almost exclusive hold on needleworking and tapestry. Female jesters and minstrels entertained kings and courtiers. Women also worked as copyists, scribes, and even as moneylenders. After the mid–fourteenth century, women worked in plowing and ironmaking. As a group, they gained more money and independence in the later Middle Ages.

There was usually a distinction between the work a married woman could do and the work an unmarried woman could do. Widows could carry on their husbands' trades. Wives sometimes worked in trades different from their husbands'. According to the law, a woman who worked at a different trade was treated as a single woman. This was to protect her husband from being held liable for her business debts, but it actually helped to advance women's rights. Unmarried women worked as wage earners, such as maids, and as shopkeepers. Middle-class women often supervised apprentices, since according to law, apprentices were entitled to her care and nurturing. Whenever unemployment was high, it became illegal to employ women. Before 1348, there were limited opportunities because many men were available for jobs. But after the plague struck, there was an extreme shortage of workers, especially in those areas hardest hit by the epidemic, and more opportunities opened to women.

Female servants were often sexually exploited as complaints to church courts show. Women worked alongside men in the fields and the workshop, leaving children unattended, with often disastrous results. Serfs were expected to continue to labor in the fields even late into pregnancy. There is little record of the work of women; women who worked with their husbands were often counted simply as "wives" on official records, and their employment was not necessarily noted. *See* Guilds.

SUGGESTED READING: Judith Bennett, *Ale, Beer and Brewsters in England:*

Women's Work in a Changing World, 1300–1600 (New York: Oxford University Press, 1997), *Sisters and Workers in the Middle Ages* (Chicago: University of Chicago Press, 1989); Martha C. Howell, *Women, Production and Patriarchy in Late Medieval Cities* (Chicago: University of Chicago Press, 1986).

Odette de Champdivers
(14th–15th century)

Known as "the little queen." When King Charles VI of France suffered attacks of madness, he was unable to endure the company of his wife, so the queen ordered Odette, a tradesman's daughter, to take her place. *See* Elizabeth of Bavaria.

Odette de Pougy (13th century)

Abbess of Notre-Dame-aux-Nonnains. Known for opposing Pope Urban IV, who in 1266 decided to build a church where his father's shoemaking shop had once stood. The church would have occupied a portion of the abbey's property. The abbess objected. She led an armed force against the workers at one site and destroyed their building. In 1268, she did the same thing when the pope sent additional workers. Furious, Urban excommunicated her and the entire convent, but she continued to oppose him for the fourteen years that the excommunication remained in effect. The church was not built until long after her death. *See* Convents and Nuns.

Olga of Kiev (d. 969)

Russian princess and regent of Viking Kiev from 945 to 964. She married Igor, the grand prince of Kiev. After he was assassinated, she seized power. Immediately, she murdered the conspirators who had killed him.

Her son Svyatoslav soon succeeded to the throne and proved to be a headstrong and militaristic ruler known for his cruelty. Olga was the only one who could restrain him.

When her grandson Vladimir succeeded to the throne, she served as his regent. During her reign, she converted to Christianity while on a trip to Constantinople, taking Helena as her baptismal name. Her grandson Vladimir imposed Christianity on his subjects. She is credited with the conversion of Russia. *See* Conversion; Religion and Women.

SUGGESTED READING: Paul Dukes, *A History of Russia: Medieval, Modern and Contemporary, c. 882–1996* (Durham, NC: Duke University Press, 1998); Vladimir Volkoff, *Vladimir: The Russian Viking* (New York: Overlook Press, 1988).

Order of Fontevrault *see* Fontevrault

Order of Saint Mary Magdalene

Also called the Penitent Sisters of Saint Magdalene and the White Ladies because of their white habits. An order whose members were primarily reformed prostitutes. The order had chapters in many cities. It was officially recognized in 1227 by Pope Gregory IV.

The Byzantine emperor, Michael IV, built a convent for prostitutes in the eleventh century, inviting them to become nuns. The idea was followed elsewhere. *See* Religion and Women.

Order of the Holy Savior *see* Brigittine Order

Order of the Poor Clares *see* Poor Clares

Order of the Poor Ladies *see* Poor Clares

Order of the White Lady

Military order created for the purpose of defending women in need. The Order of the White Lady was named after an episode witnessed by Crusaders in Tunisia during which two women in white came down from heaven to stop the Saracens (Muslims) from attacking.

P

Penitent Sisters of Saint Magdalene *see* Order of Saint Mary Magdalene

Peretta Peronne (15th century)

One of many unlicensed female surgeons during the fifteenth century. The University of Paris prosecuted her on several occasions, although she continued to work. The university controlled medicine and licensure and would not grant licenses to women. Surgery was considered an inferior occupation, and few men entered it, unless they were unable to become physicians. Thus, a pressing need for experienced surgeons caused many women to take up the occupation. *See* Medicine and Health.

Péronelle d'Armentières
(14th century)

Noblewoman of Champagne who engaged in a love affair with Guillaume de Machaut, an elderly poet, when she was about eighteen. She had poetic aspirations as well and sent a roundel to him as a means of introducing herself. A lengthy exchange of letters and poems followed. After a time, they met, fell in love, and went so far as to use a pilgrimage for a rendezvous, but she brought their relationship to an end because she was getting married. He vowed to love and adore her forever and tells the story in *Le livre de voir-dit* (The Book of the True Poem), which illustrates many of the motifs of courtly love.

SUGGESTED READING: Laurence de Looze, *Pseudo-Autobiography in the Fourteenth Century: Juan Ruiz, Guillaume de Machaut, Jean Froissart and Geoffrey Chaucer* (Gainesville: University Press of Florida, 1997); Guillaume de Machaut, *Le Livre dou Voir Dit: The Book of the True Poem* (New York: Garland, 1998).

Pest Maiden

The bubonic plague was believed to be caused by the Pest Maiden, who flew from the mouth of a dead person to infect the living. Such superstitions were readily believed since people had no other way of explaining the cause of the epidemic. *See* Medicine and Health.

Petronila Ramirez (b. 1136)

Queen of Aragón. Daughter of Ramiro the Monk, king of Aragón, and Agnes of Poitiers. In 1137, when she was barely a year old, she was betrothed to Ramon Berenger IV, the count of Barcelona. Her father then ceded rulership of Aragón to him and withdrew to a monastery.

The marriage itself took place in 1150. It unified Aragón and Catalonia (Barcelona was a county of Catalan at the time).

Petronila retained the right to rule her kingdom until she specifically gave it to her son, even though she was married and her husband would ordinarily have become ruler. She appointed her son ruler in 1164 and withdrew from political life. *See* Agnes of Poitiers.

SUGGESTED READING: Stephen Bensch, *Barcelona and Its Rulers: 1096–1291* (New York: Cambridge University Press, 1995).

Petronilla of Chemillé (1093–1149)

Abbess of Fontevrault. She became abbess when she was twenty-two years old and continued as such for the next thirty-five years, until her death. The double order was kept strictly segregated except at the church itself. The founder of the monastery, Robert d'Arbrissel, deliberately created the monastery and stipulated in his will that it should remain that way. He handpicked Petronilla to head the monastery and specified that all future abbesses should be widows. *See* Convents and Nuns; Fontevrault; Religion and Women.

Philippa of Hainaut (d. 1369)

Queen of England. She married Edward III of England and became a much-admired, popular queen. By all accounts the two loved each other and enjoyed a good marriage, notwithstanding Edward's mistresses. The couple had seven sons and five daughters, although not all of them survived to adulthood.

Queen Philippa accepted the notorious Alice Perrers into the court as her ward. After Philippa's death, Alice became Edward's mistress and wielded considerable influence and power.

Chaucer was a member of Philippa's household and dedicated several of his works to her. Jean Froissart, the French historian and chronicler, became her secretary in 1361. *See* Alice of Perrers.

SUGGESTED READING: Nigel Saul, *Fourteenth-Century England* (London: Boydell and Brewer, 2000); J. W. Sherbourne, *War, Politics and Culture in Fourteenth-Century England* (London: Hambledon, 1994).

Pilgrimage

The act of pilgrimage — visiting sacred sites for the sake of spiritual rewards — was a common practice among both Christians and Muslims in the Middle Ages. Muslims usually traveled to Mecca and sometimes to Medina; European Christian pilgrims visited holy sites throughout Europe, such as Canterbury and Santiago de Compostela, as well as the Holy Land. Because travel was dangerous and expensive, usually only very religious or very wealthy people were able to undertake pilgrimages. People traveled the pilgrimage routes in groups for protection and companionship. Over time, pilgrimages became an opportunity to carouse. The church objected, saying that pilgrims should pay attention to spiritual matters.

Although the pilgrimage routes were generally well traveled, it was possible to become lost. It was also possible to run out of money or to be robbed by the ever-present highwaymen. Women sometimes turned to prostitution as a result. Female pilgrims were sometimes abducted and sold into slavery. Occasionally, they were murdered. In the eighth century, Saint Boniface proposed forbidding women from making pilgrimages for these reasons. Although women were never officially prevented from embarking on pilgrimages, women on pilgrimages and pilgrimage in general were sometimes denounced by the clergy because of the worldly temptations and problems that resulted. *See* Religion and Women.

Placidia (d. 450)

Regent for the Western Empire. Daughter of Theodosius the Great. At the court of Constantinople, she met and married Constantius, who became her second husband. Placidia was elevated to the rank of augusta in 421, becoming co-ruler in 423. She manipulated her relatives and court officials to gain complete control of the kingdom.

She governed for her son, Valentinian III, the Western emperor, who was weak and ineffectual.

Plectrudis (8th century)

Frankish queen and regent. She married Pippin of Herstal, who is sometimes called Pippin II. After Pippin's death in 714, Plectrudis assumed control of the Frankish Empire in the name of her grandson Theudoald. She imprisoned Pippin's illegitimate son Charles Martel in order to prevent him from seizing power. Plectrudis's supporters were defeated in battle by the Neustrians, who named Raganfred as mayor of the palace. Soon, Martel seized control of the kingdom and ruled as mayor of the palace for many years. Plectrudis was probably exiled or murdered.

Poor Clares

Franciscan order of nuns founded by Saint Clare of Assisi. *See* Clare of Assisi, Saint

Premonstratensians

Monastic order noted for expelling all female members of their communities in 1134. The Catholic church insisted that women's orders could only exist as chapters of men's orders. The Premonstraten-sians attempted to maintain a combined order but eventually decided that sister communities led to too much temptation, and they expelled women from all of their monasteries. One abbot claimed that this was because the wickedness of women was greater than any other evil in the world, and they needed to be avoided like snakes. *See* Convents and Nuns; Religion and Women.

Prioress

The superior in smaller convents. They and abbesses (the superiors in larger convents) were responsible for discipline. Early in the Middle Ages, they were usually elected by committee. Later they were appointed. They usually served for life. *See* Convents and Nuns.

Prostitution

Prostitutes were considered a necessary evil in the Middle Ages. They abounded in cities, towns, and villages. Their clothing was regulated so that their occupation was easily recognizable; they had to be distinguished from respectable women. Brothels were kept in the guise of bathhouses. Ordinances required prostitutes to pay taxes, to reside in certain areas, and to restrict their comings and goings. There was even a guild for prostitutes in Paris.

Serving girls, tradeswomen, and peasants made extra income through prostitution. Prostitutes had no legal standing could not inherit property, could not make legal accusations, and could not appear in person in court.

Promiscuity was often considered the same thing as prostitution. Prostitution itself was tolerated by clerics, who felt that if prostitutes were not available, more harm than good would follow. The church feared that men would become homosexual without this outlet. The men who used prostitutes, procurers, brothelkeepers, and the prostitutes themselves could all be punished for their crimes, but for the most part, authorities left them alone.

Rape of prostitutes was not recognized, since they sold sexual services. Procurers — pimps — pretended to be embroiderers and employed prostitutes as so-called apprentices in order to keep up appearances and prevent prosecution. Barbers were often procurers.

In fifteenth-century Venice and Rome, prostitutes — courtesans — had social status and worldly success. There were over 11,000 prostitutes in Venice alone during this period. *See* Sexuality.

SUGGESTED READING: Ruth Mazo Karras, *Common Women: Prostitution and Sexuality in Medieval England* (New York: Oxford University Press, 1996).

Pulcheria (399–453)

Byzantine ruler. Sister to Emperor Theodosius II. In 414, when she was barely fifteen, she ousted the Praetorian prefect, Anthemius, who was regent and guardian to Theodosius, who was two years younger than she. Her brother was weak and indecisive. Pulcheria was strong, determined, and pious. Her two younger sisters were similar in temperament and encouraged her ambitions.

Pulcheria built many churches. Her numerous charitable actions gave her considerable political clout. Theodosius left all the affairs of state in her hands, even after he married and produced an heir. Pulcheria resented his wife, Athenais (Eudocia), as a threat to her rule. She conspired to have Athenais banished from court and exiled to Jerusalem.

Pulcheria took a vow of virginity in order to prevent an arranged marriage. When her brother was killed in a fall from his horse in 450, her rule was threatened. Thereafter, she contracted a marriage with a Thracian senator and former soldier named Marcian, who she named augustus and placed on the throne with herself, saying, Theodosius had wanted it thus. *See* Athenais.

SUGGESTED READING: Michael Grant, *From Rome to Byzantium: The Fifth Century AD* (New York: Routledge, 1998); Stephen Williams, *The Rome That Did Not Fall: The Survival of the East in the Fifth Century* (New York: Routledge, 2000).

Q

Queens and Queenship

Royal women usually achieved position through marriage rather than inheritance. Medieval queens often wielded power through personal influence. In France, the treasurer was under her supervision, and she awarded knights their annual gifts, in essence, their salaries. The queen also supervised the manors. The names of queens often appear in court documents as "intervening" or "assisting." *See* Social Class.

SUGGESTED READING: John Carmi Parsons, *Medieval Queenship* (New York: St. Martin's, 1994); Theresa M. Vann, *Queens, Regents and Potentates* (London: Boydell and Brewer, 1995).

Querrelle des Femmes

"Argument about women." Debate among fourteenth-century French writers and literary figures regarding the role and importance of women in society. Christine de Pizan contested the views stated by Jean de Meun in his continuation of *Roman de la Rose*. Many well-known authors argued their views. *See* Christine de Pizan.

R

Radegund of Poitiers (520?–587)

Thuringian princess, Frankish queen, and legendary ascetic. One of the seven wives of Clothar (Lothar) I, some of whom he had at the same time. She was a noblewoman who founded one of the earliest convents in France.

Radegund was born in the kingdom of Thuringia during the reign of Justinian. During a brutal battle in 531, she and her brother were kidnapped by Clothar, the king of Neustria (northwestern France). Such kidnappings were common during this period, even among royalty, as a way to unify territories or to bring about a marriage desired by one side. Such was the case for Radegund. She was taken to Soissons, where she was educated until her late teens, when Clothar married her. After their marriage, he apparently converted her to Christianity. His own Christianity was purely nominal — she was the fifth of his seven wives.

Clothar married Radegund so that he might claim the Thuringian throne. She disliked being married to him, and he accused her of behaving more like a nun than a queen. After some years of marriage, Clothar killed Radegund's brother, causing her to flee. After bribing Bishop Medard, she was consecrated as a deaconess. She embarked on a pilgrimage and on her return settled for some time in Tours, where she tended to the sick. Her husband still hoped to win her back, but he eventually donated buildings in Poitiers for her convent.

Radegund ran her house by the first monastic rule for women, that of Saint Caesarius, which required strict cloister and literacy. Thus, the convent became a center for learning and literature. Her biographers picture her as wiping floors, carrying wood, and doing other chores not usual to her station; thus, she was shown as the model of humility.

Numerous miracles were attributed to Radegund, whose community of women attracted many high-ranking nobles. She is also known for her poetry, of which two examples survive, *The Fall of Thuringia* and *Letter to Artachis*. *See* Convents and Nuns; Religion and Women.

SUGGESTED READING: Rosamund McKitterick, *The Frankish Kings and Culture in the Early Middle Ages* (New York: Variorum, 1995); Pauline Stafford, *Queens, Concubines and Dowagers: The King's Wife in the Early Middle Ages* (Oxford: Blackwell, 1998).

Ragnhild (9th century)

Viking queen. She married Halfdan the Black, the legendary Viking leader. She was his second wife. According to legend, she was kidnapped by the berserker

Haki, who had murdered her father. When Halfdan rescued her, Haki killed himself at her loss. Together, Halfdan and Ragnhild had Harald Fairhair, the first king of all of Norway, and Erik I Bloodaxe, who became king of Denmark.

Rauni

In medieval Viking mythology, the wife of a thunder god, Ukko. *See* Religion and Women.

Religion and Women

Christianity and the Medieval Catholic Church

Christianity is a major world religion that derived from Judaism. It is based on the life, death, and resurrection of Jesus Christ, known as the Son of God. The central doctrine of Christian faith is that by the grace of God, people are saved through faith and their sins are forgiven.

After the death of Jesus, his followers traveled throughout the world, spreading the religion. Christian groups were established throughout the Roman Empire. A structure began to form, with weekly meetings led by a priest. Soon, bishops supervised the priests and had greater authority than they did. Areas were divided into parishes and dioceses in order to facilitate preaching and winning converts.

Although early in the history of Christianity, women held positions of power, their power declined throughout the Middle Ages as the church and its popes instituted many rulings restricting the ways in which women could contribute to the church. Since they could not be ordained as priests, they were banned from performing the sacraments and could never achieve important positions in the church.

Early in the Middle Ages, priests were likely to be married and to have families. Over time, the Christian church began enforcing celibacy. It was thought that married priests would use church property to support their wives and families. They would also try to pass their churches on to their children as if they were heritable, instead of allowing the appointment of clergy to various offices. This was in fact the case in Iceland, where it took orthodox Christianity many years to establish a firm foundation. There, priests were likely to be married farmers who often built churches and passed them on to their sons.

In addition, marriage was banned because unmarried priests, it was felt, would be more likely to devote their time and effort to the church. In effect, they were married to the church. Bans on marriage and concubinage became more and more strident in the eleventh century to the resentment of clergy members, some of whom even threatened to murder bishops who tried to enforce unmarried clergy and celibacy.

Throughout the Middle Ages, the Catholic church was confronted with many heresies and heretics. Heresy could be something as seemingly minor as possession of a Bible in a vernacular language or as serious as the denial of Christ's divinity. Heretics usually believed they were following Christ's teachings. They did not necessarily believe they were wrong even if the church's representatives said they were. Often heresy occurred in the Mediterranean, where people had many contacts with the religions of the East. It also took place in areas where the orthodox church had few representatives or when church doctrine alienated people. In areas where secular learning was widespread, but the clergy were poorly educated, heresy was more common. It was rampant in areas with weak political authority.

Numerous women turned to heresy since the orthodox church did not always fill their needs nor give them important roles. Many of the heretical movements of the later Middle Ages, led by women, contributed to the reform movements that would eventually undermine the authority of the church in the sixteenth century.

Christian women suffered according to the rules of their religion. In the Byzantine Empire, women had more freedom and more power, but overall, Christian women were prevented from holding positions of power and authority, either secular or religious, and were expected to obey their fathers, brothers, husbands, and social superiors. According to church fathers, women were corrupt and evil; they pointed to the story of Adam and Eve to prove their point. Although women and men had an equal chance of reaching heaven, only fifteen percent of all saints canonized in the Middle Ages were women.

Christianity allowed one outlet for wealthy women, however, and that was the convent. Women who did not wish to marry, those who were widowed, or those who had been repudiated by their husbands could live in a convent and enjoy a great deal of freedom. Many nuns owned considerable personal property, had personal servants, kept pets, and traveled frequently to visit family and friends. Poorer women — who could not afford the fees necessary to join a convent — did not have this choice. However, they were less likely to be forced into inappropriate marriages for political gain than their wealthier sisters.

Judaism

Judaism, as a religious and cultural tradition, came under attack throughout the world during the Middle Ages. According to Jewish theology, there is one Creator who governs the world. The purpose of God and the world can be understood by the inquiring mind, and everything ultimately has meaning and purpose.

The Torah is the Jewish book of revelation. Jews also follow commandments, called mitzvoth, that regulate moral and ethical behavior. The Mishnah, or the oral tradition of Jewish doctrine, is studied by rabbis who produced two Talmuds, which are commentaries on the Mishnah. The Babylonian Talmud, compiled in the sixth century, became the orthodox document of Judaism.

A person's Jewish heritage was matrilineal — acquired through the mother. For this reason, women had a special position in medieval Judaism as those responsible for passing the religion to subsequent generations. However, medieval Judaism was strongly male-oriented. Only men could become rabbis, and only men could study Jewish doctrine and attend Jewish schools and universities.

Jews were persecuted throughout the Middle Ages by Christians and Muslims. They were the ultimate outsiders since they chose to be not Muslim nor Christian but instead preferred to adhere to Mosaic law. They were deprived of their civil rights in Europe as early as the fourth century. They were called "Christ killers" by early Christians and were classified as enemies of Christianity. They were noncitizens in a universal Christian state.

In the Frankish Empire under Charlemagne, Jews prospered as merchants, traders, and agents of the king. They also served as slave traders in the early Middle Ages. Parents sold unwanted children to them; the children were then shipped to Muslim countries. Many Jews were prominent landowners in southern France until the eleventh century. They were forced from the land when oath taking became a prerequisite for landholding — Jews could not take Christian oaths. Jews were tolerated because some of them performed an important function as money lenders and could increase revenues for nobles. But as Christians began participating in banking and money lending, Jews became less necessary, and persecution against them increased.

During the eleventh century, anti-Semitism became more virulent. The Jews, hated by Christians, were forced to live in separate areas in towns and cities. They could not bring charges against Christians, and they could not give testimony that prevailed over a Christian's in a court case. They were legally like serfs to the king, but he had no reciprocal obligation to them. They became targets of frustration because they frequently accumulated wealth as bankers and traders. Despite laws persecuting Jews and barring them from various kinds of employment, many Christians continued to employ them as physicians, tax collectors, diplomats, and managers.

Jews had their own judges and laws, but Muslim and Christian courts took precedence in cases involving Jews and non–Jews.

In Spain, during the mid–thirteenth century, Jews fared slightly better. Small but important groups of Jews lived mostly in cities, where they were officially tolerated. The professions they were allowed to pursue included medicine, money lending, administration, and tax collecting, for which they were resented by the population at large.

By the mid–fourteenth century, massacres and pogroms against the Jews occurred more and more frequently, the result of unrest throughout Europe because of the plague and unending wars. By the beginning of the sixteenth century, Jews

had been expelled from most European countries.

Jewish women faced special problems in the Middle Ages. As members of a despised group, they faced persecution. Many were forcibly converted to Christianity. If they refused, they could be exiled. Their children were stolen by Christians, who raised them as Christians. Women often killed themselves and their children rather than be forcibly converted or baptized by Christians.

Jewish laws affected Jewish women more than the laws of the Christian lands in which they lived. Like Christian women, Jewish women had few rights. According to Jewish law, a civil marriage was invalid, so a woman who did not participate in a Jewish wedding ceremony had no greater status than that of a mistress. Polygamy was allowed until the eleventh century, when Jewish doctrine developed under the influence of the Talmudic scholar Gershom ben Judah. A man could divorce a woman simply on the grounds of dislike. Women did not have this luxury. In addition, they were expected to wait on their husbands, bathing them and making certain that all of their needs were met. Any earnings they made belonged to their husbands.

Islam

A major world religion that was founded in the Middle Ages by the prophet Muhammad, Islam saw explosive growth in the early Middle Ages. The word *islam* means "to surrender," and Muslims, the followers of Islam, submit or surrender to the will of God.

Muhammad (c. 570–632) was forty years old when, as he believed, he was visited by the archangel Gabriel. He revealed these visions, as well as later ones, to his family and close friends. Within a few years, he had converted thirty or forty people, and he began preaching openly in Mecca, the city of his birth. In 622, the ridicule and opposition of the Meccans forced him to leave the city and travel to Medina. This journey, called the Hejira, marks the beginning of the Islamic calendar.

In Medina, Muhammad's spiritual and political power grew. Arabs and Jews who opposed him were persecuted, and a war was launched against Mecca. From this beginning came the religion's later emphasis on military conquest. By the time of Muhammad's death in 632, he had created a powerful Islamic state. Over the next few centuries, the basic Islamic doctrines were identified, developed, and formalized.

As in Christianity and Judaism, Islam was a male-dominated, male-oriented religion. Only men could become mullahs and caliphs, important positions in the Islamic hierarchy. Women were not allowed to worship in mosques and had to be kept segregated from men at all times.

The main doctrines of Islam were set down by Muhammad as a series of prophecies, which became the Koran. The religion teaches that anyone who worships the old gods will go to hell. Islam is firmly monotheistic. No god but Allah may be worshipped. It also insists on the brotherhood of the religion superseding the ties of tribe, family, or race. One of the practices of medieval Muslims that differed from Christians and later medieval Jews was taking more than one wife; according to the Koran, they could have as many as four as long as they could afford them. No one asked any of the wives for their permission.

For most of the Middle Ages, Islam was an aggressive, expansionist religion, not unlike Christianity. Its emphasis on jihad or holy war gave followers an excuse to fight infidels, primarily Christians, and to forcibly convert members of other religions. The expansion of Islam throughout the Middle East, Asia, and parts of Europe threatened the Western Christians, who responded by undertaking the Crusades.

Muslims in Christian lands were subject to the same types of persecution that befell Jews. The difference was that Muslims were more likely to be lower-class members of society and therefore already less powerful. They were slaves, sharecroppers, and poor peasants. They lived in separate quarters and were not often employed by Christians. Many of them were uneducated. Christians were not allowed to become Muslim, according to church law, under the threat of property confiscation and even death.

Christian laws required Muslims to wear their hair short. They could not wear brightly colored clothes, employ Christians, live in Christian houses, nor purchase lands from Christians. If a Muslim man had sexual intercourse with a Christian virgin, he could be stoned to death; she lost half of her possessions for a first offense and all of her possessions on a second offense. A married Christian woman who had an affair with a Muslim man was turned over to her husband, who could repudiate her, kill her, or otherwise dispose of her as he saw fit.

Muslims were eventually expelled from the Christian states in Spain. Their money was confiscated. Many were made slaves. Their mosques were converted into Christian churches. They were not allowed to have the muezzin call the faithful to prayer, they could not use the name of the prophet in public, nor could they go on pilgrimage as required by their religion.

Christians and Jews living in Muslim lands were also persecuted. They could be forcibly converted. Overall, however, the Muslim countries were more tolerant of the Christians in their midst, even allowing the marriage of Muslims to non–Muslims, as long as the children of the union were raised as Muslims.

Muslim women faced many special restrictions. Women were expected to dress very conservatively so as not to provoke sexual thoughts in men. According to Islamic law, called Sharia, men were responsible for women and could beat their wives, unless their wives obeyed them. However, Muslim women were allowed to transact business, as long as there were witnesses involved. Daughters received an inheritance, usually half of what sons received. Women could only marry one husband at a time, although men were allowed to take multiple wives. Women were discouraged from marrying non–Muslims. Since they had little legal control over their children, they could not promise to raise them as Muslims. A woman married to a non–Muslim would be encouraged to convert him or to abandon him and marry a Muslim. Her marriage to a non–Muslim was not always recognized as valid.

Muslims were encouraged to marry. They could even marry slaves if they so desired. A divorced woman could remarry but only after waiting a designated period of time — long enough to prove she was not pregnant. A divorce could be retracted, but only twice. A divorced woman was allowed to stay in the home of her ex-husband, who was expected to continue supporting her, or she could leave. Widows were allowed to remarry, but again they were expected to wait a designated period of time — usually four months — to prove they were not pregnant. Women were excluded from working in the government and from all positions of authority.

Muslim women in Islamic Spain had considerably more freedom than their sisters in the Middle East. They were often well educated and even became poets and scholars.

Paganism
Pagan forms of worship dominated in the early Middle Ages, when much of society was still tribal. In Scandinavia, paganism persisted well into the eleventh century, and in Hungary and the Balkans, it continued into the fourteenth century. Anglo-Saxons also continued pagan magical practices despite church disapproval. The same was true in the distant outposts of the Byzantine Empire.

Ancestor worship, the veneration of dead relatives, was common in the Nordic region, even among Christianized Scandinavians and the Germanic tribes. Believers thought their ancestors had great power, could influence events, and protect the family. If one's ancestors were not respected, they could cause harm and misfortune. If treated with appropriate respect, they could assure the well-being of their descendants. Ancestors were sometimes believed to serve as intermediaries between people and God (or the gods). Ancestor worship was practiced by individuals and families and did not have a formal doctrine. It was frequently part of another religion.

In Scandinavia, a bride brought her clan's ancestral spirits with her when she went to live with her husband. These spirits resided in the woman's section of the house. Later in the medieval period, the wedding ceremony involved the bride saying good-bye to her clan's spirits and being introduced to the spirits of her husband's clan. Pregnant women were particularly susceptible to visions. They would see a dead relative and name their child after that relative. In this way, the dead relative could return to the family.

Pagan beliefs varied from region to region. In most cases, a shaman or priest was a specialist in religious ritual and could negotiate with the deities and the dead. Scandinavia had priests who performed rituals for the community. The role was usually inherited. Some Viking priestesses existed as well, but usually they were leaders of family cults. Women were barred from public worship and from sacred sites so they developed their own cults. In Scandinavia, guardian spirits of male warriors were often female (e.g., Valkyries). The Vikings also believed in Valhalla, literally, "the hall of corpses." This was the Viking afterlife, a hall of feasting and battling for the slain followers of Odin.

Over time, pagan and Christian rituals and religious practices overlapped. There are Viking myth stories that have Christian imagery and vice versa. There are scenes of the Virgin Mary in Scandinavia in which she resembles a Valkyrie. In Viking lore, the Last Judgment is conflated with the legend of the Æsir and their allies, who battle against Loki and his allies. In Sweden, Christ and Thor are juxtaposed in art. Christ's cross was the equivalent of Thor's hammer. Throughout Scandinavia, molds for making amulets have been discovered with the cross and hammer side by side. Clearly, the two symbols were closely related in the minds of medieval Scandinavians.

Overall, male-oriented and male-dominated religions of the medieval time period sought to control and subordinate women. That they did so is not surprising; that so many women still lived powerful, happy, and fulfilled lives within the confines of these religions (and societies) is more surprising. *See* Convents and Nuns; Heresy; Inquisition; Marriage and Family; Mystics and Mysticism.

SUGGESTED READING: Caroline Walker Bynum, *Jesus as Mother: Studies in Spirituality of the High Middle Ages* (Berkeley: University of California Press, 1984); Austin P. Evans, *Heresies of the High Middle Ages* (New York: Columbia University Press, 1991); Richard Fletcher, *The Barbarian Conversion: From Paganism to Christianity* (New York: Holt, 1998); Judith Herrin, *The Formation of Christendom* (Princeton, NJ: Princeton University Press, 1989); R. I. Moore, *The Birth of Popular Heresy* (Toronto: University of Toronto Press, 1995); William F. Pollard and Robert Boenig, *Mysticism and Spirituality in Medieval England* (London: Brewer, 1997); Adil Salahi, *Muhammad, Man and Prophet: A Complete Study of the Life of the Prophet of Islam* (Rockport, MA: Element Books, 1998); Jane Tibbetts Schulenburg, *Forgetful of Their Sex: Female Sanctity and Society, c. 500–1100* (Chicago: University of Chicago Press, 1998); Lesley Smith and Jane H. M. Taylor, *Women, the Book and the Godly* (London: Brewer, 1995).

Religious Communities

Women's religious communities flourished in the seventh and eighth centuries, then began a slow decline. *See* Convents and Nuns.

Roman de la Rose (Romance of the Rose)

An allegorical poem begun in 1237 by the poet Guillaume de Lorris and finished around 1277 by Jean de Meun, also known as Jean Clopinél.

Guillaume de Lorris (1212?–1237) was born in the village of Lorris near Orléans. Little is known about him except what can be inferred from his writing. He was well read and was obviously familiar with the Roman poet Ovid, who had described the "rules" of courtly love in his works. In Guillaume's part of the poem, he describes his love affair in a dream-vision, a popular narrative type in the Middle Ages. He uses allegory to present the story. Personifications symbolize actions.

In *Romance of the Rose*, the object of the lover's attention, the Lady (who is the Rose), responds to the lover as a personification called Fair Welcome. Her modesty, however, as represented by the figure of Shame, denies him. The love affair is thus highly ritualized. Guillaume's skill as a writer makes these abstractions seem concrete.

An anonymous conclusion to Guillaume's unfinished work appeared sometime after his death. The seventy-nine lines quickly conclude the affair, but are not of the same skill as the first part of the book.

Jean de Meun, from the village of Meun, also near Orléans, completed *Romance of the Rose*. In doing so, he considerably enlarged the work and added his own anti-courtly sentiments to it. Thus the first part of the book celebrates courtly love while the second part of the book denigrates it. Jean's depiction of women is also the opposite of Guillaume's. Guillaume tells the story of a humble lover pleading for a woman's favors; Jean advises a more direct (and more misogynistic) approach to love affairs.

Jean, a scholar and professional writer, was born at about the time Guillaume de Lorris died. The personifications that he uses in the book speak like scholars, with analytical, rational, and logical statements and arguments. The question of courtly love is described from all points of view. Reason shows that love is foolish and even harmful while Genius (Imagination) points out that it is necessary. The Duenna (Chap-

erone) describes the sordid ways in which lovers go about achieving their ends while Forced Abstinence complains of the danger of denying love. In the end, Jean believes that the love of God, not earthly love, is the proper concern of all individuals.

Romance of the Rose was an extremely popular work in the Middle Ages and influenced countless later poets, including Chaucer. *See* Courtly Love.

SUGGESTED READING: Kevin Brownlee, *Rethinking the "Romance of the Rose": Text, Image, Reception* (Philadelphia: University of Pennsylvania Press, 1992); Guillaume de Lorris and Jean de Meun, *The Romance of the Rose* (Princeton, NJ: Princeton University Press, 1995); Douglas Kelly, *Internal Difference and Meaning in the "Roman de la Rose"* (Madison: University of Wisconsin Press, 1995).

Rosamund   (6th century)

Queen of the Lombards. She married Alboin, king of the Lombards, after Alboin killed her father, Cunimund, king of the Gepids, whose kingdom was in the present-day Balkans. According to legend, after defeating the Gothic Gepidae, Alboin beheaded Cunimund and forced Rosamund to drink from her father's skull.

In 572, Alboin was murdered at her instigation. One chronicler asserts that she poisoned him herself. Another chronicler states that she was involved in a conspiracy to murder him and that after his death, she married a co-conspirator, Himagis. They apparently fled the kingdom, possibly with part of the army, taking the Lombard treasury with them. They settled in Ravenna, which was still under the control of the Roman emperor.

SUGGESTED READING: Neil Christie, *The Lombards: The Ancient Langobards* (Oxford: Blackwell, 1995).

Rule of Nuns

One of the earliest known written rules of monastic life. It set clear and comprehensive guidelines for contemplative living and was used to structure Byzantine monasteries for many years. Caesarius of Arles is believed to have written the work in the early part of the sixth century.

The rule was written specifically for women. It set the length of the novitiate (at least one year). The rule counseled nuns to avoid oaths and swearing. Members had to give away all personal possessions. Luxuries were not acceptable, including anything embroidered or made of silk. Nuns — including the abbess — were not to have personal servants. No girls under the age of six or seven would be allowed. Novices had to be old enough to understand and follow the rules of the order and old enough to learn how to read and write. All members of the convent were to learn to read.

The rule specified that nuns should not live in single cells but should all share one room. No loud talking was permitted. Quarrels were to be kept to a minimum and resolved as quickly as possible. Men were not allowed into any private part of the grounds. No banquets were to be given except in honor of religious women visiting from other cities. The rule was adapted and used by many monasteries throughout the Middle Ages. *See* Convents and Nuns.

Rule of Saint Clare

First religious rule written by a woman. It was devised by Clare of Assisi in 1253 and approved by the pope in the same year. It describes how nuns are chosen, how divine offices should be celebrated, and how the abbess and other officials are elected. The rule also offers regulations about appropriate work, punishment for wrongdoing, and penance for sinning; it emphasizes that nuns should practice charitable works and take vows of poverty. *See* Clare of Assisi, Saint.

S

Saints

In Christian theology, a person entitled to veneration and capable of interceding for believers. In the early Middle Ages, saints were unofficially honored. Only much later was a process of beatification and canonization put in place in order for the church to officially recognize holy people. The criteria came to include martyrdom, a holy life, and miracles in life and after death.

Many saints' days and festivals were celebrated in the Middle Ages. Most saints were men, although occasionally women were canonized (very rarely were married women and mothers officially accepted as saints). Women were more likely to be venerated as saints early in the Middle Ages, and many women were given the honorific title of "saint" even though the church did not officially recognize them as such. *See* Martyrs, Martyrdom, and Martyrology; Religion and Women.

SUGGESTED READING: Barbara Abou el-Haj, *The Medieval Cult of Saints* (New York: Cambridge University Press, 1994);

Damon Duffy, *Saints and Sinners: A History of the Popes* (New Haven, CT: Yale University Press, 1997).

Salic Law

Law codes written by Salian Franks in the sixth century. The codes detailed the blood price or fine for crimes and injuries. It also banned women from inheriting land in order to prevent the Crown from passing to a foreigner by marriage. In the fourteenth century, Philip V, king of France, used the law to legitimize his claim to the throne. His brother Louis X died, leaving a small daughter to inherit the throne. Philip declared that women could not succeed to the throne in France. An assembly at the University of Paris agreed with him. Later, Edward III, king of England, was denied the French Crown for the same reason — his mother was the daughter of the French king, Philip IV, and had, according to Salic law, no claim to the throne. Edward III disagreed and launched the Hundred Years' War. *See* Wars and Warfare.

SUGGESTED READING: Theodore John Rivers, *Laws of the Salian and Ripurian Franks* (New York: AMS Press, 1987).

Sáráhkká

Female household spirit in medieval Scandinavia, protector of unborn females and of women in childbirth and menstruation. Similar to Mother Fire cult. The spirit lived under the hearth. Sáráhkká was the protector of families and of women even as late as the seventeenth century. She was invoked as Saint Sara by Christian women. *See* Religion and Women.

Scheherezade

Female protagonist who tells the stories in *Arabian Nights*. *See Arabian Nights*.

Schweister Katrei

(13th–14th century)

Member of the Brethren of the Free Spirit and a major theologian for the movement. She and Marguerite Porete wrote the most important gospels. The movement was condemned by the church, and she was convicted of heresy and executed. *See* Brethren of the Free Spirit; Marguerite Porete.

Second Order of Franciscans

Name given to the Poor Clares. *See* Poor Clares.

Seiðr

A medieval Scandinavian pagan ritual used for divination or to control other people. Most practitioners were women. The ritual was used in times of crisis. A religious specialist was necessary to appeal to spirit helpers. *See* Religion and Women.

Seoxburh (7th century)

Queen of Wessex. She married Cenwallah, king of Wessex. Upon his death in 672, she ruled the kingdom.

Seraglio

Turkish harem; women's quarters. *See* Harem; Women's Quarters.

Sessrúmnir

In medieval Scandinavian folklore, the hall of the goddess Freyja. The Viking slain went there after death. *See* Religion and Women.

Sexuality

Sexuality presented difficulties for the medieval church. It was natural, people enjoyed it and procreated by it, and yet it caused many problems. To allow unchecked sexual expression was to mock

God and ignore his commandments. To eliminate it meant the end of humanity. Therefore, church authorities undertook the restriction of sexuality, ideally to the marital sphere and only for the purpose of procreation. Members of religious communities, therefore, did not meet these conditions and had to live chastely.

Sexual relations were believed to interfere with one's spiritual relationship to God, so sex even in marriage posed difficulties for medieval theologians. Nonetheless, partners in a marriage owed each other the marriage debt. That is, they were required to engage in sexual relations with one another, unless both agreed to holy chastity. A marriage could be set aside if one member failed to pay the marriage debt.

Although women were thought to be naturally promiscuous, they were held to a higher standard of sexual conduct than men. This was one way that women could gain virtue, according to theologians.

All varieties of sexual conduct were practiced. Among young unmarried men, homosexuality was rampant if the legislation against it is to be believed. Nuns were also frequently accused of carrying on affairs with other nuns. How much homosexuality actually existed is difficult to determine. During this period, the word *Florence*, as in Florence, Italy, became a German word, *florenzer*, which means homosexual, indicating that it was widely believed that homosexuality was prevalent in some parts of Italy.

Church authorities thought lack of access to intercourse with women caused male homosexuality, so they sanctioned sexual intercourse in marriage and tolerated prostitution.

Many sexual practices were banned, including homosexuality and masturbation, since theologians had concluded that the only purpose for sexual intercourse was procreation. Anal intercourse was prohibited because it was used as a form of birth control. Incest was occasionally complained about, although it is hard to know how common it was. Certainly the male right to control women contributed to women's sexual exploitation and abuse. The presence of female slaves, servants, and dependents, such as nieces and cousins, afforded opportunities for predatory sexual encounters.

Virginity was highly valued. This high value probably stemmed from the fact that only free women could control or attempt to control their virginity. Slaves and serfs could be raped at will. Virginity also became conflated with chastity and the accepted moral and Christian values during the Middle Ages. Further, a prospective bridegroom wanted to be sure that any children of the marriage were truly his, so premarital virginity was important. Remaining a virgin as an adult — that is, refusing marriage — was a way for women to remain autonomous. Often, however, a woman's desires in this respect were disregarded. *See* Marriage and Family; Religion and Women.

SUGGESTED READING: Vern L. Bullough and James A. Brundage, eds., *Handbook of Medieval Sexuality* (New York: Garland, 1996); Pierre J. Payer, *The Bridling of Desire: Views of Sex in the Later Middle Ages* (Toronto: University of Toronto Press, 1993).

Shiko (6th century)

Japanese empress who ordered the construction of Buddhist temples throughout Japan at the end of the sixth century. Her son Prince Shotoku carried out her orders. He brought artists and architects from Korea and other parts of Asia to Japan, where they built numerous temples, similar to the ones in China. Japan, which is a series of islands made of volcanic rock, has little stone, so the structures were made of wood. Japanese architects soon became famous for the elaborate, durable structures they could create from wood.

Sichelgaita of Salerno (11th century)

Italian noblewoman. A Lombard, she married Robert Guiscard, the Norman duke of Apulia, Calabria, and Sicily. According to contemporary reports, she was large, indomitable, and always accompanied her husband into battle with notable zeal. Medieval historians said she was the reason the siege of Durazzo (1081–1082) was successful, because she encouraged the soldiers in their endeavors. Once the siege ended, the Normans met little resistance on their march to Constantinople. However, a rebellion back home forced Robert and Sichelgaita to withdraw, and their dream of conquering the Byzantine Empire went unfulfilled.

SUGGESTED READING: Kenneth Baxter Wolf, *Making History: The Normans and Their Historians in Eleventh-Century Italy* (Philadelphia: University of Pennsylvania Press, 1995).

Simonis Paleologus (1294–1341)

Byzantine noblewoman and princess of Serbia. Daughter of Andronicus II and Irene, the Byzantine emperor and empress. When she was five years old, her father forced her to marry the ruler of Serbia, Stephen Milutin. The church objected to the marriage, as did her mother, Empress Irene. Nonetheless, it went forward as Andronicus had planned. Stephen consummated the marriage with the child, and the injuries she sustained made it impossible for her to have children.

Simonis traveled to Thessalonica for her mother's funeral in 1317. She did not wish to return to Serbia, but her husband sent a delegation to bring her back. She tried to escape, dressed as a nun, but her half brother Constantine betrayed her, and she was forcibly returned to Serbia. Three years later, her husband died. She returned to Constantinople, became a nun, and lived another twenty years. *See* Irene Paleologina; Marriage and Family.

SUGGESTED READING: John V. A. Fine, *The Late Medieval Balkans: A Critical Survey from the Late Twelfth Century to the Ottoman Conquest* (Detroit: University of Michigan Press, 1994).

Skaði

In medieval Viking mythology, a female giant who lived in the mountains and married a Viking god, Njörðr. *See* Religion and Women.

Skuld

In medieval Scandinavian folklore, female spirit associated with fate, similar to the Greek Fates. There are three: Urðr, Verðandi, and Skuld, equivalent to Past, Present, and Future. Collectively, they are called Nornor. *See* Religion and Women.

Slavery and Women

In the Middle Ages, the practice of slavery (involuntary servitude), which had been widespread among the Romans, was modified but not eliminated. It was distinct from serfdom. Serfs, although unfree, were tied to the land and could not be separated from it. The serf and the serf's lord were bound by reciprocal obligations. Slaves and their masters were not bound by these mutual obligations, and slaves could be bought and sold at will.

In Italy and Spain, large numbers of slaves came from the Near East, almost all of them women. They worked primarily as household maids but also served as storytellers and entertainers. Female slaves were sexually abused and exploited. In areas where slavery was widespread, as many as a third of all foundlings or orphans belonged to slave women and their masters. In Arab and Turkish states, slaves were used as domestic servants and as soldiers. Female slaves, often of Christian heritage, were common in Muslim lands.

Slaves usually served the same family for most of their lives. Many were emotionally disturbed by their experiences and the conditions of slavery. Sometimes they were treated like family members and were educated; other times they were treated like animals.

The Irish raided England for slaves, who they used themselves or sold to Muslims or Vikings. Captives in wars who could not be ransomed, such as those who had no money nor social status, could be made slaves if not killed outright. Women caught in wars became forced wives and concubines. Debtors could become slaves. Children of slaves were automatically slaves, as were children born of mixed parentage. Piracy and trade further supplied slaves. In the Baltic, slavers hunted the Slavonic people, who they forced into slavery. In Spain, slaves included Africans from the Sudan, Slavs, Franks, and Normans. Very poor people sold themselves into slavery. They would conduct a ritual, such as showing up at the church with a rope around their necks, to indicate their willingness to become slaves. Criminals unable to pay fines were sentenced to slavery.

Especially early in the Middle Ages, after their owners died, slaves would be executed in order to serve their master in the next life, too. Usually, slave women were burned on the funeral pyre of their owners, although sometimes slave men also were burned to death.

Slaves were exempt from fines since they could own no property, but they could be maimed or killed instead as punishment for crimes. They had no rights; equally, they had no obligations. By law they were things, not people.

Slavery was still present in the twelfth century, but it practically disappeared in the thirteenth century. After the plague devastated Europe in the fourteenth century, the slave trade increased because of the acute labor shortage. The church eased restrictions against slaves and only prohibited the keeping of Christian slaves. Slaves were imported to Europe and the Middle East from Spain, Africa, Greece, and other countries. By the end of the fourteenth century, every wealthy Italian household had at least a few slaves.

Sometimes clergy members and others sympathetic to their plight bought slaves and freed them. Sometimes they escaped. A slave who escaped and lived in a free city for a year and a day became a free peasant. *See* Feudalism and Women; Social Class.

SUGGESTED READING: Allen Frantzen and Douglas Moffat, eds., *The Work of Work: Servitude, Slavery and Labor in Medieval England* (Rochester, NY: University of Rochester Press, 1994); Ruth Mazo Karras, *Slavery and Society in Medieval Scandinavia* (New Haven, CT: Yale University Press, 1988); Kishori Saran Lal, *Muslim Slave System in Medieval India* (Columbia, MO: South Asia Books, 1994); David A. E. Pelteret, *Slavery in Early Mediaeval England: From the Reign of Alfred Until the Twelfth Century* (London: Boydell and Brewer, 1995).

Social Class

Throughout the Middle Ages, social class in Europe was rigidly hierarchical. It was primarily a matter of birth, although commoners could be ennobled for extra-ordinary service to the Crown (which sometimes took the form of a large sum of money).

In Anglo-Saxon England, social stand-ing was identified partly by a person's wergild, the price to be paid to his or her family should he or she be murdered. An earl might have a wergild three times that of a commoner. Slaves had no wergild, but their owners had to be compensated for the loss, usually with a gold coin.

Early on, there were few nobles but many thanes, who owned land and were prosperous. Ceorls (churls) were a step below thanes. They were mostly farmers, freemen who could own land. Serfs were the next lowest level. They were bound to the land and were bought and sold (or given and taken) with it. Slaves were the lowest level of all. They were bought and sold, like property. Very poor people some-times sold themselves into slavery.

Later in the Middle Ages in Europe, the classes became more stratified. Thou-sands of landowners held land as knight service, that is, with the obligation to serve as a knight. Only a few thousand were dubbed knights at any one time. Being dubbed was a costly process, and a dubbed knight had more obligations, so many el-igible people declined the honor. Receiv-ing a knighthood was the easiest way for a commoner to enter the ranks of the no-bility, although marrying into the nobil-ity was also a time-honored process.

The ranks of nobility were as fol-lows: the earl was the highest rank below the prince or king. Earldoms were con-ferred only on members of the royal fam-ily, until later in the Middle Ages. Next came dukes, who could be extremely pow-erful, with their own followers and their own private armies. Then came barons, knights, and squires, in that order. In the

late Middle Ages, gentlemen, who were below knights in the social order, became considered members of the lesser gentry, along with squires (or esquires, as they came to be known). Nobles made up about one percent of the population, but most of what historians know about the Mid-dle Ages concerns them.

Royalty

Rulers of a kingdom or empire. Most European royal customs derived from the rituals of medieval Germanic tribes, such as loyalty to the clan chief, which trans-formed into loyalty to the king. The idea of a hereditary monarchy was a medieval invention. Formerly, tribal chieftains had been selected by merit, valor, worth, and warrior success.

Early kings ruled for life or until they proved unworthy of the job. By the four-teenth century, only the Holy Roman em-peror was elected — because the church insisted on it — and this was done by care-fully controlled electors.

The royalty were concerned about making statements of status. Their ret-inues wore their livery. They sponsored feasts, tournaments, hunts, and other pop-ular entertainments. They were liberal in gifts to gain support; followers depended on these gifts to survive. In some areas, queens awarded the gifts to the ruler's fol-lowers; more often, the king determined who would receive what. Queens often ruled as regents for minor sons and dur-ing periods in which the king was trav-eling. How much power she could actually succeed in wielding depended on the woman, since female regencies were almost always under attack by male relatives and others eager to gain their share of power.

Nobility

The aristocracy that ruled and made decisions about government came to be called the nobility. In the Middle Ages, many Roman and other European families intermarried with Goths, Vandals, Huns, and other Germanic tribes. If they were rich enough and had enough followers, they could become members of the privileged class. People who were good at war became nobles.

Early in the period, ennoblement ended when the person who had earned it died. Later, some forms of ennoblement were passed on from father to son. Women were not eligible for titles, but as the wife or daughter of a man who had one, they could pass a title on to another man (a husband or a son).

Nobles owned the land or held it as a fief from the king, and they controlled the revenues derived from it. They ruled over non-nobles in their territory, except for the clergy and the merchants who were citizens of free towns or communes. Noblemen lived by their swords and rode on horseback in battle, since to go on foot was non-noble. Traditionally, a gentleman or noble was a feudal warrior or the descendant of one, who lived in a rural castle or manor.

Nobles were encouraged to spend by the culture's emphasis on status, generosity, and expectations, such as having many well-dressed servants. They had to balance this with prudence and economy. Budgeting was understood but not always followed.

There was some movement through the social classes. Soldiers were knighted during battles, and rich traders and merchants married into the gentry. Outsiders could be ennobled for service to the king. They frequently paid for the privilege. This was lucrative to the Crown. Nobles could sink into peasantry, if they became bankrupt. They could also lose their status by undertaking certain actions, such

as going into trade. Class loyalty often transcended national boundaries.

In urban settings, the merchant had status similar to that of the lesser gentry (knights, squires, and gentlemen). Master craftsmen were the equivalent of yeomen, whereas journeymen and laborers were the equivalent of rural laborers or cottars.

The clergy had a similar arrangement of social class. The archbishop was similar to an earl in the power he held. Archbishops were, in fact, almost always noble. Bishops were similar to dukes, abbots were like barons, rectors and vicars similar to the lesser gentry, and parish priests and the lesser clergy were like peasants or craftsmen.

Peasants

Of peasants or commoners there were several categories. Yeomen, sometimes called franks, franklins, or freemen, held land outright and were free peasants. They could sell their land with the lord's approval and could leave the manor. Villeins or villains (the word later came to have a negative connotation) were neither slave nor free; they are commonly called serfs. They had to have the permission of the lord to leave the land. They paid rent for the use of the land or worked for the lord in exchange for the use of the land, much like a sharecropper.

If a woman inherited land, she often had to marry to take possession of the land on the theory that she could not cultivate it herself. She could be fined if she did not marry. The lord chose her husband.

A man who married an heiress often took her family's name to keep the holding clearly attached to her family. If there were no children, the land reverted to her family. If there were children, he had a lifetime right to use the estate, the same as a widow. Women who married heirs sometimes took their names, again to keep a holding clearly attached to a particular family. A widow was merely the custodian of her husband's land. After death, the holding reverted to her husband's family or passed to the husband's eldest son.

Peasants paid a household tax, tithed to the church, and raised the ransom if their lord were captured in battle. They were required to pay fees to use the lord's mills and ovens and were not allowed to build their own. Peasants were required to tend to the lord's fields and harvest them before their own. The church taught that not doing this would cause them to burn in hell. At death, the peasant owed his or her best possession, called the heriot, to the lord.

Most peasants lived in buildings that also housed their animals. All the members of a family shared one big bed. There was no idea of privacy. In the summer, peasants went naked. Otherwise they wore a loose tunic and blouse. The less prosperous among them lived in huts with dirt floors without even a pallet on which to sleep.

Wealthier peasants owned plows. They might own sixty acres plus a few plow horses and some livestock. They would employ others to work for them. From this group came the franklins, who were freemen, plus artisans and merchants. Below the plow line were the poorest peasants, who eked out a subsistence on the lord's estate.

Marriages were arranged for peasants. The prospective groom's father usually began the negotiations. Unlike nobles, peasants were often in their twenties or thirties before marriage. Men often did not marry until after their father died. Sometimes an elderly father would give

his son his holding in return for maintenance. Often they entered a legal agreement recognized by the courts. If the son did not live up to his promise, he could be fined.

After a marriage agreement was worked out, the two were betrothed, at which time they often began living together. The actual wedding sometimes did not take place until the woman was pregnant or even after a child was born.

Many peasant women did not marry because of a shortage of unmarried men with holdings that would support a family. If a peasant woman did not marry, she would work on her father's or brother's land or leave with her dowry to live in a town, become a servant, or hire out as a laborer. An unmarried woman could live in a lord's manor or in a village as a lodger. Usually poorer women could not become nuns.

Late marriage and short life spans meant fewer children. Also, abortion and contraception were used because family holdings would not support many people. If a peasant woman survived childhood, she often lived to an old age, surviving many husbands. She was supported by the use of her husbands' land throughout her life. She could also purchase a maintenance agreement with a monastery, which would provide a room, food, and sometimes a servant, in exchange for an inheritance. A widow might continue to work the land or give it to her son in return for support. Often she was pressured to remarry. If unable to provide the services owed to her lord in exchange for the holding, she could be forced to forfeit the land.

Independence, inheritance rights, legal standing, and obligations favored peasant women as compared to noblewomen. A peasant woman often inherited a holding and could work it or dispose of it as she pleased (with of course the lord's approval) whereas a noblewoman's holdings were often disputed or stolen or she was otherwise prevented from inheriting. Christine de Pizan said that, although they had many worries and much work to do, peasant women had more control over their lives than noble women.

Husbandmen held enough land to support themselves and their families and were free peasants. Laborers or cottars had no land and existed solely on wages. They were free peasants and lived in cots, hovels, or huts. They worked as day laborers, serving as herders or farmhands. They were the worst off of the free peasants.

Servants worked in the household of the noble. They had no land and worked mainly for their keep, earning little in wages—a pound a year was considered generous. They were free peasants and, depending on the lord, could become if not wealthy then at least comfortable. Peasant women milked cows, fed chickens and geese, sheared sheep, made cheese and butter, tended vegetable gardens, combed flax, spun, and wove. They also assisted with reaping and sowing.

In cities, peasant women dominated the textile trade. Dyers were easily recognized by their stained fingers. Spinning was almost all done by women. Dyeing and weaving were done equally by both men and women.

The worker's clock in town hall regulated work hours. Workers conducted their businesses like factory pieceworkers. A merchant would purchase raw wool. He hired one family to clean it, another to stretch it, another to tease it, another to card it, another to weave it, and another to cut it. The merchant then sold the finished piece at a fair. Workers could only work for one merchant, however, and

merchants ran the town government. If a merchant decided not to continue the process (for instance, he ran out of money), the worker was left with the cloth and no payment. This occurred often enough to create class tensions.

Working-class women in cities experienced similar conditions to rural peasants. Many women sold food and beverages and worked as innkeepers and teachers. There are even records of female blacksmiths and armorers.

In English guilds, women had less status than in continental guilds, although there were many restrictions on women's participation in guilds everywhere.

Women worked the land with their husbands and followed them into trade. Women ran their households and businesses while their husbands were away on business. Often they learned to read and write in order to correspond and keep each other informed.

Serfs and Slaves

Serfs were a level below free peasants. They were unfree peasants. They were bound to the land and could be bought and sold with it, but they were not exactly slaves. They had guaranteed rights and privileges. In England they were called villeins. They were loaned land by the lord, and they worked it as well as the lord's land. Serfs were supposed to provide every service needed by the lord. The lord could marry them off as he wished. A law called formariage prevented a serf from marrying outside the lord's estate. Female serfs rarely married. They were often sexually exploited. They were considered on a par with beasts. Their mates were arranged by the lord.

All the serf owed reverted to the lord if the serf died without children. Children of serfs belonged to the lord's land. Serfs could purchase their freedom, marry a free man or free woman to become free, enter the church (with their lord's approval), or flee and live for a year and a day in a free town or on royal property. Women of servile origin had to pay their lord in order to marry, since he would lose her labor and had to be compensated for it.

Slaves were the lowest social class. They had no rights and could be bought and sold like property. *See* Feudalism and Women; Occupations; Queens and Queenship; Slavery and Women; Wars and Warfare.

SUGGESTED READING: Theodore Evergates, ed., *Aristocratic Women in Medieval France* (Philadelphia: University of Pennsylvania Press, 1999); R. H. Hilton, *Class Conflict and the Crisis of Feudalism: Essays in Medieval Social History* (London: Hambledon, 1986); David Nicholas, *The Evolution of the Medieval World: Society, Government and Thought in Europe, 312–1500* (New York: Longman, 1992).

Sophia *see* **Zoë**

Steinunn

In *Njal's Saga,* which describes Icelandic Christian missionaries, a pagan woman who defends paganism and tries to convert the missionary priest Þangbrandr. *See* Conversion.

Subh (10th century)

Muslim political figure. She married Al-Hakam II, caliph of Cordoba, who died in 976. She was the mother of Hisham II, who she wanted to succeed to the caliphate. She allied with several political leaders in order to defend against a conspiracy. One of the leaders, Ibn Abi Amir, became romantically involved with her, and she acted as his protector. With her help, he became appointed first minister.

Sumptuary Laws

Legal rules regulating what members of various social classes could wear and eat. For a fee, one could petition for an exemption. *See* Clothing.

T

Tale of the Genji

First known novel ever written, it was composed in 1010 by Murasaki Shikibu, a female courtier in Japan. The work depicts a fictional court based on the Heian imperial court. The adventures of the fictional Prince Genki are recounted. The novel grows more philosophical as it progresses. *See* Murasaki Shikibu.

Teresa of Castile   (d. 1130)

Illegitimate daughter of Alfonso VI, king of León (also known as Alfonso I of Castile, when he assumed the throne there in 1072). Teresa married Henry of Burgundy. In 1094, Alfonso gave them rulership of what is now Portugal. This was the beginning of the independent kingdom of Portugal. After her father died, Teresa and her husband sought control of León. She continued to seek power there even after Henry's death in 1114.

In 1128, her son Alfonso Henriques forced her out of Portugal. She died in 1130. He refused to acknowledge the overlordship of Alfonso VII and worked to create an independent Portugal, which was finally recognized in 1143.

Thamar (d. 1313)

Also Ithamar; Caterina. Princess of Taranto in southeast Italy. The second daughter of Nicephorus Comnenus Ducas, the son and successor of Michael II, despot of Epiros. Her mother, Marie, was a niece of the Byzantine emperor, Michael VIII, and dominated rulership of the despotate.

In 1294, Thamar was betrothed to Philip of Anjou, the prince of Taranto. Philip's father, heir to the Angevin kingdom, wished to reestablish the empire of his family; Nicephorus needed an ally against Andronicus II, emperor of Byzantium, who had threatened the independence of Epiros. Thamar's dowry included the lands of her aunt Helena Doukaina, plus an annual income and several castles. To his subjects, it looked as if Nicephorus were selling the despotate in order to maintain its independence. Thamar's mother was desperate to prevent this. She wanted Thamar to marry the heir to the Byzantine throne, Michael IX. This would have made Epiros part of the Byzantine Empire, but both the emperor and the church declined.

Philip promised that he would allow Thamar to continue practicing her orthodox faith. Their marriage took place in 1294, as arranged. Thamar was forced to change her name to Caterina. Philip did not abide by his promise to allow her to practice her faith, causing tension between the two families. Nonetheless, Thamar and Philip had five children.

Two years later, Thamar's father, Nicephorus, died, and her mother became regent. Thamar's brother Thomas became heir to the despotate. In 1299, her husband, Philip, was captured by the Arago-

nese and remained in captivity for three years as Thamar attempted to ransom him.

Marie, still seeking to link Epiros to the Byzantine Empire, proposed that her son should marry the granddaughter of Emperor Andronicus II, but again the emperor showed little interest in such an alliance. Marie then refused Philip's rights to the dowry lands, wanting her son to have them instead. As a result, Philip waged war in 1304 but was defeated. He made another try in 1306 but was again forced to withdraw. He made Thamar sell her jewelry and personal possessions to pay for the war. Marie was eventually successful in linking the despotate to Constantinople. In 1307, her son Thomas did indeed marry a granddaughter of Andronicus II. Thomas remained despot until his murder in 1318.

In 1309, Thamar's husband, Philip, charged her with adultery, claiming she had sexual intercourse with forty different lords of his court. This was merely a pretext to divorce her. After their marriage ended, Thamar became a nun. Four years later her former husband married Catherine of Valois, but by then Thamar was dead.

SUGGESTED READING: Guglielm Cavallo, *The Byzantines* (Chicago: University of Chicago Press, 1997); Warren T. Treadgold, *A History of the Byzantine State and Society* (Stanford, CA: Stanford University Press, 1997).

Theodelinda (c. 570–620)

The daughter of Duke Garibald of the Bavarian ducal house of Agilolfings. She married Authari, king of the Lombards, who died in 590. After his death, she "chose" the new king by marrying him. Although chroniclers claim she made the choice, more probably the choice was made for her. She married Agilulf in 590. He was an Arian Christian. Theodelinda was able to convert him to Catholicism. Under his rule, Lombardy achieved a period of relative peace and stability. He reigned until Theodelinda's son Adaloald reached maturity in 616. Adaloald then became king and ruled until 626. Theodelinda's daughter Gundiperga married two men, each of whom became kings of Lombardy. When these lines died out, the descendants of Theodelinda's brother Gundoald became monarchs.

SUGGESTED READING: Neil Christie, *The Lombards: The Ancient Langobards* (Oxford: Blackwell, 1995).

Theodora (500–548)

Byzantine empress. Her father was a bearkeeper and her mother an acrobat. She herself was a notorious courtesan vilified for her insatiable appetites. She had a stage act of farce and burlesque in which she performed bizarre sexual antics. Later, she became mistress to a man who abandoned her in North Africa. She earned her way home as a prostitute, but apparently underwent a spiritual conversion.

She met Justinian when she was in her late twenties. He wanted to marry her but was opposed in this by his aunt Empress Lupicina. The two married in 525 after Lupicina's death. Theodora and Justinian became empress and emperor after Justin's death in 527. Theodora ruled equally at Justinian's side.

In 532, a mixture of high taxes, religious conflict, and political hostilities caused the Nika Insurrection, in which 30,000 people died. Although Justinian wanted to leave Constantinople during the rioting, Theodora convinced him to stay. If he had left, historians agree, he would probably have lost the throne.

Theodora was a Monophysite and

punished those who denounced the religion as heresy. This put her into conflict with Pope Silverius, who refused to support Monophysitism. Theodora had him deposed and exiled in 537. Later, he was venerated as a martyr. She supported the Jakobites in the face of official Byzantine persecution. This medieval Christian sect was founded by Jakob bar Adai, a sixth-century Monophysite leader. Jakob established a church in Syria that has survived as the Syrian Orthodox church because of the intervention of Empress Theodora.

After her death, it was discovered that she had kept an ex-patriarch, convicted of heresy, in her gynaceum for twelve years. *See* Heresy; Lupicina.

SUGGESTED READING: Lynda Garland, *Byzantine Empresses: Women and Power in Byzantium, AD 527–1204* (New York: Routledge, 1999); John Moorhead, *Justinian* (Reading, MA: Addison-Wesley, 1994).

Theodora (7th century)

Byzantine empress. She married emperor Justinian II in 693, after he escaped from exile and sought aid from Khazar Khagan Ibuzir. Theodora was the khazar's sister. After her marriage, she changed her name to Theodora.

In 704, Justinian returned to Constantinople to reclaim the throne. Theodora, pregnant at the time, remained behind with her brother. Two years later, she arrived in Constantinople, her husband restored to the throne. She became the first foreign-born empress of the Byzantine Empire. Her son Tiberius was murdered when he was six years old. Justinian II was again overthrown in 711.

SUGGESTED READING: J. F. Haldon, *Byzantium in the Seventh Century: The Transformation of a Culture* (New York: Cambridge University Press, 1991).

Theodora (9th century)

Byzantine empress. She married Emperor Theophilus, an Iconoclast (an opponent of figurative religious art). Theodora was an Iconodule, a venerator of religious icons. When Theophilus died in 842, Theodora became regent for their two-year-old son. She made it a point of her reign to eradicate Iconoclasm. In 843, she convened an ecclesiastical council that condemned the practice of Iconoclasm.

In 843, with the support of her uncle and her brother, she deposed the patriarch of Constantinople, John the Grammarian, and condemned prominent Iconoclasts (excluding her late husband) as heretics.

Her brother and uncle were soon stripped of their power. She continued to rule, however, with the Logothete Theoctistus, a eunuch and patrician.

The two co-rulers improved education, increased the treasury, and defeated Muslim attacks on the empire. Theodora in particular persecuted the Paulicians, a Christian sect that opposed much of church doctrine. Over 100,000 members were reportedly murdered during her reign.

Her brother Bardas killed Theoctistus in 855. The following year her son Michael III was named emperor, and she lost power.

SUGGESTED READING: Nicolas Oikonomides, *Byzantium from the Ninth Century to the Fourth Crusade: Studies, Texts, Monuments* (New York: Variorum, 1992); Spring Symposium of Byzantine Studies, *Byzantium in the Ninth Century: Dead or Alive?* (Brookfield, CT: Ashgate, 1998).

Theodora (973–1056)

Byzantine empress. Sister of Empress Zoë, she had been banished to a convent around 1025 by her jealous sister. In 1042,

Zoë's adopted heir, Michael the Caulker, banished Zoë from the empire. When the populace found out what had happened, they restored Zoë and blinded Michael. Because Zoë was too old to govern effectively by herself, the populace sought out Theodora and, over Theodora's protests, crowned her co-emperor. Later, Zoë married Constantine Monomachus (Constantine IX) in order to add stability to the empire. After Zoë died, Constantine had no claim to the throne, and Theodora ruled in her own right. Although seventy-seven years old, she ruled effectively until her death.

On her deathbed, she named Michael VI Stratioticus as her successor, although some historians dispute that she was capable of naming an heir at that point. Theodora died in 1056. Michael was overthrown the following year. *See* Zoë (978–1050).

Theodora Raoulaina (c. 1240–1300)

Byzantine noblewoman, nun, and scholar. Born in the empire of Nicaea, she was a niece to Emperor Michael VIII Paleologus. In 1256, she married George Mouzalon, a man of inferior status. When the reigning emperor (Theodore II) died in 1258, George Mouzalon assumed the regency of the heir apparent, John IV. The army revolted, murdering all the members of the Mouzalon family who they could find, including Theodora's husband. Theodora protested the massacre, but her uncle Michael did nothing to stop the army. When it was over, he assumed regency of Theodora's infant son and became the sole emperor of Byzantium.

John Raoul supported Michael's claim to the throne and as a reward, he was given Theodora to marry. He was a better match for her, of a higher social class than her first husband. Theodora was apparently amenable to the marriage. They were married in 1261 and had two daughters. In 1274, he died. Theodora became a nun after his death but continued to actively oppose many of her uncle's policies.

Michael attempted to unify the Byzantine church with the Roman church, to the dismay of his subjects. Theodora opposed him, as did his own sister. Together with her mother, they incited others to rebel against him. As a result, Theodora and her mother were banished to a prison fortress on the coast of the Black Sea. In 1281, Michael was excommunicated. The following year he died, and Theodora and her mother were freed.

At heart, Theodora was a member of the Arsenites, a fanatical Christian sect, but she was more tolerant of orthodox Christians than most members. At the time of her mother's death in 1284, she restored a monastery in Constantinople, becoming known as the second founder of the monastery of Saint Andrew of Crete. She indulged her love of learning there, pursuing a monastic, scholarly life. She acquired a library of her own and corresponded with other intellectuals. In 1295, she attempted to intervene in a rebellion by convincing the insurgents to leave in peace, but she failed. She died five years later.

SUGGESTED READING: Donald M. Nicol, *The Last Centuries of Byzantium: 1261–1453* (New York: Cambridge University Press, 1993); E. J. Stormon, *Towards the Healing of Schism: The Sees of Rome and Constantinople, Public Statements and Correspondence* (Mahwah, NJ: Paulist Press, 1987); Warren T. Treadgold, *A History of the Byzantine State and Society* (Stanford, CA: Stanford University Press, 1997).

Theodotë (8th century)

Byzantine empress. A court lady and mistress to Emperor Constantine VI, who divorced his wife (Mary of Amnia) in 795 and married her. The following year, Theodotë had a son. The clergy were horrified at Constantine's conduct. Her marriage was not acceptable, and her son could not be considered the heir. Constantine was soon deposed by his mother, Irene. *See* Irene, Empress.

Theophano (d. 897)

Byzantine empress. She married Byzantine Emperor Leo VI, called Leo the Wise. His father, Emperor Basil, forced Leo to marry her when he was sixteen. Later, when he fell out of favor and was imprisoned, she and her daughter insisted on sharing his sufferings. She grew increasingly pious, going so far as to sleep on a mat in her husband's bedroom. She retired to the convent at Blachernae and died there in 897.

Theophano (b. 940)

Notorious Byzantine empress. A Peloponnesian innkeeper's daughter, she married Emperor Constantine VII, choosing the name Theophano for herself at the time of her marriage. She was known as ambitious and unscrupulous. Almost immediately after her marriage, she banished her husband's five daughters by Helena Lecapenus into different convents. Many officials lost their posts because of her.

She probably began an affair with Constantine's son Romanus. Constantine soon died. Theophano and Romanus reportedly conspired to poison him. In 958, Theophano married Romanus, who had become Emperor Romanus II after the murder of his father. Theophano held most of the power in the Byzantine Empire.

After Romanus died in 963, she was

suspected of poisoning him. She seemed wholly capable of such a crime, never mind that she had given birth to their fourth child just two days before Romanus's death.

Her two sons, Basil and Constantine, who then became co-emperors, were six and three years old, respectively. Such a long minority was perilous to the stability of the empire. In order to maintain power, Theophano summoned Nicephorus Phocas, the renowned general, to help solidify her position. That same year, she married him, but the legality of the marriage was challenged by the patriarch, who said they were within the proscribed bounds of consanguinity, and Phocas must repudiate her or face excommunication. Phocas called a council of bishops who determined, not surprisingly, that the marriage was acceptable. Nonetheless, the patriarch refused to yield. Eventually he was forced to allow the marriage when information showed that they were not within the proscribed degrees.

Shortly after her marriage to Phocas, Theophano fell in love with his friend John Tzimisces. The two plotted to murder Phocas, which they managed in December 969. The patriarch refused to crown John as emperor until Theophano was sent away. She was forced into exile at the island of Proti. Her daughter, also called Theophano, married the German king, Otto II. *See* Theophano of Byzantium (956–991).

SUGGESTED READING: Adelbert Davids, *The Empress Theophano: Byzantium and the West at the Turn of the First Millennium* (New York: Cambridge University Press, 1995); Lynda Garland, *Byzantine Empresses: Women and Power in Byzantium, AD 527–1204* (New York: Routledge, 1999).

Theophano of Byzantium   (956–991)

Queen of Germany and Holy Roman empress. The daughter of the notorious Byzantine Empress Theophano, who married and murdered three emperors.

When Theophano was sixteen, Byzantine Emperor John Tzimisces, with whom her mother had had an affair, arranged for her to marry Otto, the son of the German king, Otto I. This would create an alliance between the Byzantine and Holy Roman empires.

In 973, Otto I died, and Theophano's husband, now Otto II, succeeded him. He died ten years later when his son, who would be Otto III, was only three years old. Theophano, with her mother-in-law, Adelaide, served as regent for the child. The Saxons were suspicious of Theophano, since she was Greek, and they did not care for a female ruler.

This tension was further exacerbated when Henry, duke of Bavaria, kidnapped the young Otto and demanded that the regents cede power to him. The other nobles objected to Henry's treatment of Otto, and the child was returned to his mother unharmed.

In 991, Theophano died, and Adelaide continued to serve as regent. Otto reached the age of majority in 994 and began ruling in his own right. *See* Adelaide of Italy, Saint; Theophano (b. 940).

SUGGESTED READING: Heinrich Fichtenau, *The Carolingian Empire* (Toronto: University of Toronto Press, 1978); Jonathan W. Zophy, *The Holy Roman Empire* (Westport, CT: Greenwood, 1981).

Theutberga   (9th century)

Frankish queen. She married Clothar (Lothar) II, king of the Franks. They had no children. Lothar tried to divorce her and marry his mistress, Waldrada, with whom he had several children, in order to secure a legitimate line of succession, but the pope refused to allow the divorce.

Thousand and One Nights see
Arabian Nights

Thyri Klacksdottir (10th century)

Queen of Denmark. A Christian of
unknown origin, she married Gorm the
Old, king of Denmark, who was a pagan.
According to tradition, Thyri was beautiful, saintly, and chaste. She was the mother
of Harald Bluetooth, who became king of
Denmark.

The Danevirke, a series of defensive
earthworks that controlled access to Jutland (the mainland of Denmark), has
been attributed to her.

A memorial that Gorm erected as a
tribute to her uses the word *Danmark* for
the first time to refer to the territory he
held.

Tibors (c. 1130–1182)

A female troubadour, probably the
earliest one, from Provence. She was the
sister and guardian of the famous troubadour Raimbaut d'Orange. She married
several times, including first to Gaufroy
de Mornas and then to Bertrand des Baux,
a powerful lord who was assassinated in
1181. Her second husband was a major patron of troubadours. She had three sons.

Touga

With her sister Bouga, part of a legendary family that included five brothers.
They drove the Avar rulers from Croatia
and subjected the others. They were from
"White Croatia," possibly an area north
of the Carpathians. They were probably
ethnically Iranian. The story is probably
based on a migration that took place
about the seventh century.

Treasure of the City of Ladies

Also called *Book of Three Virtues*.
Written by Christine de Pizan in 1405, the
book served as a sequel to *The Book of the
City of Ladies*. Instead of being a collection
of exempla, however, it is more of a practical guide for women living in the day-
to-day world. Christine advises women to
stick together instead of gossiping about
each other and to be tolerant of one another, whether older or younger. She gives
suggestions to new widows, derived from
her own experience, and offers advice for
going to court. *See Book of the City of
Ladies*; Christine de Pizan.

Trobairitz

Female troubadours, of whom twenty
are known to have been writing in the
Languedoc (southern) region of France in
the twelfth and thirteenth centuries.

Trota *see* Trotula of Salerno

Trotula of Salerno (11th century)

Also Trota. A physician who practiced medicine in Salerno. She made gyne-
cology her specialty (many female practitioners were midwives and gynecologists).
She wrote about medicine, something few
of her colleagues did. Some historians insist she must have been a man. *See* Medicine and Health.

Tzu-Yeh

Chinese poet who wrote in the early
medieval period. Her most famous work is
Ballad of Mulan, which is about a woman
soldier disguised as a man and the adventures she has.

U

Uksáhkká

Female household spirit in medieval Scandinavia who protected young children and the entrance to the home. She lived near the doorway. *See* Religion and Women.

Urðr

Female spirit associated with fate in medieval Scandinavian folklore, similar to the Greek Fates. There are three: Urðr, Verðandi, and Skuld, equivalent to Past, Present, and Future. Collectively, they are called Nornor. *See* Religion and Women.

Urraca (11th century)

Queen of León. Sister to Sancho III Garcés, called Sancho el Mayor, king of Navarre, one of the Christian states. She married Alfonso V, king of León. When she was widowed in 1027, she became the regent for her stepson Vermudo III.

She hired an assassin to kill her brother Sancho in a conspiracy to help Alfonso VI, her son, gain the throne in the same year. Her bid was successful. Her granddaughter, also named Urraca, ruled León.

Urraca (1081–1126)

Heiress to the kingdom of León and Castile and the territory of Burgundy and queen of Aragón and Navarre. As the daughter of Alfonso VI of León and Castile, she had a legitimate claim to his throne. She was the granddaughter of Queen Urraca of León. She married Raymond of Burgundy in 1091. Together they ruled Galicia as a petty kingdom subordinate to Alfonso. They had a son, Alfonso Raimúndez, who would become Alfonso VII.

In 1107, Raymond died. A year later, Urraca was acknowledged as his heir by the nobles. Circumstances indicated that she should marry again, so her father chose Alfonso I, the king of Aragón and Navarre. They married in 1109. She retained sovereignty of her own kingdom.

Urraca and her new husband were temperamentally unsuited to each other. Their marriage was uncanonical, and the pope nullified it within the year and threatened to excommunicate both of them if they did not terminate their relationship. Then Urraca and her husband went to war against each other. In 1114, her husband finally withdrew, and both ruled their own realms separately.

Weak and vacillating, Urraca kept supporting different factions, abandoning one group to enlist the support of another. In 1117, the citizens revolted, and she was attacked and beaten. Her son restored order, and she continued to rule.

She died in 1126, and her son assumed sole rulership of León and Castile, marking the beginning of the Burgundian dynasty that lasted well into the fourteenth century.

SUGGESTED READING: Simon Barton, *The Aristocracy of Twelfth-Century Leon and Castile* (New York: Cambridge University Press, 1997); Bernard Reilly, *The Kingdom of León-Castilla Under King Alfonso VII, 1126–1157* (Philadelphia: University of Pennsylvania Press, 1998).

V

Valkyries

Supernatural warrior princesses who took human form and magically assisted their chosen male warriors in medieval Scandinavia. Associated with the Norse god Odin, they were responsible for a warrior's conduct and death in battle. *See* Religion and Women.

Verina (5th century)

Empress mother. She married Byzantine Emperor Leo. Basiliscus, her brother, was an important political influence. Her son-in-law Zeno became emperor through the manipulations of his wife, Verina's daughter Ariadne. Verina and her brother became Zeno's implacable enemies. Basiliscus himself wanted to be emperor, whereas Verina wanted her lover, Patricius, (then master of the office) to be emperor.

Verina and her brother thus conspired to depose Zeno. In 475, she sent Zeno a message, saying the army and the people were rising against him. Zeno believed her and left Constantinople to seek refuge in Isauria. Basiliscus was named emperor and had Verina's lover assassinated. Two years later, Zeno returned and reclaimed the throne.

The Isaurian general Illus helped depose Zeno, then helped restore him. Later, Verina tried to have Illus assassinated, but she was unsuccessful. In 479, Zeno asked for Illus's military help. He agreed, under the condition that Verina be handed over to him as his prisoner; this request Zeno was happy to grant. For some years, she was held prisoner in a fortress in Isauria. Her daughter Ariadne, herself an empress, tried unsuccessfully to have Illus mur-

dered for his treatment of her mother. Later, Zeno freed Verina, who crowned the usurper Leontius in 484 and helped him establish a rival court. She died soon thereafter. *See* Ariadne.

SUGGESTED READING: Michael Grant, *From Rome to Byzantium: The Fifth Century AD* (New York: Routledge, 1998); Stephen Williams, *The Rome That Did Not Fall: The Survival of the East in the Fifth Century* (New York: Routledge, 2000).

Verðandi

In medieval Scandinavian folklore, female spirit associated with fate, similar to the Greek Fates. There are three: Urðr, Verðandi, and Skuld, equivalent to Past, Present, and Future. Collectively, they are called Nornor. *See* Religion and Women.

Violante Visconti (1355–1386)

Notorious member of the famous Visconti family, known as the "Vipers of Milan," she was suspected of killing three husbands. The family ruled Milan and its environs for almost two hundred years.

Violante married Lionel of England, duke of Clarence, in 1368. When he died of a fever four months after the wedding, she was suspected of foul play. Relations between England and Milan grew strained during this period. Then she married a sadistic seventeen-year-old, the marquis of Montferrat, who died violently. Finally, she married one of her uncle Bernabò's sons, who was killed, probably at her urging, by her brother.

Virgin Mary *see* Cult of the Virgin Mary

Virginity *see* **Sexuality; Marriage and Family; Religion and Women**

W

Waldrada (9th century)

Mistress to Chlotar (Lothar) II, king of the Franks, with whom she had several children. Chlothar attempted to divorce his wife in order to marry her, so that he could assure a legitimate line of succession, but the pope would not allow it.

Wars and Warfare

The political history of the Middle Ages is one of almost constant warfare. In the absence of their husbands, sons, and fathers for military reasons, medieval noblewomen routinely ruled in their place. In peasant households, the burden of work fell to women when men were conscripted to serve in the lord's army. Often, even if a peasant soldier was not killed in war, he never found his way home again. However, nobles relied more upon their knights than upon their peasants to wage war.

Numerous accounts exist of women leading troops into battle, not least Joan of Arc and Matilda of Tuscany. However, this was by no means common. Instead, women usually protected castles and manors and conducted business and court dealings as regents for their absent male relatives.

Warfare often meant siege. Women suffered along with men when a castle or walled town was attacked by soldiers. As victims of war, women were raped, murdered, abducted; sold into slavery, or forced to become wives, concubines, and camp followers. Rape and torture were typical instruments of terror. Women were sometimes burned to death to provide an example. Men were sometimes ransomed, but more frequently killed, since prisoners were an encumbrance. Babies and children were usually murdered, often brutally (by being speared or crushed under wagon wheels). These atrocities were meant to reduce resistance.

Such warfare brought land and treasure to the victor and therefore was an important source of revenue. By the later Middle Ages, however, war was so detrimental to trade and the economy — which required stability and peace — that it actually impeded material gain. *See* Crusades; Joan of Arc; Matilda of Tuscany.

SUGGESTED READING: Charles Oman, *Art of War in the Middle Ages, AD 378–1515* (Ithaca, NY: Cornell University Press, 1960); Charles Osman, *Armies and Warfare in the Middle Ages: The English Experience* (New Haven, CT: Yale University Press, 1999).

Wergild

Also referred to as blood money or blood price. The payment rendered to the family of a crime victim by the perpetrator of the crime, especially common among Germanic tribes, such as the Anglo-Saxons, in the early Middle Ages. It was given instead of a blood penalty and was supposed to prevent ongoing feuds and retaliations. The clan or tribe of a person who had injured or killed another person would raise the money for the penalty and give it to the victim or the victim's family. Tribal laws stated the appropriate payment or man-price (also known as honor price). According to Frankish law codes, a free Frank was worth 200 soldi (gold Roman coins). A free Anglo-Saxon was worth 200 shillings, and a free Irishman was worth 6 sets. Free women were worth slightly less. Nobles were worth three or four times that amount. Peasants and slaves were worth smaller amounts, although their owners or lords had to be compensated for their loss. The value of an oath in court was related to a person's man-price. *See* Crime, Punishment, and Violence; Law and Women.

White Ladies *see* Order of Saint Mary Magdalene

Wife of Bath

Character in Chaucer's *Canterbury Tales*. She tells the "Wife of Bath's Tale." In Chaucer's story, the Wife points out that all of the books are written by men, so they give women a bad reputation. She tells the story of a knight who is tricked into marriage with an ugly woman (a witch). The witch asks him to make a choice: she can turn into a beautiful woman by day, so that he can be proud of appearing at court with her, or she can turn into a beautiful woman by night, so that he can enjoy sexual relations with her. After thinking about the dilemma, he asks her to make her own choice. As a reward for his letting her choose, she turns into a beautiful woman permanently. This parody of courtly romance reveals some of the misogyny prevalent in the Middle Ages.

SUGGESTED READING: Geoffrey Chaucer, *The Riverside Chaucer* (New York: Houghton Mifflin, 1987).

Wife's Lament

Anglo-Saxon poem composed around 900. It is tentatively ascribed to a female poet; it echoes the complaints typical of other Anglo-Saxon poems, including betrayal and exile.

Winter's Nights Festival

Household ritual mentioned in the Icelandic sagas. The festival took place during winter with only family members and invited guests present. A sacrifice of some kind was made. These sacrifices (and the entire festival) were the responsibility of women, although men could participate in the ritual. *See* Religion and Women.

Wise Women

Older women in villages who knew herbal remedies. They have been called "part-time witches." *See* Witchcraft and the Arcane Arts.

Witchcraft and the Arcane Arts

The practice of witchcraft, magic, and sorcery was accepted without question in the Middle Ages. The belief in witchcraft stemmed partly from the conviction that the devil was active on earth and partly as a result of a rudimentary understanding of science. Witchcraft explained otherwise inexplicable events. Natural disasters such as storms or unusual weather patterns were attributed to fairies or goblins. A sudden death was the work of a demon.

Evil spirits surrounded people in the Middle Ages. Water nymphs lured men to death by drowning. Thirteen was an evil number and Friday an evil day. Shooting stars were bad omens, as were vultures, cats, howling wolves, comets, and eclipses.

Werewolves and vampires existed. Satyrs, tritons, incubi, and giants inhabited the world. The church even encouraged such superstitions, saying that evil events were satanic in origin. The fear of Satan kept people better behaved than the fear of God.

Practitioners of witchcraft were often — almost always — women. The Germanic people viewed women as powerful magicians, oracles, and fortunetellers. Women were also considered prone to evil and to spiritual and supernatural manipulation, so they were more susceptible to becoming practitioners.

Witchcraft, magic, and sorcery were practiced throughout Europe. In Scandinavia, the arcane arts had mostly died out by the thirteenth century. In other parts of Europe, the worst persecutions of witches occurred in the sixteenth and seventeenth centuries. Witches were persecuted because they committed crimes, but also because the practice of witchcraft gave them an unfair advantage over other people.

Many rituals were communal and stemmed from pagan religious rituals. Witches were suspected of flying to covens and of coupling with demons, from whom they obtained their power.

Magic and witchcraft affected people's daily lives. Lawful magic was practiced by doctors and faith healers. Medieval people believed that the angels guided the stars, so astrology could reveal divine intent. Even Pope Honorious III was thought to be a sorcerer, and several grimoires, or books of magic, were attributed to him. Legitimate sorcerers believed their images of wax or lead required baptism, exorcism, and other rites of the church to work. They felt that the celebration of mass was necessary for them to have powers, and they invoked God to help them control demons.

The Christian root of some charms is obvious. For instance, a corruption of a line from the Greek mass was used in an Anglo-Saxon charm recorded in the twelfth century. Many liturgical elements were used in the practice of magic, such as holy water mixed with healing herbs. The sign of the cross was used as a potent symbol.

But some theologians opposed this, saying that even if sorcery were used for good — to find a stray goat, for example — the fact that the help came from outside the church (which insisted on prayer, saints, priests, and the pope) made it wrong.

In addition to lawful sorcery, diabolical witchcraft was practiced. Later in the Middle Ages, all sorcery, magic, and witchcraft was considered to come from a contract with the devil. Accused practitioners of diabolical magic were forced to confess during torture. The accused sometimes believed in their powers or were willing to acknowledge powers attributed to them. They were accused of consorting with the devil, of flying at night, and of shape changing. Sometimes the accused were practicing witches. The herbs they took as part of their rituals probably induced hallucinations that made them believe they could fly or that they possessed supernatural powers. Such witches were the willing accomplices of the devil. They participated in assemblies (covens) of witches and had intercourse with other members and "demons." In exchange they believed they were given the power to cast spells on neighbors, make men impotent, and cause livestock to die.

Early in the fifth century, Saint Augustine condemned the practice of all magic, even so-called good magic, but throughout the Middle Ages, it was accepted as part of life.

By the thirteenth century, most people were opposed to witchcraft. Those people who practiced simple sorcery or folk magic were viewed with suspicion. Mostly women were accused of witchcraft and sorcery because thinkers and theologians considered them more easily tempted by the devil. Accused witches were often old women who were burdens to their families. The Inquisition, established in 1227, sought out witches as heretics. Other changes in medieval society during this time led to an escalating fear of witchcraft and the increased persecution of women, who were often perceived as dangerous and unreliable.

At the Council of Chartres in 1366, a document was issued that anathema be pronounced against sorcerers and sorcery in every church each Sunday. Sorcery, demonology, witchcraft, and the like took on new life during this part of the Middle Ages as survivors of the plague and the interminable warfare tried to control events that were uncontrollable. People terrified by the events of the fourteenth century blamed witches. Hysteria increased. In 1486, two inquisitors, Johann Sprenger and Heinrich Kraemer, wrote *Malleus Maleficarum* (The Witches' Hammer), a handbook on identifying and destroying witches. They also advocated executing the mentally ill and the disabled. Witches were viciously suppressed in the fourteenth and fifteenth centuries, but the worst persecution of witches came in the Renaissance. *See* Heresy; Inquisition; *Malleus Maleficarum*; Medicine and Health; Religion and Women.

SUGGESTED READING: Alberto Ferreiro and Jeffrey Burton Russell, eds., *The Devil, Heresy and Witchcraft in the Middle Ages* (Boston: Brill, 1998); Valeries I. J. Flint, *The Rise of Magic in Early Medieval Europe* (Princeton, NJ: Princeton University Press, 1994); Henricus Institoris and Montague Summers, *The Malleus Maleficarum of Heinrich Kramer and James Sprenger* (New York: Dover, 1971); Alan C. Kors, *Witchcraft in Europe, 1100–1700: A Documentary History* (Philadelphia: University of Pennsylvania Press, 1972).

Witches' Hammer see *Malleus Maleficarum*

Women's Quarters

Area of the home in which women were secluded. In many parts of the world, women were kept separate from men and public life. Sometimes they were virtually imprisoned in the women's quarters to keep them from forming relationships or alliances with inappropriate people and also as a means of simple social control. The women's quarters were variously known as the harem, the seraglio, and the chambre des dames.

X

Ximena *see* **Jimena**

Y

Yang Kuei-fei (8th century)

Mistress to Chinese Emperor Hsüan-Tsung the Brilliant. According to legend, he became so distracted by her that although normally a wise and able ruler, he allowed her enormous influence. He appointed many of her friends and relatives to important positions in the government. In 755, a Chinese general, An Lushan, fomented a rebellion and captured the imperial capital. The emperor was forced to flee and murdered Kuei-fei for the problems she had caused. Civil war followed. The imperial government never recovered from this blow. Hsüan-Tsung's reign and their tragic affair became the inspiration for many legendary and romantic stories.

Yolanda (d. 1219)

Regent for the Latin Empire of Constantinople. The sister of the first two Latin emperors, Baldwin I and Henry of Flanders, also called Henry of Hainault. After their deaths, she became the heir to the Crown. Her husband, Peter of Courtenay, therefore succeeded to the throne, but in 1217, he was captured by the emperor of Nicaea while attempting to recover the city of Durazzo. He spent the rest of his life as a prisoner. Yolanda served as his regent until her death.

Yolanda of Montferrat *see* **Irene Paleologina**

Z

Zoë (6th century)

Byzantine empress. She married Emperor Justin II, who gradually went insane. In 572, the Persian War resumed. Two years later, Zoë made a truce with the Persian ruler, Chosroes. She had her husband name Tiberius as Caesar and ruled jointly with him. Justin died in 578, and Tiberius became his successor. Zoë, however, had retained the keys to the treasury, and a power struggle ensued. Soon power shifted to Tiberius, and she was imprisoned and kept under guard for the rest of her life.

Zoë (978–1050)

Byzantine empress. Daughter of Constantine VIII and sister to Emperor Basil II, called the Bulgar Slayer. She was to marry the Saxon Otto III in 1002, but he died before the wedding, thwarting all hope of a unification of the Eastern and Western empires.

After Basil II died, Constantine ordered her to marry Romanus Argyrus, a senator in his sixties, although he was already married. Constantine threatened to blind him if he did not divorce his wife, who solved the problem by leaving Romanus and entering a nunnery.

Zoë and Romanus were married in 1028. The day after their wedding, Constantine died. Zoë and Romanus ruled jointly. Zoë, now about fifty, needed an heir, but it was impossible for her to conceive. Her husband took a mistress, leaving her alone.

Zoë soon fell in love with Michael, the younger brother of the eunuch John the Orphanotrophus. Michael, who was epileptic, was in his teens at the time. Zoë may have poisoned her husband, Romanus. He conveniently died in 1034. Just hours after his death, she married Michael. Because she had been her father's heir, whoever she married became emperor. Thus Michael became emperor upon their marriage. Now known as Michael IV, he almost immediately confined her to the gynaceum and began ruling in his own right. Despite his epilepsy, he was a wise and talented ruler.

Subsequently, Zoë adopted as her heir the son of Michael's brother-in-law, also named Michael, called the Caulker after his father's occupation. After Michael IV died in 1041, Michael the Caulker became Emperor Michael V, although few people had less claim to the throne.

In 1042, Michael had Zoë arrested on the trumped-up charge of attempted regicide. She was exiled to a convent on the island of Prinkipo.

When her exile was announced, the population rebelled, looting and destroying everything the emperor's family owned. Zoë was immediately recalled, but she was too old to govern effectively by herself. The populace wanted Michael off the throne, so they took Theodora, Zoë's sister, from the convent where Zoë had banished her fifteen years earlier. Theodora became co-ruler against her own wishes.

Michael fled and sought refuge in a monastery but the populace found him and dragged him out. They blinded him so that he could not attempt to usurp the throne, and it was done.

The two sisters governed reasonably well, but they disliked each other, and their tension created factions. To add stability, Zoë married Constantine Mono-machus in 1042. He became Emperor Constantine IX. She even invited Constantine's mistress, Sclerina, to the court. The populace did not care for this arrangement, but Sclerina soon died of pulmonary disease and relieved them of their distress. Zoë died a few years later, in 1050, and Theodora ruled in her own right. *See* Theodora (973–1056).

SUGGESTED READING: Lynda Garland, *Byzantine Empresses: Women and Power in Byzantium, AD 527–1204* (New York: Routledge, 1999); Barbara Hill, *Imperial Women: Byzantium 1025–1204: Power, Patronage and Ideology* (Reading, MA: Addison-Wesley, 1999).

Zoë Carbonopsina (875?–after 920)

Byzantine empress and regent. She became mistress to Leo VI after his third wife died in 901 without an heir. In 905, she had a son, but she was forced to leave the palace in order to appease the patriarch, who then baptized the child. A few days later, she returned to the palace. Leo and Zoë married in order to make their son, Constantine, legitimate. When the secret wedding was announced, the Eastern church, which condemned multiple marriages, furiously refused to recognize the marriage. A special dispensation was needed, and after appealing to the pope, to whom Leo promised military support, the dispensation was granted.

After Leo's death in 912, his brother Alexander seized power and banished Zoë from the palace. Alexander died in 913, and Zoë returned to protect her son. Alexander had named a council of regents for Constantine, which did not include Zoë. This was the only time in Byzantine history that the mother of an emperor — and an Augusta, at that — was not allowed a place on the regency council.

Patriarch Nicholas had Zoë arrested

and incarcerated in a convent, where she was known as Sister Anna. The council disapproved of the patriarch's actions and recalled her in 914, restoring her to her position. Then Nicholas made the fatal error of accommodating Symeon, the Bulgarian ruler, by arranging for Constantine to marry Symeon's daughter. Zoë, still furious at Nicholas for refusing to acknowledge her marriage to Leo, orchestrated a palace coup and ousted Nicholas. She took over the regency of her son.

In 913, Nicholas had unofficially coronated Symeon in order to appease his desire to be emperor. Zoë immediately repudiated Symeon's title and canceled the marriage plans. Symeon went to war against her. The war lasted ten years.

By 915, Zoë had defeated a Muslim army, but two years later, her armies lost two successive, crucial battles. In 918, her power was in serious jeopardy.

Then, with the support of his tutor, Theodore, Constantine told his mother her regency was over. He was thirteen.

Romanus Lecapenus, a Byzantine military leader, was one of Constantine's supporters. In 920, he accused Zoë of trying to poison him. Again, she was immured as Sister Anna in a convent (Saint Euphemia), where she stayed until her death.

SUGGESTED READING: Lynda Garland, *Byzantine Empresses: Women and Power in Byzantium, AD 527–1204* (New York: Routledge, 1999).

Zoë Zautsina (d. 899)

Also Zoë Zautzes. Mistress to Leo, the son of Emperor Basil of Byzantium. After Leo was married, she was banished and married off. Her father was suspected of conniving at the murder of Basil in 886, with the approval of Leo, who became Leo VI.

After Leo VI's wife, Theophano, died in 897, Zoë was recalled to Constantinople. Her husband conveniently died shortly thereafter. In 898, Leo and Zoë had a daughter, Anna. The following year, Zoë died. *See* Theophano (d. 897).

Appendix: Genealogical Charts

This appendix provides genealogical charts for the royal houses of various countries and for specific women covered in this book. Although each entry in these genealogies has been verified in at least two other sources, inevitably discrepancies will exist between these charts and some charts produced by others. Genealogical records are not always clear, and often a person must make an educated guess about spouses, parents, and children.

In these charts, not every spouse or child is listed. The charts do provide a representative idea of the number of children a woman typically had and of how the royal houses intermarried.

The symbol = indicates a sexual relationship, not necessarily a marriage. The record is not always clear on whether a couple was legally married.

Women covered in the text are shown on the charts in **boldface.**

Two boldface horizontal lines enclosing the name at the top of a page indicate that the chart is a continuation from the previous page or from another geneology (identified by a see reference).

Adelaide of Italy
(*See also* Ottonian Holy Roman Empire)

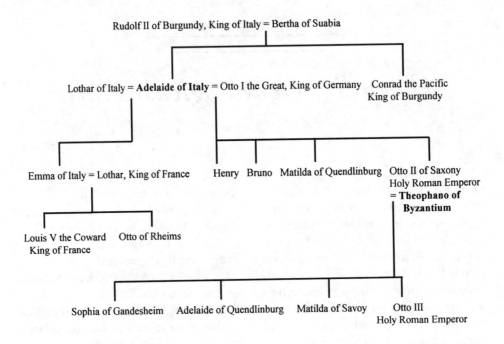

Rudolf II of Burgundy, King of Italy = Bertha of Suabia

Lothar of Italy = **Adelaide of Italy** = Otto I the Great, King of Germany   Conrad the Pacific
King of Burgundy

Emma of Italy = Lothar, King of France   Henry Bruno Matilda of Quendlinburg   Otto II of Saxony
Holy Roman Emperor
= **Theophano of
Byzantium**

Louis V the Coward   Otto of Rheims
King of France

Sophia of Gandesheim   Adelaide of Quendlinburg   Matilda of Savoy   Otto III
Holy Roman Emperor

Æthelflæd
(*See also* Mercia)

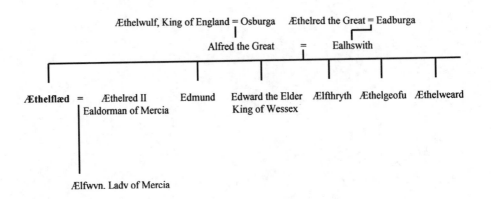

Æthelwulf, King of England = Osburga   Æthelred the Great = Eadburga

Alfred the Great   =   Ealhswith

Æthelflæd = Æthelred II   Edmund   Edward the Elder   Ælfthryth Æthelgeofu Æthelweard
Ealdorman of Mercia   King of Wessex

Ælfwyn. Lady of Mercia

Anna Comnena
(*See also* Byzantine Empire)

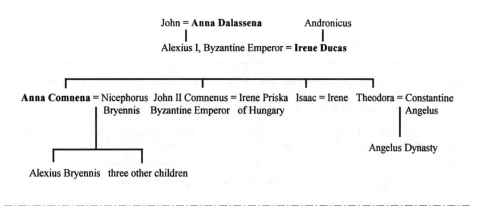

John = **Anna Dalassena**   Andronicus

Alexius I, Byzantine Emperor = **Irene Ducas**

Anna Comnena = Nicephorus   John II Comnenus = Irene Priska   Isaac = Irene   Theodora = Constantine
Bryennis   Byzantine Emperor   of Hungary   Angelus

Angelus Dynasty

Alexius Bryennis   three other children

Antioch

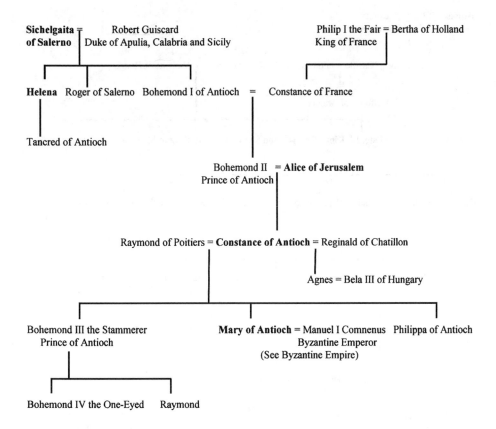

Sichelgaita = Robert Guiscard   Philip I the Fair = Bertha of Holland
of Salerno   Duke of Apulia, Calabria and Sicily   King of France

Helena   Roger of Salerno   Bohemond I of Antioch   =   Constance of France

Tancred of Antioch

Bohemond II   = **Alice of Jerusalem**
Prince of Antioch

Raymond of Poitiers = **Constance of Antioch** = Reginald of Chatillon

Agnes = Bela III of Hungary

Bohemond III the Stammerer   **Mary of Antioch** = Manuel I Comnenus   Philippa of Antioch
Prince of Antioch   Byzantine Emperor
                                              (See Byzantine Empire)

Bohemond IV the One-Eyed   Raymond

Aragon
(chart 1)

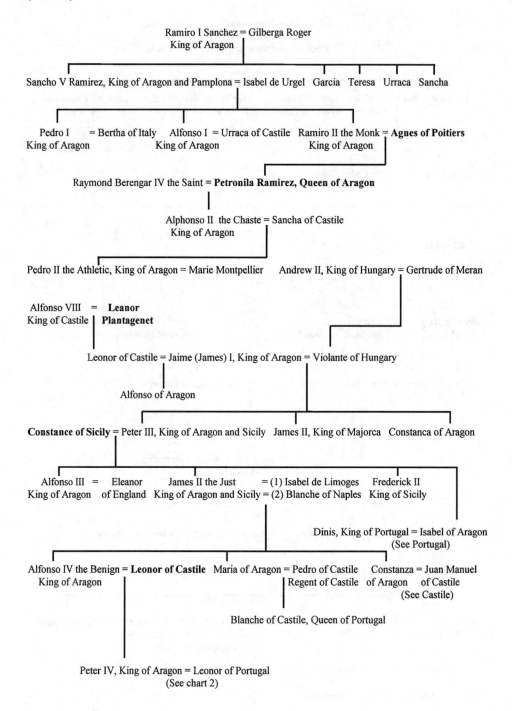

Aragon
(chart 2)

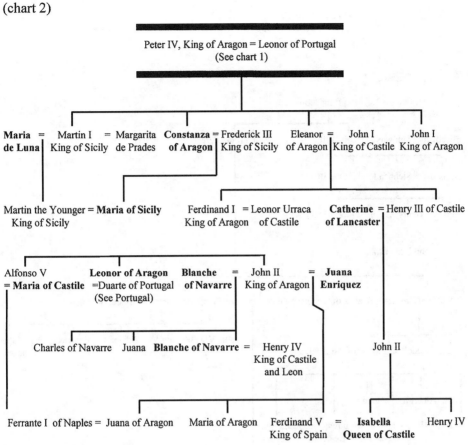

Bavaria

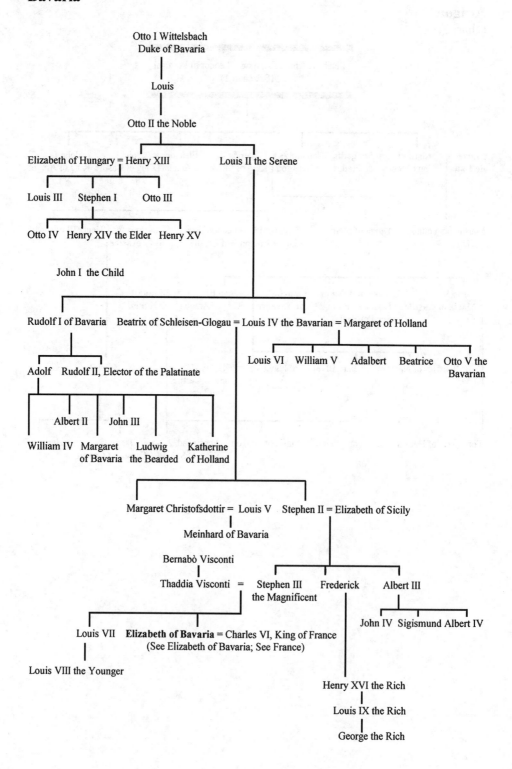

Berenguela
(See also Castile *and* Eleanor of Aquitaine)

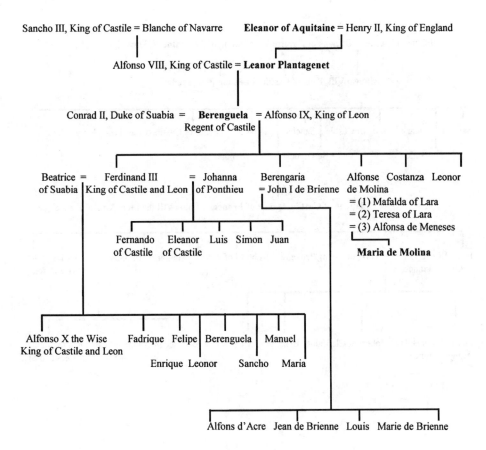

Blanche of Castile
(*See also* Castile, France *and* Eleanor of Aquitaine)

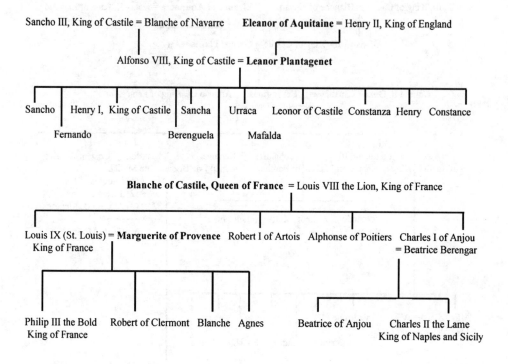

Bohemia
(chart 1)

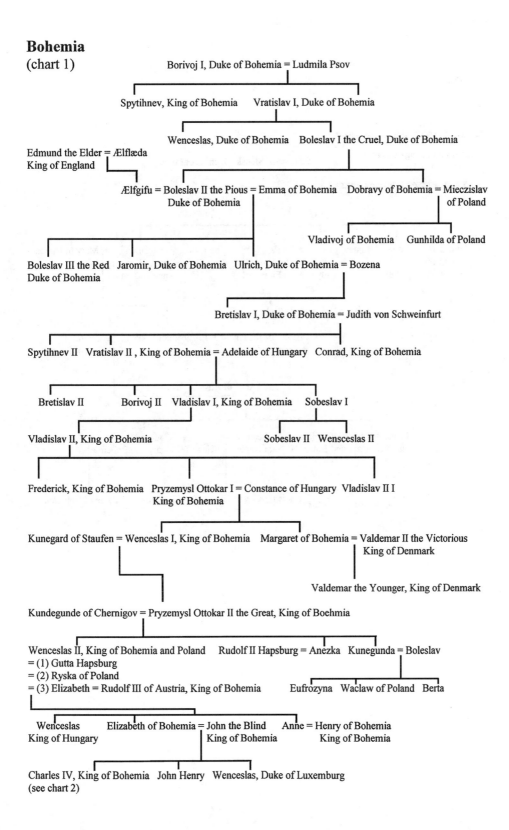

Borivoj I, Duke of Bohemia = Ludmila Psov

Spytihnev, King of Bohemia   Vratislav I, Duke of Bohemia

Wenceslas, Duke of Bohemia   Boleslav I the Cruel, Duke of Bohemia

Edmund the Elder = Ælflæda
King of England

Ælfgifu = Boleslav II the Pious = Emma of Bohemia   Dobravy of Bohemia = Mieczislav
Duke of Bohemia   of Poland

Vladivoj of Bohemia   Gunhilda of Poland

Boleslav III the Red   Jaromir, Duke of Bohemia   Ulrich, Duke of Bohemia = Bozena
Duke of Bohemia

Bretislav I, Duke of Bohemia = Judith von Schweinfurt

Spytihnev II   Vratislav II , King of Bohemia = Adelaide of Hungary   Conrad, King of Bohemia

Bretislav II   Borivoj II   Vladislav I, King of Bohemia   Sobeslav I

Vladislav II, King of Bohemia   Sobeslav II   Wensceslas II

Frederick, King of Bohemia   Pryzemysl Ottokar I = Constance of Hungary   Vladislav II I
King of Bohemia

Kunegard of Staufen = Wenceslas I, King of Bohemia   Margaret of Bohemia = Valdemar II the Victorious
King of Denmark

Valdemar the Younger, King of Denmark

Kundegunde of Chernigov = Pryzemysl Ottokar II the Great, King of Boehmia

Wenceslas II, King of Bohemia and Poland   Rudolf II Hapsburg = Anezka   Kunegunda = Boleslav
= (1) Gutta Hapsburg
= (2) Ryska of Poland
= (3) Elizabeth = Rudolf III of Austria, King of Bohemia   Eufrozyna   Waclaw of Poland   Berta

Wenceslas   Elizabeth of Bohemia = John the Blind   Anne = Henry of Bohemia
King of Hungary   King of Bohemia   King of Bohemia

Charles IV, King of Bohemia   John Henry   Wenceslas, Duke of Luxemburg
(see chart 2)

Bohemia
(chart 2)

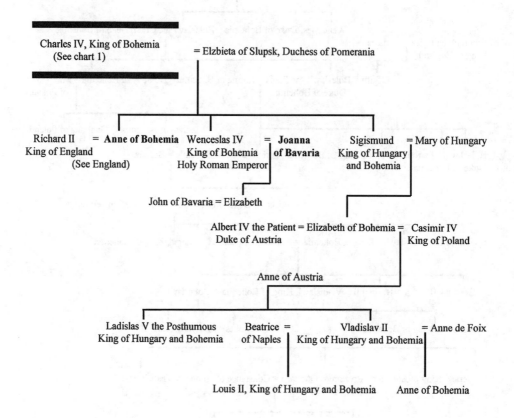

Charles IV, King of Bohemia (See chart 1) = Elzbieta of Slupsk, Duchess of Pomerania

Richard II King of England (See England) = **Anne of Bohemia**   Wenceslas IV King of Bohemia Holy Roman Emperor = **Joanna of Bavaria**   Sigismund King of Hungary and Bohemia = Mary of Hungary

John of Bavaria = Elizabeth

Albert IV the Patient Duke of Austria = Elizabeth of Bohemia = Casimir IV King of Poland

Anne of Austria

Ladislas V the Posthumous King of Hungary and Bohemia   Beatrice of Naples = Vladislav II King of Hungary and Bohemia = Anne de Foix

Louis II, King of Hungary and Bohemia   Anne of Bohemia

Byzantine Empire
(chart 1)

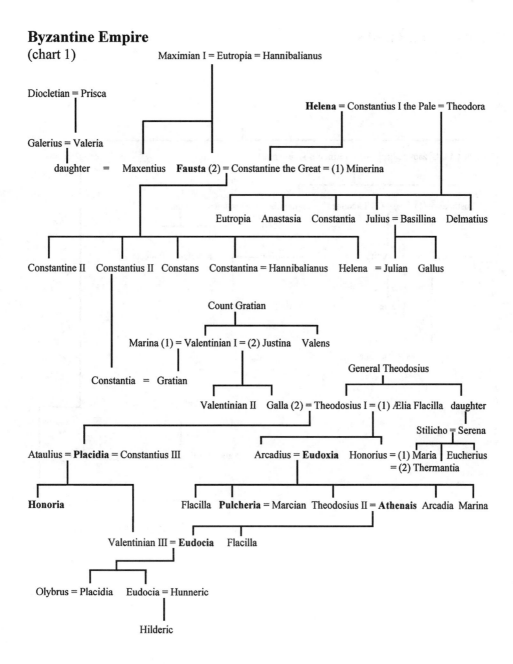

Byzantine Empire
(chart 2)

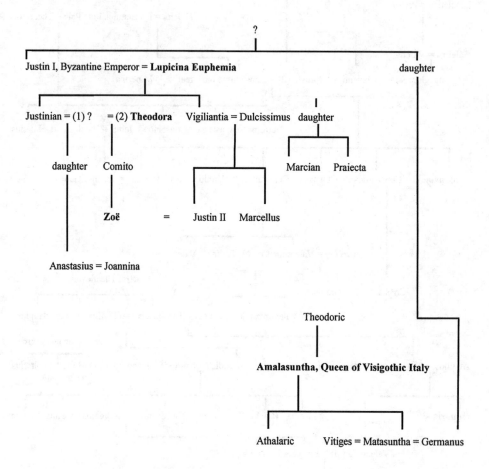

Byzantine Empire
(chart 3)

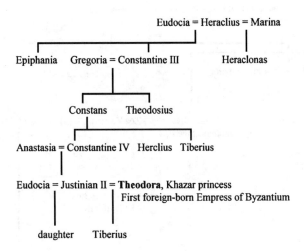

```
                              Eudocia = Heraclius = Marina
                           ┌──────────────┴──────┐            │
   Epiphania    Gregoria = Constantine III                Heraclonas
                      ┌────────┴────────┐
                  Constans       Theodosius
              ┌────────┴────────────────┐
 Anastasia = Constantine IV   Herclius   Tiberius
          │
 Eudocia = Justinian II = Theodora, Khazar princess
                              First foreign-born Empress of Byzantium
          │              │
      daughter       Tiberius
```

Byzantine Empire
(chart 4)

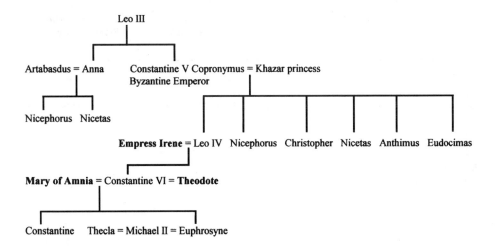

```
                         Leo III
          ┌────────────────┴──────────────┐
 Artabasdus = Anna      Constantine V Copronymus = Khazar princess
       │                 Byzantine Emperor
   ┌───┴───┐       ┌──────┬──────┬──────┬──────┬──────┐
 Nicephorus Nicetas
         Empress Irene = Leo IV  Nicephorus  Christopher  Nicetas  Anthimus  Eudocimas
                   ┌─────┴─────┐
 Mary of Amnia = Constantine VI = Theodote
          ┌───────┴───────┐
   Constantine   Thecla = Michael II = Euphrosyne
```

Byzantine Empire
(chart 5)

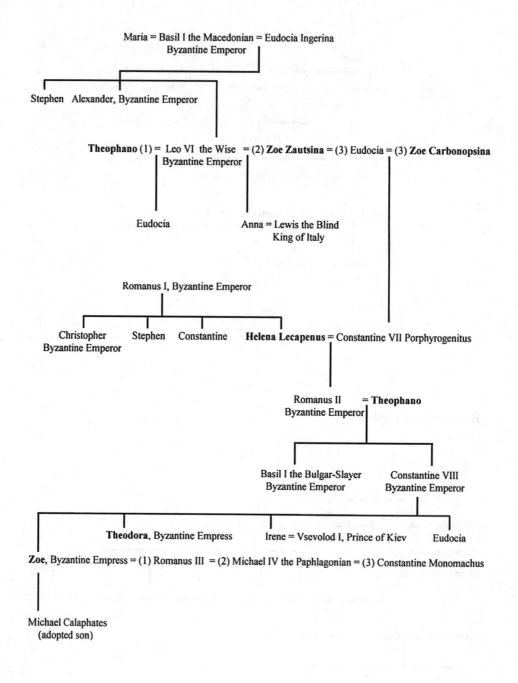

Maria = Basil I the Macedonian = Eudocia Ingerina
Byzantine Emperor

Stephen   Alexander, Byzantine Emperor

Theophano (1) = Leo VI the Wise = (2) **Zoe Zautsina** = (3) Eudocia = (3) **Zoe Carbonopsina**
Byzantine Emperor

Eudocia   Anna = Lewis the Blind
King of Italy

Romanus I, Byzantine Emperor

Christopher   Stephen   Constantine   **Helena Lecapenus** = Constantine VII Porphyrogenitus
Byzantine Emperor

Romanus II   = **Theophano**
Byzantine Emperor

Basil I the Bulgar-Slayer   Constantine VIII
Byzantine Emperor   Byzantine Emperor

Theodora, Byzantine Empress   Irene = Vsevolod I, Prince of Kiev   Eudocia

Zoe, Byzantine Empress = (1) Romanus III = (2) Michael IV the Paphlagonian = (3) Constantine Monomachus

Michael Calaphates
(adopted son)

Byzantine Empire
(chart 6)

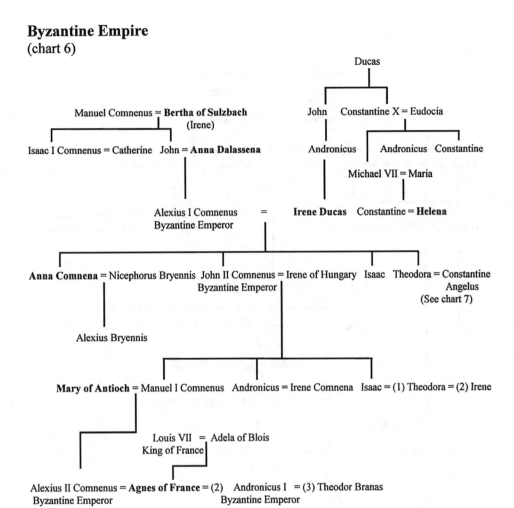

Byzantine Empire
(chart 7)

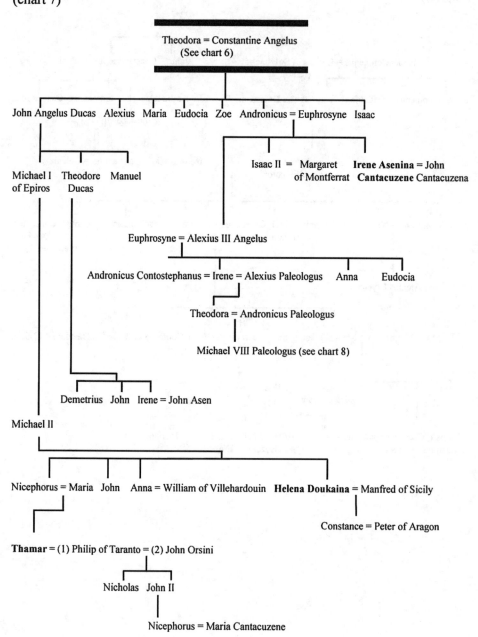

Theodora = Constantine Angelus
(See chart 6)

John Angelus Ducas   Alexius   Maria   Eudocia   Zoe   Andronicus = Euphrosyne   Isaac

Michael I   Theodore   Manuel
of Epiros   Ducas

Isaac II = Margaret   **Irene Asenina** = John
of Montferrat   **Cantacuzene** Cantacuzena

Euphrosyne = Alexius III Angelus

Andronicus Contostephanus = Irene = Alexius Paleologus   Anna   Eudocia

Theodora = Andronicus Paleologus

Michael VIII Paleologus (see chart 8)

Demetrius   John   Irene = John Asen

Michael II

Nicephorus = Maria   John   Anna = William of Villehardouin   **Helena Doukaina** = Manfred of Sicily

Constance = Peter of Aragon

Thamar = (1) Philip of Taranto = (2) John Orsini

Nicholas   John II

Nicephorus = Maria Cantacuzene

Byzantine Empire
(chart 8)

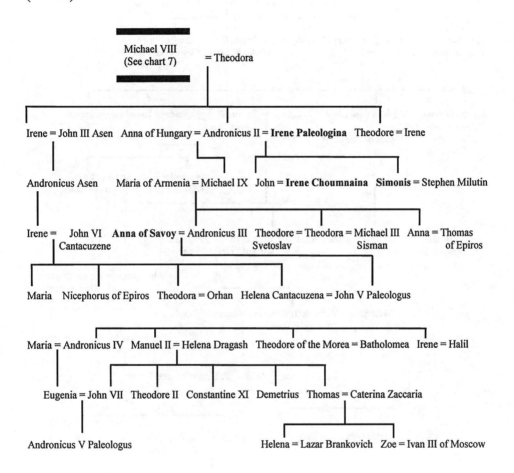

Michael VIII (See chart 7) = Theodora

Irene = John III Asen   Anna of Hungary = Andronicus II = **Irene Paleologina**   Theodore = Irene

Andronicus Asen   Maria of Armenia = Michael IX   John = **Irene Choumnaina**   **Simonis** = Stephen Milutin

Irene =   John VI   **Anna of Savoy** = Andronicus III   Theodore = Theodora = Michael III   Anna = Thomas
           Cantacuzene   Svetoslav   Sisman   of Epiros

Maria   Nicephorus of Epiros   Theodora = Orhan   Helena Cantacuzena = John V Paleologus

Maria = Andronicus IV   Manuel II = Helena Dragash   Theodore of the Morea = Batholomea   Irene = Halil

Eugenia = John VII   Theodore II   Constantine XI   Demetrius   Thomas = Caterina Zaccaria

Andronicus V Paleologus   Helena = Lazar Brankovich   Zoe = Ivan III of Moscow

Castile and Leon
(chart 1)

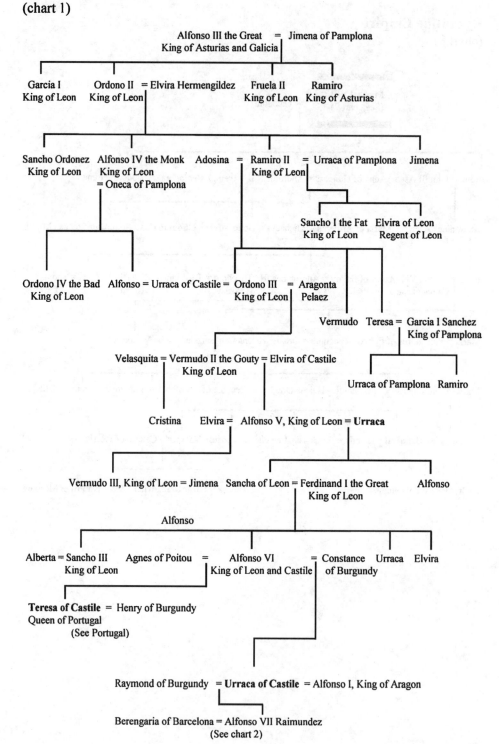

Alfonso III the Great = Jimena of Pamplona
King of Asturias and Galicia

Garcia I   Ordono II = Elvira Hermengildez   Fruela II   Ramiro
King of Leon   King of Leon   King of Leon   King of Asturias

Sancho Ordonez   Alfonso IV the Monk   Adosina = Ramiro II = Urraca of Pamplona   Jimena
King of Leon   King of Leon   King of Leon
                 = Oneca of Pamplona

Sancho I the Fat   Elvira of Leon
King of Leon   Regent of Leon

Ordono IV the Bad   Alfonso = Urraca of Castile = Ordono III = Aragonta
King of Leon   King of Leon   Pelaez

Vermudo   Teresa = Garcia I Sanchez
                    King of Pamplona

Velasquita = Vermudo II the Gouty = Elvira of Castile
            King of Leon

Urraca of Pamplona   Ramiro

Cristina   Elvira = Alfonso V, King of Leon = **Urraca**

Vermudo III, King of Leon = Jimena   Sancha of Leon = Ferdinand I the Great   Alfonso
                                         King of Leon

Alfonso

Alberta = Sancho III   Agnes of Poitou = Alfonso VI = Constance   Urraca   Elvira
       King of Leon   King of Leon and Castile   of Burgundy

Teresa of Castile = Henry of Burgundy
Queen of Portugal
(See Portugal)

Raymond of Burgundy = **Urraca of Castile** = Alfonso I, King of Aragon

Berengaria of Barcelona = Alfonso VII Raimundez
(See chart 2)

Castile and Leon
(chart 2)

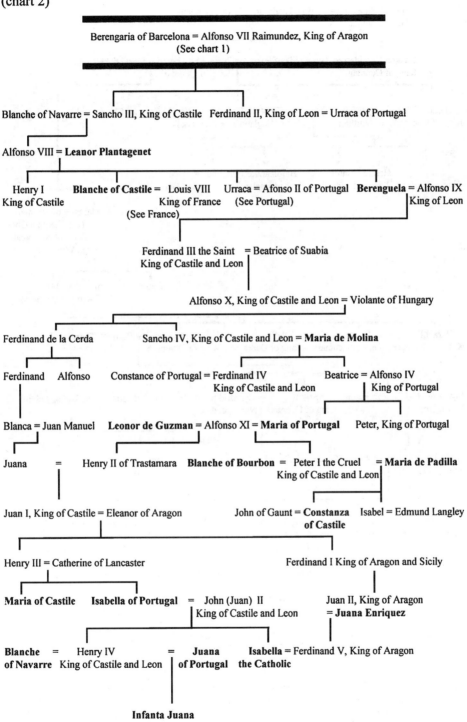

Berengaria of Barcelona = Alfonso VII Raimundez, King of Aragon
(See chart 1)

Blanche of Navarre = Sancho III, King of Castile   Ferdinand II, King of Leon = Urraca of Portugal

Alfonso VIII = **Leanor Plantagenet**

Henry I   **Blanche of Castile** = Louis VIII   Urraca = Afonso II of Portugal   **Berenguela** = Alfonso IX
King of Castile   King of France   (See Portugal)   King of Leon
                        (See France)

Ferdinand III the Saint   = Beatrice of Suabia
King of Castile and Leon

Alfonso X, King of Castile and Leon = Violante of Hungary

Ferdinand de la Cerda   Sancho IV, King of Castile and Leon = **Maria de Molina**

Ferdinand   Alfonso   Constance of Portugal = Ferdinand IV   Beatrice = Alfonso IV
                                                King of Castile and Leon   King of Portugal

Blanca = Juan Manuel   **Leonor de Guzman** = Alfonso XI = **Maria of Portugal**   Peter, King of Portugal

Juana   =   Henry II of Trastamara   **Blanche of Bourbon** = Peter I the Cruel   = **Maria de Padilla**
                                                                   King of Castile and Leon

Juan I, King of Castile = Eleanor of Aragon   John of Gaunt = **Constanza**   Isabel = Edmund Langley
                                                                   of Castile

Henry III = Catherine of Lancaster   Ferdinand I King of Aragon and Sicily

Maria of Castile   **Isabella of Portugal** = John (Juan) II   Juan II, King of Aragon
                                                King of Castile and Leon   = **Juana Enriquez**

Blanche   =   Henry IV   =   **Juana**   **Isabella** = Ferdinand V, King of Aragon
of Navarre King of Castile and Leon   **of Portugal** the Catholic

Infanta Juana

Denmark
(chart 1)

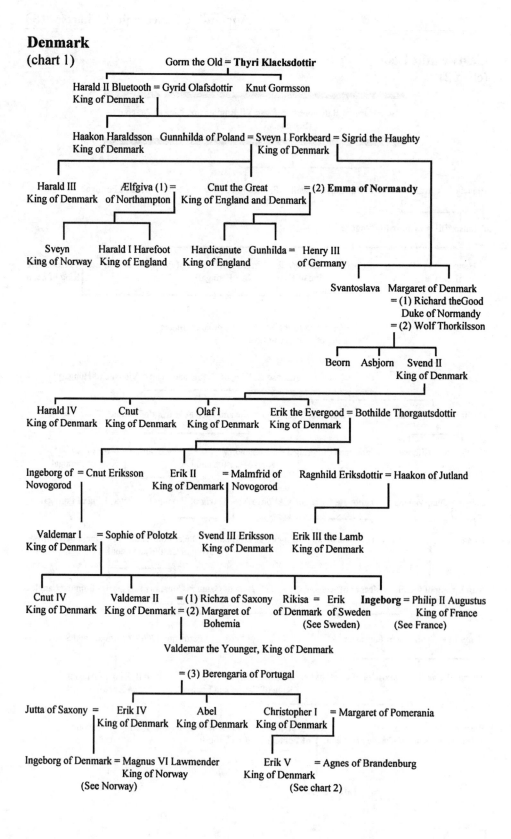

Gorm the Old = **Thyri Klacksdottir**

Harald II Bluetooth = Gyrid Olafsdottir   Knut Gormsson
King of Denmark

Haakon Haraldsson   Gunnhilda of Poland = Sveyn I Forkbeard = Sigrid the Haughty
King of Denmark   King of Denmark

Harald III   Ælfgiva (1) =   Cnut the Great   = (2) **Emma of Normandy**
King of Denmark   of Northampton   King of England and Denmark

Sveyn   Harald I Harefoot   Hardicanute   Gunhilda = Henry III
King of Norway   King of England   King of England   of Germany

Svantoslava   Margaret of Denmark
               = (1) Richard theGood
                 Duke of Normandy
               = (2) Wolf Thorkilsson

Beorn   Asbjorn   Svend II
                    King of Denmark

Harald IV   Cnut   Olaf I   Erik the Evergood = Bothilde Thorgautsdottir
King of Denmark   King of Denmark   King of Denmark   King of Denmark

Ingeborg of = Cnut Eriksson   Erik II   = Malmfrid of   Ragnhild Eriksdottir = Haakon of Jutland
Novogorod   King of Denmark Novogorod

Valdemar I   = Sophie of Polotzk   Svend III Eriksson   Erik III the Lamb
King of Denmark   King of Denmark   King of Denmark

Cnut IV   Valdemar II   = (1) Richza of Saxony   Rikisa =   Erik   **Ingeborg** = Philip II Augustus
King of Denmark   King of Denmark = (2) Margaret of   of Denmark of Sweden   King of France
                                        Bohemia   (See Sweden)   (See France)

Valdemar the Younger, King of Denmark

= (3) Berengaria of Portugal

Jutta of Saxony =   Erik IV   Abel   Christopher I   = Margaret of Pomerania
                     King of Denmark   King of Denmark   King of Denmark

Ingeborg of Denmark = Magnus VI Lawmender   Erik V   = Agnes of Brandenburg
                      King of Norway   King of Denmark
                    (See Norway)   (See chart 2)

Denmark
(chart 2)

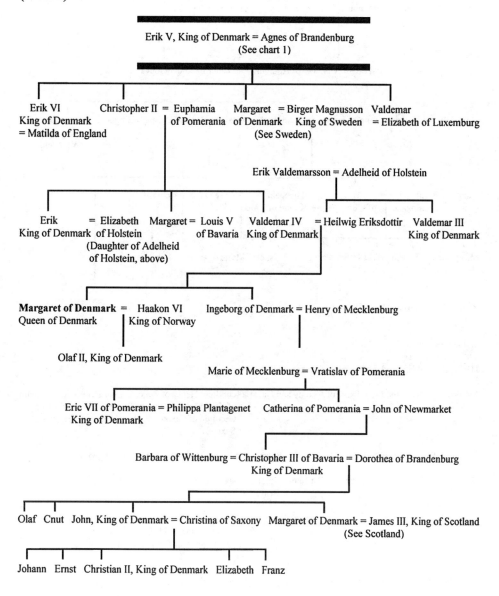

Erik V, King of Denmark = Agnes of Brandenburg
(See chart 1)

Erik VI
King of Denmark
= Matilda of England

Christopher II = Euphamia
of Pomerania

Margaret = Birger Magnusson
of Denmark   King of Sweden
(See Sweden)

Valdemar
= Elizabeth of Luxemburg

Erik Valdemarsson = Adelheid of Holstein

Erik   = Elizabeth
King of Denmark of Holstein
(Daughter of Adelheid
of Holstein, above)

Margaret = Louis V
of Bavaria

Valdemar IV
King of Denmark

= Heilwig Eriksdottir

Valdemar III
King of Denmark

Margaret of Denmark =   Haakon VI
Queen of Denmark   King of Norway

Ingeborg of Denmark = Henry of Mecklenburg

Olaf II, King of Denmark

Marie of Mecklenburg = Vratislav of Pomerania

Eric VII of Pomerania = Philippa Plantagenet
King of Denmark

Catherina of Pomerania = John of Newmarket

Barbara of Wittenburg = Christopher III of Bavaria = Dorothea of Brandenburg
King of Denmark

Olaf   Cnut   John, King of Denmark = Christina of Saxony   Margaret of Denmark = James III, King of Scotland
(See Scotland)

Johann   Ernst   Christian II, King of Denmark   Elizabeth   Franz

Eleanor of Aquitaine
(*See also* England *and* France)

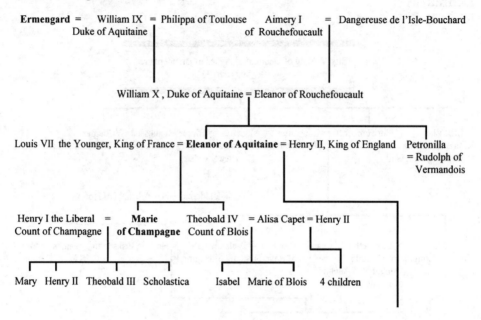

Eleanor's children by Henry II:

William of Poitiers

Henry, King of England = Margaret of France (child: John)

Matilda = Henry V the Lion, Duke of Saxony and Bavaria (children: Henry of Zelle, Otto of Brunswick, William of Winchester, Luther of Saxony, Maud of Saxony, Gertrude of Saxony, Richza of Saxony, Eleanor of Saxony)

Richard I the Lionhearted, King of England = **Berengaria of Navarre** (child: Philip of Cognac)

Geoffrey II of Brittany = Constance of Brittany (children: Eleanor of Brittany, Matilda Plantagenet, Arthur of Brittany)

Leanor Plantagenet = Alfonso VIII, King of Castile (children: Sancho; Fernando; Henry I, King of Castile; **Berenguela**; Sancha; Urraca; **Blanche of Castile**; Mafalda; **Leonor of Castile**; Costanza of Castile,; Henry; Constance)

Joan Plantagenet = (1) William II the Good, King of Naples and Sicily (child: Bohemond of Apulia)

= (2) Raymond VI, Count of Toulouse (children: Raymond VII, Wilhelmina of Toulouse, Richard of Toulouse)

John I Lackland, King of England = (1) Isabella of Gloucester

= (2) **Isabella of Angouleme** (children: Henry III, King of England; Richard of Cornwall; **Joan**; Isabella of Germany; Eleanor)

Elizabeth of Bavaria
(*See also* Bavaria)

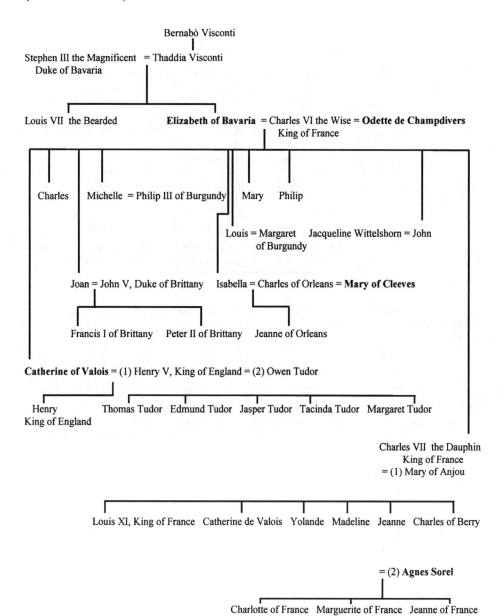

Bernabò Visconti

Stephen III the Magnificent = Thaddia Visconti
   Duke of Bavaria

Louis VII the Bearded   **Elizabeth of Bavaria** = Charles VI the Wise = **Odette de Champdivers**
                                                             King of France

Charles   Michelle = Philip III of Burgundy   Mary   Philip

                                   Louis = Margaret   Jacqueline Wittelshorn = John
                                            of Burgundy

        Joan = John V, Duke of Brittany   Isabella = Charles of Orleans = **Mary of Cleeves**

        Francis I of Brittany   Peter II of Brittany   Jeanne of Orleans

Catherine of Valois = (1) Henry V, King of England = (2) Owen Tudor

Henry   Thomas Tudor Edmund Tudor Jasper Tudor Tacinda Tudor Margaret Tudor
King of England

                                                   Charles VII the Dauphin
                                                      King of France
                                                   = (1) Mary of Anjou

Louis XI, King of France Catherine de Valois Yolande Madeline Jeanne Charles of Berry

                                                   = (2) **Agnes Sorel**

Charlotte of France   Marguerite of France   Jeanne of France

England
(chart 1)

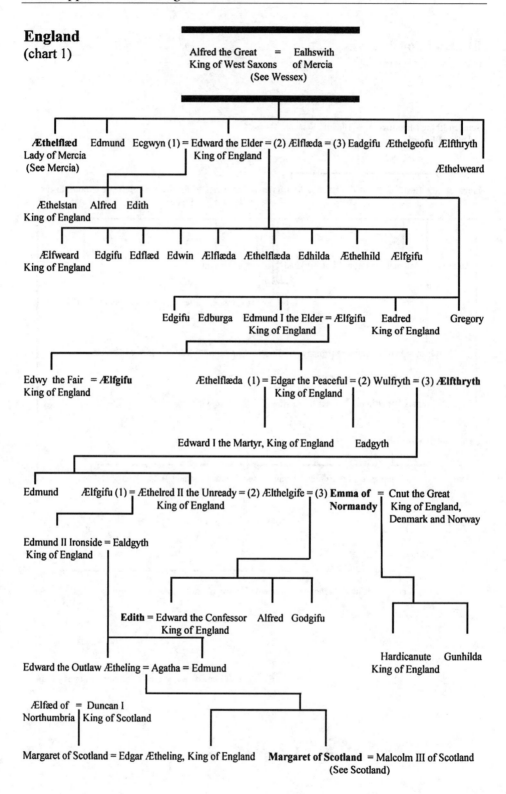

Alfred the Great   =   Ealhswith
King of West Saxons   of Mercia
(See Wessex)

Æthelflæd   Edmund   Ecgwyn (1) = Edward the Elder = (2) Ælflæda = (3) Eadgifu   Æthelgeofu   Ælfthryth
Lady of Mercia   King of England
(See Mercia)

Æthelweard

Æthelstan   Alfred   Edith
King of England

Ælfweard   Edgifu   Edflæd   Edwin   Ælflæda   Æthelflæda   Edhilda   Æthelhild   Ælfgifu
King of England

Edgifu   Edburga   Edmund I the Elder = Ælfgifu   Eadred   Gregory
                         King of England   King of England

Edwy the Fair = Ælfgifu   Æthelflæda (1) = Edgar the Peaceful = (2) Wulfryth = (3) Ælfthryth
King of England   King of England

Edward I the Martyr, King of England   Eadgyth

Edmund   Ælfgifu (1) = Æthelred II the Unready = (2) Ælthelgife = (3) Emma of = Cnut the Great
                        King of England   Normandy   King of England,
                                                                                 Denmark and Norway

Edmund II Ironside = Ealdgyth
King of England

Edith = Edward the Confessor   Alfred   Godgifu
        King of England

Hardicanute   Gunhilda
King of England

Edward the Outlaw Ætheling = Agatha = Edmund

Ælfæd of = Duncan I
Northumbria | King of Scotland

Margaret of Scotland = Edgar Ætheling, King of England   Margaret of Scotland = Malcolm III of Scotland
                                                                                 (See Scotland)

England
(chart 2)

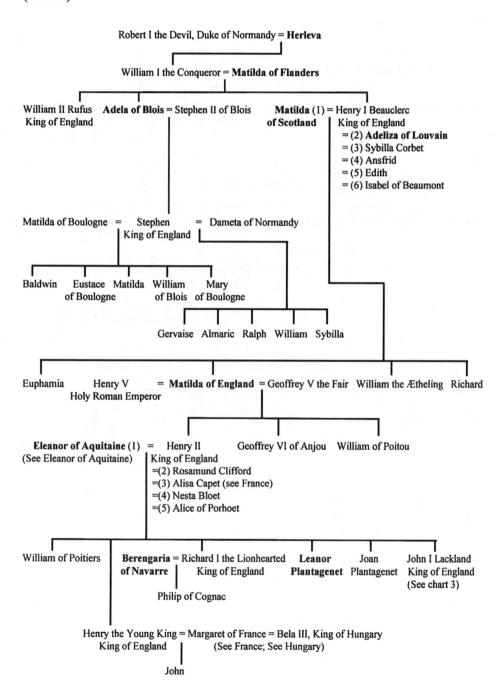

England
(chart 3)

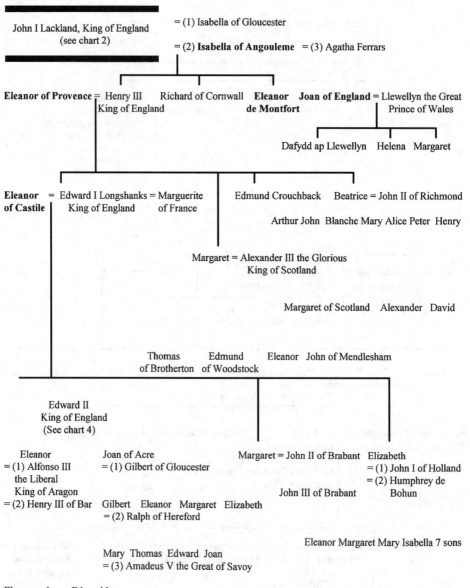

John I Lackland, King of England
(see chart 2)

= (1) Isabella of Gloucester

= (2) **Isabella of Angouleme**   = (3) Agatha Ferrars

Eleanor of Provence = Henry III   Richard of Cornwall   **Eleanor**   Joan of England = Llewellyn the Great
King of England   **de Montfort**   Prince of Wales

Dafydd ap Llewellyn   Helena Margaret

Eleanor   = Edward I Longshanks = Marguerite   Edmund Crouchback   Beatrice = John II of Richmond
of Castile   King of England   of France

Arthur John Blanche Mary Alice Peter Henry

Margaret = Alexander III the Glorious
King of Scotland

Margaret of Scotland   Alexander   David

Thomas   Edmund   Eleanor   John of Mendlesham
of Brotherton   of Woodstock

Edward II
King of England
(See chart 4)

Eleanor   Joan of Acre   Margaret = John II of Brabant Elizabeth
= (1) Alfonso III   = (1) Gilbert of Gloucester   = (1) John I of Holland
the Liberal   = (2) Humphrey de
King of Aragon   John III of Brabant   Bohun
= (2) Henry III of Bar   Gilbert Eleanor Margaret Elizabeth
= (2) Ralph of Hereford

Eleanor Margaret Mary Isabella 7 sons

Mary Thomas Edward Joan
= (3) Amadeus V the Great of Savoy

Eleanor   Joan   Edward I
of Bar   of Bar   of Bar

England
(chart 4)

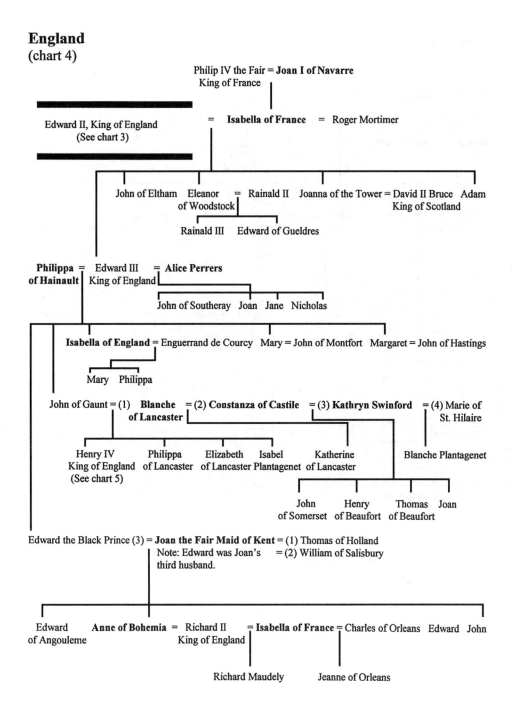

England
(chart 5)

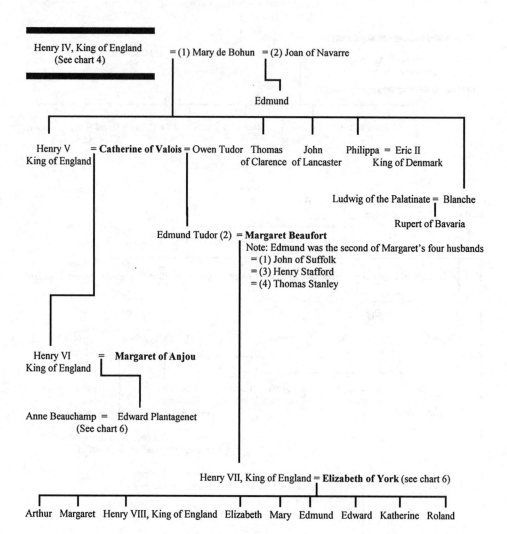

Henry IV, King of England
(See chart 4)   = (1) Mary de Bohun   = (2) Joan of Navarre

Edmund

Henry V   = **Catherine of Valois** = Owen Tudor   Thomas   John   Philippa = Eric II
King of England   of Clarence of Lancaster   King of Denmark

Ludwig of the Palatinate = Blanche

Rupert of Bavaria

Edmund Tudor (2) = **Margaret Beaufort**
Note: Edmund was the second of Margaret's four husbands
= (1) John of Suffolk
= (3) Henry Stafford
= (4) Thomas Stanley

Henry VI   =   **Margaret of Anjou**
King of England

Anne Beauchamp =   Edward Plantagenet
(See chart 6)

Henry VII, King of England = **Elizabeth of York** (see chart 6)

Arthur   Margaret   Henry VIII, King of England   Elizabeth   Mary   Edmund   Edward   Katherine   Roland

England
(chart 6)

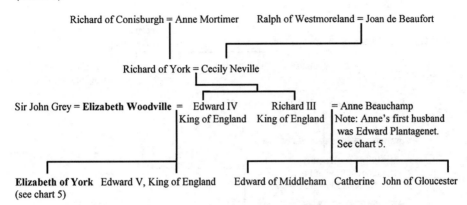

Richard of Conisburgh = Anne Mortimer   Ralph of Westmoreland = Joan de Beaufort

Richard of York = Cecily Neville

Sir John Grey = **Elizabeth Woodville** =   Edward IV   Richard III   = Anne Beauchamp
                                        King of England   King of England   Note: Anne's first husband
                                                                               was Edward Plantagenet.
                                                                               See chart 5.

Elizabeth of York Edward V, King of England   Edward of Middleham   Catherine   John of Gloucester
(see chart 5)

France
(chart 1)

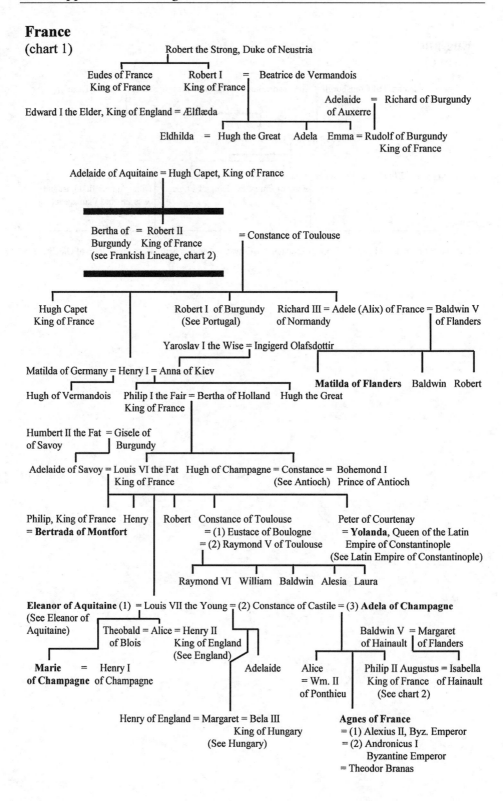

France
(chart 2)

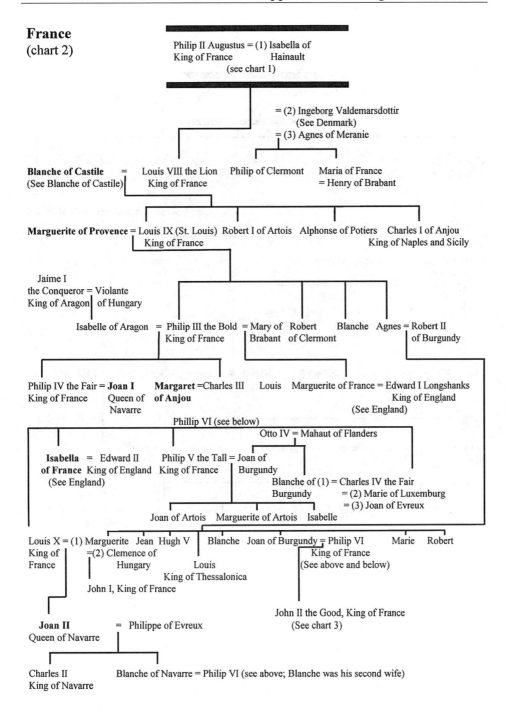

Philip II Augustus = (1) Isabella of
King of France   Hainault
(see chart 1)

= (2) Ingeborg Valdemarsdottir
    (See Denmark)
= (3) Agnes of Meranie

Blanche of Castile   =   Louis VIII the Lion   Philip of Clermont   Maria of France
(See Blanche of Castile)| King of France   = Henry of Brabant

Marguerite of Provence = Louis IX (St. Louis)   Robert I of Artois   Alphonse of Potiers   Charles I of Anjou
                            King of France   King of Naples and Sicily

Jaime I
the Conqueror = Violante
King of Aragon| of Hungary

    Isabelle of Aragon   =   Philip III the Bold   = Mary of   Robert   Blanche   Agnes = Robert II
                             King of France   Brabant   of Clermont   of Burgundy

Philip IV the Fair = **Joan I**   **Margaret** = Charles III   Louis   Marguerite of France = Edward I Longshanks
King of France   Queen of   **of Anjou**   King of England
                     Navarre   (See England)
                                 Phillip VI (see below)

                                            Otto IV = Mahaut of Flanders

      Isabella   =   Edward II   Philip V the Tall = Joan of
      of France King of England King of France   Burgundy
      (See England)   Blanche of (1) = Charles IV the Fair
                                                      Burgundy   = (2) Marie of Luxemburg
                                                                       = (3) Joan of Evreux

                    Joan of Artois   Marguerite of Artois   Isabelle

Louis X = (1) Marguerite   Jean   Hugh V   Blanche   Joan of Burgundy = Philip VI   Marie   Robert
King of | =(2) Clemence of   King of France
France | Hungary   Louis   (See above and below)
        | King of Thessalonica
            John I, King of France

                                                      John II the Good, King of France
      Joan II   =   Philippe of Evreux   (See chart 3)
      Queen of Navarre

      Charles II   Blanche of Navarre = Philip VI (see above; Blanche was his second wife)
      King of Navarre

France
(chart 3)

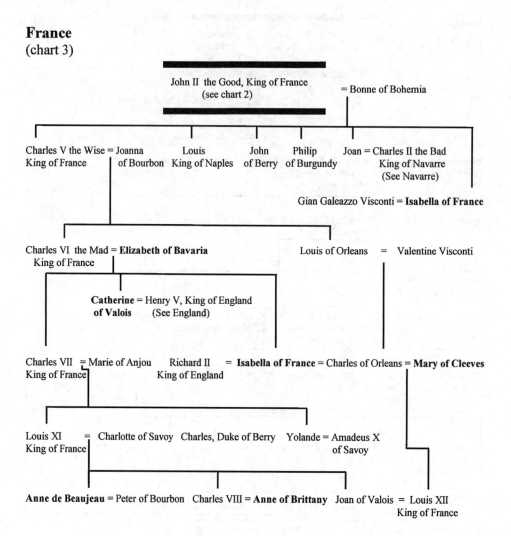

John II the Good, King of France
(see chart 2) = Bonne of Bohemia

Charles V the Wise = Joanna   Louis   John   Philip   Joan = Charles II the Bad
King of France   of Bourbon   King of Naples   of Berry   of Burgundy   King of Navarre
                                                      (See Navarre)

Gian Galeazzo Visconti = **Isabella of France**

Charles VI the Mad = **Elizabeth of Bavaria**   Louis of Orleans   =   Valentine Visconti
King of France

Catherine = Henry V, King of England
of Valois   (See England)

Charles VII   = Marie of Anjou   Richard II   = **Isabella of France** = Charles of Orleans = **Mary of Cleeves**
King of France   King of England

Louis XI   = Charlotte of Savoy   Charles, Duke of Berry   Yolande = Amadeus X
King of France   of Savoy

Anne de Beaujeau = Peter of Bourbon   Charles VIII = **Anne of Brittany**   Joan of Valois   =   Louis XII
                                                                  King of France

Frankish Lineage
(chart 1)

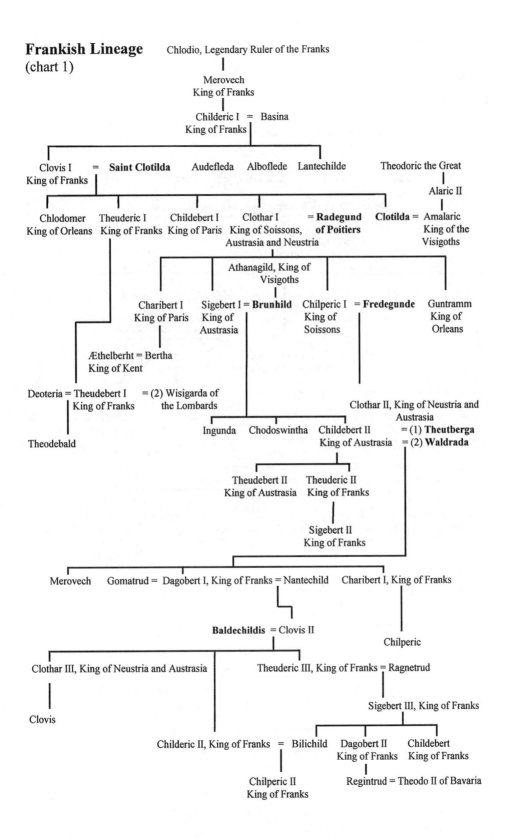

Chlodio, Legendary Ruler of the Franks

Merovech
King of Franks

Childeric I = Basina
King of Franks

Clovis I = **Saint Clotilda**   Audefleda   Alboflede   Lantechilde   Theodoric the Great
King of Franks

Alaric II

Chlodomer   Theuderic I   Childebert I   Clothar I   = **Radegund**   **Clotilda** = Amalaric
King of Orleans   King of Franks   King of Paris   King of Soissons,   **of Poitiers**   King of the
                                              Austrasia and Neustria   Visigoths

Athanagild, King of
Visigoths

Charibert I   Sigebert I = **Brunhild**   Chilperic I = **Fredegunde**   Guntramm
King of Paris   King of   King of   King of
              Austrasia   Soissons   Orleans

Æthelberht = Bertha
King of Kent

Deoteria = Theudebert I   = (2) Wisigarda of   Clothar II, King of Neustria and
           King of Franks   the Lombards   Austrasia

Theodebald   Ingunda   Chodoswintha   Childebert II   = (1) **Theutberga**
                                                              King of Austrasia   = (2) **Waldrada**

Theudebert II   Theuderic II
King of Austrasia   King of Franks

Sigebert II
King of Franks

Merovech   Gomatrud = Dagobert I, King of Franks = Nantechild   Charibert I, King of Franks

Baldechildis = Clovis II

Chilperic

Clothar III, King of Neustria and Austrasia   Theuderic III, King of Franks = Ragnetrud

Clovis

Sigebert III, King of Franks

Childeric II, King of Franks = Bilichild   Dagobert II   Childebert
                                            King of Franks   King of Franks

Chilperic II   Regintrud = Theodo II of Bavaria
King of Franks

Frankish Lineage
(chart 2)

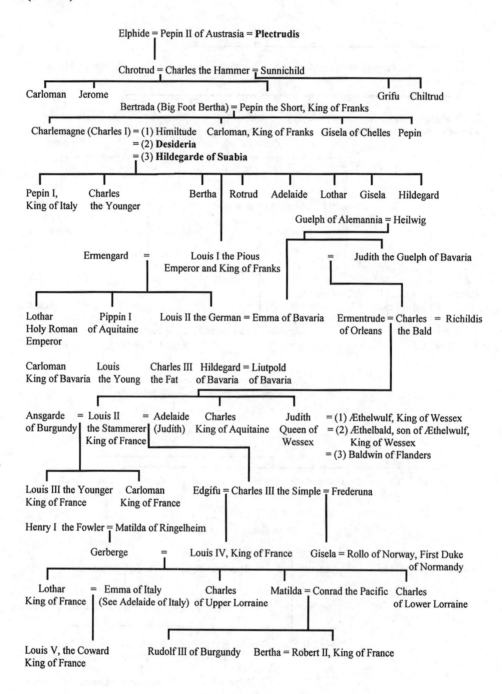

Hungary
(chart 1)

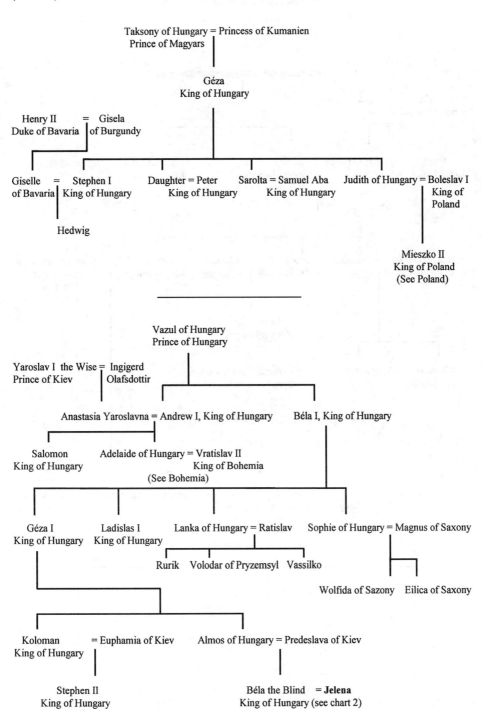

Hungary
(chart 2)

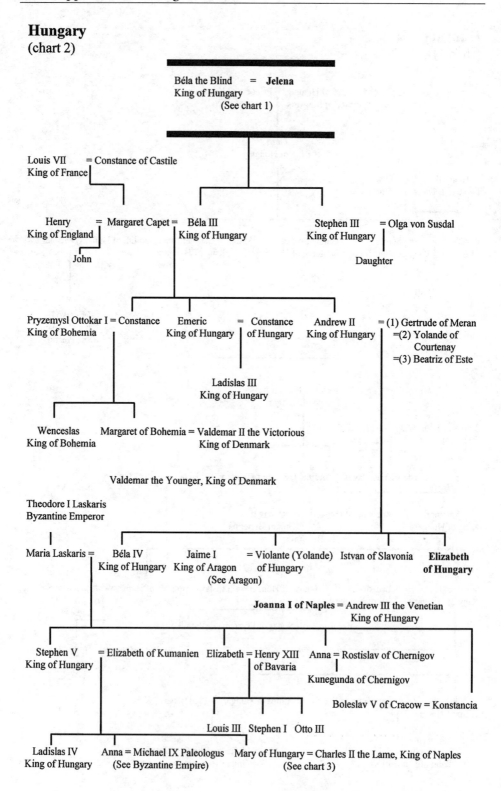

Béla the Blind   =   **Jelena**
King of Hungary
(See chart 1)

Louis VII   = Constance of Castile
King of France

Henry   = Margaret Capet =   Béla III   Stephen III   = Olga von Susdal
King of England   King of Hungary   King of Hungary

John   Daughter

Pryzemysl Ottokar I = Constance   Emeric   =   Constance   Andrew II   = (1) Gertrude of Meran
King of Bohemia   King of Hungary   of Hungary   King of Hungary   =(2) Yolande of
                                                                                        Courtenay
                                                                                     =(3) Beatriz of Este

Ladislas III
King of Hungary

Wenceslas   Margaret of Bohemia = Valdemar II the Victorious
King of Bohemia   King of Denmark

Valdemar the Younger, King of Denmark

Theodore I Laskaris
Byzantine Emperor

Maria Laskaris =   Béla IV   Jaime I   = Violante (Yolande) Istvan of Slavonia   **Elizabeth**
                    King of Hungary King of Aragon   of Hungary   **of Hungary**
                                    (See Aragon)

Joanna I of Naples = Andrew III the Venetian
                          King of Hungary

Stephen V   = Elizabeth of Kumanien Elizabeth = Henry XIII Anna = Rostislav of Chernigov
King of Hungary   of Bavaria

                                                                     Kunegunda of Chernigov

                                                            Boleslav V of Cracow = Konstancia

                                    Louis III   Stephen I   Otto III

Ladislas IV   Anna = Michael IX Paleologus Mary of Hungary = Charles II the Lame, King of Naples
King of Hungary   (See Byzantine Empire)   (See chart 3)

Hungary
(chart 3)

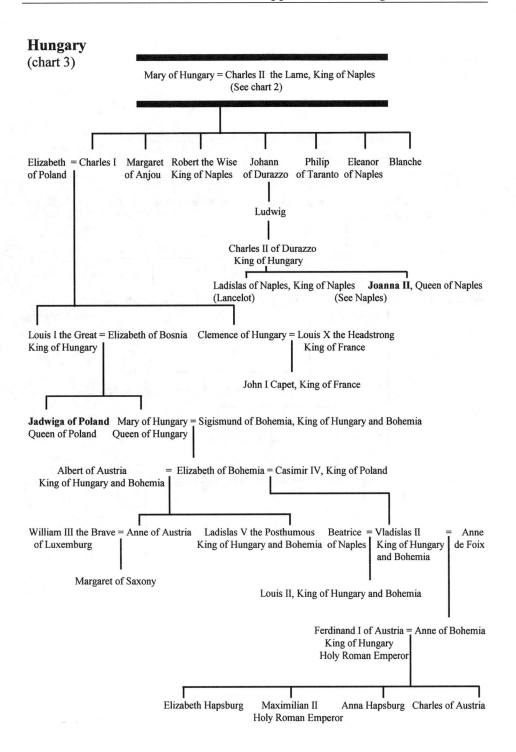

Isabella of France
(*See also* France *and* England)

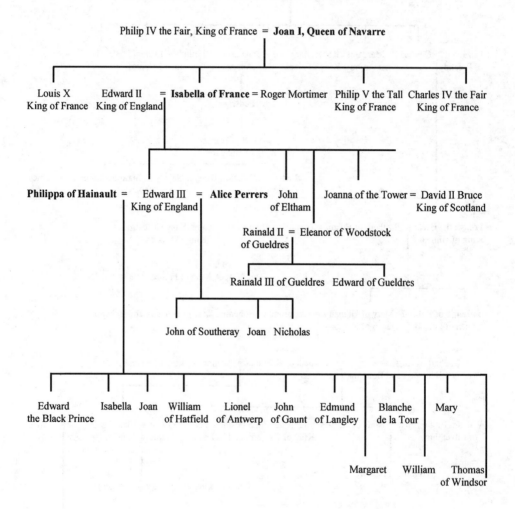

Philip IV the Fair, King of France = **Joan I, Queen of Navarre**

Louis X, King of France | Edward II, King of England = **Isabella of France** = Roger Mortimer | Philip V the Tall, King of France | Charles IV the Fair, King of France

Philippa of Hainault = Edward III, King of England = **Alice Perrers** | John of Eltham | Joanna of the Tower = David II Bruce, King of Scotland

Rainald II of Gueldres = Eleanor of Woodstock

Rainald III of Gueldres   Edward of Gueldres

John of Southeray   Joan   Nicholas

Edward the Black Prince | Isabella | Joan | William of Hatfield | Lionel of Antwerp | John of Gaunt | Edmund of Langley | Blanche de la Tour | Mary

Margaret   William   Thomas of Windsor

Kent

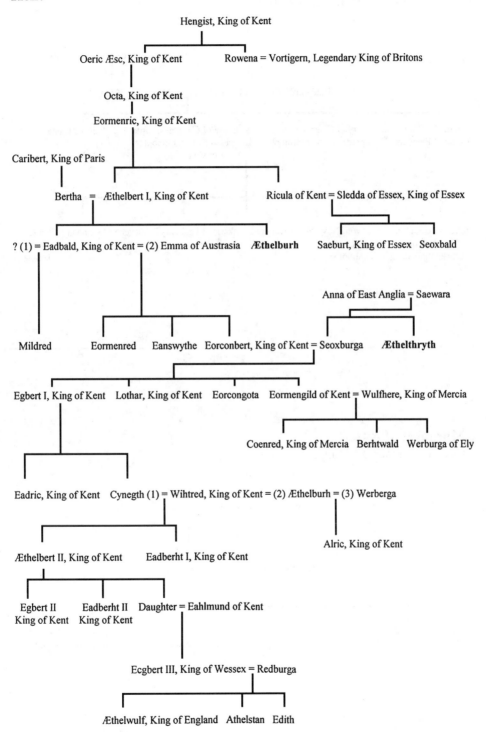

Latin Empire of Constantinople

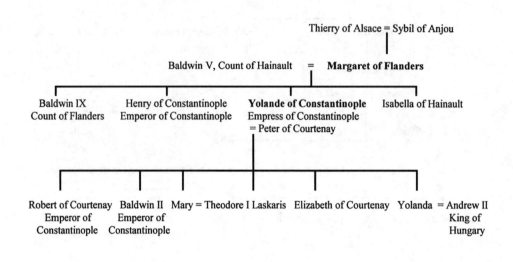

Margaret of Anjou
(*See also* France *and* England)

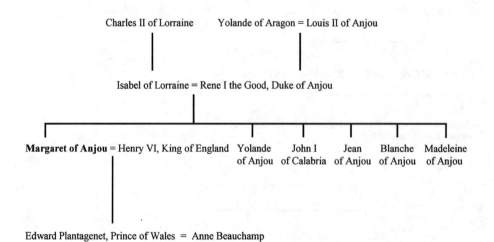

Matilda of England
(*See also* England)

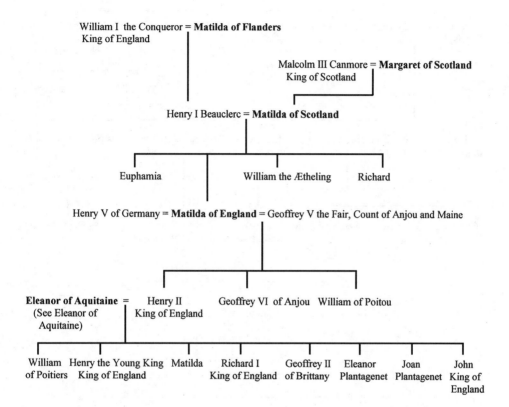

Mercia
(chart 1)

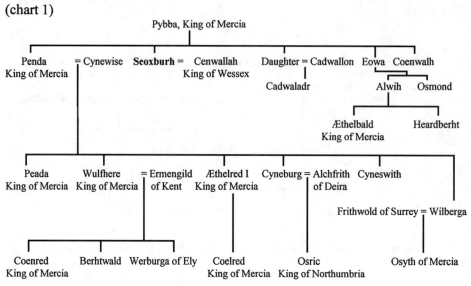

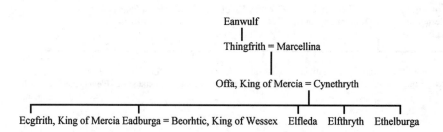

Mercia
(chart 2)

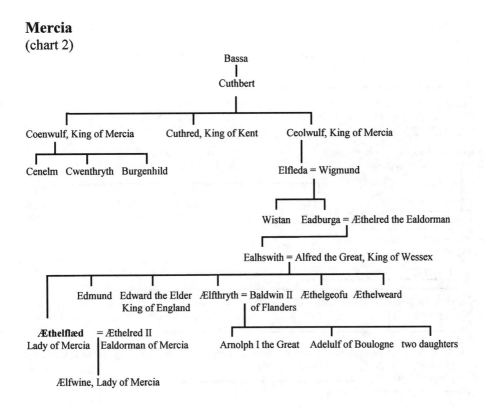

Bassa

Cuthbert

Coenwulf, King of Mercia   Cuthred, King of Kent   Ceolwulf, King of Mercia

Cenelm Cwenthryth Burgenhild   Elfleda = Wigmund

Wistan   Eadburga = Æthelred the Ealdorman

Ealhswith = Alfred the Great, King of Wessex

Edmund   Edward the Elder   Ælfthryth = Baldwin II   Æthelgeofu Æthelweard
King of England   of Flanders

Æthelflæd   = Æthelred II   Arnolph I the Great   Adelulf of Boulogne   two daughters
Lady of Mercia Ealdorman of Mercia

Ælfwine, Lady of Mercia

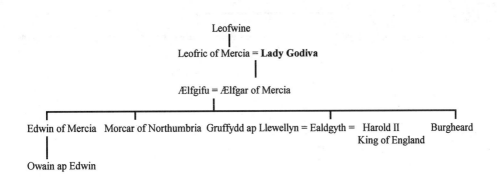

Leofwine

Leofric of Mercia = **Lady Godiva**

Ælfgifu = Ælfgar of Mercia

Edwin of Mercia   Morcar of Northumbria   Gruffydd ap Llewellyn = Ealdgyth =   Harold II   Burgheard
                                                                              King of England

Owain ap Edwin

Navarre
(chart 1)

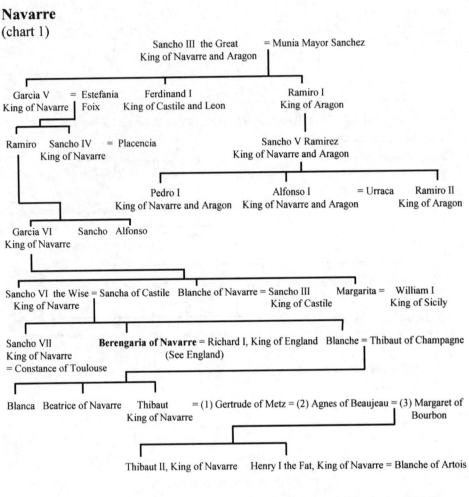

Sancho III the Great = Munia Mayor Sanchez
King of Navarre and Aragon

Garcia V = Estefania   Ferdinand I   Ramiro I
King of Navarre | Foix   King of Castile and Leon   King of Aragon

Ramiro   Sancho IV = Placencia   Sancho V Ramirez
         King of Navarre   King of Navarre and Aragon

                Pedro I   Alfonso I   = Urraca   Ramiro II
          King of Navarre and Aragon   King of Navarre and Aragon   King of Aragon

Garcia VI   Sancho Alfonso
King of Navarre

Sancho VI the Wise = Sancha of Castile   Blanche of Navarre = Sancho III   Margarita = William I
King of Navarre   King of Castile   King of Sicily

Sancho VII   Berengaria of Navarre = Richard I, King of England   Blanche = Thibaut of Champagne
King of Navarre   (See England)
= Constance of Toulouse

Blanca   Beatrice of Navarre   Thibaut   = (1) Gertrude of Metz = (2) Agnes of Beaujeau = (3) Margaret of
                            King of Navarre   Bourbon

                Thibaut II, King of Navarre   Henry I the Fat, King of Navarre = Blanche of Artois

                            Thibaut   Joan I, Queen of Navarre =   Philip IV
                                                              King of France

Marguerite of Burgundy = Louis X   = Clemence of Hungary Philip V Charles IV   Isabella = Edward II
                     King of France   King of
                     and Navarre   England
                                                                                           (See England)

        Joan II   = Philip d'Evreux   John I, King of France
    Queen of Navarre

Charles II the Bad = Joan of France Philip Louis   Blanche of Navarre = Philip VI, King of France
King of Navarre   (See France)
        (See chart 2)

Navarre
(chart 2)

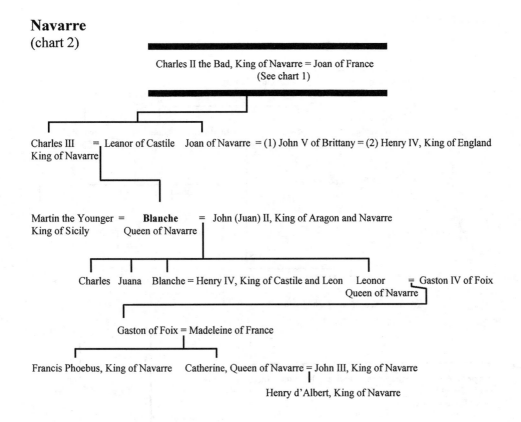

Northumbria

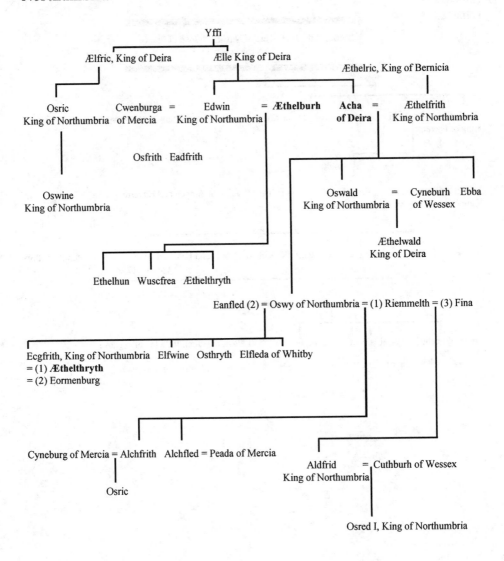

Norway
(chart 1)

Gudrod = **Asa**

Halfdan the Black = **Ragnhild**

Harald I Fairhair = (1)Ragnhild Eriksdottir = (2) Thora Mostaff =(3) Swanhilda
King of Norway

Erik I Bloodaxe = Gunnhild Ozursdottir
King of Norway

Haakon I the Good
King of Norway

Bjorn Haraldsson

Harald II Greycloak
King of Norway

Gurdrod Bjornsson = Cecilie

Harald Gudrodsson = Asta Gudbrandsdottir = Sigurd Halfdansson

Astrid Olafsdottir = St Olaf the Holy = Alfhild
King of Norway

Ulfhild

Magnus I the Good
King of Norway

Ragnhild Magnusdottir

Thora Thorbergsdottir = Harald III Hardrada = Elizabeth Jaroslavana   Guthorm   Gunnhild   Halfdan   Ingirid
King of Norway

Magnus II
King of Norway

Olaf the Gentle = Thora Johnsdottir
King of Norway

Maria   Ingigerd

Haakon Magnusson
King of Norway

Thora (1) = Magnus III Barelegs = (2) Sigrid Saxisdottir = (3) Irish woman
King of Norway

Sigurd I the Crusader
King of Norway

Olaf Magnusson
King of Norway

Harald IV
King of Norway
(See chart 2)

Norway
(chart 2)

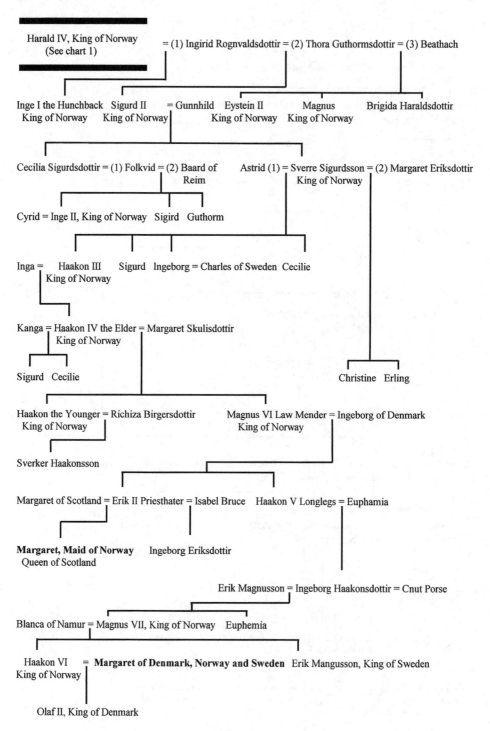

Harald IV, King of Norway (See chart 1) = (1) Ingirid Rognvaldsdottir = (2) Thora Guthormsdottir = (3) Beathach

Inge I the Hunchback, King of Norway   Sigurd II, King of Norway = Gunnhild   Eystein II, King of Norway   Magnus, King of Norway   Brigida Haraldsdottir

Cecilia Sigurdsdottir = (1) Folkvid = (2) Baard of Reim   Astrid (1) = Sverre Sigurdsson, King of Norway = (2) Margaret Eriksdottir

Cyrid = Inge II, King of Norway   Sigird   Guthorm

Inga =   Haakon III, King of Norway   Sigurd   Ingeborg = Charles of Sweden   Cecilie

Kanga = Haakon IV the Elder, King of Norway = Margaret Skulisdottir

Sigurd   Cecilie

Christine   Erling

Haakon the Younger, King of Norway = Richiza Birgersdottir   Magnus VI Law Mender, King of Norway = Ingeborg of Denmark

Sverker Haakonsson

Margaret of Scotland = Erik II Priesthater = Isabel Bruce   Haakon V Longlegs = Euphamia

Margaret, Maid of Norway Queen of Scotland   Ingeborg Eriksdottir

Erik Magnusson = Ingeborg Haakonsdottir = Cnut Porse

Blanca of Namur = Magnus VII, King of Norway   Euphemia

Haakon VI = **Margaret of Denmark, Norway and Sweden**   Erik Mangusson, King of Sweden
King of Norway

Olaf II, King of Denmark

Ottonian Holy Roman Empire

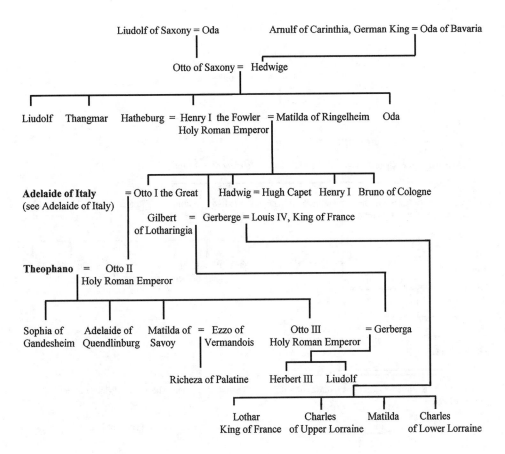

Poland
(chart 1)

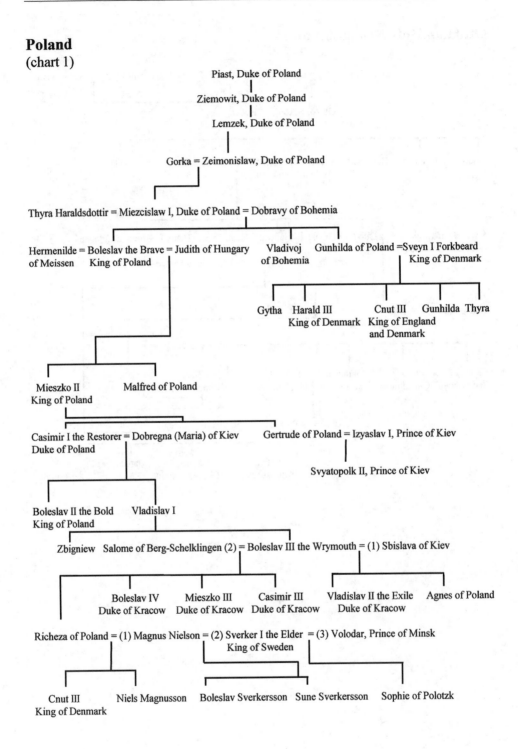

Piast, Duke of Poland

Ziemowit, Duke of Poland

Lemzek, Duke of Poland

Gorka = Zeimonislaw, Duke of Poland

Thyra Haraldsdottir = Miezcislaw I, Duke of Poland = Dobravy of Bohemia

Hermenilde = Boleslav the Brave = Judith of Hungary   Vladivoj   Gunhilda of Poland = Sveyn I Forkbeard
of Meissen   King of Poland   of Bohemia   King of Denmark

Gytha   Harald III   Cnut III   Gunhilda   Thyra
         King of Denmark   King of England
                           and Denmark

Mieszko II   Malfred of Poland
King of Poland

Casimir I the Restorer = Dobregna (Maria) of Kiev   Gertrude of Poland = Izyaslav I, Prince of Kiev
Duke of Poland

Svyatopolk II, Prince of Kiev

Boleslav II the Bold   Vladislav I
King of Poland

Zbigniew   Salome of Berg-Schelklingen (2) = Boleslav III the Wrymouth = (1) Sbislava of Kiev

Boleslav IV   Mieszko III   Casimir III   Vladislav II the Exile   Agnes of Poland
Duke of Kracow   Duke of Kracow   Duke of Kracow   Duke of Kracow

Richeza of Poland = (1) Magnus Nielson = (2) Sverker I the Elder = (3) Volodar, Prince of Minsk
                                          King of Sweden

Cnut III   Niels Magnusson   Boleslav Sverkersson   Sune Sverkersson   Sophie of Polotzk
King of Denmark

Poland
(chart 2)

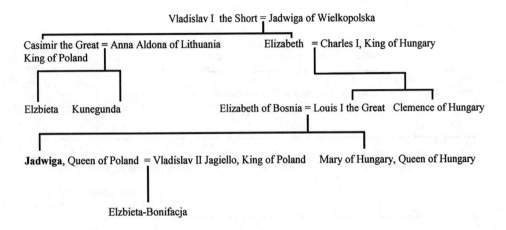

Portugal
(chart 1)

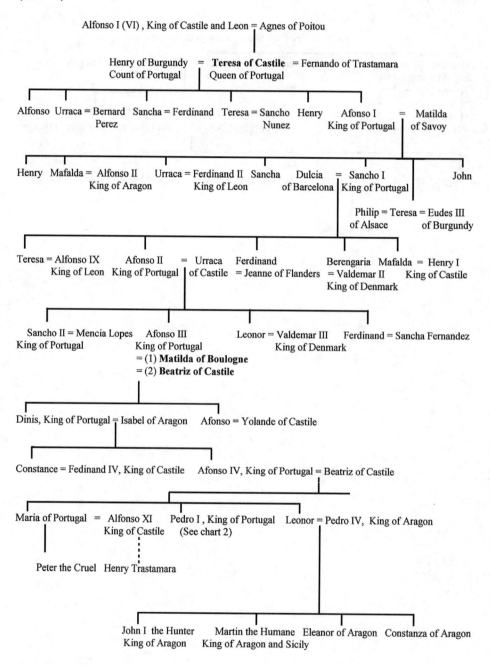

Alfonso I (VI) , King of Castile and Leon = Agnes of Poitou

Henry of Burgundy   =   **Teresa of Castile**   = Fernando of Trastamara
Count of Portugal   Queen of Portugal

Alfonso   Urraca = Bernard   Sancha = Ferdinand   Teresa = Sancho   Henry   Afonso I   =   Matilda
                        Perez   Nunez   King of Portugal   of Savoy

Henry   Mafalda = Alfonso II   Urraca = Ferdinand II   Sancha   Dulcia   =   Sancho I   John
                  King of Aragon   King of Leon   of Barcelona   King of Portugal

Philip = Teresa = Eudes III
of Alsace   of Burgundy

Teresa = Alfonso IX   Afonso II   =   Urraca   Ferdinand   Berengaria   Mafalda = Henry I
        King of Leon   King of Portugal   of Castile   = Jeanne of Flanders   = Valdemar II   King of Castile
                                                                    King of Denmark

Sancho II = Mencia Lopes   Afonso III   Leonor = Valdemar III   Ferdinand = Sancha Fernandez
King of Portugal   King of Portugal   King of Denmark
                          = (1) **Matilda of Boulogne**
                          = (2) **Beatriz of Castile**

Dinis, King of Portugal = Isabel of Aragon   Afonso = Yolande of Castile

Constance = Fedinand IV, King of Castile   Afonso IV, King of Portugal = Beatriz of Castile

Maria of Portugal   =   Alfonso XI   Pedro I , King of Portugal   Leonor = Pedro IV, King of Aragon
                        King of Castile   (See chart 2)

Peter the Cruel Henry Trastamara

John I the Hunter   Martin the Humane   Eleanor of Aragon   Constanza of Aragon
King of Aragon   King of Aragon and Sicily

Portugal
(chart 2)

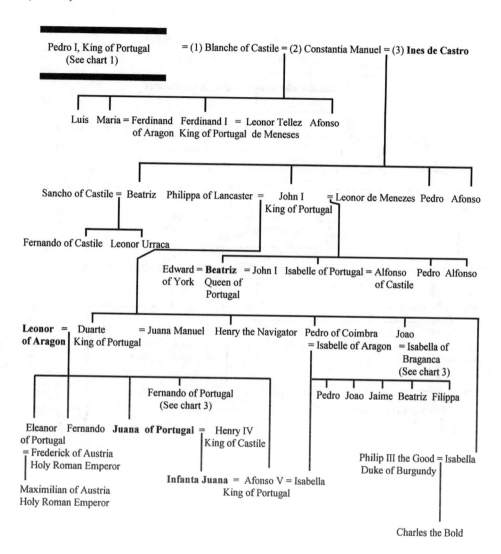

Portugal
(chart 3)

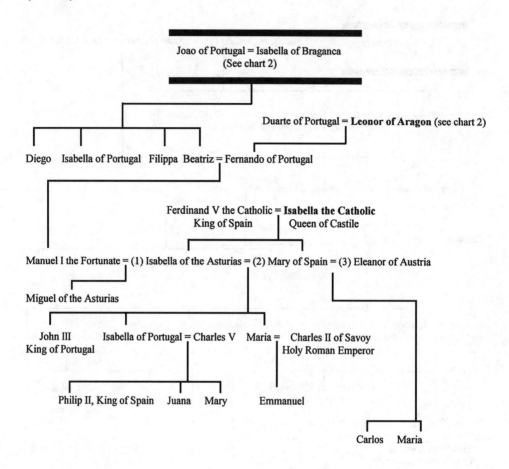

Joao of Portugal = Isabella of Braganca
(See chart 2)

Duarte of Portugal = **Leonor of Aragon** (see chart 2)

Diego   Isabella of Portugal   Filippa   Beatriz = Fernando of Portugal

Ferdinand V the Catholic = **Isabella the Catholic**
King of Spain   Queen of Castile

Manuel I the Fortunate = (1) Isabella of the Asturias = (2) Mary of Spain = (3) Eleanor of Austria

Miguel of the Asturias

John III   Isabella of Portugal = Charles V   Maria =   Charles II of Savoy
King of Portugal   Holy Roman Emperor

Philip II, King of Spain   Juana   Mary   Emmanuel

Carlos   Maria

Russia

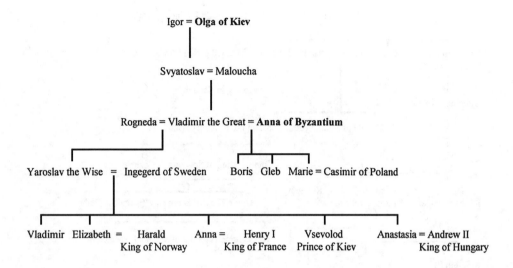

Igor = **Olga of Kiev**

Svyatoslav = Maloucha

Rogneda = Vladimir the Great = **Anna of Byzantium**

Yaroslav the Wise = Ingegerd of Sweden   Boris   Gleb   Marie = Casimir of Poland

Vladimir   Elizabeth =   Harald   Anna =   Henry I   Vsevolod   Anastasia = Andrew II
                    King of Norway   King of France   Prince of Kiev   King of Hungary

Scotland
(chart 1)

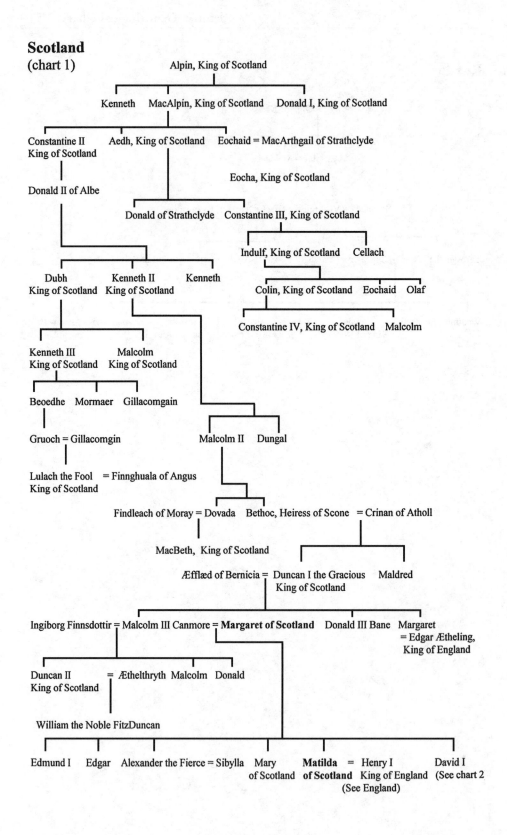

Alpin, King of Scotland

Kenneth MacAlpin, King of Scotland   Donald I, King of Scotland

Constantine II
King of Scotland

Aedh, King of Scotland   Eochaid = MacArthgail of Strathclyde

Donald II of Albe

Eocha, King of Scotland

Donald of Strathclyde   Constantine III, King of Scotland

Indulf, King of Scotland   Cellach

Dubh   Kenneth II   Kenneth
King of Scotland   King of Scotland

Colin, King of Scotland   Eochaid   Olaf

Constantine IV, King of Scotland   Malcolm

Kenneth III   Malcolm
King of Scotland   King of Scotland

Beoedhe   Mormaer   Gillacomgain

Gruoch = Gillacomgin

Malcolm II   Dungal

Lulach the Fool   = Finnghuala of Angus
King of Scotland

Findleach of Moray = Dovada   Bethoc, Heiress of Scone   = Crinan of Atholl

MacBeth, King of Scotland

Æfflæd of Bernicia = Duncan I the Gracious   Maldred
King of Scotland

Ingiborg Finnsdottir = Malcolm III Canmore = **Margaret of Scotland**   Donald III Bane   Margaret
= Edgar Ætheling,
King of England

Duncan II   = Æthelthryth   Malcolm   Donald
King of Scotland

William the Noble FitzDuncan

Edmund I   Edgar   Alexander the Fierce = Sibylla   Mary   **Matilda** = Henry I   David I
of Scotland   **of Scotland**   King of England   (See chart 2
(See England)

Scotland
(chart 2)

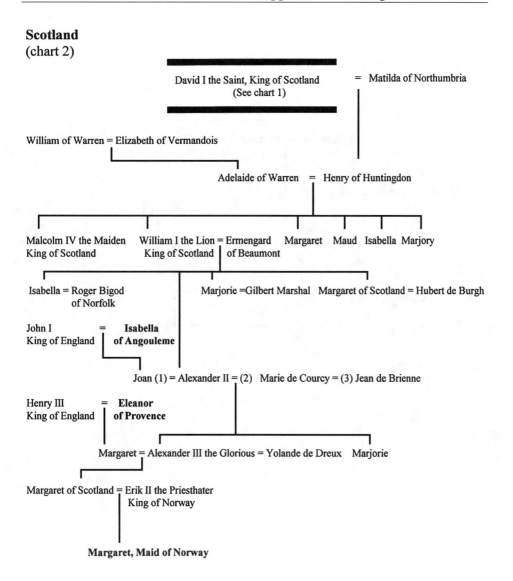

David I the Saint, King of Scotland (See chart 1) = Matilda of Northumbria

William of Warren = Elizabeth of Vermandois

Adelaide of Warren   =   Henry of Huntingdon

Malcolm IV the Maiden King of Scotland   William I the Lion = Ermengard King of Scotland   of Beaumont   Margaret   Maud   Isabella   Marjory

Isabella = Roger Bigod of Norfolk   Marjorie = Gilbert Marshal   Margaret of Scotland = Hubert de Burgh

John I King of England   =   Isabella of Angouleme

Joan (1) = Alexander II = (2)   Marie de Courcy = (3) Jean de Brienne

Henry III King of England   =   Eleanor of Provence

Margaret = Alexander III the Glorious = Yolande de Dreux   Marjorie

Margaret of Scotland = Erik II the Priesthater King of Norway

Margaret, Maid of Norway

Scotland
(chart 3)

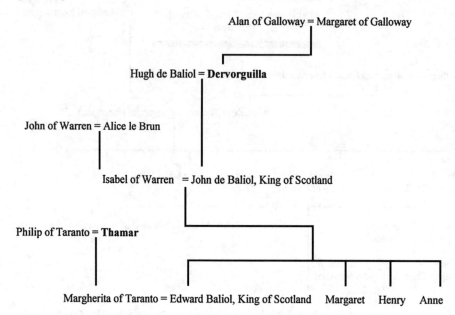

Scotland
(chart 4)

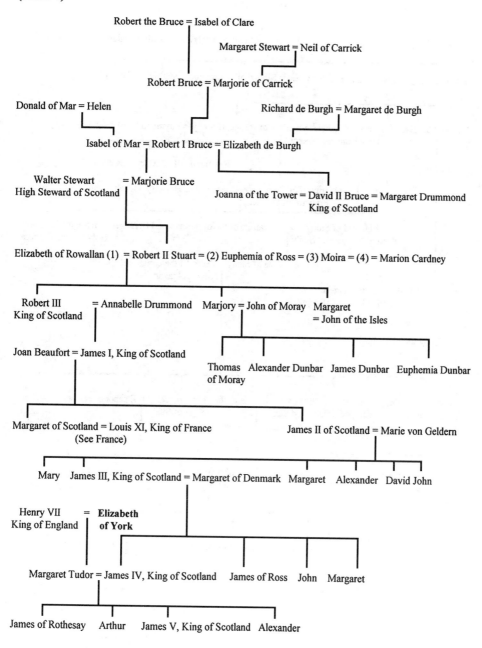

Sicily

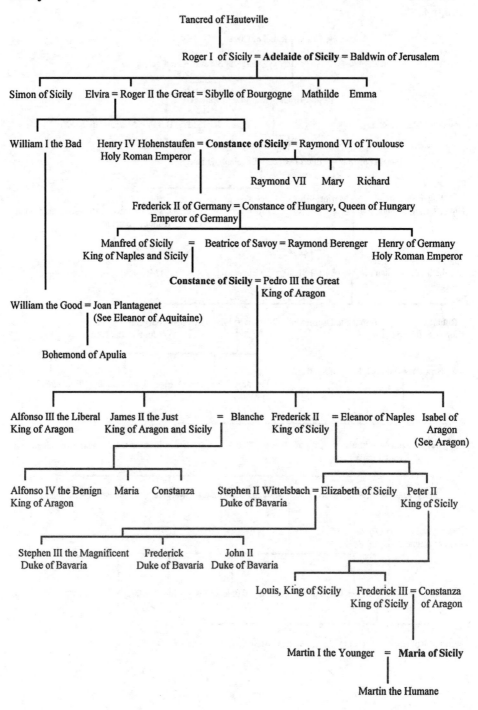

Sweden
(chart 1)

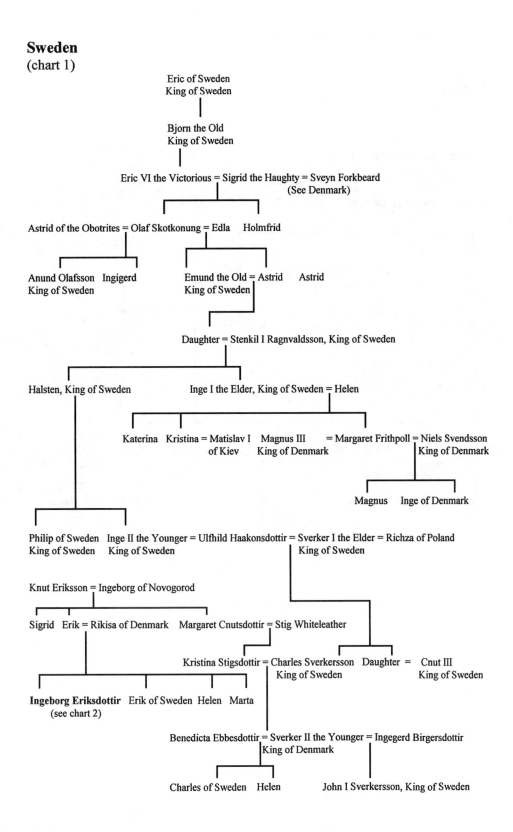

Eric of Sweden
King of Sweden
|
Bjorn the Old
King of Sweden
|
Eric VI the Victorious = Sigrid the Haughty = Sveyn Forkbeard
(See Denmark)

Astrid of the Obotrites = Olaf Skotkonung = Edla   Holmfrid

Anund Olafsson   Ingigerd   Emund the Old = Astrid   Astrid
King of Sweden   King of Sweden

Daughter = Stenkil I Ragnvaldsson, King of Sweden

Halsten, King of Sweden   Inge I the Elder, King of Sweden = Helen

Katerina   Kristina = Matislav I   Magnus III   = Margaret Frithpoll = Niels Svendsson
                      of Kiev   King of Denmark   King of Denmark

                                                          Magnus   Inge of Denmark

Philip of Sweden Inge II the Younger = Ulfhild Haakonsdottir = Sverker I the Elder = Richza of Poland
King of Sweden   King of Sweden   King of Sweden

Knut Eriksson = Ingeborg of Novogorod

Sigrid   Erik = Rikisa of Denmark   Margaret Cnutsdottir = Stig Whiteleather

                          Kristina Stigsdottir = Charles Sverkersson Daughter = Cnut III
                                                 King of Sweden   King of Sweden

Ingeborg Eriksdottir Erik of Sweden Helen Marta
     (see chart 2)

                    Benedicta Ebbesdottir = Sverker II the Younger = Ingegerd Birgersdottir
                                            King of Denmark

                        Charles of Sweden   Helen   John I Sverkersson, King of Sweden

Sweden
(chart 2)

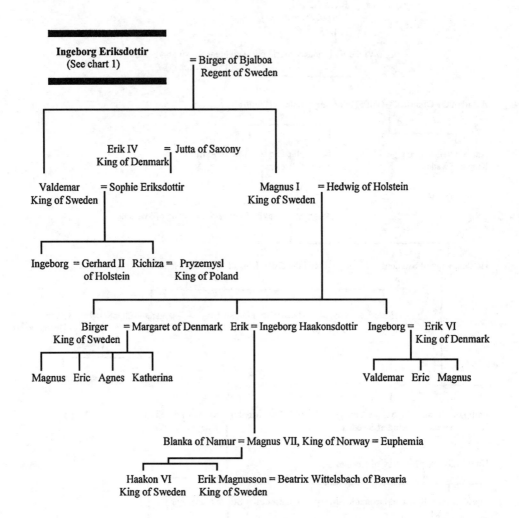

Wessex

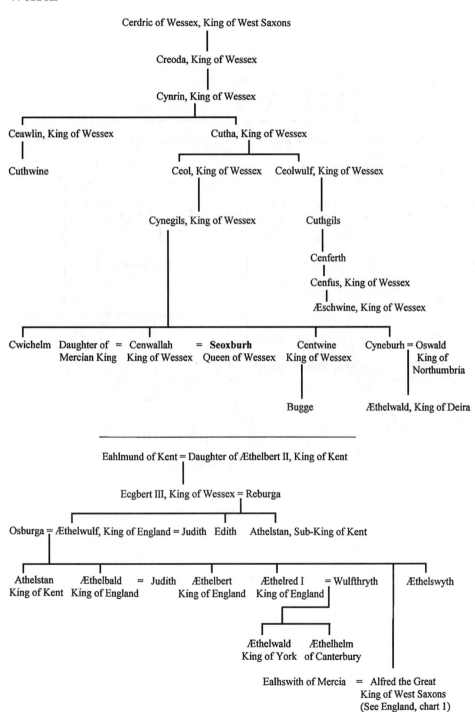

Cerdric of Wessex, King of West Saxons

Creoda, King of Wessex

Cynrin, King of Wessex

Ceawlin, King of Wessex   Cutha, King of Wessex

Cuthwine   Ceol, King of Wessex   Ceolwulf, King of Wessex

Cynegils, King of Wessex   Cuthgils

Cenferth

Cenfus, King of Wessex

Æschwine, King of Wessex

Cwichelm   Daughter of = Cenwallah = **Seoxburh**   Centwine   Cyneburh = Oswald
          Mercian King King of Wessex Queen of Wessex King of Wessex   King of
                                                                    Northumbria

Bugge   Æthelwald, King of Deira

Eahlmund of Kent = Daughter of Æthelbert II, King of Kent

Ecgbert III, King of Wessex = Reburga

Osburga = Æthelwulf, King of England = Judith Edith   Athelstan, Sub-King of Kent

Athelstan   Æthelbald   = Judith   Æthelbert   Æthelred I   = Wulfthryth   Æthelswyth
King of Kent King of England   King of England King of England

Æthelwald   Æthelhelm
King of York   of Canterbury

Ealhswith of Mercia = Alfred the Great
                        King of West Saxons
                        (See England, chart 1)

Western Rulers of Jerusalem

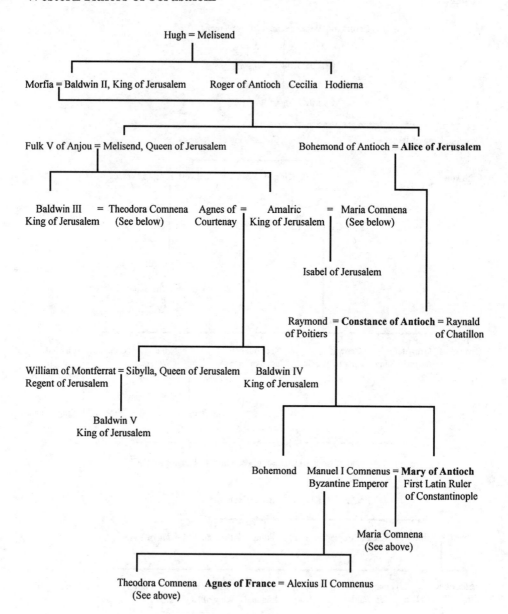

Zoë
(*See also* Byzantine Empire)

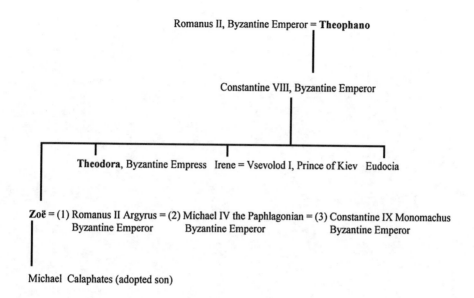

Romanus II, Byzantine Emperor = **Theophano**

Constantine VIII, Byzantine Emperor

Theodora, Byzantine Empress   Irene = Vsevolod I, Prince of Kiev   Eudocia

Zoë = (1) Romanus II Argyrus = (2) Michael IV the Paphlagonian = (3) Constantine IX Monomachus
           Byzantine Emperor   Byzantine Emperor   Byzantine Emperor

Michael Calaphates (adopted son)

Glossary

Ætheling In Anglo-Saxon England, anyone of noble birth. After the Norman Conquest, the term was used to identify members of the royal family. The beginning of the word — *Æthel* — was used as part of the name of many Anglo-Saxon kings to indicate their royal blood.

Alba A popular type of medieval song, especially among the troubadours in Provence.

Almshouse Also poorhouse. Institution that provided shelter and food for the poor, established during the Middle Ages by religious orders trying to fulfill their vows of charity.

Althing In Iceland, a national assembly of freemen established in 930 for the purpose of governing. It is the oldest legislature in the world.

Anti-pope Any pope elected in opposition to the canonically chosen pontiff. In the Middle Ages, a number of anti-popes were elected by French cardinals to counter the Roman popes.

Apostasy The act of defying faith. In early Christianity, apostasy was one of three unpardonable sins, along with murder and unlawful sexual intercourse. The term "the Apostasy," or the Riddah, is also used to refer to the period in Islamic history after the death of Muhammad during which many converts to Islam reverted to their former religions.

Archon Term used for a Slavic prince.

Ban Term used for a Hungarian duke.

Banovina Hungarian duchy. Mostly independent of the Crown, but subject to the king in matters of foreign policy.

Bard Poet, singer, and musician. A bard served as an oral historian and chronicler, a balladeer, a political and social critic, and an entertainer. In Wales, bards were often of the nobility, and they created guilds to maintain their standards. In England, they were outlawed for inciting their listeners to rebellion, so they gradually lost their importance. In Anglo-Saxon society, they were called scōps.

Bastard Feudalism Name coined by historians to describe the economic relationship that occurred when the members of a lord's retinue supported his causes but instead of being enfeoffed (rewarded with a grant of land), they were financially supported by the lord, lived in his household, took gifts of money, and were appointed to generously paid posts.

Benefices Any of the offices or rewards, such as bishoprics and episcopal sees, that could be given to worthy individuals in the Roman Catholic church. Such offices could be extremely lucrative to the holder. In the Middle Ages, they became appointed posts. This led to bribery, corruption, and conflict, as people not suited for the posts were awarded them for political reasons.

Boyar Also Bojar. Term used to identify members of the military aristocracy in Bulgaria and Russia.

Caliph In Islam, the successor to Muhammad the Prophet.

Caliphate The highest office in Islam. The individual who holds the office, the caliph, is known as the Commander of the Faithful. The caliph is the leader of the Muslim community and is considered the spiritual successor to Muhammad.

Canonization In the Roman Catholic church, the official pronouncement of the sanctity or sainthood of a dead person. A lengthy process of investigation is carried out before such a pronouncement is made. Early Christians venerated martyrs and called holy people "saints" without any official recognition by the church. The canonization procedure was not developed until 993, when Pope John XV declared Ulric, bishop of Augsburg, a saint. Strict procedures of investigation before beatification and canonization were not introduced until the seventeenth century.

Cantiagas Spanish poems of heroic deeds.

Cathay Medieval term for the Orient or Asia.

Ceorl A freeman ranking just above a serf in England during the Anglo-Saxon period. The word *churl* comes from this designation.

Chanson de Geste "Song of deeds." French poems, dating from the eleventh to the fifteenth century, that celebrate heroic and legendary events. They were important sources for medieval romances.

Coat of Arms *see* **Heraldry**

Column of the Universe *see* **Irminsul**

Concordat Agreement between the Roman Catholic church and secular government. Concordats negotiated terms regarding matters of the church in a specific country.

Condottieri Italian mercenaries. In the Middle Ages, they made up mercenary armies and were involved in the continual warfare among Italian city-states. Leaders of these mercenary armies were sometimes able to seize power and depose rightful rulers.

Count of the Palace High-ranking government official. In Charlemagne's court, it replaced the office of the mayor of the palace, but was a less-powerful position. The count of the palace presided over the palace court when the king could not be present personally.

Count Palatine Position below the king in Hungary. In the king's absence, the count palatine served as regent.

Court of Common Pleas Established during the reign of Henry III of England, it was a separate court that heard the cases of the common people. Instead of following the King's Court, which traveled with the king wherever he went, the Court of Common Pleas had a fixed location. It was overseen by a chief justice and as many judges as were needed to handle the cases brought before it.

Court of Star Chamber Created in the late fifteenth century by Henry VII in order to regain some power from Parliament. The court had an extensive jurisdiction and could try nobles too powerful to be prosecuted elsewhere. It was restricted in the penalties it could impose. Although it could order torture, imprisonment, and mutilation, it could not execute criminals. Court proceedings were public.

Curfew Restrictions placed on activities after certain hours. From the cry "Cover fires!" (in French, *couvrir feu*). In the Middle Ages, people were not allowed to work once the sun had set since they would be unable to see well enough to do their jobs correctly, nor could they leave their homes after dark.

Danegeld Monetary tributes paid to the Vikings by European rulers. In exchange for this tribute, the Vikings would stop raiding a particular city or country. Over time, European rulers developed a system of taxation in order to pay this tribute. To the Vikings, danegeld also meant any treasure or booty, which they shared among themselves, that they captured during raids.

Danelaw Territory in England under the control of the Vikings, who the Anglo-Saxons called Danes. The territory consisted of the northeast and the Midlands. It was eventually reconquered by the Anglo-Saxons under Æthelstan, who won the decisive battle at Brunanburh.

Danevirke A feature of early Denmark consisting of a series of defensive earthworks that controlled access to Jutland (the mainland of Denmark) from the south. The Danevirke has been attributed to King Godefred in 808, but it was probably constructed around 737. Credit for construction has also been given to Thryi, wife of Gorm the Old, king of Denmark.

Dark Ages Period of the Middle Ages commonly considered to be between AD 400 and 1000. The term is rarely used by modern historians.

Dauphin Term used to refer to the heir apparent to the French throne.

Despot Honorary title given to the person second in command to the Byzantine emperor.

Divine Office Also divine hours. Series of prayers recited at specified times throughout the day. The day was divided into nine "hours," and the church bell rang at each hour to summon the faithful to prayer. *Vigils* took place at midnight; *matins* was held at dawn; *lauds* followed shortly thereafter; *prime* started the workday; *terce* was held at the third hour; *sext* at lunchtime; *none* or *nonce* at the ninth hour; *vespers* was at sunset; and *compline* was at bedtime.

Do-Nothing Kings Called *rois fainéants* in French. Term used to describe the Frankish kings who succeeded Clovis, especially in the seventh century; who were characterized by a lack of aggressive leadership and disinterest in ruling. Pippin, the famous mayor of the palace, deposed the last Merovingian king and established the Carolingian dynasty, which lasted for several centuries.

Eastern Empire Term used to refer to the Byzantine Empire.

Edda Two famous compilations of old Icelandic literature. The Poetic or Elder Edda consists of thirty-four lays on mythological, legendary, and heroic subjects. It includes poems that were composed between the ninth and thirteenth centuries and was probably compiled early in the thirteenth century. The Younger or Prose Edda is a treatise on the subject of poetry. It is also a compilation of Norse mythology and was written about 1220 by Snorri Sturluson.

Eisteddfod From the Welsh, "assembly of learned men." A festival held annually at which bards or minstrels competed among themselves, set standards for poetry and music, and earned licenses as recognized bards.

Exarch Official of the Byzantine Empire, similar to a governor, who oversaw Byzantine territories. The *exarchate* was the territory governed. The Italian exarch was deposed in 608 as the Goths threw off Byzantine rule.

Fable Short tale in prose or verse that possesses a moral or exemplary value. Fables were extremely popular in the Middle Ages.

Fabliaux Short, risqué stories told in verse. They depict realistic details and ordinary people while making fun of human foibles and ridiculing authority figures. They were composed by minstrels and were especially popular in France during the Middle Ages.

Fifth Court Court of appeals established in Iceland around 1005. Verdicts in cases were determined by a simple majority of judges, who were farmers.

Fifth Element Also philosopher's stone. A substance believed by alchemists to be capable of turning base metals into gold, essential to the science of alchemy.

Filid Irish "seer" who was the equivalent of a minstrel or the Anglo-Saxon scōp. The filids memorized laws, history, genealogies, heroic epics, and poems, performing a vital function in a preliterate society.

Frank   Meaning "free," as opposed to the subject peoples of Rome. The Franks were a group of Germanic tribes which appeared in the middle of the third century and invaded Roman territory. Defeated, they withdrew into Gaul and formed two branches, the Salian and the Riparian Franks. The former settled in northern Gaul, and the latter settled in northeastern Gaul. By the sixth century, they controlled most of Gaul under Clovis. About this time they converted to Christianity and defeated the Arian Visigoths. The kingdom that the Franks ruled was the forerunner of France.

Free Companies   Sometimes called freebooters. Groups of brigands, former military men who were released from the armies and left to plunder on their own. Groups numbering up to fifty gathered under the command of quasi-military leaders. They seized castles, robbed travelers, and raided villages. They ransomed people and villages; robbed abbeys and monasteries; and killed, tortured, and raped citizens. They abducted women as forced camp followers (prostitutes) and men as forced servants. Free Companies were excommunicated as a whole by Pope Urban V in 1364, but they continued to be an ongoing torment to order and stability well into the sixteenth century.

Free-lance   Mercenaries and professional warriors for hire. They were so called because they used a lance, which was a warrior's weapon, a weapon of knights. Since they were free, with no oath of loyalty to any one lord, they could engage in any battle on any side.

Friars   Term used to indicate members of certain religious orders who lived monastic lives while serving people in the outside world. Like monks, they lived under the rule of an order and wore identifying clothing called habits, but instead of dwelling on the salvation of their own souls, they went out into the world and tried to save others. Unlike monks, who belonged to a specific monastic house and lived a cloistered life, friars belonged only to a general order and lived and worked in the secular world. Although the words *monk* and *friar* are often used interchangeably, they refer to two different types of religious practices.

Frith   Anglo-Saxon word meaning "peace." In the early medieval period, it referred to a monetary payment or tribute.

Glosses and Glossators   Commentaries and interpretations, called glosses, were made on important writings, especially theological and philosophical treatises, although scientific and literary works were not immune. The commentators, called glossators, often translated the texts they glossed. In the Middle Ages, these analytical interpretations were important in the development of philosophical and religious thought as well as secular and canon law.

Goliards   Wandering scholars and students in Western Europe, especially predominant in the twelfth and thirteenth centuries, known for writing verses that celebrated drinking and fornication while complaining about their mistreatment at the hands of their professors, the townspeople, and other adults or authority figures. Their appellation derived from the name Golia, used to refer to the devil.

Grail, Holy   In Arthurian romance, the grail is a cup or dish used by Christ at the Last Supper and sought by the Knights of the Round Table. The word *grail* is simply a corruption of the medieval Latin word *cratella*, which means "bowl." Joseph of Arimathea was believed to have preserved the Holy Grail and to have collected blood from Christ's body in it. The blood was thought to have magical qualities.

Greek Fire   An incendiary substance used before gunpowder became common. Invented in the seventh century, this flammable mixture was often used in naval battles. The substance ignited spontaneously, and the resulting fire could not be put out with water. The formula was kept secret and is still unknown.

It probably consisted of tar and petroleum, sprayed on the enemy using pumps.

Grimoires   Books of magic that were popular in the Middle Ages. They were variously ascribed to Albertus Magnus, Pope Honorius III, and other practitioners of witchcraft and sorcery. Given their subject matter, they were kept and copied in secret, making them expensive.

Hamasa   Collection of Arabic poems put together by Abu Tamman in the ninth century. It serves as a remarkable record of early Arabic verse.

Hans   Stations and hospices provided throughout Seljuk Turkey for travelers. Some were built, supported, and maintained by the sultan for his personal use; these were highly decorated and well supplied.

Hegira   Arabic word meaning "flight," used specifically to refer to the flight of Muhammad the Prophet from Mecca in 622. The year of the Hegira is the first year of the Muslim era. In the Islamic calendar, AD 622 is 1 AH (anno hegirae).

Heraldry   Also known as coats of arms. Symbolic and ornamental insignia associated with a specific person or family line, originally worn on armor. In the fourteenth century, knights began placing a family symbol on the surcoat or tunic worn over chain mail. This became known as the "coat of arms." For a few centuries, knights wore whatever symbols or insignia they wished. Near the beginning of the sixteenth century, the practice became regulated. Heraldic symbols, called heraldic devices, became inherited emblems of social status. A heraldic device usually consisted of a shield, helm, crest, motto, and several other ornaments.

Heriot   After the death of a peasant, the lord received a tribute to reimburse him for the loss. The tribute could be a service performed by the family of the deceased, but it was usually the peasant's best or most substantial possession.

Holy Grail *see* **Grail, Holy**

Holy Island *see* **Lindisfarne**

Holy Office   Another term for the Inquisition.

Hospitalitas   Literally, "hospitality." A Roman/Byzantine system of determining and rendering the money due from taxpayers under obligation to provide a fixed proportion of their revenues or produce either in cash or in kind. The system eliminated the necessity for the state to collect and distribute the revenue, since it was paid directly to the recipients. Based on a Roman model, the system spread throughout the Middle Ages and became a common method of tax collection.

Iconoclasm   Literally, "image hatred." Movement that denounced the depiction of images in religious art. Iconoclasm was particularly popular in the Byzantine Empire in the eighth and ninth centuries, leading to a violent controversy.

Iconodules   Literally, "image venerators." In the Iconoclastic Controversy, Iconodules opposed the Iconoclast policies of Byzantine Emperor Leo III and his successors. Two of the most famous Iconodules, Empress Irene and Empress Theodora, were eventually successful in restoring the depiction of natural forms in religious art and in restoring the practice of the veneration of images.

Indulgence   In the Roman Catholic church, the remission of punishment for sins. Although in the Middle Ages it was often confused with the remission of sins, it was a different practice entirely. In early Christian practice, strict penances were imposed by the confessor on a person guilty of a serious sin. Over time, the church began substituting prayer, alms giving, and charitable work, granting indulgences for the more severe penances. Later, indulgences were sold instead of granted; a wealthy person could purchase indulgences while a poor person might be forced to undergo physical punishment. The sale and granting of indulgences was one of the practices of the church that the reformer Martin Luther demanded be abandoned entirely.

Infidel An unbeliever. In the Middle Ages the term was used by Christians to refer to Muslims and by Muslims to refer to Christians. An infidel was also any person who disagreed with a particular doctrine or principle of the church. To Muslims, infidels needed to be converted or destroyed. To Christians, all infidels were heretics and were treated as such.

Interdict In the Roman Catholic church, a serious penalty that withdraws all public religious services and the administration of sacraments to a place or group of people in retaliation for certain crimes or sins. It is similar to a large-scale excommunication. In the Middle Ages, interdict was used in a much more ordinary way and for political as well as religious reasons. Travelers during the Middle Ages were forced to go around any areas that were under interdict, or they traveled at the peril of their souls.

Interregnum Term used to refer to any interruption in the succession of rulers or popes resulting in a lack of leadership for a period of time. The term is also used to refer specifically to the period between the fall of the Roman Empire and the Renaissance (i.e., the Middle Ages).

Irminsul World pillar, or column of the universe. The symbol of the power of the Saxon gods, it was the trunk that held up the heavens. Charlemagne destroyed it and announced that all Saxons who did not convert would be annihilated.

Jihad In Islam, the spiritual struggle against evil. In the Middle Ages, jihad referred to Islamic holy wars against infidels, including Christians.

Jongleurs French minstrels.

Just Price A medieval belief that capitalist enterprise offended God. Therefore, prices were set at a fair or "just" level, which would be the value of the labor plus the value of the materials used. No one gained an advantage over anyone else. Laws prohibited gaining competitive advantage through the use of new tools, technology, or processes and did not allow working late, employing extra workers, or advertising.

Karkhan Leadership position below khan in Turkey. The karkhan ruled in the absence of the khan.

Khagan Chieftain of a Slavic or Bulgarian tribe.

Khan Literally, "lord." Term used by Turkish rulers. The title "great khan" was used as the equivalent of overlord. The khan ruled over a territory called a khanate.

Kharjas Type of poetry common in Andalusia, in which a young girl tells her mother about the friend with whom she has fallen in love.

Kin Shame Law passed at the Althing in Iceland in the late tenth century in response to overzealous missionaries, requiring relatives to persecute Christians they knew if the Christians denigrated the Norse gods or pagan practices.

Knez Title for a Serbian prince.

Knight of the Road An outlaw or thief.

Knight's Fee The fief or land granted by a lord to a knight, sufficient in size to support the knight and his retinue.

Königsschutz Also called Munt. German word, important to Franks and Goths, meaning the king's duty to protect his followers. During the later Middle Ages, the importance of this duty was largely forgotten by kings, leading to numerous rebellions and civil wars.

Konungsbók "The King's Book." So named because it was owned by the Dutch Crown and was kept in the Old Royal Library. One of two extant manuscripts that preserve Icelandic law codes (the other is *Staðarjólsbók*). These law books are not official codices but are private productions that cover the judicial and constitutional system in Iceland. Both are mid–thirteenth century, well kept and ornamented.

Koran The sacred scripture of Islam. Revelations given to Muhammad the Prophet by

God and written down by his followers. The collection of revelations now known as the Koran was probably compiled around 640. An authorized version was created in the 650s, and earlier versions were destroyed (a few survive). The Koran is the earliest known work in Arabic prose. It consists of fourteen chapters of religious, social, military, and legal codes and describes the main doctrines of Islam.

Law Rock Also lögberg. Symbol of the rule of law in Iceland. During the meeting of the Althing, the Icelandic legislative assembly, any individual in Iceland could introduce new legislation or propose laws by announcing them at the law rock. The law rock was also the place where the law speaker, who presided over the law council, confirmed his ability to do the job by reciting one-third of the laws of Iceland each year.

Lindisfarne Sometimes called Holy Island. Island off the coast of Northumberland in northeast England. Saint Aidan established a Celtic Christian monastery there in 635. It was later famous for its illuminated manuscript. The Danes pillaged and destroyed Lindisfarne in 793, having learned of its many riches.

Livery Uniforms provided by medieval lords to their servants to distinguish them and identify their household.

Makar Literally, "maker." Scottish court poet.

Mären German stories that are similar to French fabliaux. They recreated everyday life and examined the power struggle between men and women. Questions of sexuality were explored, usually with a risqué and ribald sense of humor.

Master In medieval guilds, the owner of a shop that employed apprentices and journeymen. The number of masters of any one craft in a town was strictly limited.

Medreses Islamic schools of theology that were established throughout the Islamic Empire in the Middle Ages.

Meistersingers Members of German poet and musician guilds during the fourteenth through sixteenth centuries. Before this time, the creation of poetry and music had rested largely with the nobles, but in the fourteenth century, artisans and middle-class people continued the traditions. Apprentice and journeymen meistersingers were taught specific requirements and rules for composition and recitation.

Mendicant Friars Members of religious orders established in the Middle Ages, who renounced possession of all property, personal or communal, and who lived on charity by begging for alms. The established clergy opposed them in the beginning, but the major orders of friars were accepted by the thirteenth century. *See* Friars.

Minnesingers German poets (and composers) of the twelfth through fourteenth centuries, normally of the noble classes. German poetry of this period was modeled after that of the French troubadours.

Minstrel A medieval traveling entertainer who journeyed from place to place, singing and reciting poetry and relating the events that were happening throughout the world. *See* Bard.

Moors Term used in the Middle Ages to identify the Muslims in Spain and North Africa. The term was applied to Berbers as well as to Arabs.

Mozarab Literally, "would-be Arab." Arabized Christians. The term applied to Christians in Muslim Spain. They lived mostly in northern Spain and adopted a modified Arab and Islamic culture, which is reflected in their art, although it is crude in comparison to Islamic Spain's art and culture.

Mudéjares Muslims living in Christian Spain.

Normans A corrupted version of the words Northman or Norseman. Originally, Scandinavians from the northern countries. In the later Middle Ages, the term was used for the inhabitants of the duchy of Normandy and was particularly applied to the French who came over to Britain with William the Conqueror in 1066. As the aristocracy, they owned much of the land and revenues of England.

Northern Scourge   Name given by medieval Europeans to the Vikings and their repeated invasions of Europe.

Oral Formulaic   Term used to refer to traditional medieval poetry performed according to memorized formulas.

Outremer   Literally, "the land overseas." Term applied to the Holy Land in the Middle Ages, especially when it was under Christian control and thought of as an extension of Western Europe.

Patriarchs   Title first used in the sixth century to refer to the bishops of the five major sees of Rome, Alexandria, Antioch, Constantinople, and Jerusalem. Later, the Roman bishop became known as the pope. The patriarch of Constantinople held supremacy over the Eastern church.

Peace of God   Also Truce of God. Agreement to abide by certain rules regarding warfare. Several ecclesiastical councils demanded that soldiers refrain from attacking priests, churches, livestock, mills, vines, merchants, and anyone going to church on threat of excommunication. Civilians and religious and public buildings were also banned from attack. Later, fighting on Sunday and during Lent and Advent were prohibited. Over time, councils declared that fighting from Wednesday evening to Monday morning was banned as was fighting on saints' days. Although some military leaders observed the Peace of God, the rules met with varying degrees of success throughout the Middle Ages.

Peter's Pence   A tithe or tribute exacted by the papacy from England and other countries. It probably originated as a household tax during the reign of Mercian King Offa and was not discontinued until the Reformation. Similar payments were made by medieval Scandinavia, Hungary, and Poland.

Philosopher's Stone   Material that medieval scientists sought, believing it would turn base metals into gold. *See* Fifth Element.

Riddah   The period following the death of Muhammad the Prophet during which many of his followers abandoned Islam and reverted to their former beliefs. *See* Apostasy.

Runes   Characters in ancient Germanic languages. The earliest runic inscriptions date from the mid–third century, but they were most widely used from about AD 300 to 1100. Runes were often used when languages, such as Anglo-Saxon and Swedish, included sounds not adequately represented by Latin letters.

Sagas, Icelandic   Also called Viking sagas. Form of literature popular in the Middle Ages. These accounts describe ordinary people and their quarrels, work, and relations with others.

Sanctuary   A place of refuge and asylum. In the Middle Ages, Christian abbeys and churches had the right to provide sanctuary to anyone who asked it, beginning in the fourth century. Secular authority could not force the church authorities to turn over a person who sought sanctuary. In the seventeenth century, this right was revoked in England, and it was abandoned by most countries in the eighteenth century.

Saracens   The term was originally applied to a specific north Arabian tribe but in the Middle Ages was used to refer to all Muslims, regardless of their actual place of origin. The Muslims in Africa and Spain were often called Moors.

Sclavinias   General term used in the Byzantine Empire to refer to any of the areas in the Balkans where Slavs lived.

Scōp   Anglo-Saxon poet, historian, and chronicler in preliterate society. The scōp memorized history, laws, genealogy, epics, and poems. *See* Bard.

Scribes   Originally copyists and annotators of the Bible and scripture. In the early Middle Ages, most scribes were monks who copied and preserved documents and manuscripts, primarily those of a religious nature. They worked in scriptoria designed for that purpose. By the fourteenth century, they had become a professional group of tradespeople with their own guilds. Although the advent of the printing press thinned the ranks of scribes somewhat, businesses continued to need them to create copies of legal documents, agreements, and letters. Many educated women became scribes, sometimes donating the works as a charitable contribution.

Simony   Buying or selling religious offices or indulgences. It was a serious problem for the medieval church. The Council of Chalcedon (451) legislated against ordination for money, legislation that was reaffirmed throughout the Middle Ages. Simony was especially widespread in the ninth and tenth centuries and was one of the abuses that reformers most wanted to see addressed.

Skjoldungs   Legendary warrior-kings of Denmark, called scyldings in the medieval poem *Beowulf*. They were descended from Odin, the warrior god. The first Danish king was called Skjold.

Strategoi   Greek term for "general."

Stylites   Early Christian ascetics who lived on top of pillars or high places, without shelter from the elements.

Sultan   Title for Islamic rulers, first used in the eleventh century and favored by Seljuk and Ottoman Turks.

Sunna   Also Sunnah. Collection of customs based on the acts of Muhammad, from which Islamic theologians decide doctrinal issues.

Talmud   Collection of Jewish secular and religious law, including commentaries on the Torah. Two versions exist, the Palestinian or Jerusalem Talmud and the Babylonian Talmud. The first was written between the third and fifth centuries. The second was written between the third and sixth centuries. The Babylonian Talmud was considered authoritative. Medieval Talmudic scholars, known as tosaphists, lived in France and Germany between the twelfth and fourteenth centuries

and provided some of the most widely known and extensive commentaries on the Talmud.

Themes   Districts of the Byzantine Empire organized under military commands. The word *theme* originally meant "army corps," then began to refer to the territory where the corps resided. The Roman system of hospitalitas was employed in order to support them. In its basic form, the state took land from the landowner and gave it, plus the serfs or peasants attached to the land, to the soldiers to support themselves, thereby reducing the need to levy taxes for military undertakings.

Thing   Local legislative assemblies in Scandinavia. They maintained laws and customs guarded the rights of freemen, and controlled feuds by awarding compensation and imposing fines for crimes and injuries. These assemblies were often held in the spring, and in some areas they were held two or more times each year.

Thing Law   Common law. These were customs preserved and legislated about during the meeting of the Thing, the Scandinavian legislative assembly.

Thingmen   Legislative representatives required to attend the Thing (legislative assembly) in Scandinavia. They were usually local elders, leaders, or chieftains. In Iceland, Thingmen were also the farmers who followed a chieftain and were eligible to travel to the Althing.

Troubadours   Medieval singer-poets who flourished in France between the eleventh and thirteenth centuries. Although they were generally court poets who performed their own compositions, they sometimes traveled from place to place. They developed a set of guidelines for the treatment of women in songs; this came to be known as courtly love. These poets, of whom a number were women, were concentrated in southern France, primarily Languedoc, and wrote in the vernacular language called Lenga d'oc, or Provençal. Troubadour culture was destroyed during the Albigensian Crusades, which concentrated on the Languedoc area of France.

Tuath   The basic social/political unit, similar to a tribe, in medieval Ireland. The king or leader of a tuath could grow powerful or might be subject to a more powerful overking.

Vernacular   Refers to the native language of a country as opposed to the more "noble" language of literature and religion, Latin.

Völkerswanderungen   "Folk migrations." The movement of Germanic tribes across Asia and Europe.

Witan   *see* Witenagemot

Witenagemot   Anglo-Saxon term meaning "assembly of wise men." Council of advisors in Anglo-Saxon England that met to confer with the king regarding legal, judicial, and administrative concerns. It appointed the king if succession were in doubt or disputed, and it had the power to create laws, levy taxes, make treaties, and adjudicate legal cases. The term *witan* is sometimes used to refer to the members of the group as well as to the group itself.

World Pillar   *see* Irminsul

Wyrd   A prophecy or fate, especially among Germanic tribes.

Župan   Croatian ruler.

Bibliography

General History

Abulafia, David. *Commerce and Conquest in the Mediterranean, 1100–1500.* New York: Variorum, 1993.

Anderson, James Maxwell. *The History of Portugal.* Westport, CT: Greenwood, 2000.

Angold, Michael. *The Byzantine Empire, 1025–1204: A Political History.* Reading, MA: Addison-Wesley, 1997.

Arnold, Benjamin. *Medieval Germany, 500–1300: A Political Interpretation.* Toronto: University of Toronto Press, 1997.

Asbridge, Thomas S. *The Creation of the Principality of Antioch: 1098–1130.* London: Boydell and Brewer, 2000.

Ayer, Eleanor H. *The Anasazi.* New York: Walker, 1992.

Bak, Janos, ed. *The Laws of the Medieval Kingdom of Hungary: 1301–1457,* vol. 2 of The Laws of Hungary Series. Schlacks, 1993.

Baker, George Philip. *The Fighting Kings of Wessex.* New York: Combined Publishing, 1996.

Barraclough, G. *The Origins of Modern Germany.* Oxford: Blackwell, 1988.

Barrell, A. D. M. *Medieval Scotland.* New York: Cambridge University Press, 2000.

Bassett, Steven. *Origins of Anglo-Saxon Kingdoms.* New York: St. Martin's, 1989.

Bede, Venerable. *Ecclesiastical History of the English People.* New York: Oxford University Press, 1992.

Bell, Andrew. *The Role of Migration in the History of the Eurasian Steppe: Sedentary Civilization versus "Barbarian" and Nomad.* New York: St. Martin's, 2000.

Bellomo, Manlio. *The Common Legal Past of Europe: 1000–1800.* Washington, DC: Catholic University of America Press, 1995.

Bensch, Stephen. *Barcelona and Its Rulers: 1096–1291.* New York: Cambridge University Press, 1995.

Berenger, Jean. *A History of the Hapsburg Empire: 1273–1700.* Trans. C. A. Simpson. Reading, MA: Longman, 1994.

Bisson, Thomas N. *The Medieval Crown of Aragon: A Short History.* London: Clarendon, 1991.

Blair, Peter Hunter. *An Introduction to Anglo-Saxon England.* New York: Cambridge University Press, 1992.

Bloch, Marc. *Feudal Society: The Growth of the Ties of Dependence.* Trans. L. A. Manyon. Chicago: University of Chicago Press, 1988.

Bloch, R. Howard. *Medievalism and the Modernist Temper.* Baltimore: Johns Hopkins University Press, 1996.

Bodiford, William M. *Soto Zen in Medieval Japan.* Honolulu: University of Hawaii Press, 1993.

Boitani, Piero. *Mediaevalitas: Reading the Middle Ages.* London: Boydell and Brewer, 1996.

Bonner, M., and Heinz Halm. *The Empire of the Mahdi: The Rise of the Fatimids.* Boston: Brill, 1997.

Brett, Michael, and Elizabeth Fentress. *The Berbers.* Oxford: Blackwell, 1997.

Brown, R. Allen. *The Normans.* Woodbridge, England: Boydell Press, 1984.

_____. *The Origins of Modern Europe: The Medieval Heritage of Western Civilization.* London: Boydell and Brewer, 1996.

Brownlee, Marina. *The New Medievalism.* Baltimore: Johns Hopkins University Press, 1991.

Bullough, D. A. *The Age of Charlemagne.* London: G. P. Putnam's Sons, 1965.

Burns, R. *Islam under the Crusaders: Colonial Revival in the Thirteenth-Century Kingdom of Valencia.* Princeton, NJ: Princeton University Press, 1973.

Burns, Thomas. *A History of the Ostrogoths.* Bloomington: Indiana University Press, 1991.

Bury, John B. *A History of the Eastern Roman Empire from the Fall of Irene to the Accession of Basil I.* New York: Russell and Russell, 1965.

_____. *Invasion of Europe by the Barbarians.* New York: Norton, 2000.

Cambridge Medieval History. 8 vols. Cambridge: Cambridge University Press, 1911–36.

Cameron, Averil. *Changing Cultures in Early Byzantium.* New York: Variorum, 1996.

Campbell, J., ed. *The Anglo-Saxons.* Oxford: Phaidon, 1982.

Cantor, Norman F. *The Civilization of the Middle Ages: A Completely Revised and Expanded Edition of Medieval History, the Life and Death of a Civilization.* New York: Harper Perennial, 1994.

_____. *Inventing the Middle Ages: The Lives, Works and Ideas of the Great Medievalists of the Twentieth Century.* New York: William Morrow, 1993.

_____. *The Medieval Reader.* New York: HarperCollins, 1995.

Cassady, R. F. *The Norman Achievement.* London: Sidgwick and Jackson, 1986.

Cavallo, Guglielmo. *The Byzantines.* Chicago: University of Chicago Press, 1997.

Chamberlain, E. R. *Florence in the Time of the Medici.* Reading, MA: Longman, 1982.

Chirovsky, N. *A History of the Russian Empire.* London: Peter Owen, 1973.

Christie, Neil. *The Lombards: The Ancient Langobards.* Oxford: Blackwell, 1995.

Claster, Jill. *Medieval Experience: 300–1400.* New York: New York University Press, 1982.

Coleman, Janet. *Ancient and Medieval Memories: Studies in the Reconstruction of the Past.* New York: Cambridge University Press, 1992.

Collins, Roger. *Early Medieval Spain: Unity in Diversity.* New York: St. Martin's, 1995.

Constable, Giles. *The Reformation of the Twelfth Century.* New York: Cambridge University Press, 1996.

Corrick, James A. *The Late Middle Ages.* San Diego, CA: Lucent, 1995.

Coss, Peter R. *The Early Records of Medieval Coventry,* vol. II of *Records of Social and Economic History.* Oxford: Oxford University Press, 1986.

Dagens, Bruno. *Angkor: Heart of an Asian Empire.* Trans. Ruth Sharman. New York: Abrams, 1995.

De Clari, Robert. *The Conquest of Constantinople.* Trans. Edgar Holmes McNeal. Toronto: University of Toronto Press, 1997.

Deroche, Francois. *The Abbasid Tradition.* New York: Oxford University Press, 1992.

Dreyer, Edward. *Early Ming China: A Political History, 1355–1435.* Stanford, CA: Stanford University Press, 1982.

Duby, Georges. *France in the Middle Ages, 987–1460: From Hugh Capet to Joan of Arc.* Oxford: Blackwell, 1991.

Dukes, Paul. *A History of Russia: Medieval, Modern and Contemporary c. 882–1996.* Durham, NC: Duke University Press, 1998.

Dumville, David N. *Wessex and England from Alfred to Edgar: Six Essays on Political, Cultural and Ecclesiastical Revival.* London: Boydell and Brewer, 1992.

Esler, Anthony. *Human Venture: The Great Enterprise, a World History to 1500.* New York: Prentice Hall, 1995.

Evans, J., ed. *The Flowering of the Middle Ages.* London: Thames and Hudson, 1966.

Farmer, David Hugh, and J. F. Webb, eds. *The Age of Bede.* New York: Penguin, 1983.

Fennell, John Lister. *A History of the Russian Church to 1448.* Reading, MA: Longman, 1995.

Ferreiro, Alberto. *Visigoths in Gaul and Spain, AD 418–711: A Bibliography.* Boston: Brill, 1988.

Fichtenau, H. *The Carolingian Empire.* Trans. P. Muntz. Toronto: University of Toronto Press, 1978.

Fine, John V. A. *The Early Medieval Balkans: A*

Critical Survey from the Sixth to the Late Twelfth Century. Detroit: University of Michigan Press, 1991.

_____. *The Late Medieval Balkans: A Critical Survey from the Late Twelfth Century to the Ottoman Conquest.* Detroit: University of Michigan Press, 1994.

Fleming, Robin. *Law and Custom in Domesday England.* New York: Cambridge University Press, 1998.

Fletcher, Richard. *The Barbarian Conversion: From Paganism to Christianity.* New York: Henry Holt, 1998.

Franklin, Simon. *The Emergence of Rus: 750–1200.* Reading, MA: Addison Wesley Longman, 1996.

Fryde, Edmund. *The Early Paleologan Renaissance: 1261–1360.* Boston: Brill, 2000.

Fuhrmann, H. *Germany in the High Middle Ages c. 1050–1200* Cambridge: Cambridge University Press, 1987.

Ganshof, Francois Louis. *Feudalism.* Trans. Philip Grierson. Toronto: University of Toronto Press, 1996.

Gernet, Jacques. *A History of Chinese Civilization.* Trans. Charles Hartman and J. R. Foster. New York: Cambridge University Press, 1995.

Gibbon, Edward. *The Decline and Fall of the Roman Empire.* New York: Modern Library, 1995.

Goetz, Hans-Werner. *Life in the Middle Ages.* Notre Dame, IN: University of Notre Dame Press, 1997.

Grant, Michael. *The Fall of the Roman Empire.* New York: Touchstone, 1997.

_____. *From Rome to Byzantium: The Fifth Century AD.* New York: Routledge, 1998.

Gregory, Tony. *The Dark Ages.* New York: Facts on File, 1993.

Gregory of Tours. *The History of the Franks.* New York: Penguin, 1983.

Grufeld, Frederic V. *The French Kings.* New York: Da Capo, 1988.

Haldon, J. F. *Byzantium in the Seventh Century: The Transformation of a Culture.* New York: Cambridge University Press, 1991.

Hanawalt, Barbara A. *The Middle Ages: An Illustrated History.* New York: Oxford University Press, 1998.

Harding, Alan. *England in the Thirteenth Century.* New York: Cambridge University Press, 1993.

Haussig, H. W. *A History of Byzantine Civilization.* Trans. J. M. Hussey. New York: Praeger, 1971.

Heather, Peter. *The Goths.* Oxford: Blackwell, 1998.

Herlihy, David. *Medieval Households.* Cambridge, MA: Harvard University Press, 1985.

Hetherington, Paul. *Medieval Rome: A Portrait of the City and Its Life.* New York: St. Martin's, 1994.

Hicks, Michael. *Bastard Feudalism.* London: Longman, 1995.

Higham, N. J. *An English Empire: Bede, the Britons, and the Early Anglo-Saxon Kings.* Manchester: Manchester University Press, 1995.

Hines, John, et al. *Anglo-Saxons from the Migration Period to the Eighth Century: An Ethnographic Perspective.* London: Boydell and Brewer, 1998.

Hodgkin, Thomas, and Tim Newark. *Huns, Vandals and the Fall of the Roman Empire.* New York: Greenhill, 1996.

Hollister, C. Warren. *Medieval Europe: A Short History.* New York: McGraw-Hill, 1997.

_____, et al. *Medieval Europe: A Short Sourcebook.* New York: McGraw-Hill, 1996.

Holmes, George, ed. *The Oxford History of Medieval Europe.* New York: Oxford University Press, 1992.

Holt, P. M. *The Age of the Crusades: The Near East from the Eleventh Century to 1517.* Reading, MA: Longman, 1986.

Honore, Tony. *Law in the Crisis of Empire 379–455 AD: The Theodosian Dynasty and Its Quaestors.* New York: Oxford University Press, 1998.

Hubatsch, Walther. *Focus on German History: Eleven Essays.* New York: St. Martin's, 1984.

Hudson, John. *The Formation of the English Common Law: Law and Society in England from the Norman Conquest to the Magna Carta.* Reading, MA: Longman, 1996.

Hughes, Michael. *Early Modern Germany: 1477–1806.* Philadelphia: University of Pennsylvania Press, 1992.

Huizina, Johan. *Autumn of the Middle Ages.* Chicago: University of Chicago Press, 1996.

Irwin, Robert. *The Middle East in the Middle*

Ages: The Early Mamluk Sultanate, 1250–1382. London: Croome Helm, 1986.

James, E. *The Origins of France.* New York: St. Martin's, 1982.

Jenkins, R. *Byzantium: The Imperial Centuries 610–1071.* New York: Random House, 1966.

Jones, Michael C. E. *The Creation of Brittany: A Late Medieval State.* London: Hambledon, 1988.

Kochan, L., and Abraham, R. *The Making of Modern Russia.* London: Weidenfeld and Nicholson, 1969.

Koenigsberger, Helmut. *Medieval Europe 400–1500.* Reading, MA: Longman, 1987.

Lawson, M. K. *Cnut: The Danes in England in the Early Eleventh Century.* London: Longman, 1993.

Le Goff, Jacques. *Medieval Civilization, 400–1500.* Oxford: Blackwell, 1990.

Lewis, Archibald. *Nomads and Crusaders, 1000–1368.* Bloomington: Indiana University Press, 1988.

Lewis, Bernard. *The Muslim Discovery of Europe.* New York: Norton, 1985.

Linehan, Peter. *History and the Historians of Medieval Spain.* Oxford: Clarendon, 1993.

Macdermott, M. *A History of Bulgaria.* London: Allen and Unwin, 1962.

MacDonald, Fiona. *The Middle Ages.* New York: Facts on File, 1993.

Mango, C. A. *Byzantium: The Empire of New Rome.* London: Weidenfeld and Nicholson, 1980.

Matthew, Donald. *The Norman Kingdom of Sicily.* New York: Cambridge University Press, 1992.

McCarthy, Justin. *The Ottoman Turks: An Introductory History to 1923.* Reading, MA: Longman, 1997.

McKisack, May. *The Fourteenth Century: 1307–1399.* New York: Oxford University Press, 1991.

McKitterick, Rosamond. *The Frankish Kings and Culture in the Early Middle Ages.* New York: Variorum, 1995.

McKitterick, Rosamond, ed. *The New Cambridge Medieval History: 700–900.* New York: Cambridge University Press, 1995.

Meyendorff, J. *Byzantium and the Rise of Russia.* Cambridge: Cambridge University Press, 1981.

Mommsen, Theodor Ernst, ed. *Imperial Lives and Letters of the Eleventh Century.* New York: Columbia University Press, 2000.

Morgan, David. *Medieval Persia, 1040–1797.* Reading, MA: Addison-Wesley, 1988.

Moriarity, Catherine, ed. *The Voice of the Middle Ages: In Personal Letters 1100–1500.* New York: Peter Bedrick, 1991.

Mundy, John Hine. *Europe in the High Middle Ages, 1150–1309.* Reading, MA: Longman, 1991.

Nardo, Don. *The Fall of the Roman Empire.* New York: Greenhaven, 1998.

Nicol, Donald M. *The Last Centuries of Byzantium: 1261–1453.* New York: Cambridge University Press, 1993.

Norwich, John Julius. *Byzantium: The Decline and Fall.* New York: Knopf, 1996.

_____. *Byzantium: The Early Centuries.* New York: Knopf, 1989.

Oakes, Catherine. *Exploring the Past: The Middle Ages.* New York: Harcourt Brace, 1989.

Oakley, Francis. *The Medieval Experience: Foundations of Western Cultural Singularity.* Toronto: University of Toronto Press, 1988.

O'Callaghan, Joseph F. *A History of Medieval Spain.* Ithaca, NY: Cornell University Press, 1983.

Oikonomides, Nicolas. *Byzantium from the Ninth Century to the Fourth Crusade: Studies, Texts, Monuments.* New York: Variorum, 1992.

Olaniyan, Richard. *Nigerian History and Culture.* Reading, MA: Longman, 1985.

Ostrogorsky, G. *History of the Byzantine State.* Trans. J. M. Hussey. East Brunswick, NJ: Rutgers University Press, 1957.

Ozment, Steve. *The Age of Reform: 1250–1550. An Intellectual and Religious History of Late Medieval and Reformation Europe.* New Haven, CT: Yale University Press, 1986.

Peters, Edward. *Europe and the Middle Ages.* New York: Prentice Hall, 1996.

Petravich, M. B. *History of Serbia.* 2 vols. New York: Harcourt, 1976.

Poly, Jean-Pierre, et al. *The Feudal Transformation, 900–1200.* New York: Holmes and Meier, 1991.

Portal, R. *The Slavs.* London: Weidenfeld and Nicholson, 1969.

Pribechevich, S. *Macedonia: Its People and History.*

University Park: Pennsylvania State University Press, 1983.

Reilly, Bernard. *The Medieval Spains*. New York: Cambridge University Press, 1993.

Rice, T. *The Byzantines*. London: Thames and Hudson, 1969.

Roberts, David D., and Willow D. Roberts. *In Search of the Old Ones: Exploring the Anasazi World of the Southwest*. New York: Simon and Schuster, 1997.

Roderick, A., ed. *Wales: A History*. London: Michael Joseph, 1986.

Rowling, Marjorie. *Life in Medieval Times*. New York: Perigee, 1973.

Runciman, J. C. S. *Byzantine Civilization*. New York: St. Martin's, 1966.

Saul, Nigel. *Fourteenth-Century England*. London: Boydell and Brewer, 2000.

Sawyer, Brigit, and Peter Sawyer. *Medieval Scandinavia: From Conversion to Reformation, circa 800–1500*. Minneapolis: University of Minnesota Press, 1993.

Sawyer, P. H. *Kings and Vikings*. New York: Penguin, 1984.

Sayer, Derek. *The Coasts of Bohemia: A Czech History*. Princeton, NJ: Princeton University Press, 1998.

Sedlar, Jean W. *East Central Europe in the Middle Ages, 1000–1500*. Seattle: University of Washington Press, 1994.

Simon, L. J. *Iberia and the Mediterranean World of the Middle Ages: Studies in Honor of Robert I Burns, S.J.* Boston: Brill, 1995.

Sims-Williams, Patrick. *Britain and Early Christian Europe: Studies in Early Medieval History and Culture*. New York: Variorum, 1995.

Smith, G. Rex. *Studies in the Medieval History of Yemen and South Arabia*. New York: Variorum, 1997.

Spring Symposium of Byzantine Studies. *Byzantium in the Ninth Century: Dead or Alive? Papers from the Thirtieth Spring Symposium of Byzantine Studies*. Brookfield, CT: Ashgate, 1998.

Stavrianos, Leften. *The World to 1500: A Global History*. New York: Prentice Hall, 1995.

Stenton, Frank M. *Anglo-Saxon England*. New York: Oxford University Press, 1989.

Storey, R. L. *Chronology of the Medieval World, 800–1400*. New York: Simon and Schuster, 1994.

Strayer, Joseph Reese. *On the Medieval Origins of the Modern State*. Princeton, NJ: Princeton University Press, 1973.

Sugar, Peter F. *Southeastern Europe Under Ottoman Rule*. Seattle: University of Washington Press, 1983.

Tabari, George Saliba. *The Crisis of the Abbasid Caliphate*. Albany: State University of New York Press, 1985.

Taylor, John. *Politics and Crisis in Fourteenth-Century England*. New York: Sutton, 1990.

Thompson, E. A., and P. J. Heather. *The Huns*. Oxford: Blackwell, 1995.

Tibble, Steven. *Monarchy and Lordships in the Latin Kingdom of Jerusalem, 1099–1291*. London: Clarendon, 1990.

Tierney, Brian. *The Middle Ages: Readings in Medieval History*. New York: McGraw-Hill, 1992.

_____. *Western Europe in the Middle Ages, 300–1475*. New York: McGraw-Hill, 1992.

Treadgold, Warren T. *A History of the Byzantine State and Society*. Stanford, CA: Stanford University Press, 1997.

Tuchman, Barbara. *A Distant Mirror: The Calamitous 14th Century*. New York: Ballantine, 1987.

Vernadsky, G. *A History of Russia*. New Haven, CT: Yale University Press, 1944.

_____. *Kievan Russia*. New Haven, CT: Yale University Press, 1959.

_____. *The Origins of Russia*. Westport, CT: Greenwood, 1975.

Webster, B. *Medieval Scotland*. New York: St. Martin's, 1997.

Wilson, D. *The Vikings and Their Origins*. London: Thames and Hudson, 1980.

_____, ed. *The Northern World: The History and Heritage of Northern Europe* AD *400-1100*. New York: Abrams, 1980.

Wilson, Thomas B. *History of the Church and State in Norway: From the Tenth to the Sixteenth Century*. Atlanta: Scholars Press, 1971.

Wolf, Kenneth Baxter. *Making History: The Normans and Their Historians in Eleventh-Century Italy*. Philadelphia: University of Pennsylvania Press, 1995.

Wolfram, Herwig. *History of the Goths*. Berkeley: University of California Press, 1990.

Yanagi, M., et al. *Byzantium*. Trans. N. Fry. London: Cassel, 1978.

Zamoyski, A. *The Polish Way*. London: John Murray, 1987.

Zophy, Jonathan W. *The Holy Roman Empire*. Westport, CT: Greenwood, 1981.

Biography

Abailard, Pierre. *The Letters of Abelard and Heloise*. Reading, MA: Addison Wesley Longman, 1998.

Abels, Richard P. *Alfred the Great: War, Kingship and Culture in Anglo-Saxon England*. Reading, MA: Longman, 1998.

Anouihl, Jean, and Lucienne Hill. *Becket or the Honor of God*. Berkeley: University of California Press, 1996.

Armstrong, Karen. *Muhammad: A Biography of the Prophet*. San Francisco: Harper San Francisco, 1993.

_____. *Visions of God: Four Medieval Mystics and Their Writings*. New York: Bantam, 1994.

Bancroft, Anne. *The Luminous Vision: Six Medieval Mystics and Their Teachings*. New York: HarperCollins, 1989.

Barber, Richard. *Edward, Prince of Wales and Aquitaine: A Biography of the Black Prince*. Rochester, NY: University of Rochester Press, 1999.

_____. *The Life and Campaigns of the Black Prince*. New York: St. Martin's, 1997.

Bauerschmidt, Frederick Christian. *Julian of Norwich and the Mystical Body Politic of Christ*. Notre Dame, IN: University of Notre Dame Press, 1999.

Bloom, Harold, ed. *Joan of Arc*. New York: Chelsea House, 1992.

Boojamra, John Lawrence. *The Church and Social Reform: The Policies of the Patriarch Athanasios of Constantinople*. New York: Fordham University Press, 1993.

Bridges, John H. *The Life and Work of Roger Bacon*. New York: AMS Press, 1991.

Bridget of Sweden. *Saint Bride and Her Book: Birgitta of Sweden's Revelations, with Interpretive Essay and Introduction*. Trans. Julia Bolton Holloway. London: Boydell and Brewer, 2000.

Byrne, Lavinia. *Margaret of Scotland*. London: Hodder and Stoughton, 1999.

Carroll, Warren. *Isabel of Spain: The Catholic Queen*. Front Royal, VA: Christendom Press, 1991.

Caterina da Genova. *Catherine of Genoa: Purgation and Purgatory. The Spiritual Dialogue*. Trans. Serge Hughes. Mahwah, NJ: Paulist Press, 1979.

Caterina da Siena. *Catherine of Siena: The Dialogue*. Trans. Suzanne Noffke. Mahwah, NJ: Paulist Press, 1988.

Cavadini, John, ed. *Gregory the Great*. Notre Dame, IN: University of Notre Dame Press, 1996.

Chibnall, Marjorie. *The Empress Matilda: Queen Consort, Queen Mother and Lady of the English*. Oxford: Blackwell, 1993.

Clanchy, M. T. *Abelard: A Medieval Life*. Oxford: Blackwell, 1997.

Clare of Assisi: Early Documents. Mahwah, NJ: Paulist Press, 1988.

Cochrane, Louise. *Adelard of Bath: The First English Scientist*. London: British Museum Publishing, 1995.

Collis, Louise. *Memoirs of a Medieval Woman: The Life and Times of Margery Kempe*. New York: HarperCollins, 1983.

Copleston, F. C. *Aquinas*. Harmondsworth, England: Penguin, 1955.

Currier, John W. *Clovis, King of Franks*. Milwaukee, WI: Marquette University Press, 1997.

Davids, Adelbert. *The Empress Theophano: Byzantium and the West at the Turn of the First Millennium*. New York: Cambridge University Press, 1995.

Davidson, Herbert. *Alfarabi, Avicenna, and Averroes on Intellect: Their Cosmologies, Theories of the Active Intellect and Theories of Human Intellect*. New York: Oxford University Press, 1992.

Dockray, Keith. *Henry VI and the Wars of the Roses: A Sourcebook*. New York: Sutton, 2000.

Dunbabin, Jean. *Charles I of Anjou: Power, Kingship, and Statemaking in Thirteenth-Century Europe*. Reading, MA: Addison-Wesley, 1998.

Erlanger, Phillipe. *Margaret of Anjou: Queen of England*. Miami: University of Miami Press, 1970.

Estow, Clara. *Pedro the Cruel of Castile: 1350–1369*. Boston: Brill, 1995.

Evans, G. R. *Alan of Lille: The Frontiers of Theology in the Later Twelfth Century.* Mahwah, NJ: Paulist Press, 1983.

Famiglietti, R. C. *Royal Intrigue: Crisis at the Court of Charles VI, 1392–1420.* New York: AMS Press, 1987.

Fields, Bertram. *Royal Blood: Richard III and the Mystery of the Princes.* New York: Regan, 1998.

Finnegan, Mary Jeremy. *The Women of Helfta: Scholars and Mystics.* Athens: University of Georgia Press, 1991.

Gameson, Richard. *St. Augustine and the Conversion of England.* New York: Sutton, 2000.

Garland, Lynda. *Byzantine Empresses: Women and Power in Byzantium, AD 527–1204.* New York: Routledge, 1999.

Gertrude of Helfta. *Gertrude of Helfta: The Herald of Divine Love.* Ed. Margaret Winkworth. Mahwah, NJ: Paulist Press, 1993.

Gouma-Peterson, Thalia. *Anna Komnene and Her Times.* New York: Garland, 2000.

Gregory VII, Pope. *The Correspondence of Pope Gregory VII: Selected Letters from the Registrum.* Trans. Ephraim Emerton. New York: Columbia University Press, 1990.

Hagen, K., ed. *Augustine, the Harvest and Theology, 1300–1650.* Boston: Brill, 1991.

Halecki, Oskar, and Tadeusz Gomada. *Jadwiga of Anjou and the Rise of East Central Europe.* East European Monographs, 1991.

Harris, Marguerite, ed. *Birgitta of Sweden: Life and Selected Revelations.* Mahwah, NJ: Paulist Press, 1990.

Hodges, Richard, et al. *Mohammed, Charlemagne and the Origins of Europe.* Ithaca, NY: Cornell University Press, 1983.

Hodgkin, Thomas. *Theodoric the Goth.* New York: AMS Press, 1992.

Howell, Margaret. *Eleanor of Provence: Queenship in Thirteenth-Century England.* Oxford: Blackwell, 1998.

Karger, M. *Novgorod the Great.* Moscow: Progress Publishers, 1973.

Kinnamos, John. *Deeds of John and Manuel Comnenus.* New York: Columbia University Press, 1976.

Kitchell, Kenneth, and Irvin Michael Resnick, trans. *Albertus Magnus on Animals.* Baltimore: Johns Hopkins University Press, 1998.

Kogan, Barry. *Averroës and the Metaphysics of Causation.* Albany: State University of New York Press, 1985.

Lawson, M. K. *Cnut: The Danes in England in the Early Eleventh Century.* London: Longman, 1993.

Leon, Vicki. *Uppity Women of Medieval Times.* Berkeley, CA: Conari Press, 1997.

Lindberg, David C. *Roger Bacon and the Origins of Perspectiva in the Middle Ages.* New York: Oxford University Press, 1996.

Magdalino, Paul. *The Empire of Manuel I Komnenos, 1143–1180.* New York: Cambridge University Press, 1993.

Markus, R. A. *Gregory the Great and His World.* New York: Cambridge University Press, 1997.

Mayeski, Marie Anne. *Dhuoda: Ninth-Century Mother and Theologian.* Scranton, PA: University of Scranton Press, 1995.

McGinn, Bernard. *Meister Eckhart and the Beguine Mystics: Hadewijch of Brabant, Mechthild of Magdeburg, and Marguerite Porete.* Chiron, 1997.

_____. *Meister Eckhart: Teacher and Preacher.* Mahwah, NJ: Paulist Press, 1988.

Mommsen, Theodor Ernst, ed. *Imperial Lives and Letters of the Eleventh Century.* New York: Columbia University Press, 2000.

Moorhead, John. *Justinian.* Reading, MA: Addison-Wesley, 1994.

Morris, Bridget. *St. Birgitta of Sweden,* vol. 1 of *Studies in Medieval Mysticism.* London: Boydell and Brewer, 1999.

Nicholas, David. *The Van Arteveldes of Ghent.* Reading, MA: Longman, 1988.

Nicol, Donald M. *The Byzantine Lady: Ten Portraits 1250–1500.* New York: Cambridge University Press, 1994.

_____. *The Reluctant Emperor: A Biography of John Cantacuzene, Byzantine Emperor and Monk, c. 1295–1383.* New York: Cambridge University Press, 1996.

Owen, D. D. R. *Eleanor of Aquitaine: Queen and Legend.* Oxford: Blackwell, 1996.

Parsons, John Carmi. *Eleanor of Castile: Queen and Society in Thirteenth-Century England.* New York: St. Martin's, 1995.

Pearsall, Derek. *The Life of Geoffrey Chaucer.* Oxford: Blackwell, 1992.

Peters, F. E. *Muhammad and the Origins of Islam.* Albany: State University of New York Press, 1994.

Peterson, Joan. *The Dialogues of Gregory the Great*. Toronto: Pontifical Institute of Medieval Studies, 1985.

Raban, Sandra. *England under Edward I and Edward II*. Oxford: Blackwell, 2000.

Reilly, Bernard. *The Kingdom of León-Castilla Under King Alfonso I, 1065–1109*. New York: Cambridge University Press, 1991.

———. *The Kingdom of León-Castilla Under King Alfonso VII, 1126–1157*. Philadelphia: University of Pennsylvania Press, 1998.

Rubin, Nancy. *Isabella of Castile: The First Renaissance Queen*. New York: St. Martin's, 1992.

Rumble, Alexander R., ed. *The Reign of Cnut: King of England, Denmark and Norway*. Madison, WI: Fairleigh Dickinson University Press, 1994.

Salahi, Adil. *Muhammad, Man and Prophet: A Complete Study of the Life of the Prophet of Islam*. Rockport, MA: Element Books, 1998.

Severin, Timothy. *In Search of Genghis Khan*. New York: Carroll and Graf, 1993.

Stafford, Pauline. *Queen Emma and Queen Edith: Queenship and Women's Power in Eleventh-Century England*. Oxford: Blackwell, 1997.

Stock, Brian. *Augustine the Reader: Meditation, Self-Knowledge and the Ethics of Interpretation*. Cambridge, MA: Harvard University Press, 1996.

Trask, Willard. *Joan of Arc: In Her Own Words*. New York: Turtle Point Press, 1996.

Trindade, Ann. *Berengaria: In Search of Richard the Lionheart's Queen*. Dublin: Four Courts Press, 1999.

Urvoy, Dominique. *Ibn Rushd: Averroës*. New York: Routledge, 1991.

Volkoff, Vladimir. *Vladimir: The Russian Viking*. New York: Overlook Press, 1988.

Wahbah, Mourad. *Averroës and the Enlightenment*. Buffalo, NY: Prometheus, 1996.

Warren, W. L. *King John*. Berkeley: University of California Press, 1982.

Waugh, Scott L. *England in the Reign of Edward III*. New York: Cambridge University Press, 1991.

Weir, Alison. *Eleanor of Aquitaine: A Life*. New York: Ballantine, 2000.

Weisheipl, James A., ed. *Albertus Magnus and the Sciences*. Toronto: Pontifical Institute of Medieval Studies, 1980.

Wheeler, Bonnie, and Charles T. Wood, eds. *Fresh Verdicts on Joan of Arc*. New York: Garland, 1996.

Wheeler, Bonnie, ed. *Listening to Heloise: The Voice of a Twelfth-Century Woman*. New York: St. Martin's, 2000.

Willard, Charity C. *Christine de Pizan: Her Life and Works*. New York: Persea, 1990.

Culture, Art, and Literature

Ackerman, Robert W., and Roger Dahood, trans. *Ancrene Riwle: Introduction and Part I*. Binghamton, NY: Medieval and Renaissance Texts and Studies, 1984.

Allen, Peter L. *The Art of Love: Amatory Fiction from Ovid to the "Romance of the Rose."* Philadelphia: University of Pennsylvania Press, 1992.

Andreas Capellanus. *The Art of Courtly Love*. New York: Columbia University Press, 1990.

Anna Comnena. *The Alexiad of Anna Comnena*. Trans. Edgar Robert Ashton Sewter. New York: Viking, 1985.

Ashe, Geoffrey. *The Discovery of King Arthur*. New York: Holt, 1987.

Ashton, Gail. *The Generation of Identity in Late Medieval Hagiography: Speaking the Saint*. New York: Routledge, 2000.

Bak, Janos M., et al. *Medieval Narrative Sources: A Chronological Guide*. New York: Garland, 1987.

Bargen, Doris G. *A Woman's Weapon: Spirit Possession in the "Tale of Genji."* Honolulu: University of Hawaii Press, 1997.

Bayless, Martha. *Parody in the Middle Ages: The Latin Tradition*. Detroit: University of Michigan Press, 1996.

Bede, Venerable. *Ecclesiastical History of the English People*. New York: Oxford University Press, 1992.

Bedier, Joseph, and Hilaire Belloc, trans. *The Romance of Tristan and Iseult*. New York: Vintage, 1994.

Berber, Chris, and David Pykitt. *Journey to Avalon: The Final Discovery of King Arthur*. York Beach, ME: Samuel Weiser, 1994.

Blumenfeld-Kosinski, Renate, and Timea Szell, eds. *Images of Sainthood in Medieval Europe*. Ithaca, NY: Cornell University Press, 1991.

Bogin, Meg. *The Woman Troubadours*. New York: Norton, 1980.

Brownlee, Kevin. *Rethinking the "Romance of the Rose": Text, Image, Reception*. Philadelphia: University of Pennsylvania Press, 1992.

Bryce, Derek. *The Mystical Way and the Arthurian Quest*. York Beach, ME: Samuel Weiser, 1996.

Cantor, Norman F. *The Medieval Reader*. New York: HarperCollins, 1995.

Carter, John Marshall. *Medieval Games*. Westport, CT: Greenwood, 1992.

Carter, Steven D., trans. *Waiting for the Wind: Thirty-Six Poets of Japan's Late Medieval Age*. New York: Columbia University Press, 1989.

Christine de Pizan. *The Book of Deeds of Arms and of Chivalry*. Trans. Sumner and Charity Cannon Willard. University Park, PA: Pennsylvania State University Press, 1999.

_____. *The Book of the City of Ladies*. Trans. Jeffrey Richards. New York: Persea Press, 1998.

_____. *The Treasure of the City of Ladies; or, the Book of the Three Virtues*. New York: Penguin, 1985.

Coghlan, Ronan. *The Illustrated Encyclopedia of Arthurian Legends*. Rockport, MA: Element Books, 1993.

Coon, Lynda L. *Sacred Fictions: Holy Women and Hagiography in Late Antiquity*. Philadelphia: University of Pennsylvania Press, 1997.

Courtenay, Lynn T., ed. *The Engineering of Medieval Cathedrals*. Brookfield, CT: Ashgate, 1997.

Curtius, E. R. *European Literature and the Latin Middle Ages*. Princeton, NJ: Princeton University Press, 1973.

Cynewulf. *Cynewulf's "Elene."* Ed. P. O. E. Gradon. London: University of Exeter Press, 1996.

Davidson, Clifford. *Technology, Guilds and Early English Drama*. Kalamazoo: Western Michigan University Press, 1997.

de Berceo, Gonzalo. *Miracles of Our Lady*. Trans. Annette Grant Cash. Lexington: University Press of Kentucky, 1997.

de Looze, Laurence. *Pseudo-Autobiography in the Fourteenth Century: Juan Ruiz, Guillaume de Machaut, Jean Froissart and Geoffrey Chaucer*. Gainesville, FL: University Press of Florida, 1997.

Desmond, Marilynn. *Christine de Pizan and the Categories of Difference*. Minneapolis: University of Minnesota Press, 1998.

Dhuoda. *Handbook for William: A Carolingian Woman's Counsel for Her Son*. Trans. Carol Neel. Washington, DC: Catholic University of America Press, 1999.

Dunn, Charles, and Edward T. Byrnes, eds. *Middle English Literature*. New York: Garland, 1990.

Eco, Umberto. *Art and Beauty in the Middle Ages*. New Haven, CT: Yale University Press, 1988.

Ettinghausen, R., and Grabar, O. *The Art and Architecture of Islam: 650–1250*. Harmondsworth, England: Penguin, 1987.

Gabrieli, Francesco. *Arab Historians of the Crusades*. Berkeley: University of California Press, 1984.

Garbaty, Thomas J. *Medieval English Literature*. New York: Heath, 1983.

Garde, Judith N. *Old English Poetry in Medieval Christian Perspective: A Doctrinal Approach*. London: Brewer, 1991.

Gardiner, Eileen. *Medieval Visions of Heaven and Hell: A Sourcebook*. New York: Garland, 1993.

Gentry, Francis G., ed. *German Epic Poetry: The Nibelungenlied, the Older Lay of Hildebrand and Other Works*. New York: Continuum, 1995.

Ghazoul, Ferial J. *Nocturnal Poetics: The Arabian Nights in Comparative Context*. Cairo: American University in Cairo Press, 1996.

Gilchrist, Roberta. *Gender and Material Culture: The Archaeology of Religious Women*. New York: Routledge, 1997.

Godwin, Malcolm. *Holy Grail*. New York: Penguin, 1998.

Goodrich, Michael, ed. *Cross-Cultural Convergences in the Crusader Period*. New York: Peter Lang, 1995.

Goodrich, Norma Lorre. *The Holy Grail*. New York: HarperCollins, 1993.

_____. *Merlin*. New York: HarperCollins, 1988.

Gottfried of Disibodenberg and Theodoric of Echternach. *The Life of Hildegard of Bingen*. Trans. Hugh Feiss. New York: Peregrina, 1996.

Gower, John. *Mirror of Mankind*. Trans. William Burton Wilson. East Lansing, MI: Colleagues Press, 1992.

Guillaume de Lorris and Jean de Meun. *The Romance of the Rose*. Trans. Charles Dahlberg. Princeton, NJ: Princeton University Press, 1995.

Guillaume de Machaut. *Le Livre Dou Voir Dit: The Book of the True Poem*. Trans. Daniel Leech-Wilkinson and R. Barton Palmer. New York: Garland, 1998.

Haddawy, Husain, trans. *The Arabian Nights*. Ed. Muhsin Mahdi. New York: Norton, 1995.

Heaney, Seamus, trans. *Beowulf*. New York: Farrar Straus and Giroux, 2000.

Heene, Katrien. *The Legacy of Paradise: Marriage, Motherhood and Woman in Carolingian Edifying Literature*. New York: Peter Lang, 1997.

Heimmel, Jennifer. *God Is Our Mother: Julian of Norwich and the Medieval Image of Christian Feminine Divinity*. New York: Prometheus, 1983.

Henryson, Robert. *The Poems of Robert Henryson*. Oxford: Clarendon, 1980.

Hildegarde of Bingen. *Book of Divine Works, with Letters and Songs*. Ed. Matthew Fox. Santa Fe: University of New Mexico Press, 1987.

_____. *Explanation of the Rule of Benedict*. Trans. Hugh Feiss. Toronto: University of Toronto Press, 1990.

_____. *Illuminations*. Ed. Matthew Fox. Santa Fe: University of New Mexico Press, 1985.

Hinde, T. *The Domesday Book*. London: Hutchinson, 1985.

Holloway, Julia Bolton. *The Pilgrim and the Book*. New York: Peter Lang, 1987.

Howard, Donald R. *Writers and Pilgrims. Medieval Pilgrimage Narratives and Their Posterity*. Berkeley: University of California Press, 1980.

Hrotswitha of Gandersheim. *The Plays of Hrotswitha of Gandersheim*. Trans. Larissa Bonfante and Alexandra Bonfante-Warren. Oak Park, IL: Bolchazy Carducci, 1986.

Hudson, Anne. *Lollards and Their Books*. London: Hambledon, 1985.

Irwin, Robert. *The Arabian Nights: A Companion*. New York: Viking Penguin, 1996.

Jessup, Helen Ibbitson, and Thierry Zephir, eds. *Sculpture of Angkor and Ancient Cambodia: Millennium of Glory*. London: Thames and Hudson, 1997.

Julian of Norwich. *Revelations of Divine Love*. Ed. Halcyon Backhouse and Rhona Pipe. London: Brewer, 1987.

_____. *Revelations of Divine Love and the Motherhood of God*. London: Brewer, 1998.

Kellogg, Robert, and Jane Smiley, trans. *The Sagas of the Icelanders*. New York: Viking, 2000.

Kelly, Douglas. *The Art of Medieval French Romance*. Madison: University of Wisconsin Press, 1992.

_____. *Internal Difference and Meaning in the "Roman de la Rose."* Madison: University of Wisconsin Press, 1995.

Kempe, Margery. *The Book of Margery Kempe*. Trans. Barry Windean. Harmondsworth, England: Penguin, 1985.

_____. *The Book of Margery Kempe*. Ed. Lynne Staley. New York: Norton, 2000.

Kretzmann, Norman. *The Cambridge Companion to Aquinas*. New York: Cambridge University Press, 1993.

Krueger, Roberta L, ed. *The Cambridge Companion to Medieval Romance*. Cambridge Companions to Literature Series. New York: Cambridge University Press, 2000.

Leaf, W., and Purcell, S. *Heraldic Symbols*. London: Victoria and Albert Museum, 1986.

Le Saux, Francois. *Layamon's Brut: The Poem and Its Sources*. London: Brewer, 1989.

Lewis, C. S. *The Allegory of Love*. Oxford: Oxford University Press, 1936.

Linda, Georgianna. *The Solitary Self: Individuality in the Ancrene Wisse*. Cambridge, MA: Harvard University Press, 1982.

Littleton, C. Scott and Linda A. Malcor. *From Scythia to Camelot: A Radical Reassessment of the Legends of King Arthur, the Knights of the Round Table, and the Holy Grail*. New York: Garland, 1994.

Maitland, Frederic William. *Domesday Book and Beyond*. New York: Cambridge University Press, 1987.

Malory, Sir Thomas. *Malory: The Morte Darthur*. Evanston, IL: Northwestern University Press, 1968.

Marguerite, Porete. *The Mirror of Simple Souls*. Trans. Ellen L. Babinsky. Mahwah, NJ.: Paulist Press, 1993.

Martinus. *The Chronicles of Rome: An Edition of the Middle English Chronicle of Popes and*

Emperors and the Lollard Chronicles. Ed. Dan Embree. London: Boydell and Brewer, 1999.

Matejic, Mateja, and Dragan Milwojevis, trans. *Anthology of Medieval Serbian Literature in English*. Columbus, OH: Slavica Press, 1979.

McConnell, Winder, trans. *The Lament of the Nibelungen*. London: Camden House, 1994.

McGinn, Bernard. *Apocalypticism in the Western Tradition*. New York: Variorum, 1994.

_____. *Meister Eckhart and the Beguine Mystics: Hadewijch of Brabant, Mechthild of Magdeburg, and Marguerite Porete*. Chiron, 1997.

McLeod, Glenda. *Virtue and Venom: Catalogs of Women from Antiquity to the Renaissance*. Detroit: University of Michigan Press, 1991.

Meisami, Julie Scott. *Medieval Persian Court Poetry*. Princeton, NJ: Princeton University Press, 1987.

Menache, Sophia. *The Vox Dei: Communication in the Middle Ages*. New York: Oxford University Press, 1990.

Mommsen, Theodor Ernst, ed. *Imperial Lives and Letters of the Eleventh Century*. New York: Columbia University Press, 2000.

Moriarity, Catherine, ed. *The Voice of the Middle Ages: In Personal Letters 1100–1500*. New York: Peter Bedrick, 1991.

Mosse, Fernand. *A Handbook of Middle English*. Baltimore: Johns Hopkins University Press, 1969.

Murasaki Shikibu. *Tale of Genji*. Trans. Edward G. Seidensticker. New York: Vintage, 1990.

Nizami, Ganjavi. *The Haft Paykar: A Medieval Persian Romance*. New York: Oxford University Press, 1995.

Parry, Kenneth. *Depicting the Word: Byzantine Iconophile Thought of the Eighth and Ninth Centuries*. Boston: Brill, 1996.

Pearsall, Derek. *The Life of Geoffrey Chaucer*. Oxford: Blackwell, 1992.

Pelikan, Jaroslav. *Imago Dei: The Byzantine Apologia for Icons*. Princeton, NJ: Princeton University Press, 1990.

Pope, John Collins. *Seven Old English Poems*. New York: Norton, 1981.

Quilligan, Maureen. *The Allegory of Female Authority: Christine de Pizan's "Cite des Dames."* Ithaca, NY: Cornell University Press, 1991.

Raw, Barbara Catherine. *Trinity and Incarnation in Anglo-Saxon Art and Thought*. New York: Cambridge University Press, 1997.

Redon, Odile, ed. and trans. *The Medieval Kitchen: Recipes from France and Italy*. Chicago: University of Chicago Press, 2000.

Sands, Donald B., ed. *Middle English Verse Romances*. London: University of Exeter Press, 1987.

Savage, Anne. *Anchoritic Spirituality: Ancrene Wisse and Associated Works*. Mahwah, NJ: Paulist Press, 1991.

Scheindlin, Raymond P. *Wine, Women and Death: Medieval Hebrew Poems on the Good Life*. Philadelphia: Jewish Publication Society, 1986.

Scully, D. Eleanor, and Terence Scully. *Early French Cookery: Sources, History, Original Recipes and Modern Adaptations*. Detroit: University of Michigan Press, 1995.

Sells, Michael A. *Mystical Languages of Unsaving*. Chicago: University of Chicago Press, 1994.

Sharpe, Richard. *Medieval Irish Saints' Lives: An Introduction to Vitae Sanctorum Hiberniae*. Oxford: Clarendon, 1991.

Spiegel, Gabrielle. *The Past as Text: The Theory and Practice of Medieval Historiography*. Baltimore: Johns Hopkins University Press, 1997.

Staley, Lynn. *Margery Kempe's Dissenting Fictions*. University Park: Pennsylvania State University Press, 1994.

Steward, R. J. *Merlin: The Prophetic Vision and the Mystic Life*. New York: Penguin, 1995.

Stock, Brian. *Augustine the Reader: Meditation, Self-Knowledge and the Ethics of Interpretation*. Cambridge, MA: Harvard University Press, 1996.

Sugawara No Takasue No Musume and Thomas Rohlich. *A Tale of Eleventh-Century Japan: Hamamatse Chunagon Monogatari*. Princeton, NJ: Princeton University Press, 1983.

Taylor, Jerome. *The Didascalicon of Hugh of St. Victor: A Medieval Guide to the Arts*. New York: Columbia University Press, 1991.

Terry, Patricia Ann, ed. *Poems of the Elder Edda*. Philadelphia: University of Pennsylvania Press, 1990.

Topsfield, L. T. *Chrétien de Troyes: A Study of the Arthurian Romances*. London: Cambridge University Press, 1981.

Turville-Petre, Thorlac. *Alliterative Poetry of the*

Later Middle Ages: An Anthology. New York: Routledge, 1989.

Uitti, Karl D. with Michelle A. Freeman. *Chrétien de Troyes Revisited.* New York: Twayne, 1995.

Usher, Mark David. *Homeric Stitchings: The Homeric Centos of the Empress Eudocia.* London: Rowman and Littlefield, 1998.

Villehardouin, Geoffroi de. *Memoirs of the Crusades.* Westport, CT: Greenwood, 1983.

Voaden, Rosalynn. *God's Words, Women's Voices: The Discernment of Spirits in the Writing of Late-Medieval Women Visionaries.* London: Boydell and Brewer, 1999.

Wagner, Peter, and Richard L. Crocker. *Introduction to the Gregorian Melodies: A Handbook of Plainsong.* New York: Da Capo, 1985.

Walters, Lon. *Lancelot and Guinevere: A Casebook.* New York: Garland, 1996.

Wang Wei. *Laughing Lost in the Mountains: Poems of Wang Wei.* Middleton, CT: University Press of New England, 1992.

Wiethaus, Ulrike. *Ecstatic Transformation: Transpersonal Psychology in the Work of Mechthild of Magdeburg.* Syracuse, NY: Syracuse University Press, 1995.

Wilhelm, James J., ed. *Lyrics of the Middle Ages: An Anthology.* New York: Garland, 1990.

Willard, Charity C. *Christine de Pizan: Her Life and Works.* New York: Persea, 1990.

Winstead, Karen A. *Chaste Passions: Medieval English Virgin Martyr Legends.* Ithaca, NY: Cornell University Press, 2000.

Wright, Craig M. *Music and Ceremony at Notre Dame of Paris, 500–1500.* New York: Cambridge University Press, 1990.

Zaleski, Carol Goldsmith. *Otherworld Journeys: Accounts of Near-Death Experience in Medieval and Modern Times.* New York: Oxford University Press, 1987.

Zimmerman, Margarete, and Dina de Rentiis, eds. *The City of Scholars: New Approaches to Christine de Pizan.* New York: Walter de Gruyter, 1994.

Economics

Abulafia, David. *Commerce and Conquest in the Mediterranean, 1100–1500.* New York: Variorum, 1993.

Bloch, Marc. *Feudal Society: The Growth of the Ties of Dependence.* Trans. L. A. Manyon. Chicago: University of Chicago Press, 1988.

Ekelund, Robert B. *Sacred Trust: The Medieval Church as an Economic Firm.* New York: Oxford University Press, 1996.

Eliassen, Fin-Einar, et al. *Power, Profit and Urban Land: Landownership in Medieval and Early Modern Northern European Towns.* Atlanta: Scholars Press, 1997.

Epstein, Steven A. *Wage Labor and Guilds in Medieval Europe.* Chapel Hill: University of North Carolina Press, 1995.

Frantzen, Allen, and Douglas Moffat, eds. *The Work of Work: Servitude, Slavery and Labor in Medieval England.* Rochester, NY: University of Rochester Press, 1994.

Ganshof, Francois Louis. *Feudalism.* Trans. Philip Grierson. Toronto: University of Toronto Press, 1996.

Gilchrist, Roberta. *Gender and Material Culture: The Archaeology of Religious Women.* New York: Routledge, 1997.

Herlihy, David. *Medieval Households.* Cambridge, MA: Harvard University Press, 1985.

_____. *Opera Muliebria: Women and Work in Medieval Europe.* Philadelphia: Temple University Press, 1990.

Hicks, Michael. *Bastard Feudalism.* London: Longman, 1995.

Hilton, R. H. *Class Conflict and the Crisis of Feudalism: Essays in Medieval Social History.* London: Hambledon, 1986.

Hinde, T. *The Domesday Book.* London: Hutchinson, 1985.

Jain, V. K. *Trade and Traders in Western India, 1000–1300.* Columbia, MO: South Asia Books, 1990.

Jordan, William Chester. *Women and Credit in Pre-Industrial and Developing Societies.* Philadelphia: University of Pennsylvania Press, 1993.

Kaplan, Marion. *Marriage Bargain: Women and Dowries in European History.* Binghamton, NY: Haworth, 1984.

Laiou, Angeliki. *Gender, Society and Economic Life in Byzantium.* New York: Variorum, 1992.

Le Goff, Jacques. *Time, Work and Culture in the Middle Ages.* Chicago: University of Chicago Press, 1982.

MacKay, Angus. *Society, Economy and Religion in Late Medieval Castile*. Brookfield, CT: Ashgate, 1987.

Maitland, Frederic William. *Domesday Book and Beyond*. New York: Cambridge University Press, 1987.

Spufford, Peter. *Money and Its Use in Medieval Europe*. New York: Cambridge University Press, 1989.

Stacey, Robert C. *Politics, Policy and Finance Under Henry III, 1216–1245*. New York: Oxford University Press, 1987.

Woolgar, C. M. *Household Accounts from Medieval England*. New York: Oxford University Press, 1993.

Military History

Abels, Richard P. *Alfred the Great: War, Kingship and Culture in Anglo-Saxon England*. Reading, MA: Longman, 1998.

Allmand, Christopher. *The Hundred Years' War: England and France at War*. New York: Cambridge University Press, 1988.

_____. *Society at War: The Experience of England and France During the Hundred Years' War*. London: Boydell and Brewer, 1999.

Baker, George Philip. *The Fighting Kings of Wessex*. New York: Combined Publishing, 1996.

Barber, Richard. *The Life and Campaigns of the Black Prince*. New York: St. Martin's, 1997.

Bume, Alfred. *The Crécy War: A Military History of the Hundred Years' War*. New York: Greenhill, 1991.

Burns, R. *Islam Under the Crusaders: Colonial Revival in the 13th-Century Kingdom of Valencia*. Princeton, NJ: Princeton University Press, 1973.

Bury, John B. *Invasion of Europe by the Barbarians*. New York: Norton, 2000.

Christine de Pizan. *The Book of Deeds of Arms and of Chivalry*. Trans. Sumner and Charity Cannon Willard. University Park: Pennsylvania State University Press, 1999.

_____. *The Treasure of the City of Ladies; or, the Book of the Three Virtues*. New York: Penguin, 1985.

Costen, Michael. *The Cathars and the Albigensian Crusade*. Manchester: Manchester University Press, 1997.

Curry, Anne. *Arms, Armies and Fortifications in the Hundred Years' War*. Rochester, NY: University of Rochester Press, 1994.

_____. *The Hundred Years' War*. New York: St. Martin's, 1993.

Dalton, Paul. *Conquest, Anarchy and Lordship: Yorkshire, 1066–1154*. New York: Cambridge University Press, 1994.

Dockray, Keith. *Henry VI and the Wars of the Roses: A Sourcebook*. New York: Sutton, 2000.

Gabrieli, Francesco. *Arab Historians of the Crusades*. Berkeley: University of California Press, 1984.

Gibbon, Edward. *The Decline and Fall of the Roman Empire*. New York: Modern Library, 1995.

Grant, Michael. *The Fall of the Roman Empire*. New York: Touchstone, 1997.

_____. *From Rome to Byzantium: The Fifth Century AD*. New York: Routledge, 1998.

Haigh, Philip A. *The Military Campaigns of the Wars of the Roses*. New York: Sutton, 1999.

Hodgkin, Thomas, and Tim Newark. *Huns, Vandals and the Fall of the Roman Empire*. New York: Greenhill, 1996.

Holt, P. M. *The Age of the Crusades: The Near East from the Eleventh Century to 1517*. Reading, MA: Longman, 1986.

Housely, Norman. *The Avignon Papacy and the Crusades*. New York: Oxford University Press, 1986.

_____. *The Italian Crusades*. New York: Oxford University Press, 1982.

_____. *The Later Crusades*. New York: Oxford University Press, 1992.

Juvani, Ata-Malik. *Genghis Khan: The History of the World-Conqueror*. Seattle: University of Washington Press, 1997.

Kaeuper, Richard W. *Chivalry and Violence in Medieval Europe*. New York: Oxford University Press, 1999.

_____. *War, Justice and Public Order: England and France in the Later Middle Ages*. Oxford: Clarendon, 1988.

Marshall, Christopher. *Warfare in the Latin East, 1192–1291*. New York: Cambridge, University Press, 1992.

McNeill, William H. *The Pursuit of Power: Technology, Armed Force and Society Since*

1000 AD. Chicago: University of Chicago Press, 1984.

Nardo, Don. *The Fall of the Roman Empire.* New York: Greenhaven, 1998.

Neillands, Robin. *The Hundred Years' War.* New York: Routledge, 1992.

Riley-Smith, J. *The Crusades: A Short History.* London: Athlone, 1987.

_____. *The First Crusade and the Idea of Crusading.* London: Athlone, 1986.

Runciman, Steven. *The First Crusade.* New York: Cambridge University Press: 1992.

_____. *The Sicilian Vespers: A History of the Mediterranean World in the Later Thirteenth Century.* New York: Cambridge University Press, 1992.

Saunders, J. J. *The History of the Mongol Conquests.* London: Routledge and Kegan Paul, 1971.

Scales, Peter C. *The Fall of the Caliphate of Córdoba.* Boston: Brill, 1994.

Setton, Kenneth. *History of the Crusades.* Madison: University of Wisconsin Press, 1969.

Sherborne, J. W. *War, Politics and Culture in Fourteenth-Century England.* Ed. Anthony Tuck. London: Hambledon, 1994.

Sumption, Jonathan. *The Albigensian Crusade.* New York: Faber and Faber, 2000.

Villehardouin, Geoffroi de. *Memoirs of the Crusades.* Westport, CT: Greenwood, 1983.

Weir, Alison. *The Wars of the Roses.* New York: Ballantine, 1996.

Williams, Ann. *The English and the Norman Conquest.* London: Boydell and Brewer, 1997.

Political, Legal, and Social History

Aidan, Francis. *The Black Death of 1348 and 1349.* New York: AMS Press, 1977.

Alexander, Michael van Cleave. *The Growth of English Education 1348–1648.* University Park: Pennsylvania State University Press, 1990.

Amundsen, Darrel W. *Medicine, Society and Faith in the Ancient and Medieval Worlds.* Baltimore: Johns Hopkins University Press, 1995.

Asbridge, Thomas S. *The Creation of the Principality of Antioch: 1098–1130.* London: Boydell and Brewer, 2000.

Atkinson, Ian. *The Viking Ships.* Cambridge: Cambridge University Press, 1986.

Bak, Janos, ed. *The Laws of the Medieval Kingdom of Hungary: 1301–1457.* Schlacks, 1993.

Bell, Andrew. *The Role of Migration in the History of the Eurasian Steppe: Sedentary Civilization versus "Barbarian" and Nomad.* New York: St. Martin's, 2000.

Bellomo, Manlio. *The Common Legal Past of Europe: 1000–1800.* Washington, DC: Catholic University of America Press, 1995.

Binski, Paul. *Medieval Death: Ritual and Representation.* Ithaca, NY: Cornell University Press, 1996.

Birashk, Ahmad. *A Comparative Calendar of the Iranian, Muslim Lunar and Christian Eras for Three Thousand Years (1260 BH–2000 AH; 639 BC–2621 AD).* New York: Mazda Publishing, 1993.

Brooke, Christopher N. L. *The Medieval Idea of Marriage.* New York: Oxford University Press, 1994.

Brundage, James A. *Medieval Canon Law.* Reading, MA: Addison Wesley Longman, 1995.

Bullough, Vern L., and James A. Brundage, eds. *Handbook of Medieval Sexuality.* New York: Garland, 1996.

Cameron, Averil. *Changing Cultures in Early Byzantium.* New York: Variorum, 1996.

Carlson, Cindy L. *Constructions of Widowhood and Virginity in the Middle Ages.* New York: St. Martin's, 1999.

Carpenter, Jennifer. *Power of the Weak: Studies on Medieval Women.* Champaign: University of Illinois Press, 1995.

Corabj, Richard. *Time, Creation and the Continuum: Theories in Antiquity and the Early Middle Ages.* Ithaca, NY: Cornell University Press, 1986.

Drijvers, J. W., and A. A. MacDonald, eds. *Centers of Learning: Learning and Location in Pre-Modern Europe and the Near East.* Boston: Brill, 1997.

Duby, Georges. *Love and Marriage in the Middle Ages.* Chicago: University of Chicago Press, 1996.

Duggan, Anne, ed. *Queens and Queenship in Medieval Europe.* London: Boydell and Brewer, 1997.

Dumville, David N. *Wessex and England from Alfred to Edgar: Six Essays on Political, Cultural and Ecclesiastical Revival.* London: Boydell and Brewer, 1992.

Edwards, Robert, and Vickie Ziegler. *Matrons and Marginal Women in Medieval Society.* Rochester, NY: University of Rochester Press, 1995.

Elliott, Dyan. *Fallen Bodies: Pollution, Sexuality and Demonology in the Middle Ages.* Philadelphia: University of Pennsylvania Press, 1999.

Erler, Mary. *Women and Power in the Middle Ages.* Athens: University of Georgia Press, 1988.

Fichtenau, Heinrich. *Living in the Tenth Century: Mentalities and Social Orders.* Chicago: University of Chicago Press, 1991.

Fleming, Robin. *Law and Custom in Domesday England.* New York: Cambridge University Press, 1998.

Flint, Valerie I. J. *The Rise of Magic in Early Medieval Europe.* Princeton, NJ: Princeton University Press, 1994.

Geary, Patrick J. *Living with the Dead in the Middle Ages.* Ithaca, NY: Cornell University Press, 1994.

Gies, Frances, and Joseph Gies. *Marriage and the Family in the Middle Ages.* New York: HarperCollins, 1989.

Gold, Penny Schine. *The Lady and the Virgin: Image, Attitude and Experience in Twelfth-Century France.* Chicago: University of Chicago Press, 1987.

Gottfried, Robert S. *The Black Death: Natural and Human Disaster in Medieval Europe.* New York: Free Press, 1985.

Gulati, Saroj. *Women and Society: Northern India in the 11th and 12th Centuries.* Columbia, MO: South Asia Books, 1985.

Haldon, J. F. *Byzantium in the Seventh Century: The Transformation of a Culture.* New York: Cambridge University Press, 1991.

Halsall, Guy, ed. *Violence and Society in the Early Medieval West.* London: Boydell and Brewer, 1997.

Hanawalt, Barbara A. *Medieval Crime and Social Control.* Minneapolis: University of Minnesota Press, 1999.

Harvey, Margaret. *England, Rome and the Papacy, 1417–1464: The Study of a Relationship.* Manchester: Manchester University Press, 1993.

Haskett, Timothy S. *Crime and Punishment in the Middle Ages: Papers Presented at the Tenth Annual Medieval Workshop.* Victoria, BC: University of Victoria Medieval Studies, 1998.

Henisch, Bridget Ann. *Fast and Feast: Food in Medieval Society.* University Park: Pennsylvania State University Press, 1986.

Herlihy, David, and Samuel Kline Cohn. *The Black Death and the Transformation of the West.* Cambridge, MA: Harvard University Press, 1997.

Honore, Tony. *Law in the Crisis of Empire 379–455 AD: The Theodosian Dynasty and Its Quaestors.* New York: Oxford University Press, 1998.

Hopkins, Andrea. *Most Wise and Valiant Ladies.* New York: Stewart, Tabori and Chang, 1998.

Horrox, Rosemary. *The Black Death.* Manchester: Manchester University Press, 1994.

Hudson, John. *The Formation of the English Common Law: Law and Society in England from the Norman Conquest to the Magna Carta.* Reading, MA: Longman, 1996.

Hunt, Alan. *Governance of the Consuming Passions: A History of Sumptuary Law.* New York: St. Martin's, 1996.

Hunt, Tony. *The Medieval Surgery.* London: Boydell and Brewer, 1992.

Innemee, Karel C. *Ecclesiastical Dress in the Medieval Near East.* Boston: Brill, 1997.

Institoris, Henricus, and Montague Summers. *The Malleus Maleficarum of Heinrich Kramer and James Sprenger.* New York: Dover, 1971.

Jaeger, C. Stephen. *Origins of Courtliness: Civilizing Trends and the Formation of Courtly Ideals, 939–1210.* Philadelphia: University of Pennsylvania Press, 1990.

Karras, Ruth Mazo. *Common Women: Prostitution and Sexuality in Medieval England.* New York: Oxford University Press, 1996.

Kazdan, Alexander P., and Ann Epstein. *Change in Byzantine Culture in the Eleventh and Twelfth Centuries.* Berkeley: University of California Press, 1990.

Kennedy, Hugh. *Muslim Spain and Portugal: A Political History of al-Andalus.* Reading, MA: Addison-Wesley, 1997.

Kessler, Adam T. *Empire Beyond the Great Wall:*

The Heritage of Genghis Khan. Seattle: University of Washington Press, 1997.

Klaniczay, Gabor. *The Uses of Supernatural Power: The Transformation of Popular Religions in Medieval and Early Modern Europe.* Princeton, NJ: Princeton University Press, 1990.

Kors, Alan C. *Witchcraft in Europe, 1100–1700: A Documentary History.* Philadelphia: University of Pennsylvania Press, 1972.

Lal, Kishori Saran. *Muslim Slave System in Medieval India.* Columbia, MO: South Asia Books, 1994.

Lev, Yaacov. *State and Society in Fatimid Egypt.* Boston: Brill, 1991.

Lewis, Archibald. *Nomads and Crusaders, 1000–1368.* Bloomington: Indiana University Press, 1988.

MacKay, Angus. *Love, Religion and Politics in Fifteenth-Century Spain.* Boston: Brill, 1998.

_____. *Society, Economy and Religion in Late Medieval Castile.* Brookfield, CT: Ashgate, 1987.

Mansfield, Mary C. *The Humiliation of Sinners: Public Penance in Thirteenth-Century France.* Ithaca, NY: Cornell University Press, 1995.

Mason, Emma. *Westminster Abbey and Its People, c. 1056–c. 1216.* London: Boydell and Brewer, 1996.

Merback, Mitchell B. *The Thief, the Cross and the Wheel: Pain and the Spectacle of Punishment in Medieval and Renaissance Europe.* Chicago: University of Chicago Press, 1999.

Mirsky, D. S. *Russia: A Social History.* London: Cresset, 1931.

Monahan, Arthur. *Consent, Coercion and Limit: The Medieval Origins of Parliamentary Democracy.* New York: Queens University Press, 1987.

Moonan, Lawrence. *Divine Power: The Medieval Power Distinction up to Its Adoption by Albert, Bonaventure and Aquinas.* Oxford: Clarendon, 1994.

Morrison, Karl Frederick. *Holiness and Politics in Early Medieval Thought.* New York: Variorum, 1985.

Musson, Anthony, and W. M. Ormrod. *The Evolution of English Justice: Law, Politics and Society in the Fourteenth Century.* New York: St. Martin's, 1999.

Nicholas, David. *The Evolution of the Medieval World: Society, Government and Thought in Europe, 312–1500.* Reading, MA: Longman, 1992.

Noble, Thomas F. X. *The Republic of St. Peter: The Birth of the Papal State, 680–825.* Philadelphia: University of Pennsylvania Press, 1986.

Oakes, Catherine. *Exploring the Past: The Middle Ages.* New York: Harcourt, 1989.

Oakley, Francis. *The Medieval Experience: Foundations of Western Cultural Singularity.* Toronto: University of Toronto Press, 1988.

Orme, Nicholas, and Margaret Webster. *The English Hospital 1070–1570.* New Haven, CT: Yale University Press, 1995.

Paden, William D., ed. *The Medieval Pastourelle.* New York: Garland, 1988.

Parsons, John Carmi. *Medieval Queenship.* New York: St. Martin's, 1994.

Payer, Pierre J. *The Bridling of Desire: Views of Sex in the Later Middle Ages.* Toronto: University of Toronto Press, 1993.

_____. *Sex and the Penitentials: The Development of a Sexual Code, 550–1150.* Toronto: University of Toronto Press, 1985.

Pelteret, David A. E. *Slavery in Early Mediaeval England: From the Reign of Alfred until the Twelfth Century.* London: Boydell and Brewer, 1995.

Platt, Colin. *King Death: The Black Death and Its Aftermath in Late Medieval England.* Toronto: University of Toronto Press, 1996.

Powell, James M. *Medieval Studies: An Introduction.* Syracuse, NY: Syracuse University Press, 1992.

Reyerson, Kathryn, and John Drendel, eds. *Urban and Rural Communities in Medieval France: Provence and Languedoc, 1000–1500.* Boston: Brill, 1998.

Roberts, David D., and Willow D. Roberts. *In Search of the Old Ones: Exploring the Anasazi World of the Southwest.* New York: Simon and Schuster, 1997.

Rosenwein, Barbara H. *Debating the Middle Ages: Issues and Readings.* Oxford: Blackwell, 1998.

Rousseau, Constance M., and Joel Thomas Rosenthal, eds. *Women, Marriage and Family in Medieval Christendom.* Kalamazoo: Western Michigan University Press, 1998.

Runciman, Steven. *The Sicilian Vespers: A History of the Mediterranean World in the Later*

Thirteenth Century. New York: Cambridge University Press, 1992.

Russell, Jeffrey Burton. *Dissent and Reform in the Early Middle Ages.* New York: AMS Press, 1983.

Sayles, G. O. *The Functions of the Medieval Parliament of England.* London: Hambledon, 1988.

Scales, Peter C. *The Fall of the Caliphate of Córdoba.* Boston: Brill, 1994.

Sherborne, J. W. *War, Politics and Culture in Fourteenth-Century England.* Ed. Anthony Tuck. London: Hambledon, 1994.

Sims-Williams, Patrick. *Britain and Early Christian Europe: Studies in Early Medieval History and Culture.* New York: Variorum, 1995.

Speros, Vryonis, Jr. *The Decline of Medieval Hellenism in Asia Minor and the Process of Islamization from the Eleventh through the Fifteenth Century.* Berkeley: University of California Press, 1986.

Spiegel, Gabrielle. *The Past as Text: The Theory and Practice of Medieval Historiography.* Baltimore: Johns Hopkins University Press, 1997.

Spring, Eileen. *Law, Land and Family: Aristocratic Inheritance in England, 1300–1800.* Chapel Hill: University of North Carolina Press, 1997.

Storey, R. L. *Chronology of the Medieval World, 800–1400.* New York: Simon and Schuster, 1994.

_____. *The End of the House of Lancaster.* New York: Sutton, 1999.

Strayer, Joseph Reese. *On the Medieval Origins of the Modern State.* Princeton, NJ: Princeton University Press, 1973.

Takayama, Hiroshi. *The Administration of the Norman Kingdom of Sicily.* Boston: Brill, 1993.

Taylor, John. *Politics and Crisis in Fourteenth-Century England.* New York: Sutton, 1990.

Tubbs, J. W. *The Common Law Mind: Medieval and Early Modern Conceptions.* Baltimore: Johns Hopkins University Press, 2000.

Ullmann, Manfred. *Islamic Medicine.* New York: Columbia University Press, 1997.

Vann, Theresa M. *Queens, Regents and Potentates.* London: Boydell and Brewer, 1995.

Watt, Diane, ed. *Medieval Women in Their Communities.* Toronto: University of Toronto Press, 1997.

Wolf, Kenneth Baxter. *Making History: The Normans and Their Historians in Eleventh-Century Italy.* Philadelphia: University of Pennsylvania Press, 1995.

Woodward, David, and J. B. Harley. *The History of Cartography.* Chicago: University of Chicago Press, 1987.

Science and Technology

Amundsen, Darrel W. *Medicine, Society and Faith in the Ancient and Medieval Worlds.* Baltimore: Johns Hopkins University Press, 1995.

Astill, Grenville, and John Langdon, eds. *Medieval Farming and Technology: The Impact of Agricultural Change in Northwest Europe.* Boston: Brill, 1997.

Birashk, Ahmad. *A Comparative Calendar of the Iranian, Muslim Lunar and Christian Eras for Three Thousand Years (1260 BH–2000 AH; 639 BC–2621 AD).* New York: Mazda Publishing, 1993.

Courtenay, Lynn T., ed. *The Engineering of Medieval Cathedrals.* Brookfield, CT: Ashgate, 1997.

Curry, Anne. *Arms, Armies and Fortifications in the Hundred Years' War.* Rochester, NY: University of Rochester Press, 1994.

Davidson, Clifford. *Technology, Guilds and Early English Drama.* Kalamazoo: Western Michigan University Press, 1997.

Harvey, P. D. A. *Mappa Mundi: The Hereford World Map.* Toronto: University of Toronto Press, 1996.

_____. *Medieval Maps.* Toronto: University of Toronto Press, 1994.

Hayton, Sian. *Cells of Knowledge.* New York: New Amsterdam Books, 1991.

Hunt, Tony. *The Medieval Surgery.* London: Boydell and Brewer, 1992.

Kennedy, Edward S. *Astronomy and Astrology in the Medieval Islamic World.* Brookfield, CT: Ashgate, 1998.

Kitchell, Kenneth, and Irvin Michael Resnick, trans. *Albertus Magnus on Animals.* Baltimore: Johns Hopkins University Press, 1998.

Kogan, Barry. *Averroës and the Metaphysics of*

Causation. Albany: State University of New York Press, 1985.

Le Goff, Jacques. *Time, Work and Culture in the Middle Ages.* Chicago: University of Chicago Press, 1982.

Lewis, Bernard. *The Muslim Discovery of Europe.* New York: Norton, 1985.

McNeill, William H. *The Pursuit of Power: Technology, Armed Force and Society Since 1000 AD.* Chicago: University of Chicago Press, 1984.

Platt, Colin. *King Death: The Black Death and Its Aftermath in Late Medieval England.* Toronto: University of Toronto Press, 1996.

Read, John. *From Alchemy to Chemistry.* New York: Dover, 1995.

Roberts, Gareth. *The Mirror of Alchemy: Alchemical Ideas and Images in Manuscripts and Books from Antiquity to the Seventeenth Century.* Toronto: University of Toronto Press, 1995.

Storey, R. L. *Chronology of the Medieval World, 800–1400.* New York: Simon and Schuster, 1994.

Sweeney, Del. *Agriculture in the Middle Ages: Technology, Practice and Representation.* Philadelphia: University of Pennsylvania Press, 1995.

Wahbah, Mourad. *Averroës and the Enlightenment.* Buffalo, NY: Prometheus, 1996.

Weisheipl, James A., ed. *Albertus Magnus and the Sciences.* Toronto: Pontifical Institute of Medieval Studies, 1980.

Wippel, John F. *Medieval Reactions to the Encounter Between Faith and Reason.* Milwaukee: Marquette University Press, 1995.

Woodward, David, and J. B. Harley. *The History of Cartography.* Chicago: University of Chicago Press, 1987.

Theology, Philosophy, and Religion

Abou El-Haj, Barbara. *The Medieval Cult of Saints.* New York: Cambridge University Press, 1994.

Ackerman, Robert W., and Roger Dahood, trans. *Ancrene Riwle: Introduction and Part I.* Binghamton, NY: Medieval and Renaissance Texts and Studies, 1984.

Amundsen, Darrel W. *Medicine, Society and Faith in the Ancient and Medieval Worlds.* Baltimore: Johns Hopkins University Press, 1995.

Anouihl, Jean, and Lucienne Hill. *Becket or the Honor of God.* Berkeley: University of California Press, 1996.

Armstrong, Karen. *Muhammad: A Biography of the Prophet.* San Francisco: Harper San Francisco, 1993.

_____. *Visions of God: Four Medieval Mystics and Their Writings.* New York: Bantam, 1994.

Ashton, Gail. *The Generation of Identity in Late Medieval Hagiography: Speaking the Saint.* New York: Routledge, 2000.

Aston, Margaret. *Faith and Fire: Popular and Unpopular Religion, 1350–1600.* London: Hambledon, 1993.

Bancroft, Anne. *The Luminous Vision: Six Medieval Mystics and Their Teachings.* New York: HarperCollins, 1989.

Bauerschmidt, Frederick Christian. *Julian of Norwich and the Mystical Body Politic of Christ.* Notre Dame, IN: University of Notre Dame Press, 1999.

Bede, Venerable. *Ecclesiastical History of the English People.* New York: Oxford University Press, 1992.

Berry, Reginald. *A Pope Chronology.* New York: Macmillan, 1988.

Biller, Peter. *Medieval Theology and the Natural Body.* London: Boydell and Brewer, 1997.

Bloom, Harold, ed. *Joan of Arc.* New York: Chelsea House, 1992.

Blumenfeld-Kosinski, Renate, and Timea Szell, eds. *Images of Sainthood in Medieval Europe.* Ithaca, NY: Cornell University Press, 1991.

Blumenthal, U. R. *The Investiture Controversy: Church and Monarchy from the Ninth to the Twelfth Century.* Philadelphia: University of Pennsylvania Press, 1991.

Bodiford, William M. *Soto Zen in Medieval Japan.* Honolulu: University of Hawaii Press, 1993.

Boland, Vivian. *Ideas in God According to St. Thomas Aquinas: Sources and Synthesis.* Boston: Brill, 1996.

Bonner, Gerald. *Church and Faith in the Patristic Tradition: Augustine, Pelagianism, and Early Christian Northumbria.* New York: Variorum, 1996.

Boojamra, John Lawrence. *The Church and Social Reform: The Policies of the Patriarch Athanasios of Constantinople*. New York: Fordham University Press, 1993.

Bornstein, Daniel. *The Bianchi of 1399: Popular Devotion in Late Medieval Italy*. Ithaca, NY: Cornell University Press, 1994.

_____, and Roberto Rusconi. *Women and Religion in Medieval and Renaissance Italy*. Trans. Catharine R. Stimpson and Marjery J. Schneider. Chicago: University of Chicago Press, 1996.

Bossy, John. *Christianity in the West, 1400–1700*. New York: Oxford University Press, 1985.

Bouchard, Constance Brittain. *Sword, Miter and Cloister: Nobility and the Church in Burgundy, 980–1198*. Ithaca, NY: Cornell University Press, 1987.

Boyd, Anne. *Life in a Medieval Monastery: Durham Priory in the Fifteenth Century*. New York: Cambridge University Press, 1987.

Braunfels, W. *Monasteries of Western Europe*. London: Thames and Hudson, 1972.

Bridget of Sweden. *Saint Bride and Her Book: Birgitta of Sweden's Revelations, with Interpretive Essay and Introduction*. Trans. Julia Bolton Holloway. London: Boydell and Brewer, 2000.

Brooke, Z. N. *The English Church and the Papacy: From the Conquest to the Reign of John*. New York: Cambridge University Press, 1989.

Brown, Dorothy Catherine. *Pastor and Laity in the Theology of Jean Gerson*. New York:Cambridge University Press, 1987.

Brundage, James A. *Medieval Canon Law*. Reading, MA: Addison Wesley Longman, 1995.

Burns, R. *Islam Under the Crusaders: Colonial Revival in the 13th-Century Kingdom of Valencia*. Princeton, NJ: Princeton University Press, 1973.

Burton, Janet. *Monastic and Religious Orders in Britain 1000–1300*. New York: Cambridge University Press, 1994.

Bynum, Caroline Walker. *Holy Feast and Holy Fast: The Religious Significance of Food to Medieval Women*. Berkeley: University of California Press, 1988.

_____. *Jesus as Mother: Studies in Spirituality of the High Middle Ages*. Berkeley: University of California Press, 1984.

_____. *The Resurrection of the Body in Western Christianity, 200–1336*. New York: Columbia University Press, 1995.

Caterina da Genova. *Catherine of Genoa: Purgation and Purgatory. The Spiritual Dialogue*. Trans. Serge Hughes. Mahwah, NJ: Paulist Press, 1979.

Caterina da Siena. *Catherine of Siena: The Dialogue*. Trans. Suzanne Noffke. Mahwah, NJ: Paulist Press, 1988.

Cavadini, John, ed. *Gregory the Great*. Notre Dame, IN: University of Notre Dame Press, 1996.

Chadwick, H. *The Early Church*. Harmondsworth, England: Penguin, 1967.

Chenu, Marie-Dominique. *Nature, Man and Society in the Twelfth Century: Essays on New Theological Perspectives in the Latin West*. Chicago: University of Chicago Press, 1983.

Clanchy, M. T. *Abelard: A Medieval Life*. Oxford: Blackwell, 1997.

Clare of Assisi: Early Documents. Mahwah, NJ: Paulist Press, 1988.

Cole, Penny J. *The Preaching of the Crusades to the Holy Land, 1095–1270*. Cambridge, MA: Medieval Academy of America, 1991.

Collis, Louise. *Memoirs of a Medieval Woman: The Life and Times of Margery Kempe*. New York: HarperCollins, 1983.

Constable, Giles. *The Reformation of the Twelfth Century*. New York: Cambridge University Press, 1996.

Coon, Lynda L. *Sacred Fictions: Holy Women and Hagiography in Late Antiquity*. Philadelphia: University of Pennsylvania Press, 1997.

Coope, Jessica. *The Martyrs of Cordoba: Community and Family Conflict in an Age of Mass Conversion*. Lincoln: University of Nebraska Press, 1995.

Copleston, F. C. *Aquinas*. Harmondsworth, England: Penguin, 1955.

Costen, Michael. *The Cathars and the Albigensian Crusade*. Manchester: Manchester University Press, 1997.

Dales, Richard C. *The Problem of the Rational Soul in the Thirteenth Century*. Boston: Brill, 1995.

Dales, Ronald C. *Medieval Discussions of the Eternity of the World*. Boston: Brill, 1990.

Davidson, Herbert. *Alfarabi, Avicenna, and Averroes on Intellect: Their Cosmologies, Theories of the Active Intellect and Theories of Human Intellect*. New York: Oxford University Press, 1992.

Davidson, Linda Kay, et al. *Pilgrimage in the Middle Ages: A Research Guide*. New York: Garland, 1992.

Davies, Oliver. *God Within: The Mystical Traditions of Northern Europe*. Mahwah, NJ: Paulist Press, 1988.

Davis, Leo Donald. *The First Seven Ecumenical Councils, 325–787*. Collegeville, MN: Liturgical Press, 1990.

Davison, Ellen. *Forerunners of St. Francis and Other Studies*. New York: AMS Press, 1978.

De Berceo, Gonzalo. *Miracles of Our Lady*. Trans. Annette Grant Cash. Lexington: University Press of Kentucky, 1997.

Dronke, P., ed. *A History of Twelfth-Century Philosophy*. Cambridge: Cambridge University Press, 1988.

Duffy, Damon. *Saints and Sinners: A History of the Popes*. New Haven, CT: Yale University Press, 1997.

Dumville, David N. *Liturgy and the Ecclesiastical History of Late Anglo-Saxon England: Four Studies*. London: Boydell and Brewer, 1992.

Echevarria, Ana. *The Fortress of Faith: The Attitude Towards Muslims in Fifteenth-Century Spain*. Boston: Brill, 1999.

Ekelund, Robert B. *Sacred Trust: The Medieval Church as an Economic Firm*. New York: Oxford University Press, 1996.

Elliott, Dyan. *Fallen Bodies: Pollution, Sexuality and Demonology in the Middle Ages*. Philadelphia: University of Pennsylvania Press, 1999.

Emery, Kent, Jr. *Monastic, Scholastic and Mystical Theologies from the Later Middle Ages*. New York: Variorum, 1996.

Evans, Austin P. *Heresies of the High Middle Ages*. New York: Columbia University Press, 1991.

Evans, G. R. *Alan of Lille: The Frontiers of Theology in the Later Twelfth Century*. Mahwah, NJ: Paulist Press, 1983.

_____. *Philosophy and Theology in the Middle Ages*. New York: Routledge, 1993.

Fennell, John Lister. *A History of the Russian Church to 1448*. Reading, MA: Longman, 1995.

Ferreiro, Alberto, and Jeffrey Burton Russell, eds. *The Devil, Heresy and Witchcraft in the Middle Ages*. Boston: Brill, 1998.

Fichtenau, Heinrich. *Heretics and Scholars in the High Middle Ages*. Trans. Denise A. Kaiser. University Park: Pennsylvania State University Press, 1998.

Frank, Isnard Wilhelm. *A Concise History of the Medieval Church*. New York: Continuum, 1995.

Franklin, M. J., and Christopher Harper-Bill, eds. *Medieval Ecclesiastical Studies*. London: Boydell and Brewer, 1995.

Frassetto, Michael, ed. *Medieval Purity and Piety: Essays on Medieval Clerical Celibacy and Religious Reform*. New York: Garland, 1998.

Friedrich-Silber, Ilana. *Virtuosity, Charisma and Social Order: A Comparative Sociological Study of Monasticism in Theravade Buddhism and Medieval Catholicism*. New York: Cambridge University Press, 1995.

Fudge, Thomas A. *The Magnificent Ride: The First Reformation in Hussite Bohemia*. Brookfield, CT: Ashgate, 1998.

Gameson, Richard. *St. Augustine and the Conversion of England*. New York: Sutton, 2000.

Garde, Judith N. *Old English Poetry in Medieval Christian Perspective: A Doctrinal Approach*. London: Brewer, 1991.

Gardiner, Eileen. *Medieval Visions of Heaven and Hell: A Sourcebook*. New York: Garland, 1993.

Gilchrist, Roberta. *Gender and Material Culture: The Archaeology of Religious Women*. New York: Routledge, 1997.

Given, James Buchanan. *Inquisition and Medieval Society: Power, Discipline and Resistance in Languedoc*. Ithaca, NY: Cornell University Press, 1997.

Glasscoe, Marion. *English Medieval Mystics: Games of Faith*. Reading, MA: Longman, 1993.

_____, ed. *The Medieval Mystical Tradition in England*. London: Boydell and Brewer, 1985.

Godwin, Malcolm. *Holy Grail*. New York: Penguin, 1998.

Gonzalez, Justo L. *The Story of Christianity: The Early Church to the Dawn of the Reformation*. San Francisco: Harper SanFrancisco, 1984.

Goodrich, Norma Lorre. *The Holy Grail*. New York: HarperCollins, 1993.

Gottfried of Disibodenberg and Theodoric of Echternach. *The Life of Hildegard of Bingen*. Trans. Hugh Feiss. New York: Peregrina, 1996.

Gregory VII, Pope. *The Correspondence of Pope Gregory VII: Selected Letters from the Registrum*. Trans. Ephraim Emerton. New York: Columbia University Press, 1990.

Guiraud, Jean. *The Medieval Inquisition*. New York: AMS Press, 1980.

Hagen, K., ed. *Augustine: The Harvest and Theology, 1300–1650*. Boston: Brill, 1991.

Haines, Roy Martin. *Ecclesia Anglicana: Studies in the English Church of the Later Middle Ages*. Toronto: University of Toronto Press, 1989.

Hamilton, Bernard. *The Medieval Inquisition*. New York: Holmes and Meier, 1982.

Harris, Marguerite, ed. *Birgitta of Sweden: Life and Selected Revelations*. Mahwah, NJ: Paulist Press, 1990.

Harvey, Margaret. *England, Rome and the Papacy, 1417–1464: The Study of a Relationship*. Manchester: Manchester University Press, 1993.

Head, Thomas, and Richard Landes, ed. *The Peace of God: Social Violence and Religious Response in France around the Year 1000*. Ithaca, NY: Cornell University Press, 1992.

Heimmel, Jennifer. *God Is Our Mother: Julian of Norwich and the Medieval Image of Christian Feminine Divinity*. New York: Prometheus, 1983.

Henisch, Bridget Ann. *Fast and Feast: Food in Medieval Society*. University Park: Pennsylvania State University Press, 1986.

Hero, Angela, ed. *A Woman's Quest for Spiritual Guidance: The Correspondence of Princess Eulogia Choumnaina Palaiologina*. Holy Cross Orthodox Press, 1986.

Herrin, Judith. *The Formation of Christendom*. Princeton, NJ: Princeton University Press, 1989.

Hildegarde of Bingen. *Book of Divine Works, with Letters and Songs*. Ed. Matthew Fox. Santa Fe: University of New Mexico Press, 1987.

_____. *Explanation of the Rule of Benedict*. Trans. Hugh Feiss. Toronto: University of Toronto Press, 1990.

_____. *Illuminations*. Ed. Matthew Fox. Santa Fe: University of New Mexico Press, 1985.

Hillgarth, J. N. *Christianity and Paganism, 350–750: The Conversion of Western Europe*. Philadelphia: University of Pennsylvania Press, 1986.

Hinson, E. Glenn. *The Church Triumphant: A History of Christianity up to 1300*. Macon, GA: Mercer University Press, 1995.

Hirsh, John C. *The Boundaries of Faith: The Development and Transmission of Medieval Spirituality*. Stanford, CA: Stanford University Press, 1997.

Hodges, Richard, et al. *Mohammed, Charlemagne and the Origins of Europe*. Ithaca, NY: Cornell University Press, 1983.

Holloway, Julia Bolton. *The Pilgrim and the Book*. New York: Peter Lang, 1987.

_____, et al. *Equally in God's Image: Women in the Middle Ages*. New York: Peter Lang, 1991.

Hollywood, Amy. *The Soul as Virgin Wife: Mechthild of Magdeburg, Marguerite Porete and Meister Eckhard*. Notre Dame, IN: University of Notre Dame Press, 1995.

Holopainen, Toivo. *Dialectic and Theology in the Eleventh Century*. Boston: Brill, 1997.

Holt, P. M. *The Age of the Crusades: The Near East from the Eleventh Century to 1517*. Reading, MA: Longman, 1986.

Hopkins, Andrea. *Most Wise and Valiant Ladies*. New York: Stewart, Tabori and Chang, 1998.

Housely, Norman. *The Avignon Papacy and the Crusades*. New York: Oxford University Press, 1986.

_____. *The Italian Crusades*. New York: Oxford University Press, 1982.

_____. *The Later Crusades*. New York: Oxford University Press, 1992.

Howard, Donald R. *Writers and Pilgrims: Medieval Pilgrimage Narratives and Their Posterity*. Berkeley: University of California Press, 1980.

Hudson, Anne. *Lollards and Their Books*. London: Hambledon, 1985.

Innemee, Karel C. *Ecclesiastical Dress in the Medieval Near East*. Boston: Brill, 1997.

Institoris, Henricus and Montague Summers. *The Malleus Maleficarum of Heinrich Kramer and James Sprenger*. New York: Dover, 1971.

Jaeger, C. Stephen. *The Envy of Angels: Cathedral Schools and Social Ideals in Medieval*

Europe. Philadelphia: University of Pennsylvania Press, 1994.

Jeremiah, Mary. *The Secret of the Heart: A Theological Study of Catherine of Siena's Teaching on the Heart of Jesus.* Front Royal, VA: Christendom Press, 1995.

Jestice, Phyllis G. *Wayward Monks and the Religious Revolution of the Eleventh Century.* Boston: Brill, 1997.

Johnson, Penelope, and Catherine R. Stimpson. *Equal in Monastic Profession: Religious Women in Medieval France.* Chicago: University of Chicago Press, 1991.

Julian of Norwich. *Revelations of Divine Love.* Ed. Halcyon Backhouse and Rhona Pipe. London: Brewer, 1987.

_____. *Revelations of Divine Love and the Motherhood of God.* London: Brewer, 1998.

Kaelber, Lutz. *Schools of Asceticism: Idealogy and Organization in Medieval Religious Communities.* University Park: Pennsylvania State University Press, 1998.

Kamen, Henry. *The Spanish Inquisition: A Historical Revision.* New Haven, CT: Yale University Press, 1999.

Kay, Richard. *Councils and Clerical Culture in the Medieval West.* New York: Variorum, 1997.

Keck, David. *Angels and Angelology in the Middle Ages.* New York: Oxford University Press, 1998.

Kelly, Kathleen Coyne. *Performing Virginity and Testing Chastity in the Middle Ages.* New York: Routledge, 2000.

Kempe, Margery. *The Book of Margery Kempe.* Trans. Barry Windean. Harmondsworth, England: Penguin, 1985.

_____. *The Book of Margery Kempe.* Ed. Lynne Staley. New York: Norton, 2000.

Kirk, James, ed. *Humanism and Reform: The Church in Europe, England and Scotland, 1400–1643.* London: Boydell and Brewer, 1992.

Klaniczay, Gabor. *The Uses of Supernatural Power: The Transformation of Popular Religions in Medieval and Early Modern Europe.* Princeton, NJ: Princeton University Press, 1990.

Kleinbert, Aviad M. *Prophets in Their Own Country: Living Saints and the Making of Sainthood in the Later Middle Ages.* Chicago: University of Chicago Press, 1992.

Lambert, Malcolm. *Medieval Heresy: Popular Movements from the Gregorian Reform to the Reformation.* Oxford: Blackwell, 1992.

Lawrence, C. H. *Medieval Monasticism: Forms of Religious Life in Western Europe in the Middle Ages.* Reading, MA: Longman, 1984.

Le Clercq, Jean. *Love of Learning and the Desire for God: A Study of Monastic Culture.* New York: Fordham University Press, 1982.

Leff, G. *Medieval Thought.* London: Merlin, 1980.

Lepine, David. *A Brotherhood of Canons Serving God: English Secular Cathedrals in the Later Middle Ages.* London: Boydell and Brewer, 1995.

Leyser, Karl, and Timothy Reuter, eds. *Warriors and Churchmen in the High Middle Ages.* London: Hambledon, 1992.

Liebschuetz, J. H. W. G. *Barbarians and Bishops: Army, Church, and State in the Age of Arcadius and Chrysostom.* New York: Oxford University Press, 1991.

Linda, Georgianna. *The Solitary Self: Individuality in the Ancrene Wisse.* Cambridge, MA: Harvard University Press, 1982.

Logan, F. Donald. *Runaway Religious in Medieval England c. 1240–1540.* New York: Cambridge University Press, 1996.

Low, Mary. *Celtic Christianity and Nature: Early Irish and Hebridean Traditions.* Edinburgh: Edinburgh University Press, 1997.

Loxton, Howard. *Pilgrimage to Canterbury.* London: David and Charles, 1978.

Lubac, Henri de. *Medieval Exegesis.* Grand Rapids, MI: Eerdmans, 1998.

Lynch, Joseph H. *The Medieval Church: A Brief History.* Reading, MA: Longman, 1992.

MacKay, Angus. *Love, Religion and Politics in Fifteenth-Century Spain.* Boston: Brill, 1998.

_____. *Society, Economy and Religion in Late Medieval Castile.* Brookfield, CT: Ashgate, 1987.

Madelung, Wilferd. *The Succession to Muhammad: A Study of the Early Caliphate.* New York: Cambridge University Press, 1996.

Mansfield, Mary C. *The Humiliation of Sinners: Public Penance in Thirteenth-Century France.* Ithaca, NY: Cornell University Press, 1995.

Markus, R. A. *Gregory the Great and His World.* New York: Cambridge University Press, 1997.

Martinus. *The Chronicles of Rome: An Edition of the Middle English Chronicle of Popes and Emperors and the Lollard Chronicles.* Ed. Dan Embree. London: Boydell and Brewer, 1999.

Mason, Emma. *Westminster Abbey and Its People, c. 1056–c. 1216.* London: Boydell and Brewer, 1996.

Matarasso, Pauline, ed. and trans. *The Cistercian World: Monastic Writings of the Twelfth Century.* New York: Penguin, 1993.

Maxwell-Stuart, Peter G. *Chronicle of the Popes.* New York: Thames and Hudson, 1997.

Mayr-Harting, Henry. *The Coming of Christianity to Anglo-Saxon England.* University Park: Pennsylvania State University Press, 1991.

McDonnell, Ernest W. *The Beguines and Beghards in Medieval Culture with Special Emphasis on the Belgian Scene.* New Brunswick, NJ: 1954, 1969.

McDonnell, Kilian, and George Montague. *Christian Initiation and Baptism in the Holy Spirit.* Wilmington, DE: Michael Glazier, 1991.

McGinn, Bernard. *Apocalypticism in the Western Tradition.* New York: Variorum, 1994.

_____. *Meister Eckhart and the Beguine Mystics: Hadewijch of Brabant, Mechthild of Magdeburg, and Marguerite Porete.* Chiron, 1997.

_____. *Meister Eckhart: Teacher and Preacher.* Mahwah, NJ: Paulist Press, 1988.

McGuire, Brian Patrick. *The Cistercians in Denmark: Their Attitudes, Roles and Functions in Medieval Society.* Spencer, MA: Cistercian Publications, 1983.

McLaughlin, Megan. *Consorting with Saints: Prayer for the Dead in Early Medieval France.* Ithaca, NY: Cornell University Press, 1994.

McLeod, Glenda. *Virtue and Venom: Catalogs of Women from Antiquity to the Renaissance.* Detroit: University of Michigan Press, 1991.

McSheffrey, Shannon. *Gender and Heresy: Women and Men in Lollard Communities, 1420–1530.* Philadelphia: University of Pennsylvania Press, 1995.

Merriell, D. Juvenal. *To the Image of the Trinity: A Study in the Development of Aquinas' Teaching.* Toronto: Pontifical Institute of Medieval Studies, 1990.

Meyerson, Mark D., and Edward D. English, eds. *Christians, Muslims and Jews in Medieval and Early Modern Spain: Interaction and Cultural Change.* Notre Dame, IN: University of Notre Dame Press, 2000.

Milis, Ludo. *Angelic Monks and Earthly Men: Monasticism and Its Meaning to Medieval Society.* London: Boydell and Brewer, 1992.

Miller, Maureen C. *The Formation of a Medieval Church: Ecclesiastical Change in Verona, 950–1150.* Ithaca, NY: Cornell University Press, 1993.

Moonan, Lawrence. *Divine Power: The Medieval Power Distinction up to its Adoption by Albert, Bonaventure and Aquinas.* Oxford: Clarendon, 1994.

Moore, R. I. *The Birth of Popular Heresy.* Toronto: University of Toronto Press, 1995.

Morris, Bridget. *St. Birgitta of Sweden.* London: Boydell and Brewer, 1999.

Morris, Colin. *The Papal Monarchy: The Western Church from 1050 to 1250.* Oxford: Clarendon, 1989.

Morris, Rosemary. *Monks and Laymen in Byzantium, 843–1118.* New York: Cambridge University Press, 1995.

Morrison, Karl Frederick. *Holiness and Politics in Early Medieval Thought.* New York: Variorum, 1985.

Muldoon, James, ed. *Varieties of Religious Conversion in the Middle Ages.* Gainesville: University Press of Florida, 1997.

Mundill, Robin. *England's Jewish Solution: Experiment and Expulsion, 1262–1290.* New York: Cambridge University Press, 1998.

Nagy, Joseph Falaky. *Conversing with Angels and Ancients: Literary Myths of Medieval Ireland.* Ithaca, NY: Cornell University Press, 1997.

Nelson, Daniel Mark. *The Priority of Prudence: Virtue and Natural Law in Thomas Aquinas and the Implications for Modern Ethics.* University Park: Pennsylvania State University Press, 1992.

Netanyahu, B. *Toward the Inquisition: Essays on Jewish and Converso History in Late Medieval Spain.* Ithaca, NY: Cornell University Press, 1998.

Newman, Martha G. *The Boundaries of Charity: Cistercian Culture and Ecclesiastical Reform, 1098–1180.* Stanford, CA: Stanford University Press, 1996.

Nicholson, Reynold Alleyne. *The Mystics of Islam.* New York: Viking Penguin, 1990.

Noble, Thomas F. X. *The Republic of St. Peter: The Birth of the Papal State, 680–825*. Philadelphia: University of Pennsylvania Press, 1986.

Oliva, Marilyn. *The Convent and the Community in Late Medieval England: Female Monasteries in the Diocese of Norwich, 1350–1540*. London: Boydell and Brewer, 1998.

Papadakis, Aristeides. *The Christian East and the Rise of the Papacy: The Church 1071–1453*. Crestwood, NY: St. Vladimir's Seminary Press, 1994.

Parry, Kenneth. *Depicting the Word: Byzantine Iconophile Thought of the Eighth and Ninth Centuries*. Boston: Brill, 1996.

Peters, Edward. *Heresy and Authority in Medieval Europe: Documents in Translation*. Philadelphia: University of Pennsylvania Press, 1980.

Peters, F. E. *Muhammad and the Origins of Islam*. Albany: State University of New York Press, 1994.

Peterson, Joan. *The Dialogues of Gregory the Great*. Toronto: Pontifical Institute of Medieval Studies, 1985.

Petry, Ray C. *Late Medieval Mysticism*. Louisville, KY: John Knox Press, 1995.

Pollard, William F., and Robert Boenig, eds. *Mysticism and Spirituality in Medieval England*. London: Brewer, 1997.

Potts, Cassandra. *Monastic Revival and Regional Identity in Early Normandy*. London: Boydell and Brewer, 1997.

Price, B. B. *Medieval Thought: An Introduction*. Oxford: Blackwell, 1992.

Raw, Barbara Catherine. *Trinity and Incarnation in Anglo-Saxon Art and Thought*. New York: Cambridge University Press, 1997.

Reitt, Jill, et al. *Christian Spirituality: High Middle Ages and Reformation*. New York: Crossroad, 1987.

Riley-Smith, J. *The Crusades: A Short History*. London: Athlone, 1987.

_____. *The First Crusade and the Idea of Crusading*. London: Athlone, 1986.

Robinson, Ian Stuart. *The Papacy 1073–1198: Continuity and Innovation*. New York: Cambridge University Press, 1990.

Roth, Norman. *Conversion, Inquisition and the Expulsion of the Jews from Spain*. Madison: University of Wisconsin Press, 1995.

Rousseau, Constance M., and Joel Thomas Rosenthal, eds. *Women, Marriage and Family in Medieval Christendom*. Kalamazoo: Western Michigan University Press, 1998.

Runciman, Steven. *The First Crusade*. New York: Cambridge University Press: 1992.

Russell, Jeffrey Burton. *Dissent and Reform in the Early Middle Ages*. New York: AMS Press, 1983.

_____. *Lucifer: The Devil in the Middle Ages*. Ithaca, NY: Cornell University Press, 1986.

Ryan, John Joseph. *Nature, Structure and Function of the Church in William of Ockham*. Atlanta: Scholars Press, 1979.

Salahi, Adil. *Muhammad, Man and Prophet: A Complete Study of the Life of the Prophet of Islam*. Rockport, MA: Element Books, 1998.

Sameer, S. Khalil. *Christian Arabic Apologetics During the Abbasid Period, 750–1258*. Boston: Brill, 1994.

Savage, Anne. *Anchoritic Spirituality: Ancrene Wisse and Associated Works*. Mahwah, NJ: Paulist Press, 1991.

Schmitt, Miriam, ed. *Medieval Women Monastics: Wisdom's Wellsprings*. Collegeville, MN: Liturgical Press, 1996.

Schulenburg, Jane Tibbetts. *Forgetful of Their Sex: Female Sanctity and Society, c. 500–1100*. Chicago: University of Chicago Press, 1998.

Setton, Kenneth. *History of the Crusades*. Madison: University of Wisconsin Press, 1969.

Shannon, Albert Clement. *The Medieval Inquisition*. Wilmington, DE: Michael Glazier, 1991.

Sharpe, Richard. *Medieval Irish Saints' Lives: An Introduction to Vitae Sanctorum Hiberniae*. Oxford: Clarendon, 1991.

Shinners, John Raymond. *Medieval Popular Religion: A Reader*. Peterborough, Ontario: Broadview Press, 1997.

Shinners, John Raymond, ed. *Pastors and the Care of Souls: In Medieval England*. Notre Dame, IN: University of Notre Dame Press, 1998.

Sims-Williams, Patrick. *Britain and Early Christian Europe: Studies in Early Medieval History and Culture*. New York: Variorum, 1995.

Sirat, Colette. *A History of Jewish Philosphy in the Middle Ages*. New York: Cambridge University Press, 1990.

Slattery, Maureen. *Myth, Man and Sovereign Saint: King Louis IX.* New York: Peter Lang, 1985.

Smith, Lesley, and Jane H. M. Taylor. *Women, the Book and the Godly.* London: Brewer, 1995.

——. *Women, the Book and the Worldly.* London: Brewer, 1995.

Smyth, Marina. *Understanding the Universe in Seventh-Century Ireland.* London: Boydell and Brewer, 1996.

Snoek, G. J. C. *Medieval Piety from Relics to the Eucharist: A Process of Mutual Interaction.* Boston: Brill, 1995.

Somerville, Robert. *Papacy, Councils and Canon Law in the 11th and 12th Centuries.* New York: Variorum, 1990.

Sommerfeldt, John R., ed. *Studies in Medieval Cistercian History.* Spencer, MA: Cistercian Publications, 1976.

Spencer, H. Keith. *English Preaching in the Late Middle Ages.* Oxford: Clarendon, 1994.

Staley, Lynn. *Margery Kempe's Dissenting Fictions.* University Park: Pennsylvania State University Press, 1994.

Stock, Brian. *Augustine the Reader: Meditation, Self-Knowledge and the Ethics of Interpretation.* Cambridge, MA: Harvard University Press, 1996

Stormon, E. J. *Towards the Healing of Schism: The Sees of Rome and Constantinople, Public Statements and Correspondence.* Mahwah, NJ: Paulist Press, 1987.

Stroll, Mary. *Symbols as Power: The Papacy Following the Investiture Contest.* Boston: Brill, 1997.

Stump, Philip H. *The Reforms of the Council of Constance.* Boston: Brill, 1994.

Sullivan, Richard E. *Christian Missionary Activity in the Early Middle Ages.* New York: Variorum, 1994.

Sumption, Jonathan. *The Albigensian Crusade.* New York: Faber and Faber, 2000.

Swanson, R. N. *Religion and Devotion in Europe, 1215–1515.* New York: Cambridge University Press, 1995.

Sweeney, Leo. *Divine Infinity in Greek and Medieval Thought.* New York: Peter Lang, 1992.

Tamburello, Dennis. *Ordinary Mysticism.* Mahwah, NJ: Paulist Press, 1996.

Tavard, George H. *The Forthbringer of God: St.*

Bonaventure on the Virgin Mary. Quincy, IL: Franciscan Press, 1989.

Taylor, Larissa J. *Soldiers of Christ: Preaching in Late Medieval and Reformation France.* New York: Oxford University Press, 1992.

Tellenbach, Gerd. *The Church in Western Europe from the Tenth to the Early Twelfth Century.* Trans. Timothy Reuter. New York: Cambridge University Press, 1993.

Thompson, Augustine. *Revival Preachers and Politics in Thirteenth-Century Italy: The Great Devotion of 1233.* Oxford: Clarendon, 1993.

Thompson, Sally. *Women Religious: The Founding of English Nunneries after the Norman Conquest.* Oxford: Clarendon, 1991.

Tierney, Brian. *The Crisis of Church and State, 1050–1300.* Toronto: University of Toronto Press, 1988.

——. *Foundations of Conciliar Theory: The Contribution of the Medieval Canonists from Gratian to the Great Schism.* Boston: Brill, 1997.

——. *Origins of Papal Infallibility, 1150–1350: A Study on the Concepts of Infallibility, Sovereignty and Tradition in the Middle Ages.* Boston: Brill, 1997.

Toon, Peter. *Yesterday, Today and Forever: Jesus Christ and the Holy Trinity in the Leading of the Seven Ecumenical Councils.* Swedesboro, NJ: Preservation Press, 1996.

Turner, Denys. *The Darkness of God: Negativity in Christian Mysticism.* New York: Norton, 1995.

Urvoy, Dominique. *Ibn Rushd: Averroës.* New York: Routledge, 1991.

Vauchez, Andre, et al. *The Laity in the Middle Ages: Religious Beliefs and Devotional Practices.* Notre Dame, IN: University of Notre Dame Press, 1997.

Venarde, Bruce L. *Women's Monasticism and Medieval Society: Nunneries in France and England, 890–1215.* Ithaca, NY: Cornell University Press, 1997.

Voaden, Rosalynn. *God's Words, Women's Voices: The Discernment of Spirit in the Writing of Late-Medieval Women Visionaries.* London: Boydell and Brewer, 1999.

Vodola, Elizabeth. *Excommunication in the Middle Ages.* Berkeley: University of California Press, 1986.

Volz, Carl A. *The Medieval Church: From the*

Dawn of the Middle Ages to the Eve of the Reformation. Nashville, TN: Abingdon, 1997.

Wadell, Paul J. *Friends of God: Virtues and Gifts in Aquinas.* New York: Peter Lang, 1991.

Wahbah, Mourad. *Averroës and the Enlightenment.* Buffalo, NY: Prometheus, 1996.

Wakefield, Walter L. *Heresies of the High Middle Ages: Selected Sources.* New York: Columbia University Press, 1991.

Wallace-Hadrill, J. M. *The Frankish Church.* New York: Oxford University Press, 1984.

Ward, Benedicta. *Miracles and the Medieval Mind: Theory, Record and Event, 1000–1215.* Philadelphia: University of Pennsylvania Press, 1987.

_____. *Signs and Wonders: Saints, Miracles and Prayers from the Fourth Century to the Fourteenth.* New York: Variorum, 1992.

Wasyliw, Patricia Healy. *Martyrdom, Murder and Magic: Child Saints and Their Cults in Medieval Europe.* New York: Peter Lang, 1998.

Waugh, Scott L., ed. *Christendom and Its Discontents: Exclusion, Persecution and Rebellion, 1000–1500.* New York: Cambridge University Press, 1995.

Wiethaus, Ulrike. *Ecstatic Transformation: Transpersonal Psychology in the Work of Mechthild of Magdeburg.* Syracuse, NY: Syracuse University Press, 1995.

_____. *Maps of Flesh and Light: The Religious Experience of Medieval Women Mystics.* Syracuse, NY: Syracuse University Press, 1993.

Wiles, Maurice. *Archetypal Heresy: Arianism through the Centuries.* Oxford: Clarendon, 1996.

Wilson, Thomas B. *History of the Church and State in Norway: From the Tenth to the Sixteenth Century.* Atlanta: Scholars Press, 1971.

Windeatt, Barry. *English Mystics of the Middle Ages.* New York: Cambridge University Press, 1994.

Winstead, Karen A. *Chaste Passions: Medieval English Virgin Martyr Legends.* Ithaca, NY: Cornell University Press, 2000.

Wippel, John F. *Medieval Reactions to the Encounter Between Faith and Reason.* Milwaukee, WI: Marquette University Press, 1995.

Wood, Ian, and G. A. Loud, eds. *Church and Chronicle in the Middle Ages.* London: Hambledon, 1991.

Women's History

Amt, Emilie, ed. *Women's Lives in Medieval Europe: A Sourcebook.* New York: Routledge, 1993.

Ashe, Geoffrey. *Kings and Queens of Early Britain.* Chicago: Academy Chicago, 1990.

Baker, D., ed. *Medieval Women.* Oxford: Blackwell, 1978.

Bennett, Judith. *Ale, Beer and Brewsters in England: Women's Work in a Changing World, 1300–1600.* New York: Oxford University Press, 1997.

_____. *Sisters and Workers in the Middle Ages.* Chicago: University of Chicago Press, 1989.

_____, et al. *Women in the Medieval English Countryside: Gender and Household in Brigstock Before the Plague.* New York: Oxford University Press, 1987.

Bitel, Lisa. *Land of Women: Tales of Sex and Gender from Early Ireland.* Ithaca, NY: Cornell University Press, 1996.

Blamires, Alcuin. *The Case for Women in Medieval Culture.* Oxford: Clarendon, 1997.

Bloch, R. Howard. *Medieval Misogyny and the Invention of Western Romantic Love.* Chicago: University of Chicago Press, 1991.

Blok, Josine H. *The Early Amazons: Modern and Ancient Perspectives on a Persistent Myth.* Boston: Brill, 1994.

Bogin, Meg. *The Woman Troubadours.* New York: Norton, 1980.

Bornstein, Daniel, and Roberto Rusconi. *Women and Religion in Medieval and Renaissance Italy.* Trans. Catharine R. Stimpson and Marjery J. Schneider. Chicago: University of Chicago Press, 1996.

Brooke, Christopher N. L. *The Medieval Idea of Marriage.* New York: Oxford University Press, 1994.

Bynum, Caroline Walker. *Holy Feast and Holy Fast: The Religious Significance of Food to Medieval Women.* Berkeley: University of California Press, 1988.

Carlson, Cindy L. *Constructions of Widowhood and Virginity in the Middle Ages.* New York: St. Martin's, 1999.

Carpenter, Jennifer. *Power of the Weak: Studies on Medieval Women.* Champaign: University of Illinois Press, 1995.

Cole, H. *History of Women in Germany from*

Medieval Time to Present. Berlin: German Historical Institute, 1990.

Conn, Marie. *Noble Daughters: Unheralded Women in Western Christianity, Thirteenth to Eighteenth Centuries.* Westport, CT: Greenwood, 2000.

Coon, Lynda L. *Sacred Fictions: Holy Women and Hagiography in Late Antiquity.* Philadelphia: University of Pennsylvania Press, 1997.

Coope, Jessica. *The Martyrs of Cordoba: Community and Family Conflict in an Age of Mass Conversion.* Lincoln: University of Nebraska Press, 1995.

Dillard, Heath. *Daughters of the Reconquest: Women in Castilian Town Society, 1100–1300.* New York: Cambridge University Press, 1985.

Duby, Georges. *Love and Marriage in the Middle Ages.* Chicago: University of Chicago Press, 1996.

Duggan, Anne, ed. *Queens and Queenship in Medieval Europe.* London: Boydell and Brewer, 1997.

Edwards, Robert and Vickie Ziegler. *Matrons and Marginal Women in Medieval Society.* Rochester, NY: University of Rochester Press, 1995.

Erler, Mary. *Women and Power in the Middle Ages.* Athens: University of Georgia Press, 1988.

Evergates, Theodore, ed. *Aristocratic Women in Medieval France.* Philadelphia: University of Pennsylvania Press, 1999.

Finnegan, Mary Jeremy. *The Women of Helfta: Scholars and Mystics.* Athens: University of Georgia Press, 1991.

Garland, Lynda. *Byzantine Empresses: Women and Power in Byzantium, AD 527–1204.* New York: Routledge, 1999.

Gies, Frances, and Joseph Gies. *Marriage and the Family in the Middle Ages.* New York: HarperCollins, 1989.

_____. *Women in the Middle Ages.* New York: Barnes and Noble, 1991.

Gilchrist, Roberta. *Gender and Material Culture: The Archaeology of Religious Women.* New York: Routledge, 1997.

Glasscoe, Marion. *English Medieval Mystics: Games of Faith.* Reading, MA: Longman, 1993.

Gold, Penny Schine. *The Lady and the Virgin: Image, Attitude and Experience in Twelfth-Century France.* Chicago: University of Chicago Press, 1987.

Goldberg, P. J. P., ed. *Woman Is a Worthy Wight: Women in English Society, c. 1200–1500.* New York: St. Martin's, 1992.

_____. *Women in Medieval English Society.* New York: St. Martin's, 1997.

Gulati, Saroj. *Women and Society: Northern India in the 11th and 12th Centuries.* Columbia, MO: South Asia Books, 1985.

Heimmel, Jennifer. *God Is Our Mother: Julian of Norwich and the Medieval Image of Christian Feminine Divinity.* New York: Prometheus, 1983.

Herlihy, David. *Opera Muliebria: Women and Work in Medieval Europe.* Philadelphia: Temple University Press, 1990.

Hill, Barbara. *Imperial Women: Byzantium 1025–1204: Power, Patronage and Ideology.* Reading, MA: Addison-Wesley, 1999.

Holloway, Julia Bolton. *Equally in God's Image: Women in the Middle Ages.* New York: Peter Lang, 1991.

Hollywood, Amy. *The Soul as Virgin Wife: Mechthild of Magdeburg, Marguerite Porete and Meister Eckhard.* Notre Dame, IN: University of Notre Dame Press, 1995.

Hopkins, Andrea. *Most Wise and Valiant Ladies.* New York: Stewart, Tabori and Chang, 1998.

Howell, Martha C. *Women, Production and Patriarchy in Late Medieval Cities.* Chicago: University of Chicago Press, 1986.

Jesch, Judith. *Women in the Viking Age.* Rochester, NY: University of Rochester Press, 1991.

Jochens, Jenny. *Women in Old Norse Society.* Ithaca, NY: Cornell University Press, 1996.

Johnson, Penelope, and Catherine R. Stimpson. *Equal in Monastic Profession: Religious Women in Medieval France.* Chicago: University of Chicago Press, 1991.

Jordan, William Chester. *Women and Credit in Pre-Industrial and Developing Societies.* Philadelphia: University of Pennsylvania Press, 1993.

Kaplan, Marion. *Marriage Bargain: Women and Dowries in European History.* Binghamton, NY: Haworth, 1984.

Karras, Ruth Mazo. *Common Women: Prostitution and Sexuality in Medieval England.* New York: Oxford University Press, 1996.

Kausar, Zinat. *Muslim Women in Medieval India.* Columbia, MO: South Asia Books, 1992.

Kelly, Kathleen Coyne. *Performing Virginity and Testing Chastity in the Middle Ages.* New York: Routledge, 2000.

Laiou, Angeliki. *Gender, Society and Economic Life in Byzantium.* New York: Variorum, 1992.

Leon, Vicki. *Uppity Women of Medieval Times.* Berkeley, CA: Conari Press, 1997.

Leyser, Henrietta. *Medieval Women: A Social History of Women in England 450–1500.* New York: St. Martin's, 1995.

McCash, June Hall. *The Cultural Patronage of Medieval Women.* Athens: University of Georgia Press, 1996.

McDonnell, Ernest W. *The Beguines and Beghards in Medieval Culture with Special Emphasis on the Belgian Scene.* New Brunswick, NJ: 1954, 1969.

McGinn, Bernard. *Meister Eckhart and the Beguine Mystics: Hadewijch of Brabant, Mechthild of Magdeburg, and Marguerite Porete.* Chiron, 1997.

McLeod, Glenda. *Virtue and Venom: Catalogs of Women from Antiquity to the Renaissance.* Detroit: University of Michigan Press, 1991.

McSheffrey, Shannon. *Gender and Heresy: Women and Men in Lollard Communities, 1420–1530.* Philadelphia: University of Pennsylvania Press, 1995.

Morris, Katherine. *Sorceress or Witch? The Image of Gender in Medieval Iceland and Northern Europe.* New York: University Press of America, 1991.

Nicol, Donald M. *The Byzantine Lady: Ten Portraits 1250–1500.* New York: Cambridge University Press, 1994.

Oliva, Marilyn. *The Convent and the Community in Late Medieval England: Female Monasteries in the Diocese of Norwich, 1350–1540.* London: Boydell and Brewer, 1998.

Parsons, John Carmi. *Medieval Queenship.* New York: St. Martin's, 1994.

Partner, Nancy F. *Studying Medieval Women: Sex, Gender, Feminism.* Cambridge, MA: Medieval Academy of America, 1993.

Petroff, Elizabeth Alvida. *Body and Soul: Essays on Medieval Women and Mysticism.* New York: Oxford University Press, 1994.

Power, Eileen Edna, et al. *Medieval Women.* New York: Cambridge University Press, 1997.

Quilligan, Maureen. *The Allegory of Female Authority: Christine de Pizan's "Cite des Dames."* Ithaca, NY: Cornell University Press, 1991.

Rose, Mary Beth. *Women in the Middle Ages and Renaissance: Literary and Historical Perspectives.* Syracuse, NY: Syracuse University Press, 1986.

Rosenthal, Joel T. *Medieval Women and the Sources of Medieval History.* Athens: University of Georgia Press, 1990.

Rousseau, Constance M. and Joel Thomas Rosenthal, eds. *Women, Marriage and Family in Medieval Christendom.* Kalamazoo: Western Michigan University Press, 1998.

Schmitt, Miriam, ed. *Medieval Women Monastics: Wisdom's Wellsprings.* Collegeville, MN: Liturgical Press, 1996.

Schulenburg, Jane Tibbetts. *Forgetful of Their Sex: Female Sanctity and Society, c. 500–1100.* Chicago: University of Chicago Press, 1998.

Shahar, Shulamith. *Fourth Estate: A History of Women in the Middle Ages.* New York: Routledge, 1984.

Smith, Lesley, and Jane H. M. Taylor. *Women, the Book and the Godly.* London: Brewer, 1995.

_____. *Women, the Book and the Worldly.* London: Brewer, 1995.

Stafford, Pauline. *Queen Emma and Queen Edith: Queenship and Women's Power in Eleventh-Century England.* Oxford: Blackwell, 1997.

_____. *Queens, Concubines and Dowagers: The King's Wife in the Early Middle Ages.* London: Leicester University Press, 1998.

Thompson, Sally. *Women Religious: The Founding of English Nunneries after the Norman Conquest.* Oxford: Clarendon, 1991.

Vann, Theresa M. *Queens, Regents and Potentates.* London: Boydell and Brewer, 1995.

Venarde, Bruce L. *Women's Monasticism and Medieval Society: Nunneries in France and England, 890–1215.* Ithaca, NY: Cornell University Press, 1997.

Voaden, Rosalynn. *God's Words, Women's Voices: The Discernment of Spirit in the Writing of Late-Medieval Women Visionaries.* London: Boydell and Brewer, 1999.

Ward, Jennifer C. *English Noblewomen in the*

Later Middle Ages. Reading, MA: Longman, 1992.

Watt, Diane, ed. *Medieval Women in Their Communities.* Toronto: University of Toronto Press, 1997.

Williams, Marty Newman, and Anne Echols. *Between Pit and Pedestal: Women in the Middle Ages.* Princeton, NJ: Markus Wiener, 1994.

Winstead, Karen A. *Chaste Passions: Medieval English Virgin Martyr Legends.* Ithaca, NY: Cornell University Press, 2000.

Index

Page numbers in italic indicate a reference in the appendix of genealogical charts.